**tax is
not a
four
letter
word**

Canadian Commentaries

Published in conjunction with the *Literary Review of Canada*, Canadian Commentaries features prominent writers exploring key issues affecting Canadians and the world. A lead essay commissioned by the LRC becomes the ground for responses by others, opening a place for a spectrum of views and debate.

We welcome manuscripts from Canadian authors. For further information, please contact the Series Editor:

Dr. Janice Gross Stein
Director, Munk Centre for International Studies
University of Toronto
1 Devonshire Place
Toronto, ON M5S 3K7
Canada
Phone: (416) 946-8908
Fax: (416) 946-8915
Email: j.stein@utoronto.ca

Alex Himelfarb and Jordan Himelfarb, editors

tax is not a four letter word

A Different Take on Taxes in Canada

WILFRID LAURIER UNIVERSITY PRESS

Wilfrid Laurier University Press acknowledges the support of the Canada Council for the Arts for our publishing program. We acknowledge the financial support of the Government of Canada through the Canada Book Fund for our publishing activities.

Library and Archives Canada Cataloguing in Publication

    Tax is not a four-letter word : a different take on taxes in Canada / Alex Himelfarb and Jordan Himelfarb, editors.

(Canadian commentaries series)
Includes bibliographical references and index.
Issued in print and electronic formats.
ISBN 978-1-55458-832-9 (pbk.).—ISBN 978-1-55458-904-3 (epub).—
ISBN 978-1-55-458-903-6 (pdf)

    1. Taxation—Canada. 2. Finance, Public—Canada. I. Himelfarb, Alexander, 1947–, editor of compilation II. Himelfarb, Jordan, 1981–, editor of compilation III. Series: Canadian commentaries series

HJ2449.T28 2013   336.200971   C2013-903715-2   C2013-903716-0

Cover design by Chris Rowat Design. Text design by Angela Booth Malleau.

Second printing 2014

© 2013 Wilfrid Laurier University Press
Waterloo, Ontario, Canada
www.wlupress.wlu.ca

This book is printed on FSC recycled paper and is certified Ecologo. It is made from 100% post-consumer fibre, processed chlorine free, and manufactured using biogas energy.

Printed in Canada

Every reasonable effort has been made to acquire permission for copyright material used in this text, and to acknowledge all such indebtedness accurately. Any errors and omissions called to the publisher's attention will be corrected in future printings.

No part of this publication may be reproduced, stored in a retrieval system, or trans-mitted, in any form or by any means, without the prior written consent of the publisher or a licence from the Canadian Copyright Licensing Agency (Access Copyright). For an Access Copyright licence, visit http://www.accesscopyright.ca or call toll free to 1-800-893-5777.

Contents

Preface ... vii

Introduction | Tax Is Not a Four-Letter Word | *Alex Himelfarb and Jordan Himelfarb* ... 1

Part I The Conversation Today

1 | The Economic Consequences of Taxing (and Spending) | *Jim Stanford* ... 17
2 | Taxes and Transfers in Canada: The Federal Dimension | *Robin Boadway* ... 39
3 | Taxes and Public Services | *Hugh Mackenzie* ... 55
4 | Benefits from Public Services | *Hugh Mackenzie* ... 69
5 | Canadian Public Opinion on Taxes | *Frank Graves* ... 83

Part II How We Got Here

6 | Taxation and the Neo-Liberal Counter-Revolution: The Canadian Case | *Matt Fodor* ... 101
7 | A Brief Potted History of Ottawa's Tax Cut Mania | *Eugene Lang and Philip DeMont* ... 119
8 | Tax Cuts and Other Cheap Parlour Tricks | *Trish Hennessy* ... 137

Part III A Different Take on Taxes

9 | Toward a Fair Canadian Tax System | *Marc Lee and Iglika Ivanova* ... 151
10 | Carbon Taxes: Can a Good Policy Become Good Politics? | *Stéphane Dion* ... 171
11 | How Small Changes Can Make a Big Difference: The Case of Financial Transaction Taxes | *Toby Sanger* ... 191
12 | We Need to Simplify and Re-focus the Tax System | *C. Scott Clark* ... 211

Part IV How to Get There

  13 | Canada's Conservative Ideological Infrastructure: Brewing a Cup of
      Cappuccino Conservatism | *Paul Saurette and Shane Gunster*   227

Conclusion   267
Contributors   271
Index   277

Preface

The idea for a book about taxes was inspired by the cuts to the GST from 7 cents on every dollar to 5 in Conservative budgets between 2006 and 2008. That the cuts happened was no surprise. The Conservatives had made this a key election promise and it was a political no-brainer—most Canadians, other than the majority of economists, hated the GST. No, what made this surprising was that this massive tax cut—a $14-billion bite out of federal revenues—was implemented by a minority government with almost no push-back and certainly no discussion of its consequences, especially coming on top of about a decade of multi-partisan and huge tax cutting.

In fact, these massive cuts were followed by other large tax slashes, all with virtually no public debate: no debate about the consequences for Canada's resiliency to deal with economic volatility and crises; no debate about the implications for the federal role in key areas, such as health and education, where the provinces face considerable challenges; no debate about what all this would mean for the shape of the federal government and its public service, and its ability to perform core operations and deliver essential services; no debate about whether we would have the room to invest for the future or to take the necessary steps to deal with climate change and environmental deterioration, growing inequality, a growing productivity gap, and an aging population. From the beginning of his mandate to the end, Kevin Page, our first and indomitable Parliamentary Budget Officer, gamely and even courageously tried to get the information our Members of Parliament needed to assess the outcomes of the cuts to programs and services that are in the works or planned. At the time of writing, it is still impossible to get a comprehensive picture.

The contributors to this book disagree about many issues. Some would see taxes go up and others want revenue-neutral reforms. They disagree, at least to some extent, about what would be the ideal mix of taxes, about who and what should be taxed most. But they all agree on two things: that we need a conversation on taxes, and that it must include a real assessment of the consequences and costs of tax cuts now and for the longer term.

At the time of writing, some provincial budgets introduced modest tax increases, sometimes temporary, usually apologetic, and we are seeing stirrings of outrage at the recent revelations of how much tax revenue is lost to offshore tax havens. Just maybe the times are ripe for a larger conversation, an unapologetic conversation on taxes and what they buy.

As Joseph Heath sets out with admirable clarity in his *Filthy Lucre*, there are difficult choices to make about how and how much to tax, but those choices cannot be divorced from a discussion of what kinds of things we believe we should do—and pay for—together. The constant and perhaps inevitable refrain that taxes are too high is little more than ideology when divorced from a discussion of what taxes buy. Taxes, in this sense, are a proxy for the things that matter in public policy, the kind of country we want, our sense of the common good, the trade-offs we need and are willing to make, and the role of our governments in helping us manage change and realize our shared goals.

We have not tried to be even-handed here. The anti-taxers need no help making their views known, and they have effectively shaped and constrained public policy in Canada as elsewhere. This book is an attempt to seed a more balanced discussion on taxes and what they buy.

The joy of putting this together was in no small measure that it has been a family affair, father and son, with help from the rest of the family and contributions from friends and trusted colleagues. We owe thanks to many others. Wodek Szemberg of TVO and Josh Knelman, then of the *Literary Review of Canada*, for pushing us to grapple with these questions for the *Big Ideas* series, and then pushing us on the ideas themselves. Ryan Chynces, at Wilfrid Laurier University Press, provided valuable and patient editorial support. We are grateful for the assistance of the staff of the *Literary Review of Canada*, and particularly for the insights of editor-in-chief Bronwyn Drainie. Thanks too to the Metcalf Foundation for its support. Finally, we are especially indebted to Frum Himelfarb, wife and mother, former public servant and scholar, without whose gentle but constant nudging this volume would not exist.

Introduction

Tax Is Not a Four-letter Word

Alex Himelfarb and Jordan Himelfarb

We do not like paying taxes. This is not big news: we do not much like paying any bills, and there's probably never been a time when we didn't grumble in particular about taxes. But somehow, "tax" has gone from irritant to four-letter word, not to be uttered in public and certainly not to be discussed favourably in politics. What changed?

Americans have always had an uncomfortable relationship with their taxes that probably reflects an historical ambivalence about government. Taxes there have always been a hard sell. Over the last few years, however, the only saleable tax policy has, it seems, been the promise of ever-lower taxes. American ambivalence turned to anger in the aftermath of the financial meltdown and the massive government bailouts. Taxes, always a problem, became an evil. We saw that play out, almost unbelievably, in the extension of the deep Bush tax cuts made by the first Obama administration in the face of trillion-dollar deficits. We were bewildered while watching the first debt ceiling crisis and amazed by the eleventh-hour agreement to cut government services over a trillion dollars while huge tax cuts were extended, including those for the country's millionaires and billionaires. Many of us were dumbfounded by the widespread no-tax pledges among Republican politicians before the 2012 election—no new taxes whatever the circumstances, whatever the need, whatever the consequences. It is as though our neighbours, always able to reinvent themselves, were stuck with the same tune playing over and over again: All taxes are bad. Tax cuts are the magic cure for all that ails.

In Canada, we have traditionally had a more benign view of taxes. Like other northern countries, we have understood that taxes, however irksome, are the price we pay for civilization and a better future, for the privilege of living in Canada and the opportunities that provides. While there are legitimate disputes regarding how much tax and of what sort, we have generally accepted higher taxes as a way of funding valued public goods and services, redistributing income to avoid the worst excesses of inequality, and shaping the future to the extent we can.

But in Canadian politics too, another story, an anti-tax story, has been unfolding. In the 2011 federal election, all parties seemed to be competing for the austerity and low-tax crown. Apart from a minor skirmish on corporate taxes, nobody wanted to be seen as a "tax-and-spender." In Toronto, Rob Ford was elected mayor in 2010 on the promise of tax cuts and an end to the gravy train (if it can ever be found). In the 2011 Ontario election, we heard our own version of no-tax pledges. The Conservatives promised deep cuts. The Liberals promised no increases. And the NDP promised tax breaks for families and small businesses, offset somewhat by higher corporate taxes. Shortly before that, British Columbia said no to the HST in a referendum on taxes; one wonders what precedent this tax referendum creates. Federally, the Conservative government is continuing a decade-long tradition of reduced taxes—even though we are still running deficits, and even as the gap between the rich and the rest grows. It has by now become a political truism that any politician would have to be nuts to propose tax increases to Canadians.

Ironically, it is in the anti-tax US that a conversation has erupted on taxes. Warren Buffett and a few other billionaires helped open the door, if only a crack, and President Obama has, finally, made taxing the rich part of funding his recovery plan. But even these small and belated steps have produced accusations of class warfare, and alternative proposals to further cut taxes, including for the very rich. Here in Canada, the tax conversation is pretty constrained; even proposals for modest increases targeting the rich or delayed cuts for corporations meet stiff opposition. Generally, we continue to reward politicians who avoid the issues, or who promise more cuts.

Of course, as many of the chapters in this volume set out, a conversation about taxes is a proxy for much larger issues: the role of government; what should be public and universally available, and what should be private and best left to the market; how best to achieve fairness and efficiency. A discussion about taxes is a discussion about the kind of Canada we want. Without an honest conversation about tax, we might just end up sleepwalking toward a Canada we would never have chosen. We ought to have the conversation, but it is not happening and doesn't appear imminent.

How did we get here? How did tax become a "four-letter word"?

The Last Free Lunch

The late 1970s are a good place to start to understand this shift in attitudes. Then and throughout the eighties, free market ideology fully bloomed, first in the US and later and more subtly in Canada in the aftermath of serious economic stagnation and inflation. The economic problems were real and serious, and the times were ripe for an alternative to the progressive (or liberal) policies that had for decades been building the social safety net and progressive state. A number of writers have explored why the liberal establishment failed to make the adjustments to stave off this free market counter-revolution. Too much success? Had they become the establishment, defenders of the status quo? Whatever the reasons, some version of market fundamentalism, variously called neo-liberalism or neo-conservatism, reshaped politics in much of the developed world and particularly in the Anglo democracies. In this volume, York University's Matt Fodor traces the rise of neo-liberalism in Canada and what this has meant for taxes. Eugene Lang and Philip DeMont provide the numbers and discuss the impact of this shift on tax policy in Canada. Trish Hennessy gives an account of how the way we talk and think about taxes and government has changed accordingly. And Frank Graves provides data on the impact neo-liberalism has had on our complex attitudes to taxes and what they buy.

The solution to economic stagnation and inflation, according to neo-liberals, was to let the market do its work and get governments out of the way. The best way to do that: cut off their revenues by cutting taxes. As Milton Friedman, chief architect of US neo-liberalism liked to put it, when governments try to solve a problem, they almost invariably make it worse. Progress would come not from our collective efforts to build a better society—there is no society, said Thatcher—but from the pursuit of our individual interests in the market. So began three decades of an unrelenting assault on government, or at least the elevation of the market as the best means for achieving the "common good."

The architects of this counter-revolution were not perfect libertarians. They understood that government had an important role in protecting life, liberty, and property—but once that door was opened, the danger, in their view, was that government would take on too much, "interfere" too much with the allocative efficiency of the market, and to stop this, taxes—public spending—should be kept as low as possible in favour of private spending. In this view, governments had already grown far too big, and too many services were being bought publicly. Governments' role and size would have to be reduced.

But there was a political challenge here: people had become quite wedded to the public goods and services their taxes bought. So how to sell the low-tax, small-government agenda? No fancy theories here about how tax cuts automatically create jobs. The sales pitch was simple, and it was perfect politics: tax cuts would be so beneficial to economic growth that they would pay for themselves. Tax cuts were free—the last free lunch.

This notion that taxes are somehow separate from the services and goods they buy is now a part of political culture. I am reminded of two images that capture the zero-tax spirit of the Tea Party and the continuing search for a free lunch. The first is a now famous video of a Tea Partier holding a sign demanding that the government keep its hands off "my medicare." More recently, another protest photo shows a group of anti-taxers with a sign that reads "Cut Taxes, Not Defense." Whether one favours "guns" or "butter," taxes apparently have nothing to do with it.

Hugh Mackenzie, a research associate at the Canadian Centre for Policy Alternatives, has contributed two chapters to this volume about how this separation of taxes from the services they buy has distorted the conversation in Canada as well. One way that the idea of tax cuts as a free good is maintained is with the false promise that only waste and inefficiency will be cut. No politician or party favours waste and inefficiency, and every government tries to reduce both—but tax cuts on the promise of ending the gravy train almost never find enough gravy. Of course efficiency matters, waste must be attacked, and of course it matters how both taxes and spending are organized, but despite the highly publicized incidents of misspending that seem to dominate the pages of our mainstream media and disproportionately shape our perceptions, the numbers about waste never add up, and the consequences of tax cuts on public goods and services are always worse than promised.

The exaggerated perceptions of government waste and the parliamentary time spent on the scandal of the day themselves have enduring costs; they erode the public's trust in one of our most powerful tools for managing change and shaping the future—our own government.

Of course deference or blind trust is dangerous—governments must be kept in check by strong democratic institutions, a vigilant citizenry, an independent judiciary, and if we are lucky, effective media. But the absence of trust is equally dangerous. It makes it hard for us to act in our own best interests. Most Canadians know that the teachers and firefighters, the soldiers, police and health care workers, the roads, bridges, and traffic lights, the help when we are down or temporarily out of work, and the child and elderly benefits we receive are all paid for through taxes. But we are still reluctant to pay our taxes. We will always say no to taxes if we believe government is inefficient and wasteful, incompetent or worse.

We are falling into what game theorists call a social trap. Even when we know that cooperating with others serves our collective interests, lacking trust, we go off on our own. The absence of trust limits our ability to act collectively and imagine new possibilities. It takes the future away from us and hands it to "the market." No trust. No taxes. Trapped.

This growing distrust is, of course, not just a result of concerns about waste, efficiency, or even ethics. Perhaps it is the product of the increasing centralization and remoteness of government, the incredible access we now have to information, or the increased anonymity of urban life, all nurtured in a culture of individualism and consumerism. Perhaps, too, it is a result of the increasing authoritarianism of government, especially after 9/11. But it is no doubt fuelled dangerously by the endless accusations and counter-accusations of waste and misspending, by the focus on what government costs without any talk about what government gives, by the almost constant assault on the very idea of government, as if governments were something hostile and foreign to us rather than a vehicle for our collective action.

In the 1980s, government leaders knew that they had to reinvent themselves for the information age as problems seemed to be more complex, unfamiliar, and conflictual; the pace of change was accelerating, and citizens wanted more direct ownership over their public services. This was a time when the talk in Ottawa, Washington, and London, for example, was about less bureaucracy, fewer rules, more flexibility to tailor services to changing and diverse needs, and, above all, more openness. This reinvention was not going to be easy or smooth.

In fact, it never happened. Instead it crashed headlong into distrust, and never quite recovered. Mistrust of government and a preoccupation with waste led not only to cuts but also, and at the same time, to expensive layers of control and oversight that made government no more accountable or transparent but certainly more risk averse and inefficient, and therefore less worthy of our trust—a self-fulfilling prophecy.

Greater transparency was supposed to be a key part of the solution, but things haven't worked out that way. In fact, our obsession with uncovering waste may blind us to the big issues. So, even as we know more than we could ever want to about how officials spend on travel and hospitality, government seems more opaque than ever—with almost no debate, for example, on the implications of the cuts to the GST that took almost $14 billion annually out of government revenue, and almost no information on the costs of the Omnibus Crime Bill or how it is supposed to make us safer, rather than just meaner. That is not real transparency. As a result, trust continues to decline.

And so next door we see President Obama making speech after speech, gamely reminding his listeners of government's positive role in pursuing justice, security, and prosperity. He is trying to break out of the trap, and that is a tough road. We all know from personal experience that trust is easier to break than it is to rebuild.

The Costs of Austerity

Sooner or later, tax cuts lead to cuts in government services, often when we can afford them least, when we most need the help government provides, and the jobs it creates (yes, government too creates jobs). The inevitable consequence of a decade of tax cuts is cuts to programs, services, and investments in the future. Canada has become the champion of austerity, which is now presented as not only the best way but the only way to deal with current economic problems, and not just for us but for our friends and allies. Austerity here in Canada does not cut as quick and deep as what we are seeing in many other countries, especially in southern Europe. Here, austerity is implemented in slow, albeit accelerating motion, but the direction is clear, even if the consequences are not as immediately visible.

Politically, the argument for some version of austerity is pretty potent. It builds on our internationally recognized success in the 1990s for balancing the budget and reducing debt (which unquestionably made us more resilient during the tough times that followed, though with equally undeniable costs to health and social programs, among other things). It draws on a powerful thread that runs through our history—one of pragmatism and frugality, and feeds off our growing disenchantment with government, along with the serious troubles we are seeing elsewhere.

Opposition voices are reluctant to offer alternatives for fear of being seen as fiscally imprudent or stuck in the past, defending "big government." And so, presented with no options, we come to believe that in fact there are none. A good rule of thumb for public policy is that when we are told there is no alternative, the opposite is usually true: not only *is* there an alternative, but it is probably one we would prefer if it was offered.

We do indeed have choices—better choices. Of course, we have to be prudent as we dig out of the current deficits that were created partly as a result of wise government action to mitigate the worst consequences of the global recession. But this is not the 1990s. Our situation is not dire. Canada is not Greece. Before the assault on the deficit in the 1990s, about one-third of every tax dollar was going to service the federal debt, and dire warnings were circulating that Canada was at risk of hitting a debt wall and falling to third world status with respect to global capital. So we cut. But the thing is, the global economy was pretty strong and getting stronger. We were contracting, the US was spending, and our dollar was low. As it turns out, economic growth—along with real sacrifice—was crucial in balancing the budget and exceeding all reduction targets. And it didn't hurt that taxes then were quite a bit higher, along with interest rates, the costs of debt much greater, and the consequences of reductions potentially offset by lowering rates. So deficits turned to surpluses more quickly than anyone expected, and those tax-fuelled surpluses were quickly bringing down our debt.

Today, our level of debt is still the envy of other countries, and interest rates are low. But now the global economy is slowing and the future is less certain, less promising than it was in the 1990s; the recession lingers like a bad cold. Even here in Canada, and we have been pretty lucky, we continue to shed good jobs and, like everywhere else, our markets can expect to be battered by continued volatility. This is not the 1990s. Neither the fiscal urgency nor the economic conditions are the same.

And most important, we ought to understand how we got back into deficit and increasing debt in the first place, at least at the federal level. It was just a few years ago that we were running surpluses year after year. In 2006, when the current federal government took the reins, the federal surplus was $14 billion. Clearly program spending was not putting us at risk. That surplus, had we kept it, would have provided great resilience in the face of economic downturns, times when we inevitably spend more and lose revenue. The federal government would have been able to help the provinces, especially those hit hardest, and would have had more fiscal room to manage the stresses of an aging population and begin to transform our programs and invest in the future.

So what happened? Certainly part of the answer is that we are paying off the costs of stimulus spending made necessary during the recession. But that spending stopped earlier than some would have hoped, and so even with moderate growth, we should be able to return to balance with a bit of prudence, not draconian measures or constant cutting.

But recession spending is not really the culprit. Our big problem is that our revenues as a percentage of GDP are far lower than they were in the 1990s, and not just because of the recession and slow recovery. In many respects, our current and future fiscal challenges at the federal level and in some provinces are self-induced, the result of a succession of unaffordable tax cuts. Just think of the tens of billions annually taken out of our budgets since 2000 in reduced income taxes, capital gains taxes, corporate taxes, and the GST/HST, not to mention the long list of boutique tax "benefits" that amount to little more than tax cuts disproportionately benefiting those who need help least.

So our fiscal situation is not dire, at least not at the federal level. We are still reaping the benefits from the 1990s decade of sacrifice, and the challenges we do have are largely self-inflicted. And if we chose to get here, we can choose to get out.

Let us be clear that all the authors in this volume share in the broad consensus that we must be fiscally prudent. But let's pause to consider what fiscal prudence really means: It means spending wisely, reducing waste, collecting sufficient taxes to pay for the public goods and services we want, keeping budgets in relative balance over time, and keeping debt coming down, at least during reasonably good times.

Of course there is always room to find efficiencies, and we have important choices to make about our priorities. We will disagree about the choices and, ideally, that is what political campaigns are all about. A case can be made, for example, that we probably overbuilt our security apparatus after 9/11, and that in particular deserves a close look. And make no mistake, the costly plan to build more prisons and penitentiaries—unjustified by the evidence—either increases our debt or diverts money from priority services such as health and education.

As for waste, it is probably time to look at the stifling layers of bureaucratic control, a result of decades of decreasing trust, that make government more risk averse than ever, less innovative and efficient—and arguably less accountable and transparent. There are savings to be had here, but as our first Parliamentary Budget Officer repeatedly reminded us, the numbers don't add up; we will not balance the books with efficiencies and cuts to operating budgets. In any case, making the public sector work better will not be achieved by gutting government, but by breaking down its hidebound hierarchical structures, opening it up, and bringing it into the information age. Yes, government has become too central, authoritarian, and remote from our everyday lives. We have a big job to do to close the gap between citizens and their governments. But these are not primarily fiscal issues.

In fact, today's austerity is not about making government more efficient, or even about fiscal prudence. If it were, service cutbacks wouldn't be proceeding in tandem with large, unaffordable, and unnecessary tax cuts for the most affluent among us. The persistent emphasis on low taxes and cuts to public services looks more like ideology masquerading as fiscal common sense. In this light, austerity seems rather to be about cutting back the state and rolling out the free market agenda. Less public, more private; less collective, more individual. It is, in other words, the fulfillment of the neo-liberal counter-revolution rather than an economic plan for the future.

We know that some pretty smart economists from outside this paradigm, Paul Krugman (2012) and Joseph Stiglitz (2012) for two, have taken on the austerity agenda and tax-cutting neo-liberal ideology that underpins it. They argue that this is in fact the time for spending, for investments in education and infrastructure, and for putting money in the hands of those in greatest need. They argue that the consequences of premature austerity could match what we saw in the 1930s, that in any case, this strategy will not yield the growth and opportunities we need. And, they add, it is also about time to stop the tax cuts and start increasing taxes generally, especially for those who benefit most from economic growth. (In the US, a growing number of rich Americans are calling on the government to raise their taxes.)

Frankly, we don't have to try to weave our way through the debates among economists to be worried about the consequences of austerity. A recent report from the (not-left-leaning) IMF has surveyed the international evidence and concluded that in tough times deep government spending cuts do not, at least in the short term, create jobs and growth; what they do create are very significant costs to society, the economy, and quality of life for the majority (Ball, Leigh, & Loungani, 2011; IMF, 2012). Whatever the benefits of austerity, its costs are real and significant, and they fall most heavily on the people who are least able to bear them. Specifically, the authors of the report show that austerity, especially when it cannot be offset by a significant lowering of interest rates, brings with it increases in unemployment—particularly enduring unemployment—suppression of wages for the majority, and deepening income inequality.

The Inequality Trap

As we cut taxes and make them less progressive, the costs of the free lunch accumulate. While the most obvious signs may be longer wait times, potholes, and crumbling bridges, more insidious and worrisome is the inevitable rise in income inequality. Historically, Canada's progressive and higher taxes and the programs they funded were pretty effective in reducing the inequalities the market yielded. But as these inequalities increased, governments have done less to mitigate them than ever before.

The Conference Board of Canada (2011) and the Organisation for Economic Co-operation and Development (OECD) (2011) are the latest to sound the alarm that inequality is on the rise here—and fast. As the British researchers Richard Wilkinson and Jane Pickett (Wilkinson, 2011) have documented, extreme inequality—in particular, the growing gap between a few very rich and the rest—is corrosive and costly. It diverts capital, stifles demand, over time deprives us of the talent we need, and undermines democracy. It also eventually turns us against one another, with the gated community only a physical manifestation of a deeper divide.

Inequality feeds and is fed by divisive and fear-based politics, what the writer Benjamin DeMott (2003) calls "junk politics," which has contempt for evidence and experts, plays to both our fear and vanity, and divides us into hard and fast moral categories: villains and heroes, criminals and victims, hard-working tax payers and freeloaders, job creators and the rest.

When the middle rungs of the ladder start to disappear and the gap between top and middle becomes too great, feelings of superiority and inferiority almost inevitably follow. Many at the top come to believe that they deserve all they have, that they are the ones who create the jobs and keep the economy running. The very successful too often forget how much they owe to others, including earlier generations that were more ready than we are to sacrifice and pay taxes. I have always been struck by how most of us believe in luck unless we become successful; then luck suddenly has nothing to do with it. In extremely unequal societies, the rich, believing that they truly are the job creators, will often exert all of their considerable influence in the fight against paying more taxes. In this, they have been very successful.

At the other end, if the rungs of the ladder seem too far apart to climb, then those lower down will wonder why they should participate at all. If we think that others will exploit the system or consistently turn it to their advantage, if we believe the game is unfair, we will not want to play. If the game is rigged, why participate, why vote, why pay taxes?

In the fifties when Canadians were, however much they grumbled, more willing to pay taxes (and vote), most thought of themselves or at least their families as being on the way up. With extreme inequality, aspiration is blunted and replaced by fatalistic grumbling or hopelessness and opting out—or acting out. Canada has always been in the middle of the pack of developed countries on the issue of inequality, just above the average. No longer, and we are now moving in the wrong direction—and our approach to taxes has more than a little to do with this.

So as we dig out, we ought to make sure that we are not stripping away the very tools necessary to withstand future shocks, and to create jobs and opportunities now and for the future. We ought to make sure that we are not hollowing out the country, allowing the erosion of those things that give meaning to our shared citizenship and should be a source of comparative advantage going forward. And we ought to make sure that we are not undermining our ability to invest in those things that will make us stronger and greener for the future.

Of course we ought to be fiscally prudent, but first that means we ought to understand where we are and how we got here.

Choices for the Future

Perhaps of all the reasons that tax has become a four-letter word, our blunted aspirations are key. The baby boomers, who still hold considerable sway, especially in government, seem today more interested in holding on to what they have than in building something new. And for the first time in generations, Canadians worry that the young will not have it as good as their parents did. Taxes are, among other things, an investment in the future. How much harder is that to sell when people believe they are managing personal and collective decline? Without aspiration, without hope, many will want to keep all they can for themselves and their families to get through the day.

Of course, we are not there yet. Canada remains more equal than our neighbours, and we still have extraordinary assets and great promise. Some provincial governments have resisted the call for more cuts. But we certainly cannot afford complacently to wait much longer as the bills for our free lunch pile up: growing inequality, sagging productivity, a deteriorating environment. We cannot build a future out of desire for more of the same and in the same way. And we cannot build a future on the belief that the future does not belong to us—that it belongs to the market.

For too long, those of us in public policy have got it wrong. Even the most compassionate argued that we have to get the economy right first, that we would look at social and environmental issues later when we could "afford" to. But we cannot get our economy right if we don't keep people, democracy, and environment at the centre. We cannot afford to do otherwise. We will not retake the future until we change the conversation, and that has to begin with a commitment to greater equality and fairness, jobs and opportunities for the many and not just wealth for the few, dignity for all those who fall out of the market in tough times or cannot get in through no fault of their own, and a concerted effort to combat poverty and its extraordinary costs to us all.

The future will need a more innovative, productive, and confident Canada—but none of that will happen without a more just and equal Canada.

Breaking Out

We have to be smart about taxes. The reluctance to rethink how we tax has meant that many of our challenges are simply never discussed: how cities with very limited revenue sources can meet their challenges, what should the balance be between federal and provincial revenue if we are to maintain social solidarity and flexibility, and how can we achieve greater intergenerational fairness while meeting the demographic challenges of our aging population.

Jim Stanford, economist for the Canadian Auto Workers, provides a broad overview of taxes and spending in Canada and offers an alternative to the neo-liberal view. Queen's economist Robin Boadway discusses some of the particular challenges facing a federation such as ours. He warns of the risks caused by the erosion of the federal share of tax revenue, and proposes some fixes to ensure greater resiliency, solidarity, and social citizenship.

If we are to meet our shared challenges, we will all have to carry some of the burden. The consensus among economists is that cutting the GST was a mistake, and the majority of them also defend the HST. Scott Clark, former deputy Minister of Finance contributes a chapter on a smarter, simpler, more efficient tax system in which the GST/HST would play a bigger role. And sooner or later we are going to have to put a price on carbon to share the costs of a new economic and energy paradigm. Member of Parliament Stéphane Dion, former Liberal Leader and Environment Minister, sketches out why a carbon tax is a good idea but a hard sell. In this era of the financialization of the economy and the growing costs and dangers of speculation, Toby Sanger makes a compelling case for relatively new sources of revenue that would have other economic benefits, such as financial transaction taxes or other taxes focused on our financial institutions. But when it comes to taxes, fairness is not a secondary consideration; a good place to start is to ask the rich to step up. When it comes to taxes, it is smart to be progressive, to ask the wealthy to pay a bit more for that lunch that no one is getting for free, and to ask those who do greatest damage to the commons to pay more for its preservation. CCPA economists Marc Lee and Iglika Ivanova take a crack at what a more progressive tax system could look like.

There is no systematic evidence that tax cuts are the road to economic growth or that low taxes for corporations or the rich produce jobs. Our love affair with low taxes is based on unproved assumptions about the benefits with no account for the costs. High-tax jurisdictions in northern Europe are outperforming us on jobs and productivity, and are more equal societies. They have been smart about which taxes they raise and which they eliminate and they have continued to reform, sometimes dramatically, how they deliver services. They understand that governing is about making choices on how to tax, spend, and regulate. Nothing good can come of taking taxes off the table.

It is time to make some hard choices about the Canada we want, what services we see as essential, how much inequality we are prepared to tolerate, choices that will determine our ability to take back the future. Already we seem to be tiring of the fairytale. Ever lower voter turnout is a sign that we are not inspired by the leadership we are getting.

What we are seeing across Europe, at least on the streets, is an intensifying rejection of the current paradigm of tax cuts and austerity with no apparent end. We see glimpses in the US and Canada in the Occupy movements, the student protests against tuition hikes, and Idle No More. People, mostly young, but also across the generations have increasingly decided not to wait for their politicians to lead. Most great change starts outside of conventional politics; the sense is growing that the economy and the environment are being wrecked by a powerful few, and it is not right that the rest have to pay the freight—and they are demanding better. These movements are beginning to tell other stories, stories of people left out, of debts too big to handle, of lost jobs, precarious jobs and stagnant incomes, of family hardship and no helping hand. They are saying a lot of things: that maybe we have it all wrong, and they no longer believe the promises.

No one knows where all this unrest will go and what its impact will be, except that it creates an opportunity, long overdue, to change the conversation. Much will depend on leaders across every sector of our society joining that conversation. The chapter by University of Ottawa's Paul Saurette and Simon Fraser's Shane Gunster provide some ideas of just what it will take to get there.

We always get more from our political leaders when we demand more. And we always get the government we deserve and the future we are willing to make and pay for.

Note

This introduction draws on notes prepared for an address at the Gardiner Museum, October 12, 2011, and various posts from Alexsblog.ca. The event was organized by the *Literary Review of Canada* and TVO, and sponsored by the Canadian Centre for Policy Alternatives. A shorter version appeared in *The Globe and Mail*.

References

Ball, L. E., Leigh, D., & Loungani, P. (2011). Painful medicine. *Finance and Development, 48*(3). Retrieved from http://www.imf.org/external/pubs/ft/fandd/2011/09/ball.htm

Conference Board of Canada. (2011). *Income inequality in Canada: Becoming more unequal.* Ottawa, ON: Author.

DeMott, B. (2003). *Junk politics: The trashing of the American mind.* New York, NY: Nation Books.

International Monetary Fund (IMF). (October 2012). *World economic outlook: Coping with high debt and sluggish growth.* Washington, DC: International Monetary Fund.

Krugman, P. (2012). *End this Depression now.* New York, NY: W. W. Norton & Co.

Organisation for Economic Co-operation and Development (OECD). (2011). *Divided we stand: Why inequality keeps rising.* Paris: Author.

Reguly, E., & Laghi, B. (2009, July 10). Stephen Harper speaks: The recession and the challenges of power. *Globe and Mail.* Retrieved from http://www.theglobeandmail.com/news/politics/harper-speaks-the-recession-and-the-challenges-of-power/article4213227/

Stiglitz, J. (2012). *The price of inequality.* New York, NY: W. W. Norton & Co.

Wilkinson, R. A. (2011). *The spirit level: Why greater equality makes societies stronger.* London, UK: Allen Lane.

Part I ▶ The Conversation Today

Everyday conversations about taxes have pretty much always been steeped in black humour and fatalistic grumbling. In the past, however, even if we complained we seemed to know what we were getting for our taxes. One might say we viewed taxes much like bad-tasting medicine: we didn't like it, but we knew it made us better.

But over the last few decades, the conversation, especially among our politicians and much of the centrist punditry, has hardened. All that seems left is the bad taste. Taxes are increasingly portrayed as a burden from which government should be granting us relief. No more do we hear about the obligations—and benefits—of our common citizenship, about how taxes tie us to one another and the common good. We have stripped out the notion that taxes are simply the way we purchase goods and services we cannot buy alone or that are better bought together. Gone is the language of citizen, replaced by the atomizing language of consumer and taxpayer. These taxpayers, we are told, know far better than some distant bureaucrat how to spend their money—as if roads, bridges, public schools, hospitals, and the like arise spontaneously. And the traditional notion that the rich pay progressively more because they can and because they benefit most from the opportunities our country affords has been reshaped by a reluctance to tax the so-called job creators, as though we were not all job creators in one way or another.

Tax cuts have become the solution to everything—to a sluggish economy and lagging productivity, to unresponsive governments, to increasingly cash-strapped families. Taxes get cut and productivity continues to lag, governments become less responsive, and family debt continues to grow. There's something wrong with this conversation.

In this section, Jim Stanford, economist with the CAW, gives us a broad overview of where we are today, taking us through the mix of taxes we pay and how these are tied to the spending our governments undertake on our behalf. In his piece he explodes a number of the current myths, exposes the danger of talking about taxes without simultaneously talking about what they are used for. He explicitly takes on the neo-liberal economic model of how free markets work. Recognizing that there are no truly free markets, Stanford proposes a real-world economics that looks at who benefits from tax cuts and who pays the price.

The tax picture in Canada is complicated by the fact that we are a federation, and that both orders of government have pretty equivalent taxing power. In Canada, then, we must ask not only how much we tax, whom we tax and how we tax, but also how each order of government uses its tax power and, in particular, what room the federal government has to pursue national goals and address inequality among provinces. Robin Boadway of Queen's University, one of this country's leading experts on taxes and fiscal federalism, shows in his chapter how the tax story in Canada has been one of decentralization, with worrisome consequences for the capacity of the federal government to promote national objectives and social citizenship, and for Canada's capacity to spread risk and respond to crises.

Hugh Mackenzie, a leader in Canadian tax policy, has contributed two related chapters. In the first he describes the ways in which talk of taxes has become divorced from the services they buy, and the distorting effect this has on our politics and policy. Mackenzie takes all our politicians across all parties to task for patronizing us, for implying that taxes can be cut with impunity, with no consequences to the services we receive and to the quality of our lives. In the second chapter, he focuses on the value of what our taxes buy, and what we lose when they are cut. He even quantifies some of those benefits to help us see the extent to which public services are the last great bargain.

Frank Graves, President and owner of EKOS Research, takes us through some historical and recent data to show that, yes, Canadians' attitudes are changing in the directions we might have predicted, but those attitudes are complex and suggest an opening for the kind of debate that our political leaders have, until now, been reluctant to initiate. In the 2012 US election, several jurisdictions with tax referenda opted for higher taxes, including California. Tax debates are emerging in the UK and Continental Europe. Perhaps, as Graves suggests, we are ready for the conversation here too.

Chapter 1

The Economic Consequences of Taxing (and Spending)

Jim Stanford[1]

Introduction

Are taxes bad for the economy? Or are they good? The answer depends, obviously, on what kind of taxes we are talking about, what rates they are set at, and—most importantly—what the money is used for. In this chapter I argue that the economic consequences of taxation cannot be considered without simultaneously analyzing the economic consequences of the programs that are funded with taxes. I also note that both the scale and the direction of fiscal policy (spending and taxing) reflect an ongoing struggle between competing segments of society about government's economic and social role. This struggle is not just over how big government should be, but whose interests it should serve.

Governments collect taxes in a myriad of different ways, and spend the money on hundreds of different programs. Not surprisingly, these diverse taxing and spending activities have an enormous economic impact on the level and stability of employment and income, on the productivity of work, on the distribution of income, and more. It is wrong to assume that just increasing the *size* of government automatically means that it will be more responsive to human and social needs. But so long as democratic processes allow citizens to ensure that fiscal policy interventions benefit the majority, the empirical evidence suggests that higher taxes (and the more extensive public programs they fund) do indeed produce better living conditions.

In short, contrary to conservative rhetoric, societies do have choices to make regarding both the scale and the direction of fiscal policy. The neo-liberal dictum that "there is no alternative" to low taxes is clearly wrong. Societies can choose to collect adequate taxes to fund extensive, high-quality programs that enhance quality of life. Indeed, I argue in this chapter that societies should ensure a level of taxation sufficient to provide high-quality programs, and that those taxes do not damage, but may even improve, economic performance.

This chapter is structured as follows. Section I positions the fiscal activities of government (taxing and spending) in the context of an ongoing struggle between competing sectors of society over the scope and direction of government policy. Section II reviews the various forms of taxes, while Section III catalogues the various types of government spending. Section IV then provides an overall analysis of the broad economic impacts made by these fiscal policy levers. Finally, Section V reports some international empirical evidence regarding the impact of government taxes (and spending) on economic and social outcomes.

I. Spending and Taxing—Contested Terrain

Conservatives often deride government as a "tax-and-spend" operation—implying that politicians' goal in life is to find ways to collect taxes from hard-working citizens, and then invent new (and presumably wasteful) projects to spend the money on. This stereotype is wrong on many counts.

No government collects taxes just for the sake of collecting taxes. In any democratic context, taxes fund a set of government activities and programs that are demanded by the citizens who elect their political leaders. If a government no longer feels compelled by public opinion to provide a specific program, they stop funding it. Taxes are then reduced, or used for some other, more important purpose.

So the order of the traditional conservative epithet should be turned around: a better description of the logical process of government fiscal policy-making is "spending and taxing." First governments decide, in the context of the conflicting and contradictory political pressures they face, what programs they will provide. Then they figure out how to fund those programs.

Neo-liberal governments, of course, have attempted to subvert this logic by cutting taxes *first*, even while the programs they fund are still in place. That creates a deficit, which these governments then invoke to justify subsequent spending cuts. This manipulative strategy can be defeated, however. First, one needs to be able to refute the artificial "deficit-phobia" used to legitimize the spending cuts. If the deficit was caused by tax cuts, then spending reductions are by no means "inevitable"; citizens can legitimately express and enforce their preference to continue paying the taxes in order to support valuable programs. If cutbacks are implemented anyway, protests are most successful when they highlight the ongoing contribution of these programs to social cohesion and economic performance. In short, one must be able to make visible the connection between tax cuts and service deterioration, even though they're often separated by many years. Many examples exist of successful campaigns to preserve important social programs (like education, health care, and public transit), and to increase the political cost on governments who play the "deficit card" in order to justify program cutbacks.

Since taxes are ultimately justified by the public programs they finance, there is little point considering the economic implications of taxes (whether specific taxes or the overall tax burden) in isolation. We need to analyze the implications of taxes (on economic performance, living standards, inequality, and other variables of interest) *together with* the impacts of the associated programs that they support.

Free market economists like to construct elaborate quantitative models that measure the so-called deadweight losses resulting from different kinds of taxes.[2] These estimated losses are always calculated relative to an idealized free market equilibrium economy that has never actually existed, nor could exist. In this fairy-tale world, markets always clear, stakeholders are always paid according to their productivity, and resources are always fully utilized in production. Thus anything that interferes with perfect market processes must, by definition, reduce well-being.[3]

Moreover, these theoretical models rarely consider the economic (and non-economic) *benefits* of the programs that are funded from taxes. They only measure the supposedly disruptive impact of collecting taxes on the workings of private markets, and hence they consider only one side of the spending and taxing equation. In contrast, this chapter will provide an integrated analysis that considers *both* halves of the fiscal equation—spending as well as taxing.

We know that governments act to enhance the economic interests of those constituencies in society that exert the most influence over them. In a truly democratic society, governments should be ultimately responsive to majority preferences, constrained by respect for certain basic rights of individuals and minorities. In flawed democracies like Canada's, governance is distorted by the ability of certain segments of society (especially those with wealth and economic power) to impose their priorities on the system through their ability to sway public opinion, influence the outcome of elections, and directly pressure decision-makers once they are elected. In every case, fiscal policy reflects the outcome of a struggle, whether fair or lopsided, between competing interests over the scope and direction of government intervention. Fiscal policy, in short, is contested terrain.

As these competing constituencies struggle to influence the shape of fiscal policy, it is important to remember that the battle is never simply about the size of government. And certainly almost nobody is fighting to do away with government altogether. Rather, it is about who benefits from public policy, and who government serves. In this light, virtually nobody is opposed to all taxes. Corporations and the mostly wealthy people who own them *want* a central state at least strong enough to perform many important functions—like protecting private property, managing social relationships, and paying for helpful government services such as training, roads, or utilities. Even if they want a smaller, less costly government, they know these functions require taxes that can amount to a considerable portion of GDP. For example, even in the US—the most aggressively pro-business jurisdiction in the developed capitalist world—government activity consumes over 30% of GDP, and that figure has not declined during the 30-year history of neo-liberalism.

In this context, the key priority for progressives is not to focus on how to make governments bigger, rather it is about showing how to use the tools of government to undertake interventions that enhance the living conditions of large portions of the population. In other words, a debate about taxes must include a debate about spending and who benefits.

Any analysis of the economic consequences of taxes must also be informed by an understanding of the real-world mechanics of investment, production, and employment in modern capitalism. Idealized free market theories pretend that capitalism operates through the spontaneous, self-directed decisions of individual actors, all striving to maximize the value of whatever endowment of productive resources they are lucky (or unlucky) enough to possess. In that regard, any barrier or cost that interferes with autonomous exchange is believed to reduce economic activity and efficiency, and hence human welfare. That starting assumption motivates strident opposition among doctrinaire neoclassical economists to virtually any government tax, program, or regulation;[4] although, as we have noted, that absolutist opposition to government is not shared by real-world business leaders, who understand well that they need a strong state to construct and regulate a suitably stable and business-friendly economic and social environment.

In fact, the modern capitalist economy operates according to a less idealized rulebook. Capitalism is not a giant "marketplace" where millions of equal exchanges occur constantly between atomistic economic agents. The process is not spontaneous and disaggregated. Rather, the economic system is driven in a top-down manner: decisions by profit-seeking companies to invest in production are the leading force in any capitalist economy. These investments are essential to setting the whole economic machine into motion. Without investment spending by private firms, the system grinds to a halt. This dependence on private investment is demonstrated vividly during a recession, when decisions by private companies to *stop* investing cause downturns in overall employment, incomes, and spending, thus creating an economy-wide downturn.

Corporate executives understand well the dependence of the whole economy on their willingness to invest. They "blackmail" others (their own workers, communities, even national governments) by threatening to disinvest unless they attain favourable concessions. In responding to this browbeating, which is a normal feature of a business-led economy, the rest of us must make independent judgments about how serious these threats are, based on our own conclusions about whether profits are adequate to elicit continuing investment.

Therefore, all other economic actors (including workers, small businesses, and governments) are fundamentally dependent on the continuing willingness and ability of capitalists to "do their thing." But the ownership of capital, and control over those crucial investment decisions, is concentrated among a small and powerful segment of society. Unless and until a strong and mobilized majority of society's members is collectively willing to challenge the dominance of private investment decisions over our entire economic trajectory (by supplementing, and ultimately supplanting, private investment with public or non-profit forms of enterprise), our collective dependence on business investment spending will constrain and tailor our fiscal policies (that is, spending and taxing) accordingly.

This fundamental *economic* inequality relates back to the *political* inequality discussed above. Because of their economic power business leaders demand, and usually win, immediate attention from governments. Governments know they must cater to businesses' demands for a hospitable, profitable economic and social climate, or else they will stop investing and the economy will experience a crisis. Hence, when business talks, government—virtually regardless of its political stripe—listens. This is reflected in the nature of modern spending and taxing programs.

But business leaders and the wealthy do not have the power simply to dictate fiscal policy to modern governments. Thanks to the (imperfect) democratic rights and powers working people have won through centuries of struggle, a mobilized majority of the population can still press governments to protect and advance their interests, rather than just those of the wealthy. It is possible for the majority of citizens to apply enough pressure to shift fiscal policy to reflect and respect their interests, despite the predisposition of government to cater to the interests of businesses and the wealthy individuals who own them. The spending and taxing measures currently in place in Canada and other modern capitalist economies thus reflect the to-and-fro of that ongoing struggle (between the 1% and the 99%) to shape government programs. Sometimes the goalposts are moved forward. Consider, for example, recent decisions in some provinces to cancel scheduled corporate tax cuts (BC and Ontario), increase income tax for high-income earners (in several provinces), and expand funding for targeted public programs (like child care in Quebec, anti-poverty programs in Newfoundland, and public transit infrastructure in many jurisdictions). Of course, more often during the neo-liberal era the goalposts have moved in the other direction. But retreat is not inevitable, it merely reflects the shifting balance of political forces in this ongoing struggle over the scope and effect of government's actions.

Some fiscal policies and programs, therefore, are aimed clearly at enhancing the power and profit of elites, while others are intended to benefit a broader segment of society. Many of our more progressive spending and taxing measures were implemented in the postwar decades, when a robust economy and pressure from confident social movements combined to push governments to focus on lifting living standards and moderating inequality. More recently, neo-liberal governments have generally (but not universally) headed in the opposite direction—reorienting fiscal policy so it enhances the power and profitability of wealth, and does less to buttress the bargaining power of working people. That more recent trend can and will be reversed if the majority of the population mobilizes its collective clout to demand fiscal policies that benefit them, not just the wealthy.

II. How Taxes Are Collected

To pay for the programs and services their voting constituents have demanded, governments collect revenues in numerous ways.

Personal income taxes are collected as a proportion of an individual's income. Most jurisdictions impose progressive personal income taxes, whereby the rate of tax rises with a person's income; well-off people thus pay a higher proportion to support government programs. An alternative system, used in more conservative jurisdictions (such as Alberta), is a flat rate personal income tax that collects income tax at a constant rate, regardless of income.

Corporate income taxes are paid as a share of a company's final bottom-line profits. These are usually levied on a flat rate, with various exemptions and loopholes for allowable expenses. In some cases, certain sectors of business (e.g., smaller firms) are granted preferential tax rates. The incidence of corporate tax payments ultimately falls on those who own corporations; income from capital is heavily concentrated among the highest-income segments of society,[5] and hence the incidence of taxation on capital falls on the same group.

Sales taxes have accounted for a larger share of total tax revenues in recent years (they are also known as value-added, or indirect, taxes). When a consumer makes a purchase, they pay a specified additional proportion in sales tax. Businesses also pay sales tax on their purchases, but in most jurisdictions—including Canada's GST and HST systems—payments on business inputs are refunded, with the effect that the tax is collected solely on the net value added at each stage of production. Sales taxes are promoted by business lobbyists and free market economists as more economically "efficient" than income taxes. This is at least debatable, and in part is a reflection of conservatives' hatred of personal income taxes and corporate taxes (because of the disproportionate burden that both place on high-income individuals).

Payroll taxes are tied to employment via premiums on wages or payroll. The tax may be paid by the employer, the employee, or is shared between the two; economic studies indicate that most of the burden falls on workers in any event, since even if the tax is nominally paid by employers, it indirectly results in lower wages.[6] Payroll tax revenues are often channelled to particular social programs, like pensions, health care, or unemployment insurance. Most are regressive in their incidence, especially those (such as CPP or EI premiums) that are capped at a certain level of income, beyond which no additional premiums are paid.

Wealth taxes may be imposed on the accumulated wealth of an individual or a business. This is morally appealing, as they allow governments to tax the most privileged members of society. However, they have fallen out of favour in recent years, mostly because wealthy people (whose political influence has grown) strongly oppose them. Annual wealth taxes, inheritance taxes, land or property taxes, and capital taxes on business are all examples of wealth taxes.

Environmental taxes have been proposed in recent years by environmentalists, to be imposed on the use of certain polluting inputs (like energy), or on the amount of pollution emitted. One example of an environmental tax is a carbon tax, which is collected on different types of energy according to their contributions to climate change. The theory is that in addition to collecting needed revenues, these taxes would have an added benefit of discouraging the undesirable activity—although their effectiveness in this regard is debated. Environmental taxes may also be regressive in their distributional impact, since lower-income households pay a higher share of their earnings for energy-related costs like home heating and gasoline.

Of course, not all government revenue needs to come from explicit taxes; some revenue can be generated through non-tax sources. For example, many governments impose user fees for certain programs and services like public transit, garbage collection, or even health care. User fees are generally regressive in their distributional impact, and inhibit the use of public services by low-income individuals, which can produce other, more costly problems down the road. Governments also generate income from their own investments, such as interest on financial investments, rent, and other income from government-owned properties, or profits from state-owned enterprises.

III. What Taxes Are Used For

Government spending consists of hundreds of different items which together account for a large share of total GDP. Several broad categories of spending can be defined, as follows:

Like businesses and consumers, most governments have debt, and they must service it with regular *interest payments*. Interest costs are perhaps the least useful type of government spending: they represent a regressive transfer of income from government to financial investors (who are disproportionately wealthy), and they do not directly provide any incremental service or source of demand.[7]

All spending other than interest payments is considered *program spending*. Program spending, in turn, can be divided into two major categories: transfer payments and government production.

Transfer payments involve collecting money (via taxes) with one hand, and then giving it back to someone else with the other. They involve no government function or expenditure other than transferring income from one group or sector to another. Transfer payments can be made to individuals (via social programs like unemployment insurance, welfare benefits, and public pensions), to businesses (through subsidies), to other levels of government (via equalization, health, and social transfers) or to other countries (as foreign aid).

Another portion of government program spending actually involves the government "doing" something—that is, undertaking the *direct production* of some product or service (rather than simply redistributing income). Some of this productive activity is undertaken "in-house" by government. Other production is undertaken by independent or semi-independent agencies that receive much or all of their funding from governments, such as hospitals or school boards. Governments hire labour to perform this production, and purchase inputs from private companies (sometimes including outsourced programs and services). Debates over "outsourcing" revolve around whether this production should be undertaken by government itself, or by private companies hired to do the job. The long running neo-liberal push for privatization is aimed at increasing the share of government production undertaken by private firms—whether financed by government (such as contracted-out garbage collection), or provided entirely through private markets (like privatized postal or transportation services). Either way, privatization creates additional profit opportunities for private firms.

Government production can, in turn, be further divided into two broad categories: *government consumption* and *government investment*. Most governments provide a range of public services that are used (or "consumed") by the public: they include health care, education, and culture. These programs are economically equivalent to consumption, since they involve the use of output to meet a current human need or desire. But this consumption occurs in a public form: instead of paying for it through their private purchasing power, the users of public services are entitled to this consumption by virtue of their status as members of society.

Not all government production is consumed, however. *Government investment* reflects the expenditure of public funds on lasting productive assets, which in turn facilitate more production (whether public or private) in future years. That is, after all, the economic definition of investment: production used to facilitate future production, rather than used up as current consumption. Governments thus allocate a portion of their revenues to long-lasting investments in infrastructure and other forms of physical capital—like buildings, schools, hospitals, roads, machinery, and equipment. Public investment is an important contributor to broader economic growth and productivity.

IV. Adding Up the Impacts

Fiscal interventions have major and varied impacts on economic behaviour and performance. Governments collect taxes from various stakeholders at various points along the economic chain, and use this revenue to undertake many different functions. Transfer payments are given back to specified households. Conversely, direct government production involves the public (or non-profit) production of goods and services—sometimes directly consumed, and sometimes reinvested in infrastructure and other lasting assets.

This high-level overview of the various components of government taxing and spending allows us to catalogue the equally varied economic consequences of fiscal interventions. Taxing and spending alters the operation of the modern capitalist economy in several important ways: affecting incentives for economic behaviour, altering the relationship between different agents in the economy, influencing the cyclical trajectory of the economy, and shaping the final distribution of income and consumption. We briefly consider these various effects in turn:

Incentives: Taxes alter the incentives facing different economic players. This is the major preoccupation of free market economists; they enjoy cataloguing a huge array of different economic activities that are purportedly discouraged by taxes. Usually these incentive effects are not a major problem within the range of normal, feasible tax rates. Certainly, real-world experience refutes the alarmist predictions of neoclassical economic thinkers who warn that high taxes discourage work and spark outward flights of capital and talent across the economy. In historical perspective, remember that the advanced capitalist economies experienced their most vibrant expansion in the initial postwar decades (from the 1950s through the 1970s) when the overall level of taxes was growing, and tax rates on corporations and high-income earners were substantially *higher* than they are today.[8]

Right-wing commentators used to invoke the spectre of high-income individuals leaving Canada altogether because of high taxes; these claims have been proven wrong, and in fact Canada has attracted more high-skill and high-income individuals than it has lost.[9] Public spending (financed with taxes, of course!) on everything from higher education facilities to research programs and public amenities in cities has been credited with helping to attract this inflow of mobile, high-skilled workers.[10] The notion that labour effort or supply will decline because the incentive to work is impeded by a "wedge" of taxes is not convincing either, especially at a time when most Canadians have no choice but to work in order to meet basic needs, and when current labour demand is clearly inadequate to employ the existing supply of willing labour.[11] (In this context, the so-called labour–leisure choice that is theorized by neoclassical economists becomes rather hypothetical.) Indeed, if labour supply "bends backward," as empirical research suggests is possible, then higher taxes may be associated with *more* labour effort, not less.[12]

In terms of a capitalist economy's overall dynamism, the impact of taxes on the profitability of private businesses—thus affecting both the motive and cash flow for new capital investment—is more important than the impact on individual labour effort. If taxes are too high on businesses, investment spending may weaken: companies may shift investments to other, more attractive jurisdictions, or else experience reduced cash flows to fund new projects. That is why even more progressive governments, like those in Scandinavia, generally pay for extensive public programs with high taxes on individuals, rather than on businesses. However, empirical evidence suggests that so long as corporate income taxes stay in a range that is broadly comparable with other jurisdictions, the impact of incremental changes in tax rates on business investment spending is hard to even detect.[13] Other factors—like the state of overall economic growth, the quality and productivity of labour, the local infrastructure, and so on—are more important to business investment decisions than the level of business taxes. And at a time when non-financial businesses in Canada are sitting on idle cash balances of nearly $600 billion, a hoard which grew steadily right through the recent recession, the claim that corporate investment is constrained by available cash flow is not credible.[14]

Incomes: With transfer payments (funded through taxes), working households are now no longer exclusively dependent on what they can earn through employment in order to survive. Government transfers now offer workers a certain degree of economic independence.[15] This can dramatically alter the economic and social relationships that underpin capitalism. Not surprisingly, workers generally appreciate strong transfer programs. But from employers' perspective, there is no more hated form of government spending than income security programs, especially those aimed at working-age people. They relax the compulsion on workers to offer their services for hire in the labour market: the old dictum "work or starve" no longer fully applies. Comprehensive income security thus makes it harder for employers to recruit workers with strong discipline at low wages. Vociferous attacks by business lobbyists in recent years on income security programs (like employment insurance or provincial welfare programs) have been motivated less by concern over the taxes required to fund these programs, than by opposition to their positive impact on the bargaining power of working people. Other transfer programs are aimed at enhancing the incomes and well-being of groups of non-working people, including child allowances, public pensions, and disability support programs.

Production: Direct government production establishes an entirely separate yet parallel chain of real economic output that supplements the productive activity of private companies. Society as a whole becomes somewhat less dependent on private businesses to set the economic cycle in motion. In Canada, direct government production accounts for about 15% of total production (measured as a share of GDP), and business lobbies try to prevent its further expansion. Nevertheless, the mere fact that production can and does occur successfully outside of the core profit-driven logic of capitalism opens up intriguing economic and political possibilities. At the same time, government production also helps to cushion total GDP and employment from the ups and downs of the private sector economic rollercoaster.

Investment and Productivity: Governments at all levels in Canada have stepped up their investment spending in recent years, partly as a response to the 2008–9 recession, and partly to make up for the deterioration in public assets that is the legacy of past decades of public sector underinvestment. In 2010, for example, public capital spending in Canada was 175% higher than it had been a decade earlier, and accounted for 27% of all non-residential fixed capital spending that year (compared to just 15% in 2000).[16] Major public investment projects generate all the same spinoff income and employment benefits as current government programs like health care and education. But there are additional benefits arising from the impact of high quality infrastructure on the productivity of the economy, including spinoffs into the private sector. Modern and efficient transportation, communications, and utility systems contribute to more reliable and efficient production throughout the economy.[17] By the same token, some government services also have beneficial spillover effects on economy-wide productivity, by helping to sustain a healthier and more cohesive population of workers.

Cyclical Stabilization: Both government production and transfer payments play an important counter-cyclical role in stabilizing the economic fluctuations that are a normal feature of capitalism. Indeed, the relative stability of public sector activity was a very important moderating force in Canada's economy during the recent 2008–9 recession. It is normal for budgets to experience deficits when the economy is in recession. Revenues decline during a downturn because tax revenues fall with reduced income and spending, while expenses for unemployment insurance and other social programs automatically increase. Tax and spending programs that respond in this way to broader economic trends are called "automatic stabilizers." The cyclical deficit experienced during a downturn actually helps the economy recover more quickly by sustaining spending levels. Perversely, trying to eliminate a cyclical deficit through proactive restraint with spending cuts or tax increases imposed during a recession only makes things worse by further undermining consumer and business spending.[18]

The stabilizing value of government spending in this regard is greater than just the direct expenditure involved. So long as unemployment exists, government spending generates *multiple* final impacts on production, employment, and income that are felt throughout the economy, including in private sector activity. The initial injections of government expenditure, whether on current programs, investment, or transfer payments, are ultimately re-spent several times over (by workers, businesses, and other economic actors), thus initiating subsequent second-order expansion in spending, production, and employment. This ultimate boost in activity from an initial input of government spending is called the "multiplier effect." Of course, even greater ultimate economic value can be attained from a steady, long-running infrastructure program, rather than short-term "make-work" projects. For example, during the 2008–9 recession, the federal government (matched by provincial governments) sponsored a temporary slate of capital spending projects. Emphasis was placed on so-called shovel-ready projects that had quick turnarounds and often high "political visibility," but did not usually reflect Canada's most pressing long-term infrastructure priorities. A better approach would be to support a steady, ongoing schedule of public investment projects—accelerating them during cyclical downturns, if need be—rather than quickly turning the funding on and then off in temporary bursts.

Employment: Another consequence of direct government production is that the government itself becomes a major employer. A significant segment of workers (around 15% of total employment in Canada) is employed by public and non-profit organizations rather than private sector businesses. Work in public sector agencies is usually, although not always, somewhat better-paying (especially for lower-wage workers) and more secure than it is in private companies, since the employer is not motivated by the same relentless pressures of profit and competition that drive private employers to ruthlessly cut costs and squeeze workers. Superior public sector employment practices thus help to lift standards elsewhere in the economy by power of example—and occasionally, when labour markets are tight, through competition for scarce workers. Today, however, public sector workers (and their wages, pensions, and benefits) have become a favoured target for austerity measures, and this will inevitably suppress wage trends across the labour force, both private and public.

Distribution: The overall spending and taxing activity of government has a generally positive impact on the overall distribution of income and opportunity in society. Despite neo-liberal efforts, both personal and corporate income taxes are still strongly progressive: they impose a proportionately larger burden on higher-income individuals. Indeed, as income distribution has shifted steadily in favour of the wealthy, their share of total income taxes paid has increased doubly, both because they earn a larger share of income, and because they are taxed at a higher rate. Other taxes are less progressive, or even regressive (such as sales taxes, which are mildly regressive, and capped payroll taxes like CPP and EI premiums, which are more strongly regressive). As others analyze in detail elsewhere in this collection, the overall tax burden has become less progressive in recent years, mostly because of the eroding importance of income taxes, both personal and corporate, in the total tax bundle.

But we must also consider the distributional impact of the spending side of the fiscal policy equation. We should not be unduly focused on demands to make the tax system *fairer*, in isolation from the *programs* that taxes fund.[19] Many forms of public spending make significant contributions to the well-being of working and poor people. Of course, well-off people and businesses also benefit from many government activities. But some programs, like income security transfers, clearly benefit poor people proportionately more than rich people. And even if we assumed that all individuals consume, on average, an *equal* share of the value of government-produced public services (that is, that government services are distributed neutrally), they still have a progressive distributional impact. This is because while public services add measurably to everyone's standard of living—supplementing the value of privately purchased goods and services—they make a *proportionately* larger contribution to the total standard of living of lower-income people.[20]

The overall impact of government spending and taxing on income distribution can be measured at three distinct stages. Begin with the total income (before tax) that individuals "earn" in the economy, including funds from employment, investments, and other private sources of income, excluding government transfers. This is called "market income," and its distribution in most capitalist countries, including Canada, is shockingly unequal. But those incomes are then adjusted by taxes paid to, and personal transfer payments received from, the government. Higher-income people pay more tax, and generally receive less transfer income. So the distribution of *total after-tax* income—that is, after taxes and transfers—is much more equal than the distribution of market income. Finally, distribution must also be adjusted to account for the real consumption opportunities provided by direct public services like health care, education, access to public facilities, and so on. These services supplement the standard of living for each household above and beyond what they can buy with their money income. This further reduces the proportionate gap between the richest and poorest households.

Despite the current regressive direction of neo-liberal fiscal policy, therefore, the overall spending and taxing activities of government continue to considerably narrow the gap between rich and poor. The difference between the richest and poorest households in market incomes is many times larger than the difference in final total consumption. In Canada in 2010, for example, the average market income of the top quintile of households was 54 times as great as the lowest quintile: a stunning degree of inequality. After taxes and transfers, however, that ratio fell to 9:1. And if we assign each household with an equal proportionate share of real public services in Canada (worth some $8,000 per Canadian in 2010), then the ratio of inequality in final consumption falls to 5:1 or lower.[21] This positive impact of government taxes and programs is not as strong as it used to be, nor as strong as it could be. But the positive distributional effect of government fiscal policy is still very powerful, and it is important to understand the different ways in which it is felt.

In sum, the effects of taxes and the programs they support are felt in numerous, interrelated ways throughout the whole economy.[22] The obsession of free market economists with the supposedly chilling impact of taxes on initiative and effort is misplaced; there are many more important, and largely positive, impacts of government programs on the level, stability, and efficiency of economic activity. Table 1.1 summarizes the economic impacts of government spending and taxing across these various broad dimensions. Unless you accept the starting theoretical assumption of free market economists that *any* interference with the perfect workings of private markets must necessarily reduce social welfare, then evidence that taxes significantly undermine economic performance is scarce. In contrast, there is compelling evidence that the programs financed from taxes provide numerous benefits: stabilizing and diversifying incomes, directly producing useful services, and significantly moderating inequality and exclusion.

V. International Evidence on the Aggregate Economic Impacts of Spending and Taxing

Figures 1.1 through 1.5 present aggregate economic data from a cross-section of 34 OECD economies illustrating the correlation (or lack thereof) between taxes and economic performance. In each case, a scatter plot illustrates the pairing of a country's overall tax burden (measured as a share of GDP averaged over the last decade to minimize the impact of cyclical factors) with some indicator of economic and social performance. The tax burden is measured along the

Table 1.1 Economic consequences of taxing and spending

Nature of Effect	Strength and Direction of Effect
Economic Incentives	
Labour supply	Negligible impact on work effort.
Business investment	Non-linear and weak negative impact on capital spending; negligible impact if taxes are broadly competitive with other jurisdictions.
Incomes	Transfer payments diversify and stabilize household incomes; support consumer spending.
Production	Government production diversifies and stabilizes total output.
Investment and Productivity	Public capital spending adds significantly to total investment. Public investment and current services can both help to boost private sector productivity.
Macroeconomic Stabilization	Automatic stabilizers offset private market cycles. Public sector output and employment are more stable.
Employment	Public sector jobs diversify employment opportunities. Public sector conditions help lift labour standards in the private sector.
Income Distribution	Taxes and transfers substantially reduce inequality in money incomes. The consumption of public services further reduces inequality in final consumption.

horizontal axis; the respective "outcome" measures are plotted along the vertical axes. A linear trend line is added to illustrate the overall direction of correlation evident in each scatter plot. Canada's position in each graph is also highlighted.

In terms of economic efficiency, there is no evidence that higher tax burdens reduce the effectiveness with which productive resources (and labour in particular) are put into motion. Figure 1.1 compares tax burdens to average realized labour productivity growth over the past decade; there is no statistically significant correlation between the two variables.[23] There are several higher-tax jurisdictions—including Finland, Sweden, Denmark, the Netherlands, Austria, and Germany—that have achieved better long-term productivity growth than Canada, despite (or perhaps because of) their higher overall level of taxes.

Figure 1.2 similarly indicates there is no correlation whatsoever between taxes and unemployment. Many OECD countries are able to combine generous public programs, including income security measures that put Canada's to shame, with efficient labour market structures and strong employment

Figure 1.1 Tax rates compared to labour productivity growth: OECD countries, 2000–2011

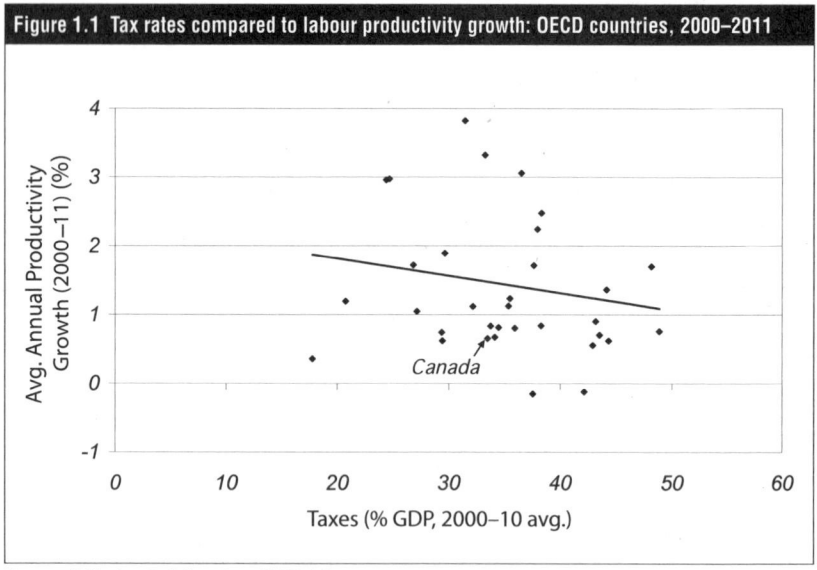

Source: Author's calculations from OECD data.

Figure 1.2 Tax rates compared to unemployment levels, OECD countries, 2000–2011

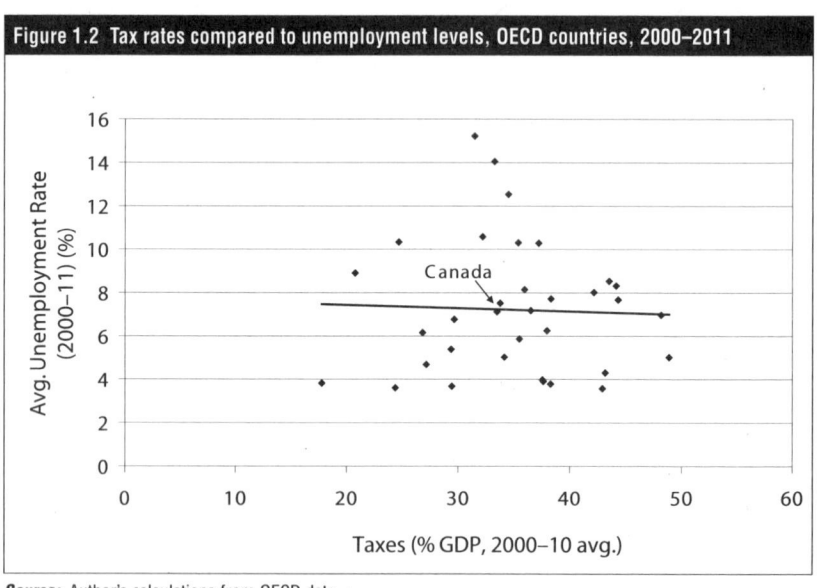

Source: Author's calculations from OECD data.

outcomes. The experience of several European countries is convincing evidence that it is possible to provide comprehensive and generous income security, while at the same time achieving strong labour market outcomes and very low unemployment.

In terms of income levels, Figure 1.3 indicates that there is a visible and statistically significant relationship between aggregate tax levels and income. Higher-tax countries tend to demonstrate, on average, higher incomes. This does not mean that high taxes *cause* higher incomes; in fact, the dominant causation in this relationship certainly runs from higher incomes to higher taxes, not the other way around. Higher-income countries have more resources that can be devoted to public programs. And many public programs, such as health care and education, have a high "income elasticity of demand." This means that societies tend to allocate a *growing* share of total income to these services as their income levels rise; public services become relatively more important social priorities as an economy becomes more developed. Higher-income countries also have more developed and (hopefully) democratic political structures, which allow the majority's interest in the provision of public services to be expressed and enforced. In other words, it appears that taxes and income can become part of a virtuous cycle in which prosperity funds the programs that sustain or enhance prosperity. Whatever the direction of causation, Figure 1.3 certainly refutes the

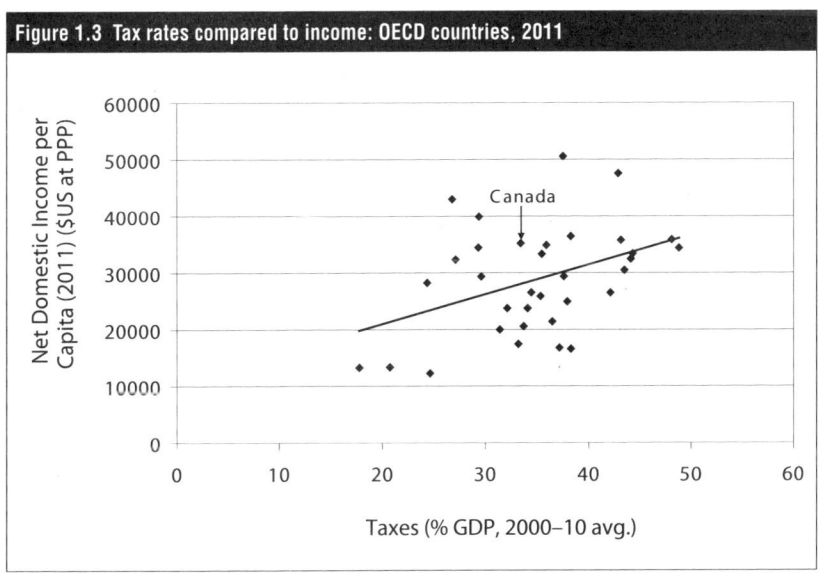

Figure 1.3 Tax rates compared to income: OECD countries, 2011

Source: Author's calculations from OECD and UNDP data.

conservative claim that low taxes are a prerequisite for prosperity; in fact, the opposite correlation is evidently true.

Figure 1.4 shows that income inequality is negatively and strongly associated with tax burdens. Not surprisingly, societies that allocate a larger share of total GDP to public programs tend to demonstrate more equal distributional outcomes. Causation in this relationship could run both ways. As I discussed in detail above, public programs themselves obviously serve to reduce inequality either directly, through transfer payments, or indirectly by allowing lower-income individuals more opportunity, thanks to accessible education and health programs, to successfully support themselves. At the same time, where income is distributed more equally, the power imbalances that can distort debates over fiscal policy (whereby a rich minority subverts the desire of the majority for a healthy network of public services and income security) are less consequential. In this regard, taxes are good for equality, but equality is also good for taxes—since higher equality helps to reinforce political support for public programs and the taxes that pay for them.

Finally, Figure 1.5 provides perhaps the most important and impressive evidence of the value of taxes and the programs they support. It plots each country's tax ratio against its score in the United Nations Development Program's Human Development Index (HDI), a composite measure of income, education, and life expectancy.[24] A statistically significant positive relationship is visible between taxes and this concrete, widely accepted measure of human well-being. This does not imply that paying higher taxes, in and of itself, improves human

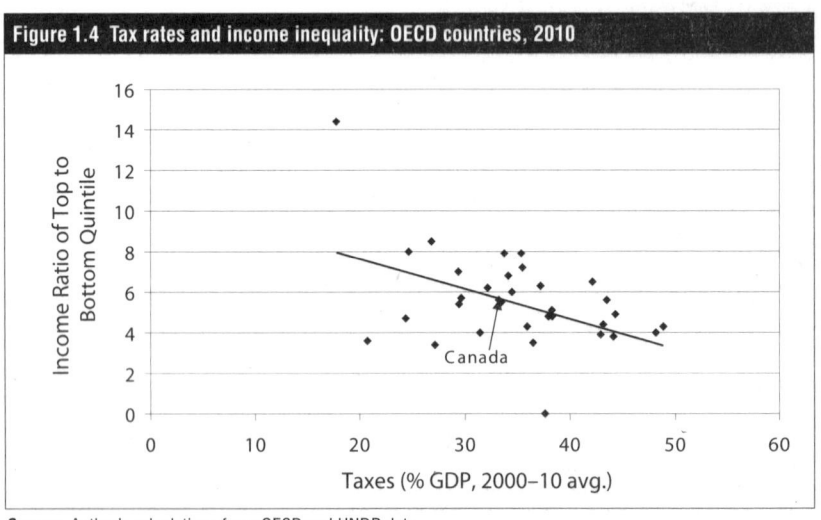

Figure 1.4 Tax rates and income inequality: OECD countries, 2010

Source: Author's calculations from OECD and UNDP data.

Figure 1.5 Tax rates and Human Development Index: OECD countries, 2011

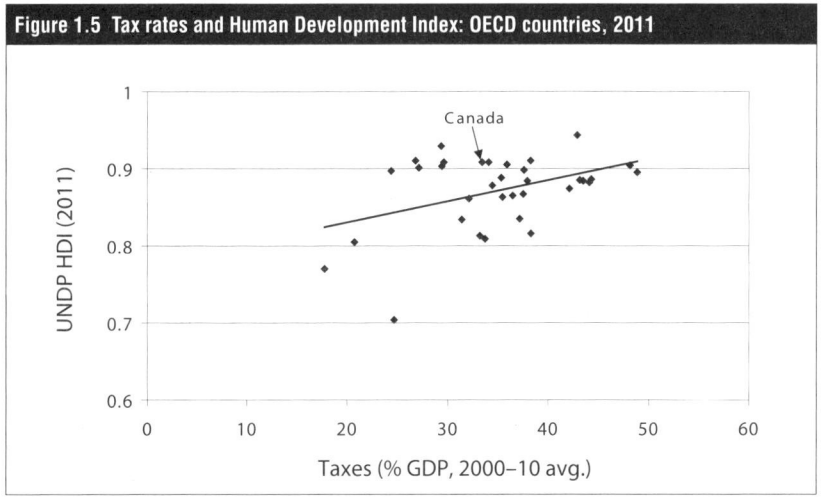

[Scatter plot: UNDP HDI (2011) vs Taxes (% GDP, 2000–10 avg.), with Canada labeled]

Source: Author's calculations from OECD and UNDP data.

living standards; rather, it is the *public programs taxes pay for* that make such an important and measurable difference to quality of life. The evidence is clear: citizens in countries that collect more taxes (and use them to finance effective, valuable public programs) live longer, and live better, than those in countries that do not.

Conclusion

The goal of progressives is not high taxes, or bigger government for its own sake. Rather we campaign for *good policies and programs*, recognizing that those programs need to be financed by taxes in order to exist. Empirical evidence and real-world experience indicate that wise public spending generates a myriad of economic benefits, measured by stronger and more stable incomes and employment, better cyclical stability, improved productivity, and better living conditions—evidenced by concrete outcomes in health, education, and life expectancy. Sufficient taxes can be collected to pay for those programs, without negating the economic benefits created by them. Countries with overall tax burdens much higher than Canada's demonstrate superior growth, income, and productivity performance. We can therefore frame fiscal debates in the following manner. First, we must demonstrate and argue for the concrete benefits that are provided by specific public programs. Second, we show that taxes are a necessary and tolerable cost of attaining those benefits, and that they can be collected in an efficient, fair, and economically sustainable manner.

Historical and international experience proves that society has the capacity and freedom to make important choices about fiscal policy. Collectively, we can make choices regarding the extent of taxes, the way taxes are collected, and the nature of the programs they fund. There are benefits and costs associated with each tax and program. It is possible to construct a composite package of taxes sufficient to fund high-quality and extensive public programs that is still consistent with strong employment, investment, and productivity outcomes. Modern-day globalization makes it more complicated to design that composite package, since we must keep an eye on the international mobility of capital, but not impossible.

Neo-liberalism was ushered in with Margaret Thatcher's famous dictum, "there is no alternative." But that claim is false. Three decades later, merely recognizing that society has the ability to make fiscal choices is, in and of itself, a radical conclusion. Making the most of that choice, and preserving the democratic freedoms that allow us to continue to exercise it, is the task we now face.

Notes

1. Economist, Canadian Auto Workers, Toronto, stanford@caw.ca. This chapter adapts and extends work I had published in 2008.
2. Auerbach and Hines (2002) provide a summary of this mode of analysis.
3. For a critique of the underlying logic of computable neoclassical welfare models, see Stanford (2003).
4. And it also explains the quantitative estimates generated by neoclassical computable general equilibrium models of the supposed costs of taxes and other government-inspired "distortions."
5. According to data published by Canada Revenue Agency (2010), two-thirds of all taxable dividend income and three-quarters of all taxable capital gains were received by tax-filers with an income in excess of $100,000 in 2008 (a group that represents just over 5% of all tax-filers).
6. See Dahlby (1993) for a summary of evidence in the Canadian context; she finds over 80% of the final incidence of payroll taxes is borne by workers.
7. Of course, whatever project was financed with the borrowed money will have generated some benefit that needs to be weighed against the subsequent cost of interest payments.
8. Data reviewed by Hungerfold (2012) indicate a historical correlation between higher tax rates on businesses and high-income households on the one hand, and faster economic growth on the other, although Hungerfold does not believe there is a causal link between the two.
9. The fact that living and social conditions in Canada are better than they are in the US and some other jurisdictions, in large part because of public programs funded by taxes, has helped to attract these individuals to Canada, the complete opposite of conservative predictions. This point is emphasized by Florida (2008), among others.
10. Lewington (2011) documents the recent inflow of foreign experts to Canadian universities.
11. At time of writing in 2013, official unemployment in Canada totaled 1.4 million. Considering other pools of unutilized or underutilized labour (including discouraged workers, the decline in labour force participation, involuntary part-time workers, those waiting for jobs to start, and others), true unemployment in Canada is at least 2 million. See Stanford (2013) for more details.
12. In a backward-bending supply situation, workers have a target level of income; if after-tax wages are lower, then they will choose to work more hours to meet that target (and vice versa); hence higher taxes can elicit more labour supply, not less. Of course, the extent to which individuals can genuinely "choose" how many hours they work is overstated by economists anyway.

13 See my 2011 report for a review of empirical evidence in the Canadian context. I found business tax reductions only had a very weak impact on business investment (mediated through higher corporate cash flows), and I argued that government would elicit more incremental business investment by allocating the same amount of funds—equivalent to the revenues lost through corporate tax cuts—to public investment projects, thus stimulating overall economic growth and "crowding in" additional business investment spending.
14 Continued growth in idle corporate cash balances recently led even the Bank of Canada's Governor, Mr. Carney, to express concern about the "dead money" sitting in idle hoards, and to challenge Canadian companies to boost their capital spending (Carmichael, Blackwell, & Keenan, 2012).
15 In the language of Esping-Anderson (1990), income security programs create an opportunity for the "decommodification" of labour, offering a prospect for survival independent of paid employment.
16 My calculations are based on data in Statistics Canada CANSIM Table 380-0017.
17 Pioneering empirical research into this effect was conducted by Aschauer (1989).
18 Even governments that support larger public programs and hence higher taxes in the long run must be careful about increasing taxes during a downturn, because of the negative macroeconomic side effects of tax increases at a time of economic weakness.
19 A progressive program funded with a regressive tax can still have a net progressive effect on distribution. This is true of social programs such as Employment Insurance and the Canada Pension Plan, both funded by capped, regressive payroll taxes—but both are very important pillars of income protection for working Canadians.
20 This argument is outlined with empirical support in Mackenzie and Shillington (2009).
21 My calculations are based on data in Statistics Canada CANSIM Tables 202-0701 and 380-0017.
22 An interesting attempt to measure many of these various impacts of government taxing and spending in Ontario is provided by the Centre for Spatial Economics (2012).
23 A weak and statistically insignificant correlation is visible in Figure 1.1, and is due solely to the recent inclusion within the OECD of several new member countries from Eastern Europe that have experienced rapid reported productivity growth in recent years. Across the set of long-established OECD members, there is no visible correlation at all between average tax burden and productivity growth.
24 The UNDP's HDI is not a perfect measure of living standards. In particular, it does not directly take into account the problem of inequality in income distribution, relying only on an average measure of real incomes. But it is certainly a more complete and valid indicator of living standards than simply ranking economies according to per capita GDP.

References

Aschauer, D. A. (1989). Is public spending productive? *Journal of Monetary Economics, 23*(1), 177–200.

Auerbach, A. J., & Hines, J., Jr. (2002). Taxation and economic efficiency. In A. J. Auerbach & M. Feldstein (Eds.), *Handbook of public economics* (Vol. 3, pp. 1347–1421). Amsterdam, NL: Elsevier.

Canada Revenue Agency (CRA). (2010). Income tax statistics for individuals, final statistics, 2008 tax year. Retrieved from http://www.cra-arc.gc.ca/gncy/stts/fnl-eng.html

Carmichael, K., Blackwell, R., & Keenan, G. (2012, August 23). This is dead money. *Globe and Mail*, p. A1.

Centre for Spatial Economics. (2012). *Budget 2012 and the public sector contribution to Ontario's economy* (OPSEU Report). Toronto, ON: Ontario Public Service Employees Union.

Dahlby, B. (1993). Payroll taxes. In A. M. Maslove (Ed.), *Business taxation in Ontario* (Research studies of the Fair Tax Commission, pp. 80–170). Toronto, ON: University of Toronto Press.

Esping-Andersen, G. (1990). *The three worlds of welfare capitalism*. Cambridge, UK: Polity Press.

Florida, R. (2008). *Who's your city: How the creative economy is making where to live the most important decision of your life.* Toronto, ON: Random House Canada.

Hungerfold, Thomas L. (2012). *Taxes and the economy: An economic analysis of the top tax rates since 1945.* Washington, DC: Congressional Research Service.

Lewington, J. (2011, February 20). Spending freely on research, Canada reverses brain drain. *Chronicle of Higher Education, 57*(24), p. 1.

Mackenzie, H., & Shillington, R. (2009). *Canada's quiet bargain: The benefits of public spending* (CCPA National Office Report). Ottawa, ON: Canadian Centre for Policy Alternatives.

Stanford, J. (2003). Economic models and economic reality: North American free trade and the predictions of economists. *International Journal of Political Economy, 33*(3), 28–49.

Stanford, J. (2008). *Economics for everyone: A short guide to the economics of capitalism.* London: Pluto Books.

Stanford, J. (2011). *Having their cake and eating it too: Business profits, taxes, and investment in Canada, 1961 through 2010* (CCPA National Office study). Ottawa, ON: Canadian Centre for Policy Alternatives.

Stanford, J. (2013). The myth of Canadian exceptionalism: Crisis, non-recovery, and austerity. *Alternate Routes,* 19–32.

Chapter 2

Taxes and Transfers in Canada: The Federal Dimension

Robin Boadway

Introduction

One cannot talk seriously about tax policy in Canada without the provinces being part of the conversation. The story of tax policy in Canada is in part about decentralization and the reduced capacity of the federal government to pursue national purpose and social citizenship. This chapter explores how we got here, what the implications may be for equity, solidarity, efficiency, and resiliency in changing times, and what steps are available to alter our course.

Canada is unique among federations in the discretion given to the provinces for revenue-raising, and the extent to which they exercise it. Contrary to the impression made by the Constitution, the revenue-raising authority of the provinces is comparable to that of the federal government.[1] The provinces can and do levy all the same types of taxes as does the federal government, including individual and corporation income taxes, sales taxes, payroll taxes, and excise taxes. In addition, they levy taxes and other charges on natural resources and, together with municipalities, property taxes.

Over the postwar period, the division of revenue-raising between the federal government and the provinces has gradually become more decentralized. From 1970 to 2009, provincial income tax collections rose from about 40% of federal collections to over 60%. The evolution of provincial revenue-raising responsibility is also reflected in the fact that transfers from the federal government now constitute about 18% of total provincial revenues, compared to 25% in 1990. Of particular importance has been the growing reliance on natural resource revenues by a handful of provinces. In 2008–9, Alberta obtained roughly as much revenue from natural resources as it did from its major tax bases (income and sales), while Newfoundland and Labrador and Saskatchewan obtained more (Treff & Ort, 2010).

At the same time, provinces have also achieved considerably more discretion over tax policy. Those provinces which have chosen to join the Harmonized

Sales Tax (HST) system to harmonize their sales taxes with the federal government have sacrificed some discretion over the tax base; however, unlike the initial signatory provinces (New Brunswick, Nova Scotia, and Newfoundland), those joining now are allowed discretion over their provincial HST rate and have been able to negotiate specific exemptions with the federal government. In the case of the individual income tax, provinces acquired greater autonomy over their rate structure with the changes in the Tax Collection Agreements in 2001. The movement from a system in which the provinces chose only a single tax rate to apply to the federal rate structure, to one in which they could choose their own rate structures was precipitated by pressures arising from the provinces' unwillingness to cede personal tax policy to a federal government whose share of income tax revenues had fallen dramatically. The provinces demanded, and got, a level of autonomy commensurate with their revenue-raising responsibility.

The decentralization of revenue-raising responsibility and tax policy discretion to the provinces was not the consequence of unilateral provincial actions. While it is true that provincial expenditure responsibilities were rising relative to the federal government, it is also true that the federal government was complicit in the transfer of revenue-raising to the provinces. There is a fundamental interdependency between federal and provincial budgets reflected in the so-called vertical fiscal balance. The federal government raises more revenue than it needs for its own program spending, and transfers the remainder to the provinces. The extent of revenue-raising done by the provinces depends on the level of transfers it receives from the federal government.

A lower fiscal gap goes hand in hand with greater self-sufficiency for the provinces, and both federal and provincial fiscal decisions contribute to the balance achieved. In principle, it is possible to imagine that the provinces move first in determining the vertical fiscal balance. That is, their expenditure choices combined with their decisions about how much revenue to raise lead to a shortfall of revenues that the federal government may feel obliged to cover through transfers. While the pressures faced by the provinces in providing health, education, and welfare programs combined with their limited capacity to raise revenues undoubtedly puts them in a vulnerable position, it is more plausible to view the federal government as the dominant partner in the determination of vertical balance. The single most important initiative that contributes to vertical balance is the level of federal–provincial transfers, which is determined by the federal government. It is reasonable to suppose the dynamics of decentralization that have characterized the Canadian federation have largely been the consequence of federal initiatives. Any future changes in fiscal balance will require the will or acquiescence of the federal government.

Why Is the Vertical Balance Important?

The extent of the vertical fiscal gap determines the division of revenue-raising responsibilities between the federal government and the provinces. While this is important for the design of good tax policy, it has much broader implications about the well-being of the federation. It is worth recounting the arguments informing the debate about the preferred amount of fiscal decentralization.

The arguments for fiscal decentralization are well known, and relate mostly to standard efficiency claims favoured by economists.[2] Accountability, the argument goes, is fostered to the extent that provinces are required to raise taxes to cover their own expenditures. In its weakest form, this applies to marginal revenues raised: provinces are alleged to have more effective control over the size of their budgets if they are responsible for raising incremental revenues. But forceful proponents of decentralization take the view that any dollars received as transfers will not be spent as responsibly as dollars raised from one's own tax revenues. Decentralists further argue, based on analogies to private markets, that fiscal competition induced by decentralization will necessarily discipline sub-national governments to behave more efficiently, reduce waste, and innovate. Merely relying on transfers for one's revenues will discourage provinces from proactively developing their own economies so as to become more self-sufficient.

These arguments no doubt have some merit, although the evidence is not at all clear. Whatever their merit may be, there are some compelling counter-arguments to suggest that revenue decentralization can have deleterious side effects, and these compound with more decentralization. The side effects have to do with tax efficiency, and more importantly with redistributive equity and social citizenship. I will discuss these in more detail in the following sections, but a brief summary is useful at the outset.

First, the decentralization of revenue-raising can compromise tax harmonization. This is an efficiency problem to the extent that agreeing about a common base is made more difficult. But more important, the decentralization of rate structures can lead to a deterioration of the equity properties in the tax system as provinces compete down redistribution standards.

Second, decentralization necessarily increases horizontal imbalances in the federation, since provinces differ in their ability to raise revenues. In principle, this could be addressed by enhancing equalization. But decentralization makes that more difficult, both since the federal government's revenue-raising ability has been reduced and because the imbalances to be corrected have increased. This is a particular problem in a setting where horizontal imbalances are being exacerbated by the growing importance of regionally based natural resource revenues and the uneven distribution of the aging population across provinces.

Third, decentralization reduces the ability of the federal government to influence the design of programs for which provinces have exclusive legislative authority, but which have national consequences. A substantial share of provincial program spending is in the areas of health, education, and welfare, largely governed by provincial legislation. The federal government has an interest in these programs because they address objectives that are at least partly of national interest, including social insurance (or risk-sharing), equality of opportunity, and equality of outcomes. As I discuss below, these objectives are a priori of national interest because they define social citizenship in Canada, and this is recognized by Section 36(1) in the Constitution Act of 1982.

Finally, there is one other concern related to the consequences of decentralization. From a long-term perspective, decentralization reduces the insurance role of a federation. It is notable that all four of the provinces that currently do not receive equalization did so in the past. Newfoundland and Labrador was a traditional have-not province for most of its early years after entering Confederation, and Saskatchewan was, more often than not, a recipient. Indeed, Alberta had to be bailed out of bankruptcy before the Second World War. Conversely, Ontario recently went from being a habitual contributor to recipient of equalization. The system of federal–provincial transfers is one of the three main mechanisms available in a federation to adjust to regional shocks. The other two are the progressive personal tax-transfer system, and migration. Since the former two are compromised, there is excessive dependence on migration as a response to large shocks.

The level and nature of decentralization in Canada is well beyond what is required to achieve the efficiency objectives attributed to it. We are approaching the range where our social fabric is in danger of being unravelled. The tendency to decentralize has been with us for some time now, and it will be difficult to reverse. It is therefore worth sounding another clarion call in the hope that policy-makers and the public take some heed.[3] However, there is an important caveat to doing so. While I emphasize the dangers of excessive fiscal decentralization in this chapter, the federal government is equally capable of behaving badly in a more centralized system. Federal tax policies may fail to meet everyone's norms of a just and efficient society. Federal transfers to the provinces may be too intrusive or susceptible to pre-emptive and disruptive unannounced changes that lead to provincial fiscal imbalances. Perhaps a return to more open and transparent federal–provincial collaboration is needed.

We now turn to a more detailed account of the problems posed for achieving sound tax policy in a decentralized federation.

Tax-Transfer Harmonization

The federal government and the provinces co-occupy the same major tax bases. It is in the interest of both, and of taxpayers, for federal and provincial taxes to be harmonized as much as possible, while leaving sufficient discretion to each region to achieve their own fiscal objectives. Canada has a highly regarded system of tax harmonization for income and sales taxes, and one that is well worth preserving. Tax Collection Agreements (TCAs) for personal and corporate taxes ensure that participating provinces—all except Quebec for the personal tax, and all but Alberta and Quebec for the corporate tax—abide by using a common tax base. As well, a single allocation method is used to assign tax bases to provinces, and importantly, a single independent tax collection agency, the Canada Revenue Agency (CRA), administers taxes for both levels of government. Provinces have the discretion to set their own tax rates.

This TCA system was put in place when the federal government was much more dominant in the income tax field than it is now. As income tax room was transferred to the provinces they demanded, and got, more income tax policy discretion. An important change occurred in 2001 when, instead of being allowed to apply a single provincial tax rate to federal tax liabilities, the provinces were allowed, within limits, to set their own rate structures and tax credits. Thus provinces can choose the progressivity of their income taxes.

Sales tax harmonization involves the six eastern provinces either adopting the HST, or in the case of Quebec, retaining their own value-added tax system harmonized to the federal Goods and Services Tax (GST). Participating provinces adopt similar though not identical tax bases, and choose different provincial tax rates. They also provide provincial refundable tax credits to offset the consequences of harmonization on the lowest-income families. This harmonized value-added tax system is only administratively feasible because all HST provinces make use of the CRA to collect taxes, so firms only have to deal with one tax authority, and cross-border transactions are properly accounted for. There is an imperfect way of allocating the provincial share of HST tax collections among participating provinces using final consumption data, but this imperfection is of limited importance since HST revenues are ultimately subject to equalization. The four western provinces remain outside of the system, and apart from Alberta levy their own retail sales taxes. Most economists agree that as sales taxes go, the HST is far superior to provincial single-stage retail sales taxes because by purging business inputs from tax, sales taxes do not interfere with production efficiency, and domestic firms are put on a level playing field with foreign ones.

Although the system of tax harmonization has served Canada well by enhancing the efficiency of the tax system, the extent of decentralization of revenue-raising creates several concerns. The most important one is that decentralization leads to competitive pressures that erode the progressivity of the tax-transfer system: the so-called race to the bottom. This is evident is a number of dimensions. First, since provinces have been allowed to set their own rate structures, virtually all of them have adopted ones with fewer brackets than the federal government; Alberta only uses a single one. In principle, one might argue that there is nothing wrong with provinces choosing less progressive income taxes than the federal government. However, given that their share of total income taxes is about 40%, they have a significant influence over the progressivity of the income tax system as a whole.

Second, there is little doubt that competitive pressures have contributed to the erosion of provincial welfare rates over the last couple of decades, particularly since the Canada Assistance Plan, which matched provincial welfare spending with a federal grant, was replaced by the non-matching Canada Health and Social Transfer, and eventually the Canada Social Transfer (CST). The incomes of welfare recipients have been falling across Canada since 1994. For example, in Ontario, the real welfare income of a single employable person fell by 35% between 1994 and 2007, and in Alberta by 21% (National Welfare Council, 2008). Welfare recipients with children have fared better owing to refundable tax credits based on the number of children, but all welfare incomes have fallen in real terms, and relative poverty levels have increased. Needless to say, there is no harmonization of welfare rates across the provinces. Moreover, the federal government's contribution to welfare recipients is provided through refundable tax credits, and these are miniscule. It has unnecessarily and consequentially ceded to the provinces responsibility for transfers to the poor.

Third, although it happened long ago, a classic case of fiscal competition eroding redistribution is the estate tax. When the federal government vacated the estate tax field in the major tax reform of 1972, it invited the provinces to take it over. Initially, all provinces except Alberta did so. However, by 1979, all provinces except Quebec had abandoned the field, and a few years later Quebec did as well. Estate taxation was effectively eliminated. (It was replaced by a system of deemed realization of capital gains on death which simply changed the timing of payment for taxes that would ultimately have to have been paid anyway.)

The point of these three examples is that revenue decentralization introduces pressures that erode redistribution. Indeed, some proponents of decentralization would see that as an advantage.

Tax harmonization may not be enough by itself to alleviate the adverse consequences of business tax decentralization. The textbook case of adverse tax competition concerns the taxation of business income. On the one hand, the mobility of capital and firms results in inevitable pressures to reduce business tax rates in order to avoid losing businesses to other jurisdictions. These pressures in turn make the apparent cost of providing public services seem high to provincial governments, whose response is naturally to economize on spending, particularly on public services and transfers to the needy. This problem is more pronounced if, as I discuss in the next section, some provinces face much greater fiscal pressures than others. Those with lower fiscal capacities and/or more expenditure needs will be especially constrained when they compete with low-tax provinces to attract business.

Tax competition by itself will discourage provinces from taxing mobile businesses and persons. More than that, they may engage in strategic beggar-thy-neighbour policies designed precisely to attract businesses to their province at the expense of others. They can do this selectively by using tax incentives or industry-specific tax credits. The overall effect is a high level of distortion. I argue in the next section that this is especially an issue with resource-rich provinces.

In short, our system of tax harmonization was born when the federal government was dominant in the income tax field. The danger is that as the provinces obtain an increasing share of the tax room, the consensus to maintain a highly harmonized system will erode.

Horizontal Imbalance

Horizontal imbalance refers to differences in the ability of provinces to provide comparable levels of public services at comparable tax rates, to paraphrase Section 36(2) of the Constitution Act, 1982. This can reflect both differences in the capacity of provinces to raise revenues, and differences in expenditure needs. The extent of horizontal imbalance is notoriously difficult to measure, especially on the expenditure side. In the case of revenue-raising, the methodology applied by the equalization program is widely accepted as a reasonable one. A province's relative revenue-raising capacity is the per capita revenues that would be raised by applying national average provincial tax rates to the province's tax bases. Horizontal imbalance reflects the differences in the per capita revenue-raising capacities thus defined.

This is not an exact measure because there may not be a commonly defined set of tax bases across provinces, but we need not be unduly concerned with the details. However common tax bases are measured, it is clear that the more revenue-raising responsibility is decentralized, the greater the horizontal imbalance. According to Section 36(2), the federal government is committed to the principle of making equalization payments so that all provinces can provide reasonably comparable public services at reasonably comparable rates of taxation. At the same time, the more decentralized revenue-raising becomes, the more costly it is for the federal government to fulfill this commitment: the extent of horizontal imbalances is larger, and the federal share of tax revenues is lower. The saliency of this problem is apparent when we see how much the Section 36(2) commitment has eroded in recent years. As horizontal imbalances have grown, equalization has become more restrictive, apparently due to perceived affordability concerns. The growth rate of equalization has been capped, and only one-half of provincial resource revenues are subject to equalization.

The other essential component of equalization, in the broad sense, is the system of equal per capita federal–provincial social transfers financed by federal general revenue. This system of transfers, made up of the Canada Health Transfer (CHT) and Canada Social Transfer (CST), is analogous to a net system of equalization: it implicitly equalizes high-capacity provinces down and have-not provinces up. Its integrity has stood up reasonably well until recently, despite the massive cutbacks in the mid-1990s, but it now seems destined to fall behind the growth of provincial social program expenditures. The provinces will be responsible for financing an increasing proportion of these programs.

This difficulty posed by revenue decentralization is exacerbated by two other factors. The first is that the equalization system is necessarily a gross system: the federal government makes payments to the recipient, or have-not, provinces, but cannot extract negative tax payments from the non-recipients. As long as the standard of equalization is a national average among all provinces, there is bound to be an imbalance between the have-not provinces and those with above-average revenue-raising capacity, and this imbalance increases with decentralization. In principle, this could be addressed by increasing the standard for equalization above the national average—ideally, to the top province's standard—but that would essentially undo the revenue decentralization that caused the problem in the first place. Here is where the federal government could recognize and exploit the CHT/CST as essential components of the equalization system by conditioning the transfer on provincial fiscal capacity. However, unless the aggregate size of the CHT/CST system increases enough so that all provinces remain significant transfer recipients, conditioning the CHT/CST on fiscal capacity could compromise its role as an instrument for exerting federal influence on provincial social policies, an issue I return to below.

The second factor exacerbating the difficulties of maintaining a viable equalization system, and one with more far-reaching consequences, is the enormous imbalance in natural resource revenues among provinces. As of 2011–12, the fiscal capacity of Alberta, Newfoundland and Labrador, and Saskatchewan were 166%, 153%, and 133% of the national average, respectively. This compares to only 67% in Prince Edward Island, 83% in Quebec, and 93% in Ontario.[4] These imbalances pose enormous challenges for the equalization system, and expose one key disadvantage of a decentralized tax system in a federation where the bulk of natural resource revenues accrue to the provinces. At the risk of straying too far afield, it is worth emphasizing some major consequences for the federation of the current resource boom.

The run-up in natural resource wealth has two broad effects. The increase in resource production and exports has real effects on other sectors and regions of the economy that are the main focus of the Dutch disease literature.[5] Although these raise serious concerns, I have set them aside for our purposes. The second effect of the resource boom arises from fact that the exploitation of natural resources generates rents, a share of which accrues to governments through leases, royalties, and taxes. In the context of natural resources, rents refer to the value of the resources net of the cost of discovering and extracting them. More generally, rents are any returns that firms obtain in excess of the costs of production, including above-normal profits resulting from market power, location, or the ownership of scarce factors of production unavailable for use elsewhere. The use of the resource rents by governments, especially provincial ones, leads to a number of implications.[6]

To the extent that resource rents accrue to the provinces, sizeable horizontal fiscal imbalances arise between resource-rich and resource-poor provinces. In an ideal world, this problem would be mitigated if the provinces saved their resource revenues in a Heritage Fund and used only the Fund's return for current purposes, so that the benefits are shared with future generations. Then equalization could be based on the imbalances that arise from the annual use of these returns, and that would be manageable for the federal government.

However, resource-rich provinces do not behave this way. They seem to be unable to collect a fair share of the resource rents from producers in their provinces,[7] and those they do collect are not saved. Instead they are used to finance current government expenditures, which has a couple of important consequences. For one, this leads to lower provincial tax rates that result in substantial horizontal imbalances. Since the resource-rich provinces are not equalization recipients, these imbalances remain unequalized. This produces not only fiscal inequities and inefficiencies across the federation of the sort that the equalization is intended to redress but also puts competitive pressure on other provinces to restrict their tax rates on businesses and higher-income persons and entrepreneurs.

Furthermore, a proportion of those resource revenues are spent explicitly for province-building; that is, to provide infrastructure and other amenities intended to attract business from other provinces and diversify the provincial economy. From a regional development perspective, the outcome can be perverse: capital and businesses are attracted from so-called core regions to peripheral regions (using Krugman's terminology [1991]) simply because the latter are where the resource rents are found. A balanced national policy would not choose to develop regions simply because they happen to have a bounty of natural resources; that would contradict the benefits of agglomeration, which is one source of the Dutch disease problem. It is important to emphasize that these effects are over and above whatever other Dutch disease consequences there are for resource versus manufacturing activities. They arise simply because of the decentralized resource-rent collecting system.

Vertical Balance

A final, and related, issue arising in a decentralized federation concerns the vertical fiscal gap; that is, the extent to which the provinces as a whole obtain revenues from federal transfers as opposed to their own taxation. Generally speaking, provincial-level governments in virtually all OECD federations—and sub-national governments in unitary states like Japan and the Scandinavian countries—are responsible for the provision of similar sorts of public services, and these include substantial ones like education, health care, and welfare. This leads to levels of provincial–municipal public expenditures that are comparable to that of the federal government. Where federations differ is in the proportion of these expenditures financed by federal transfers, or the size of the fiscal gap. The fiscal gap in Canada is at the low end relative to federations like Australia and Germany.

To some, a vertical fiscal gap merely reflects the fact that the benefits of decentralizing public service provision to the provinces outweigh the limited benefits of decentralizing taxes. However, one can also take the view that, rather than being residual, the vertical gap is itself important because of the crucial role that federal–provincial transfers play. The argument can be put succinctly: the legislative responsibilities of the provinces include the provision of public services that fulfill important social objectives, like redistributive equity, equal opportunity, and social insurance. Indeed, a sizable majority of provincial public expenditure programs are in this category, including education, public health insurance, social services, and targeted transfers. The reason for assigning this responsibility to the provinces is the presumption that they are able to deliver these services more effectively than the federal government, given their closeness to the constituents being served and their ability to cater to different local needs.

The federal government's interest in the delivery of these services arises from the general interest it has in matters of national equity or social citizenship. It is the federal government whose responsibility extends to matters affecting all Canadians, and includes the expectations citizens have to reasonably comparable levels of social protection, fairness, and equality of opportunity no matter in which province they reside. This is explicitly recognized in Section 36(1) of the Constitution Act, which commits the federal and provincial governments together to (a) promoting equal opportunities, (b) furthering economic development to reduce disparities, and (c) providing essential public services of reasonable quality to all Canadians, all without altering existing legislative authorities. Given that the provinces have legislative authority over the main instruments for achieving these objectives, namely education, health, and welfare, the federal government must rely on other policies to fulfill its commitment. The most effective and flexible one is the spending power; that is, the use of federal–provincial transfers as an instrument for influencing provincial legislation in areas of national interest. The spending power is controversial among some observers, especially the government of Quebec.[8] But, if one takes the commitment expressed in Section 36(1) seriously, the judicious use of the spending power is the only real alternative the federal government has for furthering its interests in national social citizenship. Indeed, that interest exists independent of Section 36.

A fiscal gap is a necessary condition for pursuing the joint federal–provincial commitment expressed in Section 36(1). But the means by which the federal government uses the spending power are varied. The most visible way is through conditional transfers. These have been used historically for transformative purposes, to encourage the provinces to establish comprehensive health insurance and welfare programs. In more recent years, they have fulfilled more of a sustaining role as block grants with very broad conditions that leave the provinces considerable discretion. Arguably more important is the implicit moral authority, or moral suasion, bought by federal contributions to provincial social programs. The greater the federal government's financial commitment is, the more likely the provinces are to abide by national standards, such as those of the Canada Health Act.

National standards need not always be explicit. For example, conditions have never been attached to the component of the CST intended for post-secondary education (PSE). Yet, as long as the federal government was making a significant contribution, provinces seemed to be willing to design their PSE systems so that students from all provinces were treated equally, even when foreign students faced higher fees. In recent years, this compact has eroded, so that increasingly provinces discriminate against out-of-province students through differential fees, preferential admissions, and incentives to retain graduates in their home province. It is, of course, impossible to know what sort of influence federal transfers to the provinces buys, especially since interactions between federal and provincial policy-makers take place behind closed doors. At the least, the existence of block CHT/CST-type transfers of significant size leads to a more cooperative approach to federal–provincial policy-making, which is critical given the joint commitments the two levels of government share.

There are a few other elements of the federal–provincial nexus to which the fiscal gap contributes. One, as we have already discussed, is equalization. A sizable fiscal gap is absolutely essential to maintain the integrity of the system, given that the size of the fiscal gap is inversely related to the amount of horizontal imbalance and therefore the need for equalization. This is especially important in the new reality of natural resource-driven imbalances. The ability to maintain the integrity of even the current system of equalization—that includes only 50% of natural resource revenues—requires a significant fiscal gap. This would be even greater were the CHT/CST system to be used to achieve some explicit equalization of the resource-rich provinces.

A second element worth recalling is the role of the federal fiscal system as a means of providing long-term insurance across the federation. In a country as diverse as Canada, the fortunes of different regions can change over time. Given that a common currency applies to the federation, local exchange rate changes cannot facilitate adjustment to regional shocks. Federal institutions provide three alternative adjustment mechanisms. First, the national income tax transfer system automatically transfers funds from lucky to unlucky regions. Second, federal–provincial equalizing transfers complement the individual tax-transfer system, the difference being that instead of equalizing personal incomes, it equalizes the ability of provinces to deliver public services. Finally, the ability of labour to migrate freely among provinces provides a third adjustment mechanism. While all three have a part to play, balance is important.

Inadequacy in the federal tax-transfer and equalization systems will result in too much reliance on migration. Households will be encouraged to migrate from less lucky to more lucky regions in response to fiscal differentials rather than productivity differentials: hence the term fiscally induced migration. Nurturing the appropriate amount of protection against regional shocks entails a minimum fiscal gap and a sufficient share of income tax room in the hands of the federal government. As always, there are trade-offs: one does not want fiscal insurance to inhibit migration from regions in long-term decline to growing regions with advantages of agglomeration. At the same time, one does not want the inadequacy of insurance to encourage inefficient migration, for example, migration for social benefits, which is costly not only for those moving but also for those left behind.

A final consideration is that the existence of a sizeable fiscal gap has useful contingent value in the event that the need arises for some transformative federal–provincial transfer in the future. One can imagine a few policy areas where new cooperative initiatives might be desired. An immediate one might be an extension of health insurance to include pharmaceuticals or home care, both relevant in an era of aging populations. A second one might be a re-invigoration of the welfare system, such as that recently proposed by Ontario (Commission for the Review of Social Assistance in Ontario, 2012). A third whose time might finally come is a major initiative in the area of post-secondary education. The federal government might find it difficult to participate meaningfully in any of these areas if the fiscal gap continues to erode. It is probably much more difficult to transfer revenue-raising power back to the federal government once it has been turned over to the provinces.

Before concluding this section, it is worth mentioning some caveats to the argument for preserving a significant fiscal gap. The case for a fiscal gap relies in good part on the argument that the federal government needs access to federal–provincial transfers to achieve its policy objectives of equalization, influence over social programs, and a fair tax-transfer system. This presumes that the federal government will use its fiscal powers judiciously. The deployment of the spending power might be more intrusive than necessary to achieve the common objectives of the two levels of government. Conditions might be too onerous and detailed, and the unilateral enforcement of transfer conditions might be heavy-handed. Transfers might be treated as discretionary rather than being formula-driven, leading to bilateral deals between the federal government and groups of provinces that are viewed as unfair and politically driven, and could potentially lead to a form of soft budget constraint. Finally, the federal government might be tempted to use federal–provincial transfers as means of responding to fiscal shocks it faces, as it did in the mid-1990s. This is tempting because transfers are a relatively easy expenditure program to cut, and the act effectively transfers the fiscal problem to the provincial governments (who may then transfer their deficits to municipalities).

These are issues that arise in every federation, and there is no recipe for avoiding them. Perhaps the best way to manage the fiscal gap is for federal–provincial fiscal relations to be cooperative and transparent, and for transfers to be formula-based and sheltered from the year-to-year budgetary decision-making. The only imaginable alternative to a federal role in achieving national equity and efficiency in the tax-transfer system and provision of important public services and social insurance is for the provinces themselves to agree to national standards, and presumably to let the equalization system deteriorate. But there is reason to doubt whether this could ever be achieved without a federal "equalizer," given the diverse and changing interests and capacities of the provinces.

Rescuing the Canadian Federation

The Canadian federation is entering unchartered territory. The natural resource boom is putting unprecedented pressure on horizontal balance in the federation, and the federal government is ill-equipped to deal with it. The equalization system is increasingly unaffordable and seemingly unsustainable given the reduced revenue capacity of the government, and it is completely inadequate in responding to the vast chasm between the recipient and non-recipient provinces. The progressivity of the tax-transfer system has been competed down. The inability of resource-rich provinces to save their resource revenues exacerbates the typical consequences of a sustained resource boom, and this is made worse by the fact that these revenues are available for province-building initiatives. The collapse of the Canadian social contract seems to be a distinct possibility.

If the federal government were to engage itself in these issues, what might it do? How could it meet its moral commitments to Section 36 of the Constitution, and more generally its obligation to be the primary guardian of Canadian social citizenship? This is asking a lot in a world where the provinces have primary access to resource revenues, which are the prime source of imbalance, and where the federation has otherwise evolved to be relatively decentralized. It is often said that all Canadians benefit from the natural resource wealth found in some provinces. That will clearly not be the case in the absence of federal policies.

What follows is a brief list of measures, in no particular order, that the federal government can undertake that would enable it to respond to the situation Canada finds itself in. Some of these ideas are expanded upon in considerably greater detail in later chapters.

The fiscal gap must be protected and enhanced in order to address the increasing horizontal imbalance and to maintain a federal presence in addressing national equity and efficiency issues. Simply put, the federal government must collect more revenue than it needs for its own direct responsibilities.

Federal tax room in the personal income tax field should be guarded and enhanced, and the fairness of the federal income tax system should be improved; at least as much emphasis should be placed on fairness at the bottom as at the top of the income distribution, for example, by making all tax credits refundable and better targeting them to low-income taxpayers. The federal government should accept more of a share in assisting the least well-off in Canada.

The federal government should obtain a higher share of resource rents; one approach, discussed elsewhere (Boadway, Coulombe, & Tremblay, 2012), is to reform the corporate tax so that its base better conforms to economic rents, and to raise the federal corporate rate. Ideally, the federal government should occupy the entire corporate tax field, but since it cannot do that unilaterally, it could increase its own share.

The implementation of a federal carbon tax would be sound on environmental grounds, and would give the federal government a "free" source of tax revenue to help it fulfill its Section 36(2) commitment to equalization.

The CHT/CST system should be viewed not only as a form of federal contribution to maintaining social programs of national interest but also as an integral element of equalization; as such, per capita transfers could be scaled back for provinces receiving equalization payments to better eliminate revenue capacity differences with have-not provinces.

The adverse consequences of inequities on resource-poor provinces would be mitigated if resource-rich provinces saved their rents in a Heritage-type fund rather than using them to reduce provincial taxes and engage in province-building. Apart from equalization, the federal government is limited in its response; it could encourage resource revenue-saving by making CHT/CST entitlements contingent on provincial saving, and it could focus its infrastructure projects on resource-poor provinces, with a view to building their capacity to grow, thereby reducing their reliance on equalization, as suggested by Dodge, Burn, and Dion (2012).

Notes

1 Part VI, s. 91(3) of the Constitution Act of 1982 permits the federal government to generate income from "the raising of money by any mode or system of taxation," while s. 92(2) gives the provinces exclusive legislative authority to make laws with respect to "direct taxation within the province in order to the raising of a revenue for provincial purposes." The latter has been interpreted to include sales and excise taxes, despite their not normally being thought of as direct taxes. In addition, s. 92A(4) permits provinces to raise money by any method of taxation in respect of non-renewable resources, forest resources and electrical energy. Note that the power of resource taxation is not exclusive.
2 Fiscal decentralization includes the decentralization of spending responsibilities. In the Canadian case, the assignment of expenditure responsibilities is largely predetermined and non-controversial, so we focus mostly on the revenue side. However, one kind of expenditure that is open to rebalancing is transfers to low-income persons.
3 I proposed some of the arguments in this chapter in my article The folly of decentralizing the Canadian federation (1996) and essay Mind the gap: Reflections on fiscal balance in decentralized federations (2011).
4 These percentages are based on data obtained from Finance Canada.
5 See, for example, recent summaries of the Dutch disease in Canada in Drohan's 9 habits of highly effective resource economies (2012), and Campbell's The petro-path not taken (2013).
6 This is discussed at greater length in a paper I co-authored with Coulombe and Tremblay, *The Dutch disease and the Canadian economy: Challenges for policy-makers* (2012).
7 The Alberta Royalty Review Panel estimated that the public sector share of rents was only 44% for conventional oil, 47% for oil sands, and 58% for natural gas, and that fairer shares would be 49%, 64%, and 63%, respectively.
8 See Commission on Fiscal Imbalance (the Séguin Commission), *Final report* (2002).

References

Alberta Royalty Review Panel. (2007). *Our fair share*. Edmonton, AB: Ministry of Finance.

Boadway, R. (1996). The folly of decentralizing the Canadian federation. *Dalhousie Review*, 75(3), 313–49.

Boadway, R. (2011). Mind the gap: Reflections on fiscal balance in decentralized federations. In T. J. Courchene, J. R. Allan, C. Leuprecht, & N. Verrelli (Eds.), *The federal idea: Essays in honour of Ronald L. Watts* (pp. 363–377). Montreal, QC: McGill-Queen's University Press and Institute of Intergovernmental Relations.

Boadway, R., Coulombe, S., & Tremblay, J-F. (2012, October 26–27). *The Dutch disease and the Canadian economy: Challenges for policy-makers*. Paper presented at Thinking Outside the Box, a Conference in Celebration of Thomas J. Courchene, Kingston, Ontario.

Campbell, B. (2013). *The petro-path not taken* (CCPA Report January 17, 2013). Ottawa, ON: Canadian Centre for Policy Alternatives.

Commission on Fiscal Imbalance (the Séguin Commission). (2002). *A new division of Canada's financial resources: Final report.* Quebec City, QC: Government of Quebec.

Commission for the Review of Social Assistance in Ontario (2012). *Brighter prospects: Transforming social assistance in Ontario.* Toronto, ON: Ministry of Community and Social Services.

Constitution Act, 1867 [en. by the Canada Act 1982, Part VI, s. 92(2)A].

Constitution Act, 1982 [en.by the Canada Act 1982, Part III, s. 36(1), (2)].

Dodge, D., Burn, P., & Dion, R. (August 2012). Federal–provincial fiscal arrangements: Thinking outside the box. *Policy Options*, 30–33.

Drohan, M. (2012). *9 habits of highly effective resource economies: Lessons for Canada.* Toronto, ON: Canadian International Council.

Krugman, P. (1991). *Geography and trade.* Cambridge, MA: MIT Press, 1991.

National Welfare Council. (2008). *Welfare incomes, 2006 and 2007.* Ottawa, ON: Author.

Treff, K., & Ort, D. (2010). *Finances of the Nation 2009.* Toronto, ON: Canadian Tax Foundation.

Chapter 3

Taxes and Public Services

Hugh Mackenzie

For most of the past two decades, public policy debate in Canada has been dominated by taxes. Tax cuts of one kind or another have featured in the platforms of every political party in almost every election. Increasing any tax has been characterized as the third rail of Canadian politics: the issue that will kill any campaign that touches it.

Remarkably, our running conversation about taxes has taken place without any serious reference to the reason we have taxes in the first place—to pay for public services. The notion that measures that reduce our fiscal capacity might have negative consequences for public services has been pushed to the periphery, left to be raised, with little impact, by organizations the tax cutters dismiss as self-serving "interest groups."

This one-dimensional conversation is not incidental to conservative or neo-liberal political strategy, it is central to it. The failure to address the direct consequences of tax cut policies is not an oversight but a decision—deliberate, dishonest, and extremely successful. The tactics have been as effective as the strategy. Using a "balanced budget" as the pivot point, services have been cut to reduce deficits when the economy is weak, while taxes have been cut to absorb surpluses when it is strong. The net effect is that without ever having had a public debate about the relative importance of public services in Canada, their role in society has been reduced dramatically since the mid-1990s.

Conversations that separate actions from consequences are familiar to any parent. They are the kinds of conversations you have with a four-year-old at the supermarket checkout as you try to explain that he can't just grab that box of Smarties; the kinds of conversations that any toddler understands.

Most four-year-olds have figured out that when you go to the store to get something you want, you have to be prepared to pay for it. Yet almost all of our political leaders and a lot of the people out there who are paid to influence them would rather stand on the corner and try to spit nickels than admit that obvious fact when it comes to the taxes we pay for public services.

We are overdue for an adult conversation about taxes and public services. A conversation that starts at A and goes to B—one that re-establishes in public discourse a connection between the public services we need and the taxes that pay for them.

The Anatomy of a One-Dimensional Conversation

Keeping the political conversation about taxes away from public services is central to neo-liberal political strategy. The tax cut has become the one-size-fits-all tube sock of public policy for conservatives in Canada. Sometimes it seems that there is no substantial public policy issue to which a tax cut is not the answer. The coda to the right's incessant clamour for tax cuts in response to every public policy issue is the insistence that we can have tax cuts without suffering any decline in public services. Conservatives claim to have ways around that problem.

Eliminate government waste, they say, and we can have lower taxes without cuts to services. Such an argument sounds good, particularly when the various provincial and federal auditors provide an annual sourcebook of public spending horror stories. The problem is, the numbers don't add up. Pressed for examples, the tax cutters always come up with spectacularly stupid-sounding things governments have done that actually don't cost very much money. In fact, overwhelmingly, public money is spent on things that Canadians value in their everyday lives.

Then there's the argument that if you lower taxes, government revenue will actually increase. This defies logic, and is also inconsistent with the evidence. Data from the Organisation for Economic Co-operation and Development (OECD) demonstrate that, since 1995, tax revenue in Canada has dropped from 36 to 31% of GDP. And while that may not sound like much, it represents a decline of more than $80 billion a year in public revenue.

And finally there's the argument that if we cut public services, it wouldn't be a bad thing because our public services aren't as good as they should be. Fair comment, perhaps, but hard to swallow from the very people whose successful campaigns to reduce public revenue have caused those services to deteriorate in the first place. It's a bit much to hear from people who have been waging war against public revenue that our roads are full of potholes or that waiting lists are too long for elective surgeries.

Without intending to, the left has actually reinforced the conservatives' strategy. It can't seem to resist the cheap populism of pocketbook politics, trying to catch the wave the conservatives are riding and amplifying it in the process. So the NDP in British Columbia makes common cause with Bill Vander Zalm, and in Ontario it shares platforms at rallies against energy taxes with the leader of the province's Conservative Party. Progressives campaign for better public services as if they can be provided for free, or on the basis that they won't cost us anything because the higher taxes needed to pay for them will all be shouldered by people we don't know, who make a lot more money than we do, and big corporations, but not small businesses.

The left makes things worse when it opposes taxes on the grounds that they impose a "burden" on average families (or whatever the code phrase is for "us" today). There are lots of problems with both the economics and the politics of this proposition. One problem with the economics is that if you set the income cut-off high enough to be politically comfortable, there aren't enough people to pay for better public services. Another problem is that if you raise taxes by a high enough amount on a small enough group of people, they'll try to find a way to avoid paying them. And because these people have lots of money, they can afford to pay others to help them skirt these obligations. If you need proof, just look at the near-hysteria generated by the investment industry in Canada when the federal government closed down an income trust tax loophole that threatened to eliminate corporate taxation altogether.

The politics aren't much better. At worst, the left's approach reinforces the idea that taxes are a burden to be avoided, and therefore undermines the case for greater investment in public services. It seems clear which ideological position will benefit from fomenting hostility toward taxes—especially when even the emotive language of "tax burdens" and "tax grabs" is borrowed from conservatives.

Attempting to frame the issue as one of tax fairness doesn't help. No matter how often you say that it is a particular tax that is unfair, what people hear is that all taxes are unfair. And if the conversation is allowed to revolve around taxes to the exclusion of services, tax fairness has the indirect effect of reinforcing the idea that tax cuts are free— that you can have them without paying anything.

Tax Cuts: The Link between Conservatism and Populism

For conservatives, separating taxes from public services accomplishes a number of tactical objectives at once. It frees them from having to confront the contradiction inherent in simultaneously heightening concerns about fiscal deficits and advocating tax cuts. Tax cuts are free. It is also a lot easier to sell the idea of taxes as a "burden" if they are presented as disconnected from any of the purposes for which they are raised.

Separating taxes from public services—presenting cuts as if they are "free"—enables the right to finesse the key question that could sink their project: who is actually benefiting from the tax cuts that are being proposed. In a world where reduced fiscal capacity has no consequences for public services, tax cuts are always worthwhile. In such a world, there's no need to address the consequences of reduced services for people with lower incomes; supposedly, everyone is getting something and tax cuts don't cost anybody anything. But that world does not exist.

The Tax-Cut/Deficit-Fighting Ratchet Effect

In the 20 years during which fiscal politics have become dominant in Canada, we have been through one complete major economic cycle—from the recession of 1991 to the depression of 2008—and a number of minor cycles.

The pattern in these major and minor cycles has consistently repeated itself. In a recession, the budgetary deficit emerges as a political problem—sometimes helped along by pay-in-advance tax cuts in the Mike Harris Ontario model. The response to the political problem is to cut services to bring the budget back into balance. As the economy recovers, the "fiscal dividend" of higher revenue is deemed to be surplus, and is used to fund tax cuts. The tax cuts both consolidate the service cuts made during the deficit fight—soaking up the fiscal capacity that could be used to restore or improve services—and eliminate any fiscal cushion that might otherwise have made a subsequent downturn easier to manage.

When the next downturn hits, with the revenue cushion gone, the budgetary deficit again emerges as a political problem, and the cycle of service cuts and tax cuts repeats itself.

At the federal level, the cycle played itself out through majority governments of both major parties and three minority governments. The Chrétien government used the fight against the deficit as the pretext for a major pullback from cost-sharing services provided under provincial jurisdiction and for a massive cut in unemployment insurance benefits. When the budget was balanced in 1999, the fiscal dividend was used to fund the largest comprehensive tax cut in Canadian history. When the federal budget produced high surpluses in the early years of Stephen Harper's Conservatives, the government responded by cutting the GST by two percentage points, and both increasing and accelerating planned corporate income tax cuts. In the wake of the 2008 market meltdown and the budgetary deficit that flowed directly from it, the Harper Conservatives embarked on another round of program and service cuts, and continued borrowing to carry on their program of tax cuts for corporations. And before the service cuts had even been approved, the Minister of Finance declared his intention to get back to the business of cutting taxes even further as soon as the budget was balanced.

In Ontario, the same process has played itself out in governments led by all three of the major political parties. As Ontario struggled to recover from the

1991 recession, the Rae NDP government kicked off the cycle of budget-cutting in response to a large and growing deficit. The Harris government upped the ante when it was elected, implementing a substantial personal income tax cut before the deficit had even begun to decline. As the budgetary balance was beginning to improve in the late 1990s, the government implemented another round of income tax cuts, and threw major cuts in capital gains and corporate income taxes into the bargain. After a departure from the script, when the newly elected McGuinty government introduced a health care tax and delayed implementation of scheduled corporate tax cuts, it embraced corporate income tax cuts at the peak of the economic cycle. Then, when the economy and its budgetary balance deteriorated in 2008 and 2009, it declared its planned tax cuts off limits and announced sweeping program and service cuts.

It is telling that despite nurturing an atmosphere of budgetary crisis, the federal government has refused to delay the implementation of its scheduled corporate tax cuts, and has insisted on relying only on the program cuts to bring the budget into balance. At the same time, only a narrow minority government prevented exactly the same thing from happening in Ontario.

In a perverse form of Keynesianism, conservative governments are using the impact of economic cycles as a weapon against public services. Rather than balance the budget over the economic cycle, accumulating surpluses in boom times and running deficits in periods of economic weakness, conservatives are using deficits as a pretext for program and service cuts and surpluses as a pretext for tax cuts.

Separating Services from the Taxes That Pay for Them Distorts Our Decisions

When the Mulroney government changed the tax system in 1989 to claw back Old Age Security benefits from higher-income seniors, it justified the change on the basis that millionaire seniors shouldn't be subsidized by other Canadians with lower incomes. When the Chrétien government ended the Family Allowance in 1995, it justified the change on the basis that millionaire parents shouldn't be subsidized by other Canadians with lower incomes. When governments across Canada imposed double-digit increases in college and university tuition and fees year after year in the 1990s, they justified the change on the basis that high-income families sending their children to university shouldn't be subsidized by Canadians with lower incomes.

It is a superficially attractive argument, and one that is dead wrong.

Why? Because it ignores the source of the revenue used to pay for these services. These arguments would make sense if we paid for these services with head taxes—taxes that levy the same amount, in dollar terms, from everyone. But we don't. We pay for public services with a menu of taxes that amount to roughly the same percentage of income, overall, for every Canadian.

Because income in Canada is so unequally distributed, when you take into account the revenue sources used to pay for broadly based public services, the argument for targeting them based on income is turned on its head. It turns out that when these benefits are reduced or eliminated for high-income earners to pay for tax cuts or to avoid tax increases, the millionaire will save far more in reduced taxes over his lifetime than he would ever receive from Old Age Security, the Family Allowance, or tuition subsidies.

The real losers in service targeting are middle-income families, because they lose all the benefits but save relatively little in reduced taxes or avoided tax increases. No wonder middle-income earners are unhappy. Over the last decade, the middle class has paid a price in two ways: they have been excluded from the benefits of economic growth—while real per capita GDP has grown by 73% since 1975, inflation-adjusted median family incomes have barely budged, growing by less than 4% in total in 36 years; and the reduction in taxes has meant that they also lose many of the benefits they had received from public goods and services.

The separation of taxes from public services also distorts our thinking about income distribution and redistribution. We typically measure income distribution before and after taxes and transfers. The before tax and transfer, or "market income" measure, is intended to capture the distribution of income that results from the operation of market forces unaffected by government policy. The after tax and transfer measure reflects the distribution of income after deducting taxes paid and adding in personal transfer payments.

This measure implicitly treats taxes paid on transfer payments received as a net loss in living standard. It ignores the contribution public services make to our standard of living in general, and the impact of public services other than cash transfers on the distribution of economic resources in our society. As studies by the Canadian Centre for Policy Alternatives (CCPA), the OECD and others have shown, ignoring the impact of public services distorts the picture both in aggregate and from the perspective of income distribution.

The CCPA study (Mackenzie & Shillington, 2009), for example, found that using the conservative accounting convention of measuring the value of public services at their cost, public services are valued between $15,000 and $20,000 per capita regardless of income, life stage, or family type. And because that value is distributed essentially equally among all Canadians, it has a powerful countervailing impact on the decidedly unequal distribution of resources produced by the market.[1]

The role of public services in the redistribution of resources in our society also complicates the way we think of tax fairness and the impact of the tax system on distribution. The decision to provide a service publicly amounts to a decision to consume that service in common, rather than privately, with significant implications for distribution.

We commonly think of taxes as influencing the distribution of resources based on the share of income represented by taxes. Taxes that increase as a share of income when income increases are considered to be progressive; taxes that decline as a share of income when income increases are considered to be regressive. Personal income taxes with graduated rates are progressive. Payroll taxes are progressive at the low end of the income scale (because they do not apply to transfer payment income), neutral in the middle, and regressive at the top (because they do not apply to income from capital). Consumption taxes in general tend to be regressive throughout the income scale because they do not apply to net savings, and net savings increase as income increases.

When we talk about tax policy, we are often mesmerized by the choice between "progressive" (good) and "regressive" (bad) taxes without reference to the services they pay for. The left has been highly critical of regressive taxes. By failing to look at what those taxes buy, they reinforce the one-sided nature of the debate. In other words, regressive taxes can be used for progressive purposes. And when we oppose regressive taxes, what people hear is agreement with the anti-tax mantra of the right, but what they don't hear is the consequences of cutting these taxes for the services they've grown to depend on.

Because we ignore the distributive impact of public services, we fall into the trap of opposing the very taxes that provide much of the financing for the more comprehensive systems of public services the countries whose systems we admire rely upon.

In the work that Richard Shillington and I did in the CCPA paper referred to above, we found that public services in Canada amount to a demogrant—most Canadians derive roughly the same dollar value from public services, regardless of their family type or income. Low-income Canadians benefit somewhat more, because of income-related transfer payments like the child tax benefit, employment insurance, and the guaranteed income supplement at the federal level and social assistance at the provincial level, but other than that, the per capita benefit is about the same—$15,000 to $20,000—regardless of income or household type. The relative benefit from different kinds of public services varies by family type and income, but the total is remarkably consistent.

It Is a Tax-Cutting Era, Not a Permanent State

Tax phobia has so dominated our political culture in the past 20 years, it is hard to remember a time when politicians weren't afraid to suggest that we should pay more taxes to receive better public services. Indeed, with such political hostility to taxes, one could be forgiven for wondering how we ended up with the public services we have now.

A 2006 Canadian Centre for Policy Alternatives study (Mackenzie) looking at the evolution of the Canadian public economy from 1961 to 2005 offers some perspective. First, it shows two distinct eras in the development of the Canadian public economy. Between 1961 and 1993, public programs as a share of GDP increased in Canada from 28 to 41%. Between 1993 and 2005, public programs as a share of GDP declined from 41 to 32%.

Second, it shows that by far the most important contributor to the growth in public programs over that period was in provincial and local government services. Between 1961 and 1993, federal government program spending as a share of GDP was consistently in the range of 10 to 13% of GDP, whereas provincial government programs increased from 8 to 18%. Local government programs increased slightly, from 6 to 8% of GDP.

After 1993, programs as a share of GDP dropped for all three orders of government: federal from 13.5 to 9.8%; provincial from 18.4 to 15%; local from 9.2 to 7.1%.

Third, the growth in provincial public services between 1961 to 1993 was accompanied by a steady increase in own-source revenue (rather than transfers) as a share of GDP. While federal own-source revenue remained bound in a range of 16 to 18% of GDP for the entire 1961 to 2005 period, and local government

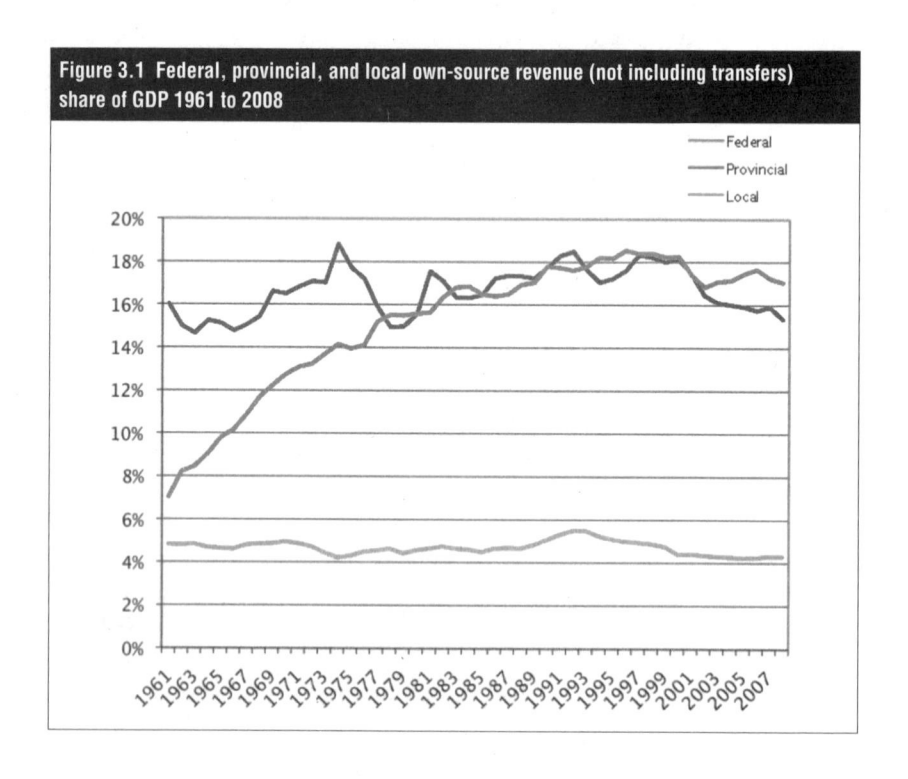

Figure 3.1 Federal, provincial, and local own-source revenue (not including transfers) share of GDP 1961 to 2008

Taxes and Public Services | 63

Figure 3.2 Federal, provincial, and local government revenue from taxation; share of GDP 1961 to 2008

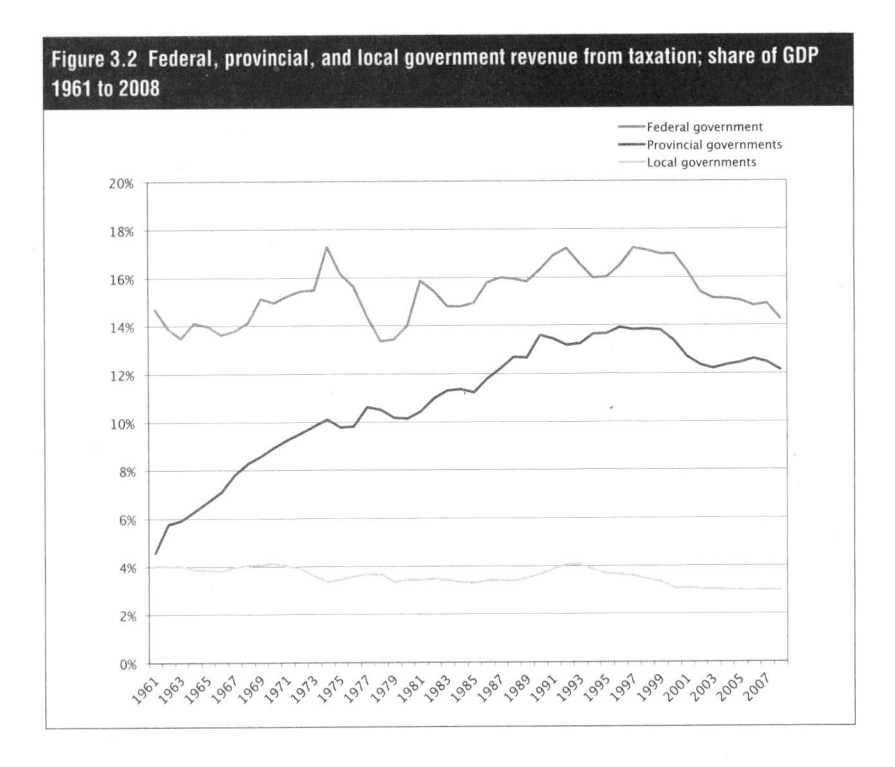

Figure 3.3 Own-source revenue percent of GDP, 1961–2005

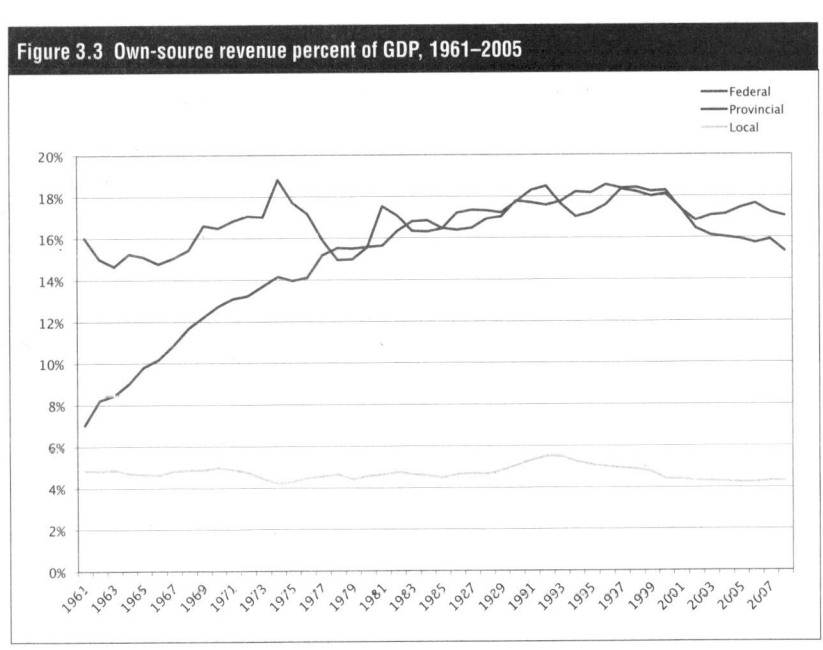

between 4.0 and 5.5%, provincial government own-source revenue increased from 7% of GDP in 1961 to peak at 18.6% of GDP in 1995.

Between the mid-1990s and 2005, own-source revenue as a share of GDP declined by 2% at each of the federal and provincial levels, and by 1.5% at the local level.

The link between taxation and public services in Canadian fiscal history could not be more obvious. Equally obvious is the link between the tax cuts that have been implemented in Canada since the 1990s and the declining role of public services in our economy.

Separating Taxes from Public Services: American Conservatives' Big Idea

Opposition from conservatives to public services spending in America is not new. American conservatives consistently opposed the growth in public spending in Roosevelt's New Deal and the more robust approach to economic regulation that accompanied it. The centrist consensus that narrowed the differences between social democrats and mainstream conservative parties in Europe and between Liberals and Progressive Conservatives in Canada from the 1950s to the 1970s never took hold in the United States. What divided the immediate postwar era from the period since 1980 was that prior to 1980, conservatives in the United States were largely unsuccessful in their opposition. Every Republican campaign against Roosevelt ended with a Democratic Party landslide. Successful Republican candidates embraced a centrist consensus, leaving conservatives out in the cold.

The failure of conservatives' fight against public services is illustrated most clearly in the 1964 campaign of conservative favourite Barry Goldwater, who directed his campaign against the Kennedy–Johnson "Great Society" programs, and who led the Republicans to a massive defeat.

In the wake of the New Deal of the 1930s and the Great Society of the 1960s, conservatives in the United States were finding it impossible to reverse the tide of public interest in and popular support for expanded public services. Conservative Republicans campaigned against government programs, only to discover that people actually liked their public services. Conservatives could get elected, but not if they held onto their big picture agenda.

The insight in the 1970s that led to conservatives dominating public discourse for the next 30 years was to separate taxes from public services in the policy debate. Instead of campaigning against public services—which people liked—they scared people silly with doomsday scenarios about government deficits and campaigned against taxes, which most people would choose not to pay if they could. Win the battle against taxes, the strategy went, and no government—no matter its political leaning—will be able to avoid cutting spending.

Conservatives used the deficit as a symbol of "unaffordable" public spending, but avoided specifics. Beginning with Reagan in the 1980 election campaign, they campaigned against the deficit and used it as the justification for cuts to public programs. And backed by the counter-intuitive (and ultimately, demonstrably counter-factual) proposition that cutting taxes would increase public revenue, they ignored the deficit and continued to cut taxes, leaving the elimination of the United States' budgetary deficit to the Clinton administration between 1992 and 2000.

The strategy continued with the Bush Administration between 2000 and 2008, with massive tax cuts leading to a budgetary crisis. In Canada, the conservatives' use of a similar strategy has been spectacularly successful. Data published in the Fiscal Reference Tables prepared by the Department of Finance show that total government outlays in Canada dropped from 52% of GDP in 1991 to 39% in 2008, before rebounding to 44% in 2010 as a result of the recession and stimulus spending. At their low point in 2008, government outlays in Canada as a share of GDP were virtually identical to those in the United States.

Between 1991 and 2008, governments in Canada collectively reduced the public economy to the share of GDP it held in the early 1970s, a dramatic change and by far the largest decline in a public sector among the OECD countries.

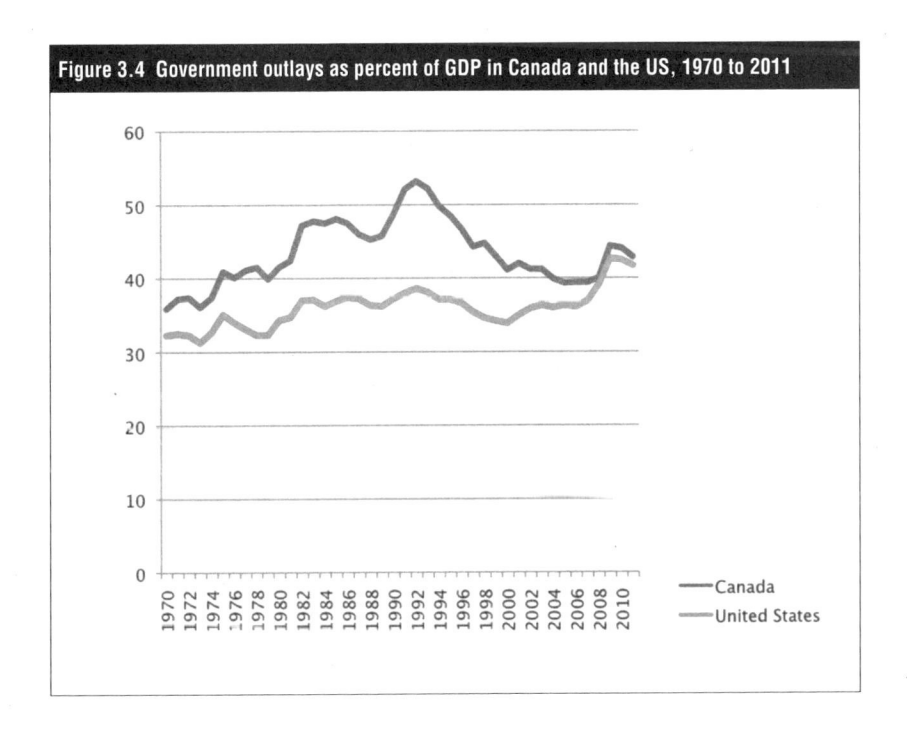

Figure 3.4 Government outlays as percent of GDP in Canada and the US, 1970 to 2011

Consequences and Conclusions

The separation of taxes from the public services they pay for fundamentally alters the terms of the debate. The consequences are wide-ranging and profound. Ignoring the public services side of the tax and services trade-off produces a kind of collective self-loathing through which we ignore many of our greatest achievements as a society and leave others to wither away. The service cut and tax cut cycle it fuels has already produced a dramatic and unprecedented reduction in the size of our public economy. Separating taxes and services reinforces an atmosphere in which political dishonesty becomes an essential tool for survival. And it leads progressives into the trap of opposing taxes on the basis of their distributive impact, supporting the anti-tax bias in the process.

Even the way we ***measure*** inequality feeds the one-armed debate. Our measure of inequality is the distribution of income after taxes and transfers—as if the taxes we pay that we don't get back through direct transfer payments are of no value, and even less defensibly, make no contribution to the moderation of market income inequality.

We undervalue the public economy in other ways as well. Even in our national accounts, we undervalue public services. By convention, public services are valued at cost; we make no attempt to measure the benefits they deliver. So we implicitly assume that we get no return for our investments in public infrastructure. We implicitly assume that we get no value from the efficiency achieved through the public provision of health care insurance. We implicitly assume we get no value from productivity improvements in the delivery of public services, to the point where productivity improvement actually shows up as a *reduction* in value.

We underinvest in what we undervalue. And we undervalue public services.

The disconnect between taxes and public services is not politically neutral. It is central to the political strategy of conservatives. And the consequences of the success of that strategy to date are already evident. As we turn our attention to the big picture trends that are sure to influence the way we live in the future—the aging of our population, growing income inequality, and the inexorably slow-moving crisis of climate change—we will need more public investment, not less. All place greater demands on our ability to accomplish things together, as a society. We must have that adult conversation about the public services we need, and the taxes we'll have to pay to provide them, and we must have it soon.

Fortunately, there is some evidence that Canadians are ahead of their politicians on the issue of taxes and public services. Public opinion surveys report repeatedly that respondents indicate a preparedness to pay more in tax in return for better public services in a wide range of areas. At a local level, where the consequences of budget cuts are much more immediately visible, the tax cutters and tax freezers have been remarkably unsuccessful. Toronto Mayor Rob Ford's inability to hold together his hand-picked right-wing coalition and ram through his agenda of cuts to services is another indication. So is the evident willingness of Toronto residents to pay more to build a better public transit system.

As Thoreau put it, "it takes two to speak the truth." It looks like Canadians are willing to listen. Are our politicians willing to lead?

Notes

1 While the most obvious conceptual problem arises with after-tax-and-transfer income, it is also conceptually difficult to isolate market-only factors in the measurement of market income because of the significance of the public sector in total employment. Since the distribution of wage and salary income is more egalitarian in the public sector than in the private sector, the commonly used distribution of income before taxes and transfers will tend to understate the degree of inequality in private sector incomes.

References

Mackenzie, H. (2006, July). *The art of the impossible: Fiscal federalism and fiscal balance in Canada*. Ottawa, ON: Canadian Centre for Policy Alternatives.

Mackenzie, H., & Shillington, R. (2009). *Canada's quiet bargain: The benefits of public spending* (CCPA Growing Gap Project). Ottawa, ON: Canadian Centre for Policy Alternatives.

Verbist, G., Förster, M., & Vaalavuo, M. (2012). *The impact of publicly provided services on the distribution of resources: Review of new results and methods* (OECD Social, Employment and Migration Working Papers, No. 130). Retrieved from http://dx.doi.org/10.1787/5k9h363c5szq-en

Chapter 4

Benefits from Public Services

Hugh Mackenzie

In a 1927 United States Supreme Court judgment, Justice Oliver Wendell Holmes famously declared, "taxes are what we pay for civilized society."[1]

While that is as true today as it was then, most of us have much less lofty reasons for paying the taxes that provide public services: we couldn't get through a day without them. Every day, we consume, use, and benefit from public services of an astonishing variety without giving it a second thought—indeed, usually without giving it any thought at all. That variety, along with the differences in our personal circumstances means that each of our interactions with public services is different, but dependence on public services in our daily lives is common to all of us.

To demonstrate this point, I'm going to invite you now to stop reading and conduct a thought experiment. Think your way through your day, from when you got up in the morning until you went to bed at night (or the other way around if you are a shift worker), making a note of every time you used, consumed, or benefited from a public service.

Here are the results of mine:[2]

The alarm clock buzzed and I turned on the light. The electricity I used was distributed to my home by a public utility, and probably generated by a public utility. I used the toilet and flushed, the waste disappearing into my home's plumbing system to be transported kilometres away and processed, all as a public service thanks to the taxes I pay. I brushed my teeth using water that came out of the tap when I turned the handle; water that was there because I paid my taxes. I walked out my front door and down a sidewalk that wouldn't be there if my neighbours and I hadn't paid our taxes. My children and I got into the car and drove down a street that wouldn't be there if we hadn't paid our taxes. I dropped off one of my children at the bus stop to go to school. To catch a bus that wouldn't be there if we didn't pay our taxes; to go to a school that wouldn't be there if we didn't pay our taxes. I managed to make it to my destination without incident, despite the fact that the roads were crowded with others doing exactly what I was doing, thanks to the traffic signals, rules of the road, and police officers that keep us safe. All paid for by taxes. Later that day, I picked up one of my daughters at school and drove her to an appointment with her doctor, the cost of which was covered by the taxes we all pay. At this point, my story becomes a bit repetitive, so I'll skip to my drive home, listening to a radio that wouldn't work if we didn't have a public regulatory system that restricted broadcasters to specific frequencies and making sure I caught the news on the CBC, Canada's public broadcaster. We sat down to dinner without a moment's thought to the safety of the food we were eating, thanks to a system of rules and regulations whose creation and enforcement was paid for through our taxes.

The variety and convenience of public services is obvious from our thought experiment. But the examples we encounter specifically each day barely scratch the surface. There's also the security provided by police, fire, and ambulance services not because of anything specific that they do for us on any specific day, but because they are there. Air quality regulation and enforcement without which life in many cities would be a living hell. The indirect benefits we receive because public services are available to others as well as ourselves, providing all of us with a better educated and healthier society.

It is also easy to miss the sheer scale of the public services enterprise. The millions of children who attend public elementary and secondary schools every day. The hundreds of thousands of teachers who meet these students every day to make the system work. The tens of thousands of Canadians who see a doctor or visit a hospital every day. The thousands of kilometres of sewers and water mains. The hundreds of thousands of kilometres of roads, streets, and highways, not to mention the system of public transportation. The millions of hectares of public parks.

Measuring the Benefit from Public Services

When we reflect on it, our day-to-day experience proves Justice Holmes' point. Life in the twenty-first century as we know it would not be possible without public services. Public services underpin our economy, make it possible for us to provide the essentials of human life to ourselves and our families, and enable us to participate in the economic, social, political, and cultural life of our communities.

Public services are pervasive. But are they a good deal? How important are public services to the lives of Canadians, compared to the goods and services we obtain directly in private markets? And in particular, given the constant and unrelenting attack on the taxes that pay for our public services from conservatives, how does the value we receive from public services compare to the taxes we pay to provide them? In other words, from a macro perspective, how do public services measure up?

A number of studies have looked in some detail at these questions. The most recent of these, published by the Organisation for Economic and Co-operation Development (OECD) in January 2012, investigates the impact of in-kind direct services to households provided through the public sector in OECD-member countries (Verbist, Förster, & Vaalavuo, 2012). It estimates both the average value of these direct public services, per household, and the effect of these services on the distribution of resources among households.[3] The study found that, on average across the OECD, these benefits increase average household disposable incomes by 29%, and that publicly provided resources have the effect of reducing household income inequality. Notably, the study found that the impact of public cash and in-kind benefits for reducing inequality increased in countries where average benefits rose between 2000 and 2007, and declined in countries where average benefits declined.

The OECD study estimates that, for Canada, expenditures on education, health care, early childhood education and care, social housing, and long-term care of the elderly alone have a value equivalent to 25% of disposable income in 2007. Including public pensions, cash transfers were equivalent to 14% of disposable income.

The power of these five categories of in-kind expenditures as a counterpoint to market income inequality is demonstrated by the study's estimates of the value of in-kind benefits as a percentage of disposable income, by income quintile.

By far the most important areas of in-kind benefit, both in aggregate and as influencers of the distribution of resources, are health care and education. Across the OECD, these five categories of public in-kind benefits are valued at

Table 4.1 In-kind benefits as a percent of disposable income in 27 OECD countries, 2007						
Quintiles	1st Q	2nd Q	3rd Q	4th Q	5th Q	Total
Education	30.0%	18.5%	14.2%	10.4%	5.6%	11.8%
Health care	34.9%	22.2%	15.8%	11.8%	7.2%	13.9%
Social Housing	1.8%	0.7%	0.4%	0.2%	0.1%	0.4%
Early Childhood Education and Care	4.5%	3.0%	2.4%	1.5%	0.8%	1.8%
Elder Care	4%	1.9%	0.7%	0.4%	0.2%	0.9%
TOTAL	75.8%	46.4%	33.5%	24.3%	13.7%	28.8%

33.5% of the disposable income for the middle income quintile; nearly half the disposable income of households in the second quintile, and more than 75% the disposable income of households in the bottom quintile.

A similar study published in 2009 by the Canadian Centre for Policy Alternatives (CCPA) focused specifically on Canada (Mackenzie & Shillington, 2009). This study was broader in scope in two respects: it estimated the distribution of the value of all public services, not simply in-kind transfers, and it provided a breakdown of those benefits by category of public service, household type, and level of government providing the service.

Using data and analytical tools from Statistics Canada, the study authors estimated that in 2007 Canadians enjoyed an average $15,000 benefit per capita from the public services that our taxes fund—roughly equivalent to the annual earnings of an individual working full time at the minimum wage.

Lower-income Canadians benefit more from personal transfer payments (most of which are income-related), but middle- and upper-income Canadians benefit fairly equally from all public services. The public services we use and benefit from change as we go through the life cycle. Seniors, for instance, benefit less directly from public education than they do from public health care—but when they were young parents raising children, the opposite was true.

The median Canadian household income (half live in households with incomes below that amount, and half live in households with incomes above it) was approximately $66,000 in a 2.6-person household. That median household realized a $41,000 benefit from public services, equivalent to roughly 63% of the household's private income.

The study authors found that more than two-thirds of Canadians benefit from public services worth more than 50% of their household's total earned income. The chart in Figure 4.1 shows the distribution of per capita benefits from public services, by income category.

The chart demonstrates the power of public services in redistributing resources. Although the per capita dollar value of services is relatively stable across all income ranges, benefit from public services declines as a share of household income as income increases.

The findings also revealed variations in both the level and distribution of benefits from public services, depending on family type.

The data show a per capita value of public services, ranging from $13,332 for families with children to a maximum of $25,386 for single seniors.

The composition of the benefit varies significantly by family type and life stage. Seniors tend to draw a substantial proportion of their benefit from income transfers and health care. For families with young children, naturally, education makes up the most significant share of benefit. For most other groups of Canadians, besides seniors, health care is the most significant service.

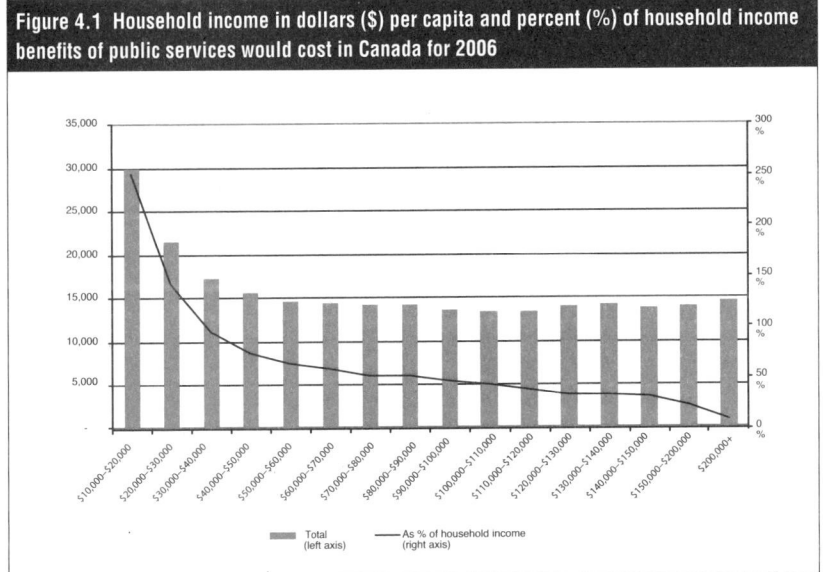

Figure 4.1 Household income in dollars ($) per capita and percent (%) of household income benefits of public services would cost in Canada for 2006

Table 4.2 Average and distribution of benefit from public services by family type

	% of Population	Per capita Benefit	% Education	% Health	% Transfers	% Other
Total	100%	16,527	16%	19%	21%	44%
Couples with Only Older Children	11%	14,758	17%	23%	7%	53%
Families with Children	41%	13,332	29%	15%	13%	43%
Lone Parents with Children	6%	20,416	28%	12%	24%	37%
Non-Senior Couple: No Children	15%	15,407	8%	25%	10%	57%
Other	2%	16,740	17%	17%	28%	38%
Senior Couple	12%	21,199	1%	21%	43%	34%
Single Senior	4%	25,386	0%	22%	50%	28%
Single Non-seniors	10%	21,929	10%	24%	9%	57%

The following three charts show the distribution of benefits from public services by income group for each of the three orders of government in Canada.

74 | Hugh Mackenzie

Figure 4.2 Per capita benefit from public spending by household income in Canada, 2006, federal government

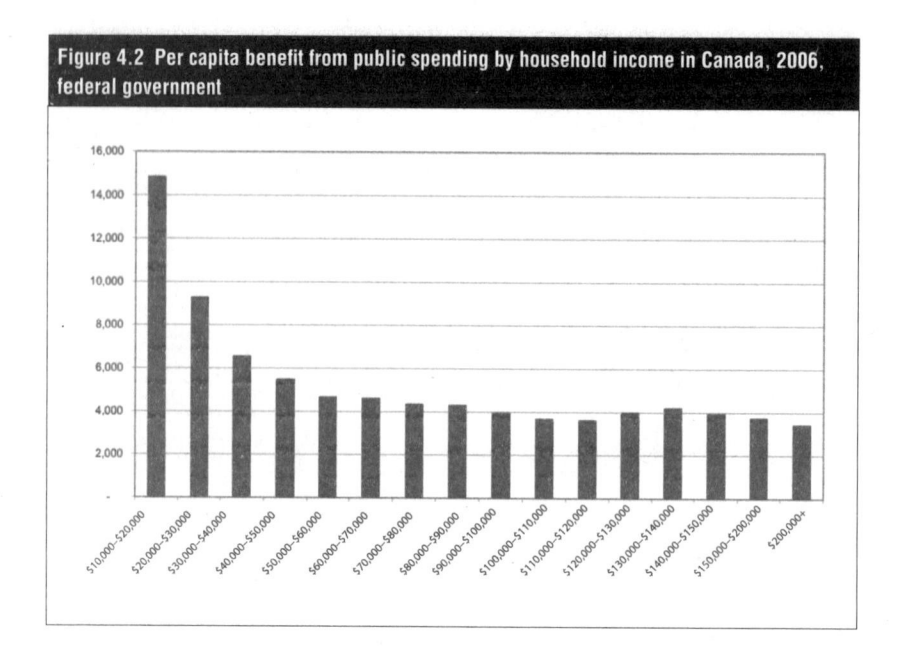

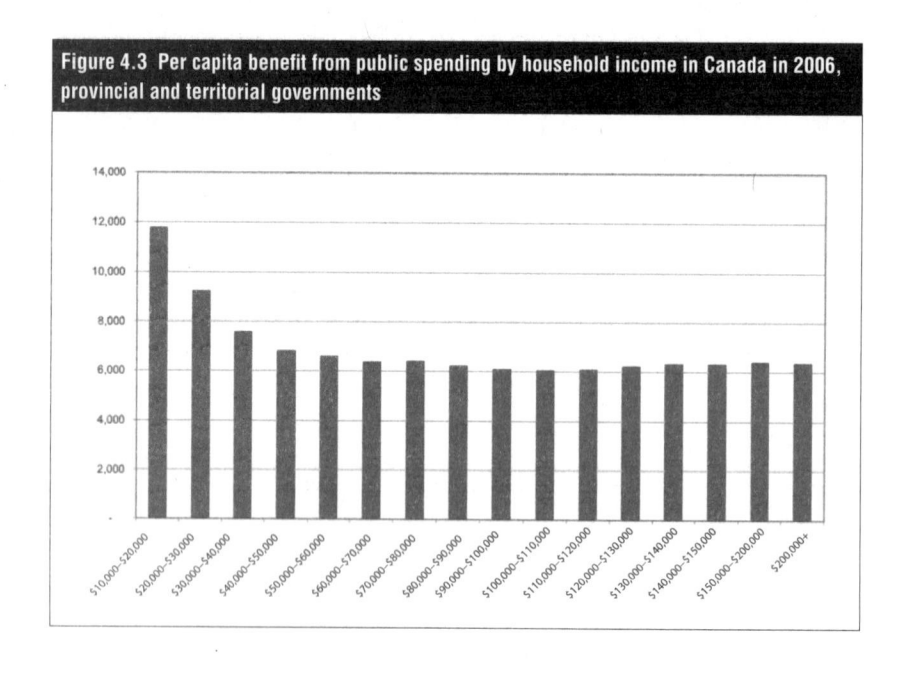

Figure 4.3 Per capita benefit from public spending by household income in Canada in 2006, provincial and territorial governments

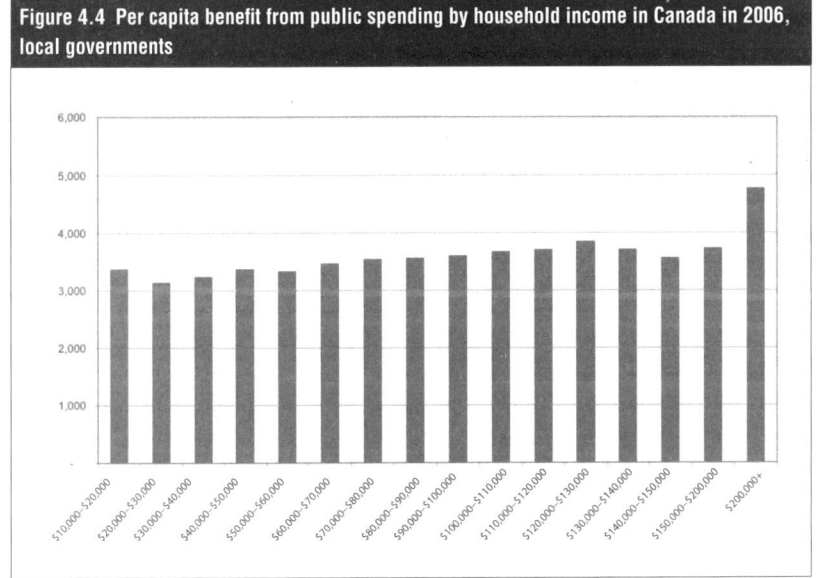

Figure 4.4 Per capita benefit from public spending by household income in Canada in 2006, local governments

While provincial governments are clearly the most important providers of public services in total, federal public services are more important when it comes to impact on income distribution. The value of local government services actually increases slightly in dollar terms as income increases, reflecting the importance of police and fire services in local services and the positive relationship between the value of those services and household income.

Public services account for a significant proportion of the living standard of most Canadians. The value we receive from public services, per capita, varies depending on income and family type, but within such a narrow range that public services deliver a virtually uniform value to all Canadians. In sum, public services amount to a demogrant—an entitlement based on citizenship.

This simple fact has profound implications for the way we think about public services in Canada and for the ongoing debate over taxes, tax cuts, and public expenditure restraint.

At a high level, the debate between taxes and public services cuts as a response to budgetary pressures is a metaphor for the tension between a citizenship democracy, represented by the democratic distribution of benefits from public services, and a dollar democracy, represented by the primacy given to the private economic interests of taxpayers; between citizenship and taxpayership. The data demonstrate that a dollar not spent on public services is not the same as a dollar raised through increased taxes. For the vast majority of Canadians, the loss in value from a dollar not spent on public services is significantly greater than the loss from an equivalent increase in taxes. Why? Because the benefit from public services is distributed roughly equally among all Canadians, while revenue from taxation is not. Because taxation is, in aggregate, roughly proportional to income, and income is distributed unequally, the net value trade-off between taxes and public services is a virtual mirror image of the distribution of income in Canada.

This basic fact has not been lost on Canadians at the top of the income scale, whose economic interests are well served by a one-sided debate over the relative roles of tax increases and spending cuts in responding to budgetary pressures. The vast majority of Canadians, however, have been notably ill-served by it.

These findings also demonstrate the power of public investment as a redistributive offset to growing inequity in market incomes. Both the OECD and CCPA studies highlight the fact that public services account for a significant share of a middle-income household's living standard, a share that increases for moderate and lower-income households. This, in turn, challenges the way the debate over tax fairness has been framed in Canada, particularly by political progressives.

We don't levy taxes for the sake of levying taxes; we levy taxes to pay for public services. The implication of this is that what matters for the role of government in redistribution is the fiscal bargain—the relationship between taxation and benefit from public services—not just the impact of taxation in isolation.

Looking at the net impact of a policy change in the fiscal bargain casts a very different light on the debate over tax cuts and public spending in Canada. The CCPA study showed that the vast majority of Canadians would have been better off without the major tax cuts introduced in the 2000s, including cuts in consumption taxes and others considered to be regressive.[4] In their analysis, the study authors estimate that 80% of Canadians would have been better off if, instead of cutting the GST, the Harper government had transferred the money to local governments to pay for more and better public services.

Compared to the broad-based income tax cuts implemented by provincial governments in the late 1990s and early 2000s, 80% of Canadians would have been better off if their provincial governments had spent the money on health care and education. And had the federal government invested in improved federal public services instead of cutting capital gains taxation by one-third in the early 2000s, 91% of Canadians would have been better off.

Of course, the advocates of tax cuts never present the real trade-off between taxation and the benefits from public services. The closest we came in Canada to a debate over this trade-off was when the Federation of Canadian Municipalities (FCM) advocated leaving the national GST rate at 7% and transferring the 2% the federal government was proposing to cut to local governments. And even in that instance, the FCM was unable to establish in the public mind the relationship between funding for local governments as institutions and benefits to Canadian households.

In the absence of a way to make the benefits from public services visible to Canadians, the debate over tax cuts becomes a contest between a very concrete "saving" in taxes and an abstraction, a loss in fiscal capacity.

The tax cuts are made to sound like free money to middle-income Canadians. But when one factors in the value of the services that would have been provided from those foregone taxes, the cuts are anything but free. The data indicate that the tax cuts implemented in the last 15 years have had the net effect of reducing the living standards of most Canadians.[5]

The Challenge of Measuring Public Services

The results highlighted by these studies underline the economic importance of public services to the living standards of most Canadians. Yet even these data tend to understate both the value of public services to Canadian households and the net fiscal bargain. Measures of the value of public services developed from aggregate economic data, including all of the measures cited above, tend to understate significantly the value of public consumption relative to market consumption.

When we measure the value of privately produced goods and services, we do so using market prices, which at least theoretically reflect the amount that a willing buyer is prepared to pay a willing seller, and thus reflect the value to the buyer of the good or service.

With public services, measurement is not nearly that straightforward.

Most public services do not trade in a traditional market. And many services that are funded by market-like user fees provide benefits that do not flow exclusively to those who pay the fees. As a result, even if there is an equivalent price charged for a service, it often does not fully capture the benefit provided by that service. The underlying issue is that transactions involving private goods and services, consumption, use, and benefit have essentially the same meaning, but that is not generally true for public services.

We interact with some public services as consumers, consuming in the sense that our use of the service precludes its use by someone else. The interaction of parents and students with education is a good example. My son or daughter's attendance at our local school means that that place is not available to another's child. So is the relationship we have as patients with the health care system. The 15 minutes that I spend with my doctor during my checkup is 15 minutes not available to someone else. Generally, we choose to provide these services publicly because we are not prepared to leave it entirely to the market and the resources it makes available to individuals to determine their use. For example, we see access to education and health care as fundamental entitlements.

In some cases, we provide market-like goods and services publicly simply because it is more efficient to do so. We could, theoretically, require every property owner to put a light on their property near the street, but it is far more efficient to provide street lighting as a public service. For example, in some Canadian provinces, automobile insurance is provided publicly, because they have determined it is more efficient to do so.

Many other public services can be used without being consumed. For example, within limits, my use of a street or road does not preclude someone else from using it as well. We share the use of the street, just as we share the use of the water and sewer system with our neighbours. Similarly, the security provided by police, fire, and ambulance services or the armed forces is enjoyed by all, but consumed to exhaustion by no one.

Finally, we may benefit from public services which we neither use nor consume. For example, as noted above, we benefit from the health and education systems not only because we or our children use them but also because the fact that these services are generally available to everyone makes us all better off. We benefit individually when we use the health care system, but we also all benefit from the fact that people in our society generally are healthier as a result. A better-educated population is more productive and better able to engage in the social, political, and cultural life of the community.

Similarly, people who choose to use private transportation benefit from the public transportation system because it takes cars off the roads, reducing congestion. Users of private transportation who have experienced the effects of labour disputes or technical problems in the transit systems of large cities understand those benefits only too well.

These characteristics make the valuation of public services very difficult. In principle, an evaluation of public services should take into account all of the benefits that all of us receive. And in some cases, when decisions are being made about new projects or programs, analysts try to do just that. They attempt to measure benefits from public goods, services, and programs that cannot be captured in a price, or even a proxy for a price.

Generally, however, we don't try to measure the benefits from public services. Instead, we adopt the oversimplified convention that public services are valued at their cost. Even in cases where benefits have been estimated in deciding whether or not to go ahead with a project, from that point on, the value of the project is measured at its cost.

The value of government services in our gross domestic product, for example, is measured using the cost of providing those services.

Measuring the Value of Public Services at Cost: Implications

The fact that we measure the value of public services at their cost has significant implications. By definition, there is no measured economic gain from expenditures on a public service, so there is no economic basis for determining whether or not we have enough of any given service. This is a particular problem with shared-use services and services that deliver general social benefits to both non-users and users. For example, relying on users to pay for public transit will inevitably result in our having less public transit than we need, because the price users are prepared to pay does not reflect the benefit to the community at large of investments in transit.

Measuring public services at their cost distorts the decisions we make about establishing new public services or expanding existing ones, because it is difficult to identify and measure all of the benefits that flow from those investments. It is particularly a problem, however, during periods of "fiscal constraint," when governments are looking for ways to "save" money. Because the budget-makers value services at their cost, by definition expenditure on any public service can be reduced without any net cost to society.

A perfect indication of this problem arose in the debate in Ontario over spending cut recommendations in the report of former TD Bank vice-president Don Drummond. Among Drummond's recommendations was the elimination of the government's new early learning program—the extension of kindergarten programming to a full day, integrated with after-school child care.

Extensive studies have shown repeatedly that the benefits to society from early learning investments, both in the short and long term, significantly outweigh program costs. In the short term, the payoff comes in the form of greater labour force participation and increased productivity for parents of children in early learning programs.[6] In the long term, the evidence of better educational outcomes for children participating in early learning programs is overwhelming. Indeed, in deciding to extend kindergarten to a full day, the Government of Ontario relied on studies that identified precisely those kinds of economic gains (Pascal, 2009).

In an accounting framework in which services are valued at their cost, however, early learning programs can be eliminated at no net cost, since the benefit foregone has the same value as the cost savings from eliminating the program. Drummond's acceptance of deficit reduction as an overriding goal tipped the balance in favour of eliminating the program. The evidence supporting a net benefit from these programs may have been critical in the adoption of the policy in the first place, but it played no role whatsoever in the recommendation for its elimination.

A similar problem underlies our chronic underinvestment in public infrastructure. Infrastructure investments are undertaken based on long-term net benefits. Often the decisions to make these investments are supported by cost-benefit studies that demonstrate a positive net return to society after all costs are taken into account. Once the investment is complete, however, those net benefits completely disappear from our accounting, which by definition indicates that we receive no net benefit. For example, a decision to invest in road widening or a higher-capacity bridge would have been based in part on the value of the time saved by road users benefiting from reduced congestion. However, in economic accounts, those benefits are not recognized. The ongoing value of the road-widening or bridge is measured only by its economic depreciation.

Again, the distortion in decision-making created by this accounting convention was evident in a recommendation from the Drummond Report to cancel or defer a substantial proportion of the Ontario Government's proposed infrastructure renewal program. Indeed, the entire Drummond review exercise was based on the premise that while tax increases are costly to households, cuts to public services can be made with no net cost.

This theme—cutting public services without reference to the benefits foregone as a result of those cuts—is not unique to Ontario. It is repeated in all three orders of government and in every part of the country.

In some instances, the consequences are immediately evident. Fees charged for services that used to be universally accessible; reduced hours or closures for public facilities; reduced entitlements to cash benefits. In other instances, it can take years, even decades, for the full impact to be felt. Toronto is paying the price today for the cancellation of transit investments by the Harris Government 15 years ago. Canadians who have suffered from the consequences of the 2008 depression have been doubly burdened by the deterioration of the social safety net through two decades of cuts to social housing, employment insurance, and social assistance programs.

Cost-based accounting for the output from public services also distorts the debate over public service productivity. Valuing services at their cost means that, under standard measures of productivity, public service productivity by definition cannot increase. Any improvement in public service operations will be reflected in lower costs, which in turn will be reflected in a lower measured value for the service.

The fact that conventionally measured public service productivity cannot increase by definition highlights the disingenuousness of conservatives who criticize the productivity of public service workers.

Conclusion

Public services are pervasive. They affect virtually every aspect of our lives. They contribute significantly to our standard of living. They act as a powerful counterweight to the tendency of market forces to produce economic outcomes that are increasingly inequitable. They democratize consumption. Yet these services are pervasive to such an extent that we take them for granted. They are invisible.

That invisibility is not benign. It distorts our perceptions of the choices that are open to us. It leads us to underinvest in public services that are critically important to our economic future. And it makes public services vulnerable to the seductive and self-serving claims of conservatives that we can balance budgets simply by reducing public spending and without consequences, that tax cuts can be implemented at no cost, that any gain from a tax cut, no matter how small, is "worth it."

Conservatives have taken full advantage of the invisibility of public services. The idea that any tax cut is worth it has been used as a smokescreen to obscure the fact that while tax cuts go disproportionately to those with high incomes, the costs of the public expenditure restraint needed to pay for them are borne disproportionately by lower- and middle-income Canadians.

And until we start to pay attention to the value we receive from the public services we use, that will continue.

Notes

1 *Compañía General de Tabacos de Filipinas v. Collector of Internal Revenue*, [1927]. Interestingly, the popular version of that quote—"I like to pay taxes. With them I buy civilization"—is directly parallel to billionaire Warren Buffett's comparison of his and his secretary's tax rates. The quote is attributed to Mr. Justice Holmes in an anecdote drawn from a conversation between Holmes and his secretary, and was reported by soon-to-be Justice Felix Frankfurter in his 1938 book, *Mr. Justice Holmes and the Supreme Court*.

2 I told a variant of this story for the first time in a presentation to the Standing Committee on Finance and Economic Affairs of the Ontario Legislature in 2002. I had been making a pitch on behalf of the Ontario Alternative Budget project for increased investments in public services, when a Conservative member of the committee accused me of suggesting that we would be better off if the government had more of our money and we had less of it to use ourselves. I replied that I wasn't sure I would have put it that way myself, but that's exactly what I was saying. And then I proceeded to take her through my day. Her question time was up before I finished.

3 The study focused on cash transfers and in-kind transfers for health, education, housing, early childhood education, and care and long-term care for the elderly. The figures presented here do not include cash transfers, which on average across the OECD were measured at 23% of disposable income.

4 A regressive tax is not one that raises more revenue from lower-income households than it does from higher-income households; it is a tax that raises *proportionally* more revenue from lower-income households than from higher-income households—that is, a tax that amounts to a higher proportion of the income of lower-income households than of higher-income households. Thus a tax can be regressive and still provide the tax side of a fiscal bargain that results in a net transfer of resources from higher-income to lower-income households.

5   A 2011 study for Canada using a standard international method for comparing living standards conducted for the Centre for the Study of Living Standards found an average total benefit of 55% of household income and an average net benefit (after taxes) of 7% of household income (Sharpe, Murray, Evans, & Hazell, 2011, p. 24).
6   These were the findings of Fortin, Godbout, and St-Cerny in their working paper, *Impact of Quebec's universal low-fee childcare program on female labour force participation, domestic income and government budgets*. Their analysis concluded that the tax/transfer return to the federal and Quebec governments from Quebec's universal low-fee child care program significantly exceeded its cost.

References

Compañía General de Tabacos de Filipinas v. Collector of Internal Revenue (1927).

Fortin, P., Godbout, L., & St-Cerny, S. (2012). *Impact of Quebec's universal low-fee childcare program on female labour force participation, domestic income and government budgets* (Working Paper 2012/02). Retrieved from http://www.usherbrooke.ca/chaire-fiscalite/fileadmin/sites/chaire-fiscalite/documents/Cahiers-de-recherche/Etude_femmes_ANGLAIS.pdf

Mackenzie, H., & Shillington, R. (2009). *Canada's quiet bargain: The benefits of public spending* (CCPA Growing Gap Project, April 15, 2009). Ottawa, ON: Canadian Centre for Policy Alternatives.

O'Toole, G. (2012, April 13). Taxes are what we pay for civilized society [Web log post]. Retrieved from http://quoteinvestigator.com/2012/04/13/taxes-civilize/

Pascal, C. E. (2009). *With our best future in mind: Implementing early learning in Ontario* (Report to the Premier by the Special Advisor on Early Learning). Toronto, ON: Government of Ontario.

Sharpe, A., Murray, A., Evans, B., & Hazell, E. (2011, July). *The Levy Institute measure of economic well-being: Estimates for Canada, 1999 and 2005* (Working Paper No. 680). Retrieved from http://www.levyinstitute.org/publications/?docid=1399

Verbist, G., Förster, M., & Vaalavuo, M. (2012). *The impact of publicly provided services on the distribution of resources: Review of new results and methods* (OECD Social, Employment and Migration Working Papers, No. 130). Retrieved from http://dx.doi.org/10.1787/5k9h363c5szq-en

Chapter 5

Canadian Public Opinion on Taxes

Frank Graves

Introduction

The study of public opinion on taxes is one of the most frustrating and confusing areas for the analyst of public attitudes, fraught with apparently ambiguous results that easily lead to diametrically contradicting conclusions. Whether it is in the service of disingenuous manipulation, or a genuine attempt to understand and reveal more about society and political choice, this is an area where one can easily construct two completely and apparently irreconcilable pictures of what the public really thinks. The data also consistently reveal a gap between what Canadians say and how they vote. Simply put, taxes do better on surveys than they seem to do in politics.

The Variety of Public Meanings of Taxation

Before I talk about the most recent data on taxes, I should contextualize the discussion by considering several factors that can further complicate the already complicated matter of gauging the public's views on taxes.

Part of the apparent ambiguity in public opinion on taxation can be explained by the variety of taxes we are talking about and the ways in which questions concerning them are framed. Another challenge is the differences in vested interests, values, and ideologies of the respondents. And there is also the fact that the public outlook on taxes is in a state of some flux; both in attitudes to taxes themselves and in outlook on closely related issues such as inequality, the role of the state, and views of the Canadian economy in a changing global context. In the next section, I will examine some partial indicators of these issues, and then turn to the historical context and some speculations about the future of this debate.

Type of Tax

Not surprisingly, attitudes toward taxes vary by the type of tax in question. For example, a majority of Canadian adults (59%) believe that the various

Figure 5.1 Attitudes toward tax rates

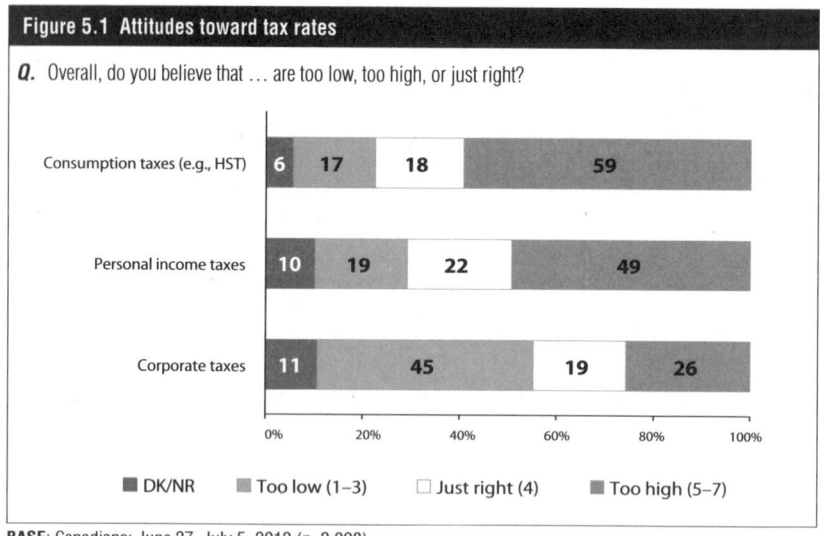

Q. Overall, do you believe that ... are too low, too high, or just right?

Tax type	DK/NR	Too low (1–3)	Just right (4)	Too high (5–7)
Consumption taxes (e.g., HST)	6	17	18	59
Personal income taxes	10	19	22	49
Corporate taxes	11	45	19	26

BASE: Canadians; June 27–July 5, 2012 (n=2,098).

consumption taxes they pay are "too high," as Figure 5.1 shows. Almost half also believe that they pay too much in personal income taxes. At the same time, they are likely to describe the taxes paid by others (particularly corporations and corporate executives), as decidedly "too low." It is also entirely likely that taxes that are visible and frequent—the GST/HST, for example—will always be less popular than taxes that are less visible, whatever their relative substantive merits.

Propositional Form of the Statements about Taxes

How questions are phrased is always important in public opinion research, but perhaps even more important when it comes to tax preferences. No simple set of questions can adequately capture the complexity of the issue, but some proven barometers can help sort through the ambiguities and divisions in public opinion. A key example is the kind of choice that the question implies. Generally, the public will respond very favourably to the option of deep cuts to spending as an alternative to tax increases, public debt, and continued—or even deepened—deficits, in large part because they believe that government is rife with waste, inefficiency, and poor spending priorities.

Figure 5.2 shows a fairly typical response to a standard question of this sort. While a prudent 30% reject answering the question at all, the overall lean is toward spending cuts. Well that was easy; the public will reward savage cuts and abhor new taxes or debt. Some have even claimed that this new austerity aspiration is significantly increased. On this latter point, my team and I asked the same question of a very large random sample in 2012, and we found that this public read was actually dead stable. So there is no new thirst for austerity. Is the

Canadian Public Opinion on Taxes | 85

Figure 5.2 Preferred approach to deficit

Q. In your opinion, what should the Government of Canada's main approach to the deficit be for the coming year?

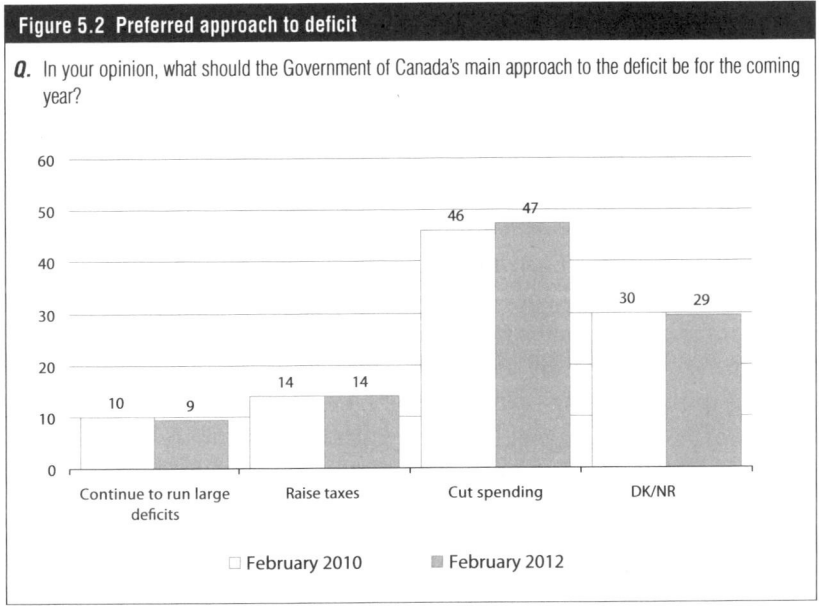

Response	February 2010	February 2012
Continue to run large deficits	10	9
Raise taxes	14	14
Cut spending	46	47
DK/NR	30	29

BASE: Canadians; most recent data point February 21–28, 2012 (n=3,699).

Figure 5.3 Preferred government priorities

Q. The federal government faces major challenges in dealing with its finances. The country also has major ongoing investment needs. Which of the following 3 priorities should be the most important principle for dealing with these challenges?

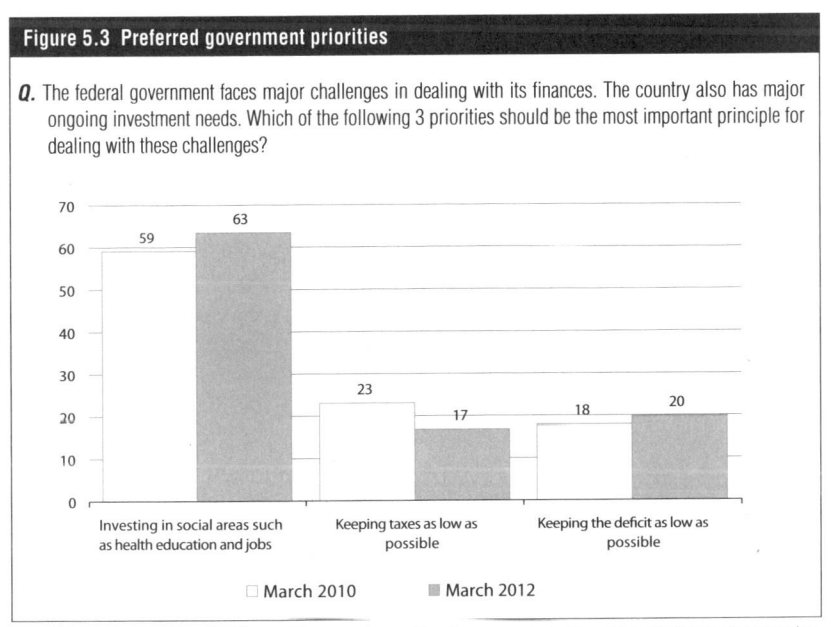

Priority	March 2010	March 2012
Investing in social areas such as health education and jobs	59	63
Keeping taxes as low as possible	23	17
Keeping the deficit as low as possible	18	20

Note: In our most recent poll, this question was changed to give respondents the option of skipping the question. The 2012 results exclude the 7% of respondents who did not provide a valid response.
BASE: Canadians; most recent data point February 21–28, 2012 (n=3,699).

apparent single-mindedness of the public on this issue really that straightforward?

Yet consider Figure 5.3. If people prefer spending cuts to tax and debt in Figure 5.2, they prefer "investment in health, education and jobs" by an even larger margin here. At 63%, that constitutes an overwhelming majority of Canadians, and that number is up, modestly but significantly (statistically), since 2010 budget time. The emphasis on social investment is dramatically higher among women, younger Canadians, university graduates, and non-Conservative supporters. So the seemingly widespread perception of a huge and growing desire for tax-cutting among Canadians in a "bloodthirsty" mood is only partially true at best. They say "yes" to cuts over tax increases, and "yes" to tax increases for investments—but the highest scores we received were for social investment, not spending cuts. It's an inscrutable set of seemingly contradictory attitudes.

Differences by Social Location

As noted in the last section, we found significant variations in attitudes to taxation and the role of government depending on age, gender, and to a lesser extent, region and locale. By far the biggest effects are political ideology and party choice. These differences become clearest when talking about the issue of taxation as it connects to the size and role of the state. Conservatives clearly lean

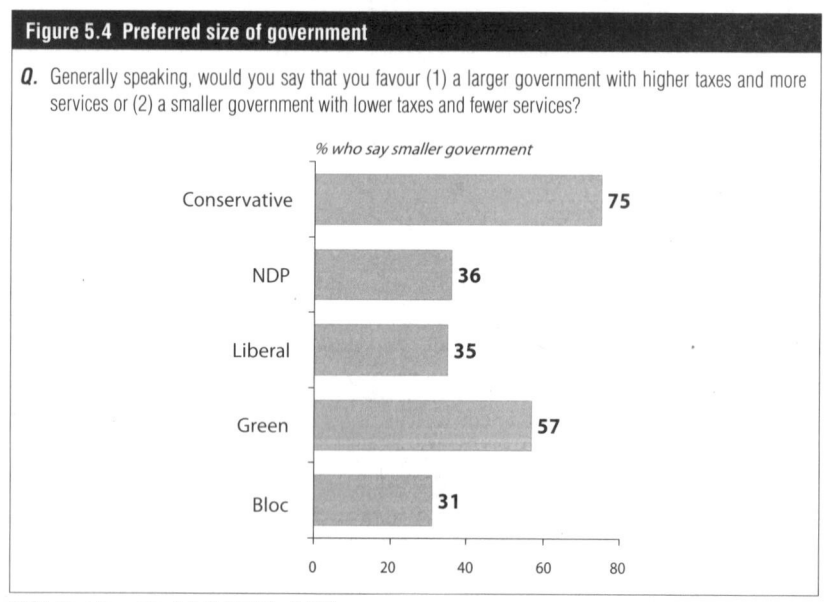

Figure 5.4 Preferred size of government

Q. Generally speaking, would you say that you favour (1) a larger government with higher taxes and more services or (2) a smaller government with lower taxes and fewer services?

% who say smaller government

Party	%
Conservative	75
NDP	36
Liberal	35
Green	57
Bloc	31

BASE: Canadians; March 5–9, 2010 (n=1,420).

toward smaller government; support for reducing government is twice as high for them as it is among NDP and Liberal supporters. This parallels a similar if even deeper difference in the United States, where the mantra for the Republicans and the Tea Party movement in particular is summed up with bumper sticker simplicity: "Less taxes, smaller government."

Canada–US comparison

I have charted North American attitudes to taxes and the role of government for some time. Although the data are a decade old, they show that Canadians were more collectivist and less averse to taxation and government generally than Americans. The data aren't shown here, but Mexicans were even more averse to taxes, and this was linked to basic issues of the government's legitimacy and perceptions of its corruption.

Figure 5.5 Tracking the meaning of national identities

Q. What does being [...] mean to you?

Rank		Canadian	American
1	Leaving a healthy environment to future generations	64	53
2	Having social & health programs to support all citizens	48	31
3	Having the opportunity to pursue a good life	58	73
4	Living in a tolerant, multicultural country	61	56
5	Being free to do and think as I please	60	64
6	Having a say in the political / social / economic development of my country	47	57
7	Sharing many values and beliefs with other citizens	50	58
8	Being able to count on your fellow citizens if you are in need	40	48
9	Living in the best society in the world	54	49
10	Feeling distinctly different from people in other countries	39	28
11	Serving my country when it needs me	37	50
12	Paying taxes	31	14

BASE: Most recent data points: Canadians November 2006 (n=2,002); Americans November 2006 (n=1,500).

Summary

The apparent contradictions in public opinion research are only partly a product of the vagaries in public opinion. The variety of meanings of taxes are also based on differences according to what sort of tax we are talking about, the propositional form of the question asked, and segmentations on fault lines around values and vested interests. While taxes, like unpleasant medicines, do not engender warm affectionate responses, the public clearly rejects the notion that they should be cut at all costs, and that all taxes are bad. In fact, Canadians generally seem to accept the notion that taxes are a necessary precondition for quality of life and a healthy society, certainly more so than other North Americans. But are these enduring value differences eroding? Are we as a nation shifting to the right? Do the historical data reflect an older Canada? In the next section I explore the most recent data.

Recent Shifts in Public Outlook and Some Conjectures about the Future

In a piece titled *Public perceptions of Canadians on economic issues: From Reaganomics to Humanomics* (Graves, 1999), I chronicled how Canadian attitudes to the role of the state and taxation had morphed during the eighties and nineties. As Western economies (particularly the United States and United Kingdom) stagnated in the post-Vietnam period, there was a distinct shift in attitudes from the post–Second World War expansionary period that culminated in the pursuit of the Great Society in American and the Canadian analogue, the "just society." The neo-liberal counter-revolution ushered in by Reagan and Thatcher called

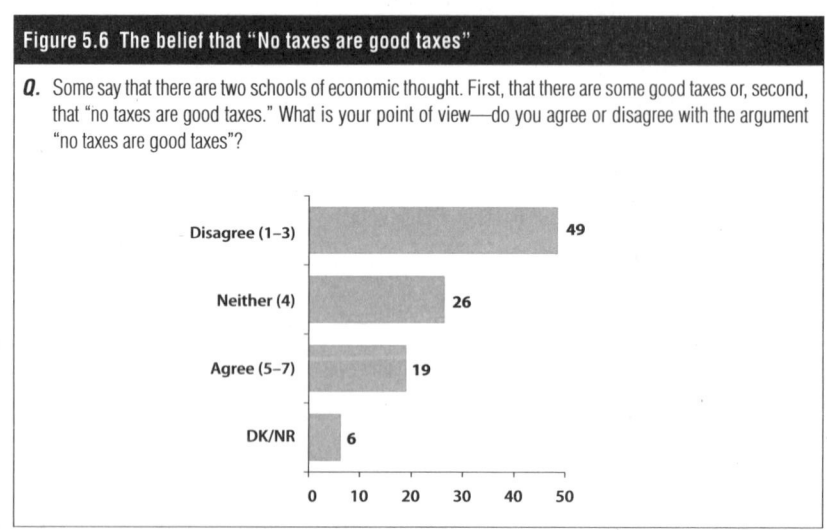

Figure 5.6 The belief that "No taxes are good taxes"

Q. Some say that there are two schools of economic thought. First, that there are some good taxes or, second, that "no taxes are good taxes." What is your point of view—do you agree or disagree with the argument "no taxes are good taxes"?

- Disagree (1–3): 49
- Neither (4): 26
- Agree (5–7): 19
- DK/NR: 6

Note: Most recent figure recalculated to exclude those who answered "Don't know/No response."
BASE: Canadians; June 27–July 5, 2012 (n=2,098).

for broad-based reductions to government spending and lower taxes, a combination that was supposed to propel the economy to growth and prosperity. In Canada, this shift was never as dramatic, but of course we were not immune. By the nineties, extreme anxieties about jobs and public finances led to a major transformation of taxes and public finances here as well. And with these there were changes in public attitudes toward government and taxes.

Broader Contextual shifts

The last few years have been marked by two extraordinary shifts in public opinion. The first is a growing sense that Western democracies are heading for what some refer to as "the end of progress." The second is a growing fear about income inequality, and particularly the growing disparity between the über rich and the rest of society.

In Canada, this longer-term erosion of confidence in the inevitability of progress and a better future has clearly been taking root. Looking back, one-third of Canadians believe they are better off than the last generation, compared to 37% who say they are worse off. Looking forward, however, Canadians feel the next generation will be worse off by a margin of four to one. See Figure 5.8.

Furthermore, amid fears that the world is in for a period of prolonged economic stagnation, a staggering 72% of Canadians agree that "American dominance peaked in the last century." The traditional economic powerhouses of Europe and North America are seen as falling into decline, while China and Southeast Asia are seen as economies on the rise.

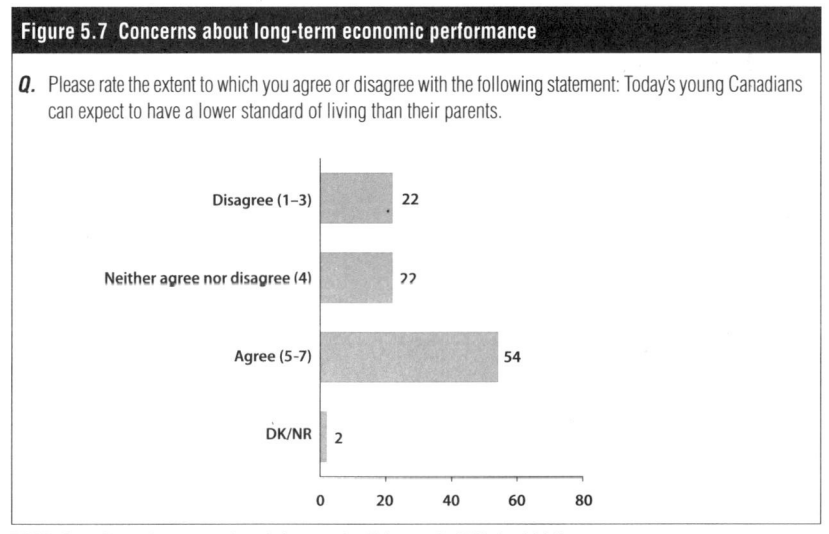

Figure 5.7 Concerns about long-term economic performance

Q. Please rate the extent to which you agree or disagree with the following statement: Today's young Canadians can expect to have a lower standard of living than their parents.

Response	%
Disagree (1–3)	22
Neither agree nor disagree (4)	22
Agree (5–7)	54
DK/NR	2

BASE: Canadians who are employed; January 27–February 8, 2012 (n=1,922).

90 | Frank Graves

Figure 5.8 Perceived changes in quality of life over time

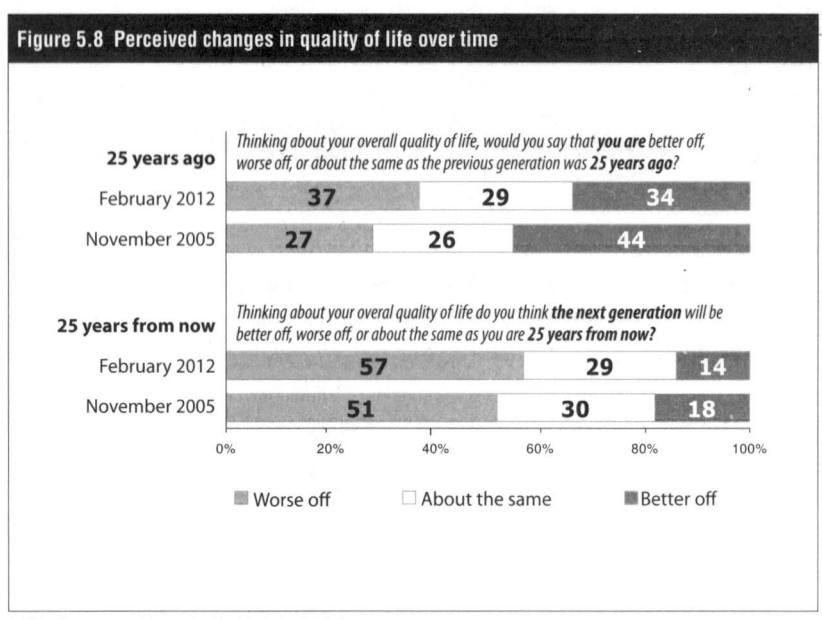

25 years ago — *Thinking about your overall quality of life, would you say that you are better off, worse off, or about the same as the previous generation was 25 years ago?*

	Worse off	About the same	Better off
February 2012	37	29	34
November 2005	27	26	44

25 years from now — *Thinking about your overall quality of life do you think the next generation will be better off, worse off, or about the same as you are 25 years from now?*

	Worse off	About the same	Better off
February 2012	57	29	14
November 2005	51	30	18

BASE: Canadians; March 6–11, 2012 (n=2,001).

Figure 5.9 A future of American dominance

Q. Since the end of the Cold War, the United States has essentially been an unrivalled superpower. However, the economic crisis, combined with the growing influence of emerging economies such as China, India, and Brazil, is leading many to believe that American dominance is ending. Which of the following statements comes closest to your point of view?

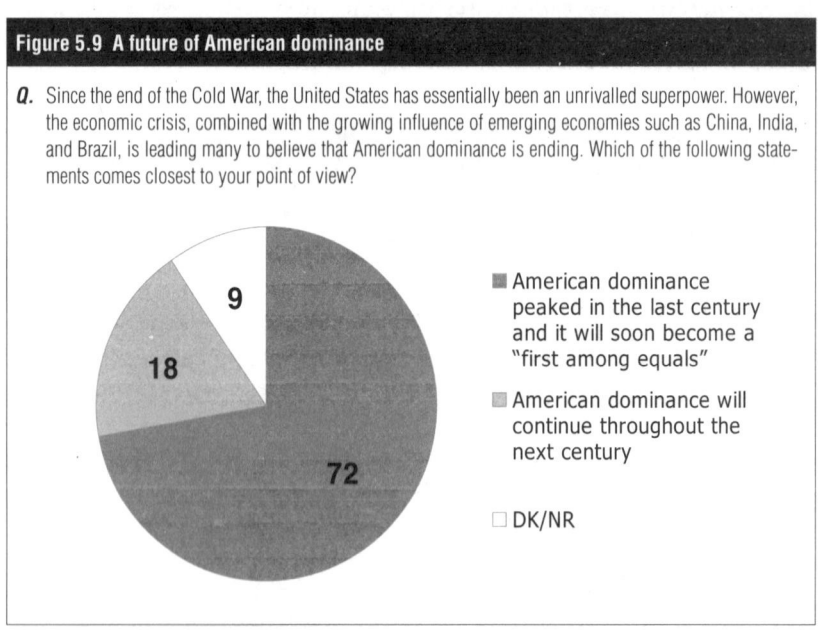

- 72 — American dominance peaked in the last century and it will soon become a "first among equals"
- 18 — American dominance will continue throughout the next century
- 9 — DK/NR

BASE: Canadians; March 6–11, 2012 (n=2,001).

Canadian Public Opinion on Taxes | 91

Figure 5.10 The future well-being of world economic zones

Q. Over the next decade, the world economy will undergo many significant changes. Do you believe that the following economic zones will be better off or worse off ten years from now than they are today?

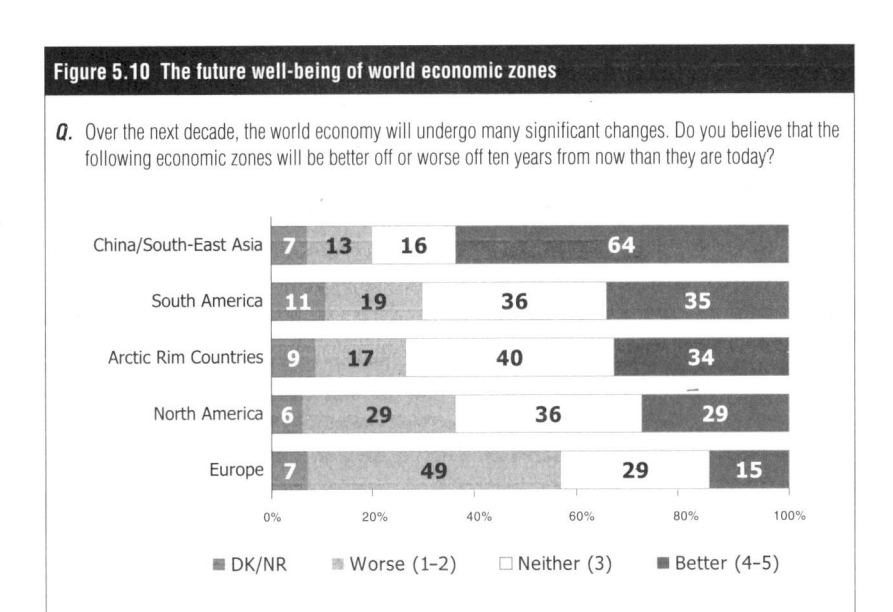

Economic Zone	DK/NR	Worse (1–2)	Neither (3)	Better (4–5)
China/South-East Asia	7	13	16	64
South America	11	19	36	35
Arctic Rim Countries	9	17	40	34
North America	6	29	36	29
Europe	7	49	29	15

BASE: Canadians; March 6–11, 2012 (n=2,001).

Figure 5.11 Preferred size of government

Q. Generally speaking, would you say that you favour (1) a larger government with higher taxes and more services or (2) a smaller government with lower taxes and fewer services?

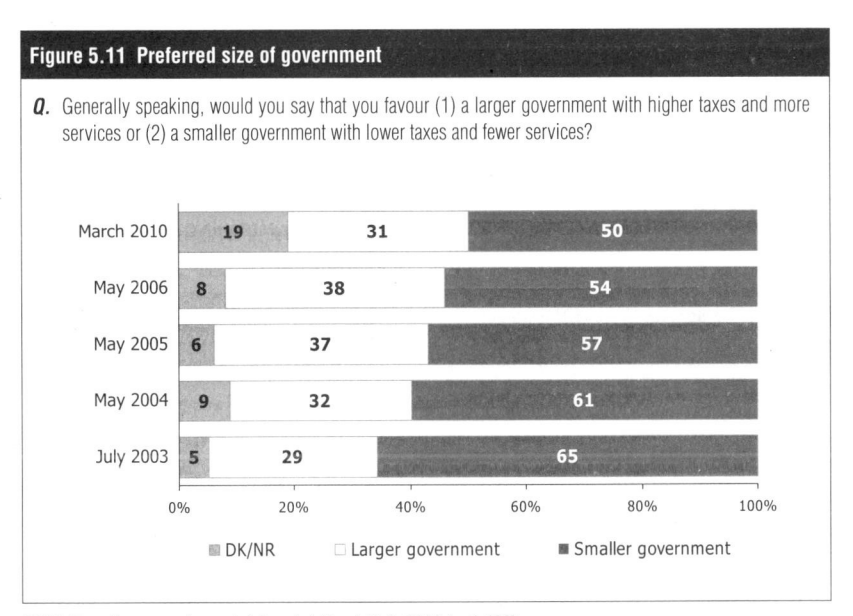

	DK/NR	Larger government	Smaller government
March 2010	19	31	50
May 2006	8	38	54
May 2005	6	37	57
May 2004	9	32	61
July 2003	5	29	65

BASE: Canadians; most recent data point March 5–9, 2010 (n=1,420).

Figure 5.11 shows an important trend line. Many have claimed that the recent success of the right reveals a "blueing" of Canadian attitudes. The time series data, however, continue to show that Canadians are less—rather than more—likely to prefer smaller government than they were in the past. They still want government to play a positive role—they do not want it to retract, but to cost less. This probably reflects the continuing belief that government is wasteful—something that is not unexpected, given the all-party emphasis on waste and its elimination—rather than any new belief that government is less important. Not surprisingly, ideology matters here. And attitudes seem to be polarizing. As I expected, self-declared conservatives are more supportive of cuts to taxes and government than liberals. However, there is no evidence of a fundamental shift in Canadian attitudes on the importance of government.

Income Inequality and the Rise of the 1%

In addition to shifts in attitudes about the end of progress, an equally profound new shift has direct bearing on the debate about taxes. A range of diverse evidence is showing that income inequality has vaulted from relative obscurity to become a top priority for Canadians. In Figure 5.12, even arrayed against the hugely important issues of the economy (jobs and growth) and health care and education (social), the growing gap between rich and poor emerged as the top priority and dramatically eclipsed fiscal issues like taxes and debt by a margin of more than three to one. What on Earth is going on here? Is this a rogue error? Inequality also placed a close second to the debt crisis as the biggest threat to the global economy (Figure 5.13). We also see evidence in the United States from both PEW and Rasmussen that inequality concerns are rising and there has been a dramatic shift to favouring taxing the wealthy. This is transforming the political landscape for a public that is increasingly skeptical of corporate tax relief and trickle-down economics.

The Top 1%

Figure 5.14 shows that this burgeoning concern with inequality can and probably will affect the political landscape in Canada. By a margin of two to one (and over three to one for those outside of the Conservative base) Canadians would be more likely to vote for a party that raised taxes on the rich than one that promised to keep taxes low.

And what about those fat executive paycheques we've been hearing about? Just 7% of Canadians say that executive pay should continue to be set by corporate boards as it is now. More than half want executive pay submitted to shareholders for their approval. And more than one-third say that any executive income over a million dollars should be taxed at 90%.

Figure 5.12 The most important issue for discussion

Q. Which of the following do you think should be the most important issue in discussions about Canada's future? Should it be (1) social issues like health and education, (2) issues related to the economy like economic growth and jobs, (3) Fiscal issues like taxes and debt, (4) issues such as the growing gap between rich and poor, or (5) none of these?

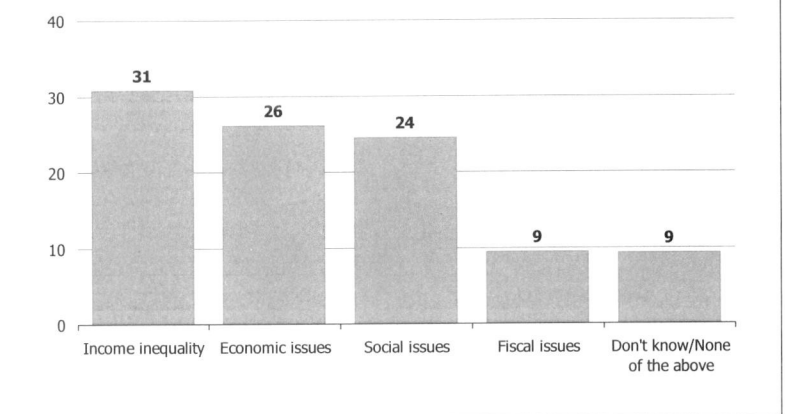

Issue	%
Income inequality	31
Economic issues	26
Social issues	24
Fiscal issues	9
Don't know/None of the above	9

BASE: Canadians; February 21–28, 2012 (n=3,699).

Figure 5.13 The biggest threat to the global economy

Q. Which of the following do you think is the biggest threat to the global economy?

Option	%
Growing debt crisis in advanced economies	36
An extreme and growing concentration of wealth in the richest 1% of the population	32
An aging population	11
A lack of innovation and productivity	5
Climate change	5
Other	9
DK/NR	3

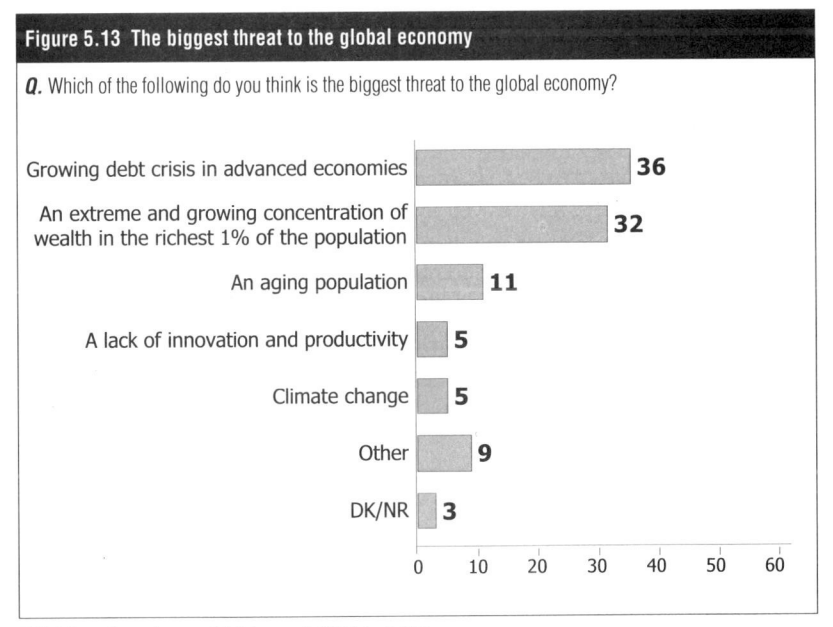

BASE: Canadians; January 27–February 8, 2012 (n=2,891).

94 | Frank Graves

Figure 5.14 No new taxes versus taxing the rich

Q. In the next federal election, would you be more likely to support a party that promised to NOT raise taxes or a party that promised to raise taxes on the rich?

- A party that promised to raise taxes on the rich: 60
- A party that promised not to raise taxes: 30
- DK/NR: 10

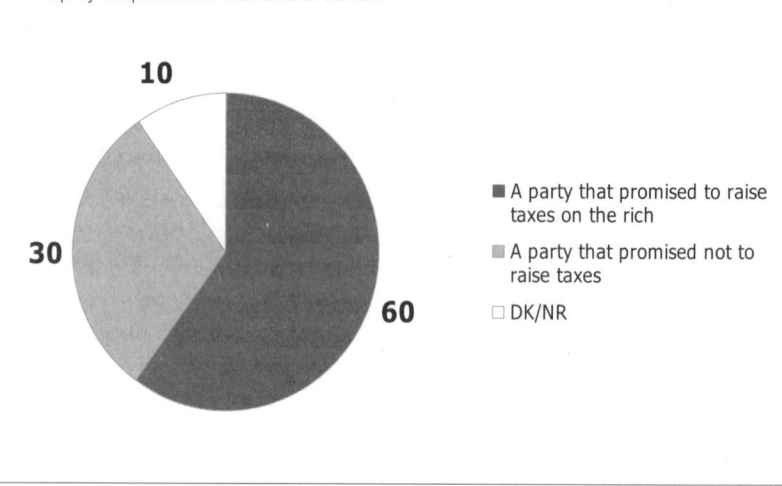

BASE: Canadians; February 21–28, 2012 (n=3,699).

Figure 5.15 Attitudes toward executive compensation

Q. There is a lot of talk about how high executive compensation has risen in recent years. From your perspective, do you think that executive pay and bonuses should be …

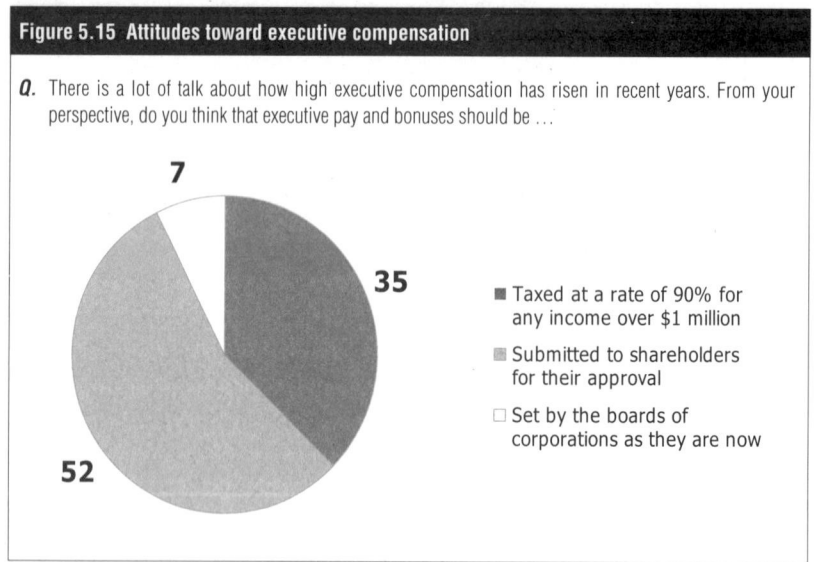

- Taxed at a rate of 90% for any income over $1 million: 35
- Submitted to shareholders for their approval: 52
- Set by the boards of corporations as they are now: 7

BASE: Canadians; April 8–13, 2009 (n=1,587).

Another revealing indicator is Canadian attitudes to what are arguably the two largest socio-political movements of the past decade. Favourable attitudes to the Occupy movement dramatically outstripped favourable attitudes to the Tea Party movement (the poster child for austerity and minimal government).

So, how does this all play out in terms of our starting questions? Contrary to expectations and what seems to be the conventional political wisdom, the desire for minimal government and lower taxes is declining, if anything, and self-professed small-*l* liberal orientations have been rising over the past decade. This leaves me to explain the inconvenient fact that political actors endorsing minimal government and lowest possible tax levels have enjoyed electoral success in Ottawa and elsewhere.

The public seem to look at their tax burdens in a mildly negative way, particularly value-added and personal income taxes. To the extent that they believe tax cuts will come from reductions in government waste and "pork," greater efficiency, and clearer priorities, they are supportive of tax cuts. And this is often the promise made, if rarely kept—tax cuts without cuts to direct services for citizens. If, conversely, citizens see that tax cuts will come at the expense of investments in the future—heath, education, and green infrastructure for example—they will no longer support them. There is also evidence that people support the role of taxation in combating extreme inequality, particularly in the case of the recent expansion of wealth among the upper echelons (the familiar 1%). Canadians also support the use of taxes to discourage dangerous or unhealthy behaviour such as smoking and alcohol consumption. We also have strong evidence that the same reasoning applies to climate change and openness to a carbon tax. Generally, Canadians are supportive of the idea that polluters should pay.

Canadians show a decisive view that corporate taxes and taxes on executive compensation and the rich are too low. A cynical explanation might be that we are always happier to see other people pay more. A less cynical interpretation is that fairness matters in understanding views regarding taxes, and many want to know that those who benefit most are also paying their fair share. As the incomes of the vast majority of Canadians are flattening, and more and more families are living paycheque to paycheque, these issues are taking on heightened urgency. No doubt the view that the majority pay too much already is significantly fuelled by the fact that even supposedly progressive parties have fought against consumption taxes or other taxes that hit the majority—without, as Hugh Mackenzie pointed out in the last two chapters, any discussion of the benefits that these taxes buy.

Views on taxes are linked to education (those who are university educated are more pro-tax than the less educated), and gender (women much more strongly favour social investment over tax relief than men). There are significant age effects, but these are more complex. Those in the family formation and child-rearing parts of the life cycle are more negative to taxation.

The largest effects are, however, based on political values and ideology. In a nutshell, support for less government and lower tax rates is much higher among conservatives in Canada. This tension across variations in attitudes to the size and role of the state and its link to tax levels is probably the largest political divide separating roughly one-third of Canadians who support the current government from the other two-thirds.

Like other unpleasant exigencies of everyday life, people would prefer to discuss other more exciting or positive things. The evidence is quite clear that although the public understands and accepts the importance of taxes to a healthy society, they don't pick it as a prominent topic for national debate. As seen in Figure 5.16, Canadians would much rather that national forums focus on social and economic issues. But of course those conversations are severely constrained if we do not link them to the question of taxes—and how we propose to pay for the investments Canadians support and need. This is an important challenge for those trying to move this conversation forward. It may also be the case that people's stated support for social and environmental investment over tax reduction and austerity is exaggerated in polls to some degree. Otherwise, I would be hard-pressed to explain why the NDP haven't held power over the past two decades. In any case, absent political leadership willing to make the

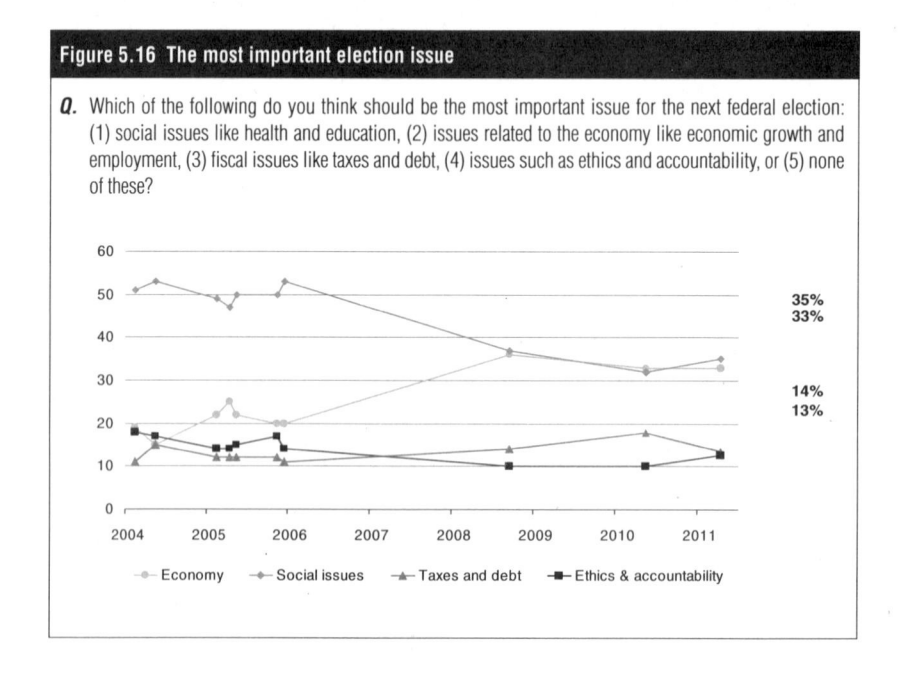

Figure 5.16 The most important election issue

Q. Which of the following do you think should be the most important issue for the next federal election: (1) social issues like health and education, (2) issues related to the economy like economic growth and employment, (3) fiscal issues like taxes and debt, (4) issues such as ethics and accountability, or (5) none of these?

Figure 5.17 Support for political movements

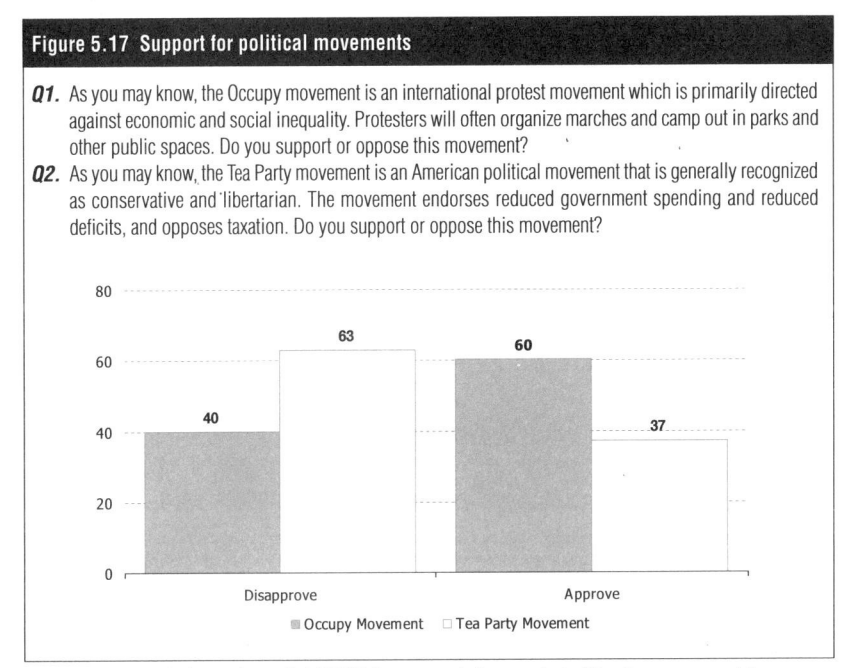

Q1. As you may know, the Occupy movement is an international protest movement which is primarily directed against economic and social inequality. Protesters will often organize marches and camp out in parks and other public spaces. Do you support or oppose this movement?

Q2. As you may know, the Tea Party movement is an American political movement that is generally recognized as conservative and libertarian. The movement endorses reduced government spending and reduced deficits, and opposes taxation. Do you support or oppose this movement?

	Disapprove	Approve
Occupy Movement	40	60
Tea Party Movement	63	37

Note: Figures exclude those who replied DK/NR. Four percent of respondents did not express an opinion regarding the Occupy movement, while 12% did not express an opinion regarding the Tea Party movement.
BASE: Canadians; December 14–21, 2011 (n=2,005).

case for taxes and tax reform, we can expect continued ambivalence or ambiguity in public attitudes.

Conclusions

There is a certain logic to the apparently contradictory aspects of public opinion on taxes. There is, of course, no consensus. Indeed, divisions seem to have become deeper than ever, depending on political ideology and values.

The dominant political assumption—that tax increases are "off the table"—is only partially true. There is significant openness to taxing corporations and the rich, and to taxing polluters and "vices." More broad-based taxes remain a harder sell so long as Canadians continue to believe that sufficient savings can come from cutting waste and stopping the "gravy train."

The emotional appeal of lower taxes and less spending is more readily accessible to voters than the more complex and less viscerally engaging arguments for progressive taxation, which sound more like rational appeals for public plumbing. Since it is emotional engagement that increasingly seems to be at the heart of modern political success, this is a critical challenge for progressives. The status quo will persist if this issue isn't dealt with more effectively by the majority who

Figure 5.18 Tracking trust in government

Q. How much do you trust the government in Ottawa/Washington to do what is right?

Those who say all/most of the time

[Chart showing trust percentages for Canadians and Americans from 1968 to 2010, with most recent values at 26% and 26%]

— Canadians —■— Americans

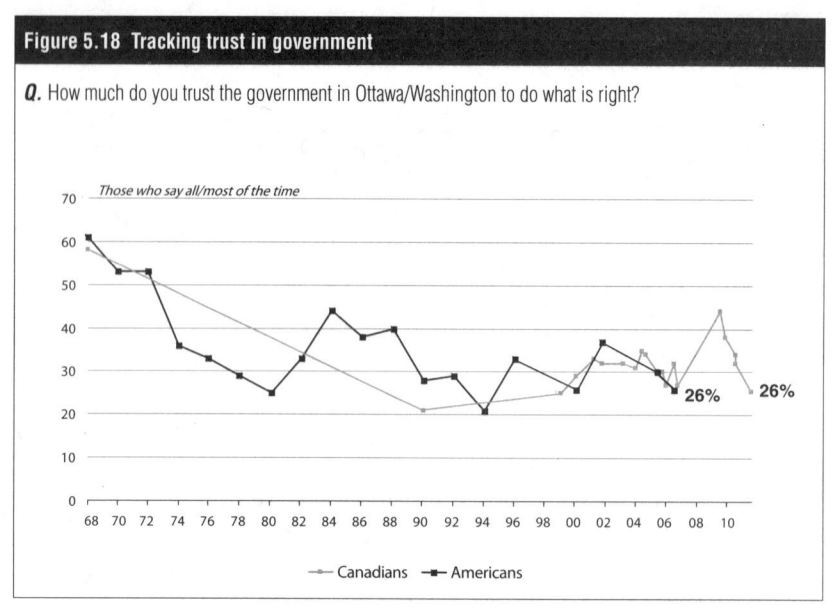

Note: The most recent figure was recalculated to exclude those who answered "Don't know/No response."
BASE: Canadians; most recent data point December 14–21, 2011 (n=2,005).

want to see it changed—those who take a view of measured support for progressive taxation and apparently reject the radical position that all taxes are bad.

A conversation about taxes will have to address the distrust of government and the growing view that governments are remote, unresponsive, and wasteful, while building on the equally widespread view that governments have an important, positive role to play in helping us manage our shared future.

A conversation about taxes, then, will have to be a conversation about how to make government work for the majority, how to strengthen public services and make wise investments—how to make government more responsive, accountable, transparent, and focused on the future.

References

Graves, F. L. (1999, September 17). Public perceptions of Canadians on economic issues: from Reaganomics to "Humanomics." *Canada in the 21st Century: A Time for a Vision, Luncheon Address.* Paper presented at the Centre for the Study Living Standards conference, Ottawa, Ontario. Retrieved from http://www.csls.ca/events/sept1999/ekos.pdf

Part II ▶ How We Got Here

The one-sided conversation on taxes did not start with the election of the current Conservative government. Even if our Prime Minister's declaration that there are no good taxes takes us to a whole new level of anti-tax thinking, it builds on the assault on taxes that started decades ago and has influenced the policies and rhetoric of all our political parties, more or less. Tax-cutting has been a multi-partisan business, and the fear of serious tax reform a multi-partisan affliction.

There is no single explanation for this evolution in our thinking about taxes. Globalization and ever more mobile capital, the rise of individualism, more savvy citizens, the inability of governments to remake themselves for the information age, and the demographic crunch; all reshape our choices and how we think about them. But the very fact that tax rates are mixed and vary so substantially from country to country, and that countries with higher taxes often do better than us in terms of both productivity and equality begs the question: how did we come to make the choices we did?

In this section, Matt Fodor, a York University political scientist, tracks how the neo-liberal (or neo-conservative, depending on your tastes) counter-revolution led by Ronald Reagan in the US and Margaret Thatcher in the UK has played out even if more subtly in Canada, and how it has reshaped policy and thinking on taxes, markets, and the role of government.

Policy experts Eugene Lang and Philip DeMont know government from the inside and out, and show how these ideological changes manifested themselves in Canadian economic policies over the last three decades. They put into a historical and international perspective just how and how much—or little—we tax, and they allude to some of the consequences of our tax decisions

Former journalist Trish Hennessy, who now heads up the Ontario Office of the Canadian Centre for Policy Alternatives (CCPA), provides a personal take on how the political rhetoric that attended these shifts played out and reshaped the psychology of taxes in Canada.

Chapter 6

Taxation and the Neo-Liberal Counter-Revolution: The Canadian Case

Matt Fodor

Understanding the current debate—or lack of debate—over taxation requires some assessment of the evolution of political ideologies in Canada and how these shape and limit our understanding of what is possible and what is not. In this chapter I examine the shift from what might be most easily described as a Keynesian or progressive frame to market fundamentalism, variously called neo-liberalism or neo-conservatism, and what the impact has been of this shift on public policy, and more specifically taxes, in Canada.

The easiest way to capture the contrast between market fundamentalism and Keynesianism is through comparing the work of its two leading figures, Milton Friedman and John Maynard Keynes, on taxation, inequality, and the role of government. For Friedman government was the problem, to put it grossly, while markets as free as possible of government intrusion were the solution. As he stated in 2003, "I am in favour of cutting taxes under any circumstances and for any excuse, for any reason, whenever it's possible. The reason I am is because I believe the big problem is not taxes, the big problem is spending" (Ruger, 2011, p. 114). In *Capitalism and Freedom,* he specifically took on what he believed were the wrong-headed attempts of the state to pursue equality of income, clearly rejecting "the belief in equality of income as a social goal and a willingness of the arm of the state to promote it" (1962/2002, p. 161).

In contrast, Keynes, whose economic ideas prevailed for three decades following the Second World War, argued that unemployment and extreme inequality were the greatest threat to our future. As he wrote in his most famous work, *The General Theory of Employment, Interest and Money,* "the outstanding faults of the economic society in which we live are its failure to provide for full employment and its arbitrary and inequitable distribution of wealth and incomes" (1936/2006, p. 341). Keynes noted the progress achieved in reducing inequality of wealth and income via direct taxation since the late nineteenth century, particularly in his native Britain, and argued strongly for progressive taxation as a key means of achieving this goal (Pressman, 2007, pp. 26–27). In his view the state had a positive role to play, and progressive taxation was a key instrument for playing that role.

Keynes' view, which dominated thinking through much of the developed world until the late seventies at least, stands in stark contrast to the current economic orthodoxy that calls for a reduction in the role of the state in social provision, lower taxes, and the privileging of "job creators"—in other words, reduced progressivity. Some version of neo-liberal market fundamentalism, as Greg Albo (2002) observed, "has come to dominate public discourse and the modalities of the state in one country after another" (p. 46). It has taken different shape in different countries and over time but, one way or another, it has dominated the conversation for decades (Albo, 2002, p. 46; Harvey, 2007, p. 87).

Margaret Thatcher in Britain and Ronald Reagan in the United States led the first postwar governments to embrace the market and step away from the Keynesian consensus. By the 1990s, these ideas became so dominant that even parties and governments of the centre-left were clearly and profoundly influenced, and these parties have not been very successful in offering a clear and compelling alternative. Just why the Keynesian consensus collapsed so thoroughly in some countries, the US and the UK in particular, while less so in others, such as the countries of northern Europe, is an open question and deserves more attention than this chapter can provide. Some have argued that the shift simply reflects the consequences of globalization, but the very fact that certain countries resisted and are doing just fine makes this an unsatisfying argument. Some have pointed to the failure of the so-called liberal establishment to renew their policy thinking. And others point to the deliberate and highly successful strategies of "the right" to change the conversation through investments in think tanks and public communications. Many of these issues are taken up by Saurette and Gunster in the final chapter of this book.

In this chapter, I will focus on describing the shift in economic thinking—from Keynes to Friedman—particularly as it relates to the issue of taxes. I start by discussing the changes in the US and Britain, and then focus on the slower and more subtle changes in Canada from the 1970s up to today.

Paradigm Shift: From Keynesianism to Neo-Liberalism

Between 1945 and 1980, Keynesianism served as the dominant economic theory in advanced capitalist countries. During this period, state intervention to reduce inequality and expand welfare was not in conflict with economic orthodoxy (Lavelle, 2008, p. 9). Indeed, for much of the postwar period, it appeared that the changes of the "Keynesian revolution" were irreversible. Its opponents had been discredited by the experience of the Great Depression of the 1930s; after the war, mainstream conservatives largely made their peace with Keynesian economics and the welfare state (Judt, 2010, p. 91; Krugman, 2009, pp. 58–59). During the postwar years, Harvey (2007) notes, a variety of state forms (social democratic, liberal, Christian democratic, etc.) all accepted

> that the state should focus on full employment, economic growth, and the welfare of its citizens, and that state power should be freely deployed alongside of or, if necessary, intervening in or even substituting for market processes to achieve these ends. Fiscal and monetary policies usually dubbed "Keynesian" were widely deployed to dampen business cycles and to ensure reasonably full employment. A "class compromise" between capital and labour was generally advocated as the guarantor of domestic peace and tranquility. States actively intervened in industrial policy and moved to set standards for the social wage by constructing a variety of welfare systems (health care, education, and the like). (pp. 10–11)

Yet by the mid-1970s, the postwar Keynesian consensus came under assault by a reinvigorated conservatism, and by the 1980s, neo-liberalism had pretty much supplanted Keynesianism as economic orthodoxy, with profound consequences for public policy (Palley, 2004). As the late historian Tony Judt (2010) commented,

> The victory of conservatism and the profound transformation brought about over the course of three decades was . . . far from inevitable: it took an intellectual revolution. In the course of little more than a decade, the dominant "paradigm" of public conversation shifted from interventionary enthusiasms and the pursuit of public goods to a view of the world best summed up in Margaret Thatcher's notorious *bon mot*: "there is no such thing as society, there are only individuals and families." In the United States, at almost the same moment, Ronald Reagan achieved lasting popularity for his claim that it was "morning in America." Government was no longer the solution—it was the problem. (pp. 96–97)

In this view, the role of the state is to protect life, liberty, and property—necessary preconditions for the market to function properly, but no more:

> Neo-liberalism is in the first instance a theory of political economic practices that proposes that human well-being can best be advanced by liberating individual entrepreneurial freedoms and skills within an institutional framework characterized by strong private property rights, free markets, and free trade. The role of the state is to create and preserve an institutional framework to such practices. . . . But beyond these tasks the state should not venture. (Harvey, 2007, p. 2)

But the state had been built up considerably through the Second World War and since, and this posed a challenge for the neo-liberal economists: how to reduce a state that had grown not only big but also popular. The era of Keynesian redistributive economics saw unprecedented growth rates; as the economic historian Angus Maddison (1995) observed, "[t]he years 1950 to 1973 were a golden age of unparalleled prosperity" (p. 73). During the postwar boom, high levels of public expenditure for redistributive ends coincided with sufficiently high levels of capital accumulation and profitability (Harvey, 2006, p. 14).

This "golden age" was eventually disrupted by global events. Starting in 1974, the twin challenges of stagnation and inflation created cracks in the Keynesian consensus. "Output, productivity, and export growth all fell sharply, instability in export volumes and GDP increased, and unemployment and inflation both rose" (Glyn, Hughes, Lipietz, & Singh, 1990, p. 45). With declining corporate profitability, the Great Social Compromise was over; business was no longer a willing participant.

Not surprisingly the neo-liberal economists gained traction, exerting increasing influence over public policy. The business community, in the words of Thomas Edsall, had "refined its ability to act as a class" (1985, p. 128). In the US, the Business Roundtable, which consisted of the CEOs of the largest corporations, was founded in 1972, and an array of well-financed right-wing think tanks, such as the American Enterprise Institute and the Heritage Foundation were established. In addition, neo-liberalism had become increasingly influential in university economics departments (Harvey, 2007, pp. 20–22, 43–44). Milton Friedman, the most prominent of the Chicago School economists, had emerged as a high-profile public intellectual, defender of the market system, and opponent of increased government intervention in the economy. The business community welcomed the economic philosophy espoused by Friedman and his followers, which blamed government rather than the private sector for the economic hard times (Laxer, 1981, p. 28). In Britain, the Institute for Economic Affairs served as the most influential proponent of neo-liberal ideology, where Keith Joseph, who went on to serve as a key adviser to Margaret Thatcher, emerged as a prominent figure (Harvey, 2007, p. 57). In 1974, Joseph and Thatcher founded the Centre for Policy Studies, with the explicit aim of transforming the Conservative Party along neo-liberal lines.

With Keynesianism seemingly discredited, neo-liberal ideas began to fill the void. For instance, as Robert Pollin (1998) pointed out, the traditional policy goal of full employment was undermined by the inability to control inflation in the 1970s, while Friedman's theory of the "natural rate of employment"—which posited that if unemployment falls below its "natural rate," inflation would accelerate—had gained acceptance. Although the primary cause of rising inflation was not low unemployment but rather spikes in oil prices, "[e]conomic policy-makers worldwide became convinced that inflation resulting from low unemployment had become severe and uncontrollable" (Pollin, 2012, p. 30).

This shift both fed into and fed off of changes in popular attitudes. In a time of high unemployment and inflation, the idea of government had become increasingly unpopular among much of the population. As Leo Panitch (1986) observed, "[t]he word 'public'—whether attached to enterprise, employees or service—became . . . a dirty one in Western political culture after a decade of denigration by businessmen, politicians, and journalists of various political stripes" (p. 91). It was in this context that a popular base could be won over to neo-liberal ideas.

Margaret Thatcher was elected prime minister of Britain in 1979; Ronald Reagan was elected president of the US a year later. Thatcher and Reagan were "revolutionaries" in the sense that they broke dramatically with the postwar consensus and even the traditions of their own parties. Keynesian economics was abandoned for monetarism. Trade union power was curtailed, while business benefited from deregulation. And taxes were dramatically cut, particularly for high earners and corporations; Reagan, for instance, cut the top individual tax rate from 70 to 28%. Meanwhile, the so-called Volcker shock at the US Federal Reserve in 1979 sharply raised interest rates and symbolized a dramatic shift toward monetarism among central banks (Harvey, 2007, pp. 23–24).

As neo-liberalism emphasizes the withdrawal of the redistributive state, the collective rights of citizenship are replaced with an emphasis on the rights of the taxpayer. Indeed, this shift was key to the political success of both Thatcher and Reagan. Anti-tax voters represented sizable constituencies that were cultivated by the Conservative and Republican parties. Framing the political debate with taxes and deficits worked to the advantage of the New Right. Meanwhile, the opposition Democratic Party in the US and Labour Party in Britain failed to articulate a coherent position on taxation, and thereby were unable to answer the question of who pays for the welfare state. As Cronin (1987) noted at the time,

> [p]arty leaders seem to know intuitively what the historical record shows in detail: that supporters of social programmes have been successful when they have been able to focus political debate on their merits or on the needs of constituencies, but have failed miserably when the question of taxation held the centre of the stage. They therefore respond to the new politics of taxation not with creative alternatives but by wishing the issue would go away. (pp. 264–265)

In contrast to the confidence of the New Right, thinking on the Left became confused. As Keynesianism fell out of favour with policy-makers, progressives "lost the luxury of not having to choose between orthodox economics and government intervention to raise living standards" (Lavelle, 2008, p. 33). To many, it appeared that the Right, with its emphasis on market freedom, was more capable than the Left in dealing with social and economic change (Miliband, 1995, p. 3). The Left started to lose confidence, to worry that its traditional approach could not handle globalization and increasing capital mobility, nor withstand the attacks on taxes and "big government" led by an increasingly confident and organized business community.

The Thatcher–Reagan "revolutions" served to solidify neo-liberalism as the dominant economic and political ideology in the English-speaking world. The policies they implemented and political coalitions they cultivated could not easily be dislodged by their Democratic and Labour Party successors, Bill Clinton and Tony Blair (Harvey, 2007, p. 62). Indeed, by the 1990s, parties of the centre-left had developed a strategic response to the challenges of globalization and declining electoral fortunes. Known as the "Third Way," this model accepts a greater role for markets and less government intervention in the economy. Clinton, Blair, and the various social democratic governments in Western Europe elected in the 1990s all maintained stringent monetary and fiscal policies (Pollin, 1998), constraining their ability to pursue progressive policy objectives.

By the 1990s, neo-liberal ideology had spread well beyond the US and Britain, and had become well entrenched in other liberal democracies, including Canada.

Neo-Liberalism in Canada

Forming a New Consensus

By the end of the Second World War, the governing Liberals had more or less adopted Keynesianism, and their early acceptance became "a distinct partisan advantage" (Brodie & Jensen, 1988, p. 262). The Liberals dominated Canadian national politics during this period, and not surprisingly, the Keynesian consensus was soon accepted by all major political parties.

In the mid-1970s, Canadian businesses, like their US counterparts, began to organize as a class. The traditional business lobbies were deemed ineffective, and the make-up of Parliament under Prime Minister Pierre Trudeau was seen as not particularly amenable to the business agenda (Dobbin, 1998, p. 165). It was the imposition of wage and price controls by Trudeau in 1975 (in order to combat inflation) that especially mobilized the business community. Trudeau had stated on national television that "it no longer works, the free market system," and mused that permanent government intervention in the economy may be necessary. The business community responded with a more aggressive defence of the free market system (Laxer, 1981, p. 31).

Following the model of the Business Roundtable in the US, the Business Council on National Issues (BCNI), made up of the CEOs of Canada's largest corporations, was formed in 1976. The main purpose of the BCNI was to exert an influence on broader public policy rather than the traditional approach of lobbying with regard to specific legislation (Laxer, 1981, pp. 36–37; Dobbin, 1998, pp. 165–167). In addition, two well-financed organizations, the National Citizens Coalition (NCC), a conservative lobby group, and the Fraser Institute, a think tank that was a bastion of Friedmanite economics, were founded. These new organizations sought to change the "ideological fabric" of the country (Dobbin, 1998, pp. 182–184). At the same time, neo-liberalism had become increasingly influential in the economics profession, both in the universities and significant economic advisory bodies such as the Economic Council of Canada and the Ontario Economic Council (Laxer, 1981, pp. 27–28; Brodie & Jenson, 1988, p. 312). Perhaps the most illustrative example is the C. D. Howe Institute, the country's most respected think tank. Founded in 1958, it had initially generally supported Keynesian economics and social programs, but began shifting to the right in the late 1970s and was thoroughly neo-liberal by the mid-1980s (Ernst, 1992).

A rightward shift in public attitudes was underway as well. New Democratic Party governments in British Columbia and Manitoba were turfed in the mid-1970s by voters resentful of the growth in public spending, and were replaced by ideologically conservative governments. A monthly Gallup poll showed Canadians held increasingly conservative views, at least toward labour unions, the unemployed, and the poor (Laxer, 1981, pp. 17, 21–22). As Laxer (1981), writing in the early 1980s, observed,

> The new right in Canadian politics gathered strength because the old economic strategy, with its balancing act between the private sector and public spending for social services, was causing growing resentment. The new right responded to the mood of the affluent segments of the population, no longer willing to put up with the pressures of high taxation. The targets of the right were public services and government spending. The ark of the covenant of the new conservatism was the free market system. (p. 17)

Yet the popular appeal of neo-liberal ideology had its limits. In the June 1979 election, the Trudeau government was defeated by the Progressive Conservatives, led by Joe Clark. However, Clark was a Red Tory and had not bought into the anti-government, anti-tax consensus that was emerging. His minority government fell less than a year later, and Trudeau led the Liberals back to power in February 1980 with a decisive victory, calling for more of a state-guided economic approach (Laxer, 1981, pp. 196–197).

The re-election of Trudeau coincided with the mobilization of an increasingly organized and confident business community. Under the leadership of Thomas d'Aquino, the BCNI increased its public profile and became influential in policy-making (Dobbin, 1998, pp. 167–168). According to Clarkson (1991), the BCNI agenda for the 1980s was twofold:

> First the BCNI wanted a Canadian-American agreement that would secure commercial access for Canadian exporters to the US market and guarantee their freedom to locate in any state. Secondly, on the home front they wanted the replacement of the social-democratic interventionist state by a regime that responded to the norms of the neo-conservative ideology which had recently become the conventional wisdom among the elites of the OECD countries. (p. 113)

An attempt at tax reform in 1981 drew the ire of the corporate elite. Then finance minister Allan MacEachen attempted to make the tax system more progressive and raise taxes on corporations and the wealthy. In particular, he had learned that billions of dollars in revenue were lost due to numerous loopholes that benefited corporations, and introduced a tax reform package that would close many of these and raise an estimated $3 billion in revenue. Despite the enormous potential revenue, ultimately, the government backed down in the face of massive business opposition (Dobbin, 1998, pp. 168–169; McQuaig & Brooks, 2011, pp. 146–147).

The 1981–82 recession, which hit Canada especially hard, struck another blow to the Trudeau government's reform agenda and the notion of government intervention. For many Canadians who had always been friendlier than Americans to the idea of government, "big government" was increasingly becoming the problem (Clarkson, 1991, p. 112). A Cabinet shuffle in September 1982 signalled to the business community that the Trudeau government had abandoned its reform agenda and MacEachen was replaced as finance minister by Marc Lalonde, who sought to make amends with the business community. As Clarkson (1991) noted,

> the decisive watershed had been crossed.... For the remaining years of the Trudeau era, the BCNI told the government directly what it wanted. It provided complete and detailed draft legislation for a new competition act that would accelerate, in the name of economic rationalization, Canada's already high level of corporate concentration. (pp. 114–115)

In November 1982, the Macdonald Commission, headed by former finance minister Donald S. Macdonald, was established to help the Liberals develop an agenda for the 1990s. As Drache and Cameron put it, "[w]hat Donald Macdonald was asked to do was nothing short of proposing a new consensus on economic policy" (1985, p. ix). The Macdonald Commission ultimately concluded, more or less, that neo-liberalism was the superior policy paradigm. Markets were deemed more efficient than government intervention. Curtailing inflation was given priority over fighting unemployment. The report called for free trade and the cutting back of the welfare state (Clarkson, 1991, pp. 112–115; Bradford, 2000, p. 68).

Brian Mulroney led the Progressive Conservatives to power in a landslide win of the 1984 election. While not nearly as ideologically committed as Thatcher and Reagan, Mulroney was nonetheless more amenable to the corporate agenda than Trudeau had been for most of his time in office. The trend toward neo-liberalism accelerated. When the Macdonald Commission released its report in 1985, Mulroney came out in support of its key recommendations. In 1987, Mulroney negotiated a free trade agreement with the US, which was the main issue of the 1988 federal election. The Liberals and NDP both opposed the deal and received between them the most the votes, but the Conservatives won a majority of seats under the "first past the post" electoral system. "Across the government's second term, an end to universality in social programs and reductions in labour adjustment programming each came, despite promises suggesting the exact opposite in the 1984 and 1988 Conservative election campaigns" (Bradford, 2000, p. 69).

Mulroney's finance minister, Michael Wilson, implemented a major tax reform package in 1987 that reduced taxes on the wealthy significantly (McQuaig & Brooks, 2011, p. 146). Wilson also appointed John Crow as governor of the Bank of Canada, who pursued an extreme—and unprecedented—"zero inflation" policy. According to McQuaig (1998), the C. D. Howe Institute played a key role in making the intellectual justification for this controversial policy (pp. 102–112; McQuaig & Brooks, 2011, pp. 179–184). Under Crow, Clarkson (2002) wrote, "the Bank became the messianic collaborator in the neo-conservative counter-revolution . . . the Bank helped to discipline wages by reducing inflation-based demands for pay increases and by creating enough unemployment to undermine the bargaining position of the labour unions" (pp. 141–142). The Mulroney government also introduced the Goods and Services Tax (GST) in 1991, replacing a former tax on manufacturers, which was highly unpopular but became an important source of revenue.

Near the end of his term, Mulroney negotiated the North American Free Trade Agreement (NAFTA) with the US and Mexico. A key component of NAFTA was the concept of "national treatment"—that is, corporations based in all three countries must be treated the same in all jurisdictions. The rights of the state, in turn, are restricted in terms of regulating business; the rights of citizens are superseded by the rights of corporations (Laxer, 1998 pp. 17–18).

Neo-Liberalism Solidified

In 1993, Jean Chrétien led the Liberals back to power with a decisive victory. The Liberals promised to scrap the unpopular GST (as did the right-wing populist

Reform Party and the NDP "from the left") and NAFTA, although they did not deliver on either promise. The party's 1993 *Red Book* platform broke largely with neo-liberal orthodoxy—calling for a focus on job creation rather than deficit-fighting, a more active industrial policy, and a reversal of federal cuts. Finance minister Paul Martin, who helped draft the 1993 platform, initially took this approach in his 1994 budget—shifting spending priorities away from defence and toward social programs (Clarkson, 2002, p. 134). Martin also did not renew Crow's term as governor of the Bank of Canada.

However, as McQuaig (1998) argued, the bureaucracy in the Department of Finance had become a bastion of monetarism and resisted a more interventionist approach; by 1995, Martin had largely, if temporarily, conceded to the prevailing neo-liberal ideology (pp. 82–90). As Clarkson (2002) explained, "[w]ith his notorious 1995 budget, Paul Martin banished Keynesian notions from government rhetoric to an even greater extent than had his Tory predecessor. Deficit reduction was to be permanent, not simply confined to the upside of the business cycle" (p. 135).

The 1995 budget included a 40% cutback in cash transfers to provinces by 1997, from $17.3 billion to $10.3 billion. The federal government's contribution to health, welfare, and education was reduced from 15 to 9% over four years; Mulroney over his nine-year term had reduced it from 20 to 15%. The budget saw the elimination of two programs that were products of the social democratic state of the 1960s and 1970s: the Canada Assistance Plan (CAP), which had set national guidelines for social assistance, and Established Programs Financing (EPF), which allocated funding to provinces specifically for health and post-secondary education. The CAP and EPF were replaced by the Canada Health and Social Transfer (CHST), a lump-sum transfer to provinces that required no accountability. The implementation of the CHST, Dobbin noted (2003), represented a fundamental break with the principle of universality:

> The CAP and EPF enshrined the very philosophy of 1960s and 1970s nation building. That philosophy was universality, the principle that everyone, regardless of income, would receive key public services and that they would be paid for by progressive taxation. In this single move, Paul Martin . . . signalled that the federal government was, with the stroke of a pen, reversing possibly the most important core principle of Canadian social democracy. The practical implications of the CHST were difficult to overstate, for the elimination of these two programs had the effect of freeing provincial governments from any commitment to the national project. (p. 78)

Martin stated that he would devote 50% of surpluses to the restoration of government spending, and split the remaining half evenly between tax cuts and debt reduction. Even this proposal would not have come close to restoring spending to pre-1995 levels; spending on government programs had fallen from 18% of national income in the mid-1980s to about 12% in 1999 (McQuaig, 1998, pp. 6–7).

In 2000, Martin introduced a budget that would cut $100 billion in federal taxes over five years. Tax cuts were touted as a "reward" for the sacrifices made by Canadians in the war on the deficit. Yet as Hugh Mackenzie pointed out in the previous two chapters, these "sacrifices" were not shared equally among the population. More than 30% of the tax cut benefits went to the top 5% of individual tax earners, and more than 70% went to the top 30%. Taxpayers in the top 0.5% of earners saved an average of $19,000, while those in the median income range ($30,000–$35,000) received a "reward" of $800. The most inequitable of tax cuts was the reduction in the capital gains tax from 75 to 50% of earned income, with 45% going to the wealthiest 0.6% of Canadians. Corporate taxes, too, were cut in the name of enhancing "competitiveness" by more than 35%, to well below the US level (Mackenzie, 2004, pp. 60–62). Mackenzie (2004) commented that the emphasis on tax cuts eliminated "the government's fiscal capacity to rebuild the services and transfers that were cut in the mid-1990s" (p. 55).

Canada was indeed the most successful among G7 countries in terms of deficit reduction during the 1990s. Yet, as Jackson noted (2010), several other OECD countries—Australia, Denmark, Finland, the Netherlands, New Zealand, and Sweden—also saw similarly large deficit reductions. In Canada, spending as a percentage of GDP fell by more than seven percentage points, from 46.6% in 1996 to 39.1% in 2007. Across the OECD as a whole, it fell by just 0.7 percentage points, and across the Euro zone, still only 2.6 points. Canada also stood out for not having tax increases as part of its deficit reduction strategy. A deficit reduction strategy that relied on spending cuts rather than tax increases contributed to a significant increase in inequality. Between 1993 and 2001, the share of after-tax and transfer income that went to the top 20% of families increased from 36.9 to 39.2%. Cuts to unemployment insurance and welfare (the latter slashed by provinces following changes in the federal funding formula) meant that there was little reduction in poverty, and incomes in the bottom half of households only increased modestly, in spite of lower unemployment. Canada had become "a much more market-driven society, moving it much closer to the US model" (Jackson, 2010).

At the provincial level too, neo-liberalism had become increasingly solidified during the 1990s. In Ontario, Mike Harris led the Conservatives to power in 1995 on a platform called the Common Sense Revolution, which tapped into anti-tax and anti-government sentiment. Welfare recipients were vilified, as were those who worked in the public sector. One of Harris' most popular pledges was a 30% cut in the provincial income tax (Laxer, 1996, pp. 32–33). The Common

Sense Revolution fundamentally changed Ontario politics. Queen's Park expert Graham White, writing in 1997, compellingly argued,

> there is an underlying dynamic to the Common Sense Revolution that promises to make the Harris government, in Ontario terms, truly radical. Again the 30% income tax cut is central. Once in place, it will be virtually impossible to reverse. In opposition, the Liberals and New Democrats attack the idea of a tax cut. Yet both parties know that even if they form the next government they will not have the nerve to boost provincial taxes back up to their old levels.
>
> Given that the revenue base is being more or less irreversibly reduced, government spending will simply be unable to return in the foreseeable future to past levels. Thus, the spending cuts that the Tories have implemented—to welfare, municipalities, hospitals, and education—are also, in practical political terms, virtually irreversible. (p. 415)

The neo-liberal turn at the provincial level was not confined to parties of the right, however. The Ontario Liberal government of Dalton McGuinty, which came into power in 2003, continued to cut corporate and personal income taxes. And NDP governments in Saskatchewan and Manitoba, for instance, have moved away from the traditional Keynesian approach of prioritizing public investments and embraced tax cuts and balanced budgets (Stanford, 2001, pp. 95–99).

While neo-liberalism had become dominant due to changing economic circumstances and a shifting outlook of the business community, its ascendance nevertheless depended upon a degree of popular consent. The overall strategy of neo-liberals was to delegitimize the positive role of government. The mainstream media, along with such organizations at the C. D. Howe Institute, the Fraser Institute, and the NCC were key players in this battle, which in Canada accelerated in the mid-1980s. The assault on the egalitarian state, as Dobbin (1998) notes, had three components. First was the deficit scare: neo-liberals insisted that excessive government spending would have catastrophic consequences (pp. 218–219). Second was the attack on public services, from a variety of angles: they were labelled overly generous, bureaucratic and unaccountable, inefficient and in need of "competition" from the more efficient private sector. As public services no longer worked, why not cut them (Dobbin, 1998, p. 229)? Third was the call for tax cuts, which became louder and more extreme in the mid-1990s. With incomes stagnating for many, tax cuts were appealing as a means of increasing one's disposable income. Ideologically, they served the purpose of appealing to individualism and changing the political culture (Dobbin, 1998, pp. 248–249). These tactics paved the way for the arrival of the Stephen Harper Conservative government and a new era in Canadian neo-liberalism.

Neo-Liberalism in the Age of Harper

For a brief interlude between 2000 and 2005, there was at least a partial break from the increasing neo-liberalization of Canadian politics. In his last term in office, Chrétien implemented much progressive legislation. This included sharp increases to the National Child Benefit, greater spending on health care, post-secondary education and the arts, and changes to electoral financing laws that limited individual donations and banned corporate donations.

Martin replaced Chrétien as Liberal Party leader and prime minister in 2004. The Liberals were reduced to a minority government after the 2004 election. The NDP, led by Jack Layton, pressured Martin to reverse a proposed $4.6 billion in corporate tax cuts and instead spend the money on affordable housing, public transit, and education and training (Boswell, 2011). There were also moves to implement a national child care program and the historic Kelowna Accord, which sought to improve living conditions for First Nations, but both were undermined by a non-confidence vote cast by all three opposition parties in November 2005.

Stephen Harper, leader of the newly established Conservative Party, which was born in 2003 out of a merger between the right-wing Canadian Alliance (formerly the Reform Party) and the Progressive Conservatives, came to power in January 2006, forming a minority government. Under Harper, the assault on the already-weakened progressive state accelerated. The child care program, for instance, was scrapped, replaced by a $1,200 per year tax credit that did not come close to meeting the costs of child care in the private market. This program was promoted as an alternative to statism, where individuals had more "choice" (Philipupillai, 2011).

Tax-cutting has been central to the Harper agenda. Beginning in 2007, Finance Minister Jim Flaherty cut corporate taxes by about one-third, dropping the federal rate from 22 to 15% over five years. In making the case for corporate tax cuts, Flaherty, in April 2012, referenced the key argument of supply-side economics, the basis for so-called Reaganomics: "What we're seeing, despite the fact that we've reduced business taxes, is we're seeing our corporate tax revenue continue to rise. And this is further proof, if anyone needed it, that reduction of taxation creates more economic activity, more investment, more jobs ..." (Beltrame, 2012) Yet this was not borne out by the numbers: revenues from corporate taxes decreased from about $40 billion in 2007–8 to $30 billion three years later; the government's own projections showed that corporate tax revenues would not approach $40 billion until 2016–17 (Beltrame, 2012).

In addition to cutting corporate taxes, Harper has enthusiastically promoted "boutique tax cuts," which are little more than backdoor tax cuts aimed at winning middle-income voters over to the Conservative Party. These include tax credits for sports equipment, children's fitness, and income-splitting for seniors.

Although the wide-ranging tax cuts were sold as a way to assist "ordinary" families, the main beneficiaries have been those with higher incomes. The right-leaning Frontier Centre for Public Policy, for instance, noted that about 65% of claimants had annual incomes over $50,000, even though only about 25% of Canadian tax filers earn more than $50,000 per year (Russell, 2011).

The most popular tax cut was a reduction in the GST, from 7 to 6%, and later to 5%. The savings to individual consumers were minimal, but the GST cut deprives the federal government of about $14 billion annually, reducing its capacity to pay for public investments (Demont, 2009). In a study conducted for the Canadian Centre for Policy Alternatives, Hugh Mackenzie and Richard Shillington (2009) found that 80% of Canadians would have been better off if the federal government had transferred the money to municipalities to pay for public services rather than cutting the GST (p. 6).

As Harper has come to dominate the Canadian political scene, anti-tax ideology has increasingly spread across the political spectrum. The NDP, ignoring the experience of the Nordic social democracies, opposed the implementation of a carbon tax in British Columbia and the Harmonized Sales Tax (HST) in Ontario and BC. And in a similar vein to Harper's GST cut, New Democrats have taken up the issue of removing the Harmonized Sales Tax (HST) from home heating. This was a key platform plank in Nova Scotia in 2009, where Darrell Dexter formed the first NDP government in the province. The neo-liberal campaign to promote individualism, and to demonize taxes as a burden rather than a positive investment in public services, had largely succeeded.

In his 2010 budget speech, Flaherty boasted that the country's federal tax-to-GDP had fallen to its lowest level since 1961. As Evans and Albo (2010) commented, "[t]his is astonishing given that 1961 precedes the advent of the important redistributive cost-sharing programs of the late 1960s that enabled an expansion in public health care, post-secondary education, social assistance and a myriad of other services and programs" (p. 20). After winning a majority government in May 2011, the constraints on the Harper government were largely lifted. The use of back-to-work legislation against Canada Post and Air Canada employees signalled the curtailment of trade union power. And the 2012 budget demonstrated the commitment to neo-liberal retrenchment. The budget includes such sweeping changes as the raising of the age of eligibility for Old Age Security from 65 to 67, though some years off, and disquieting warnings that the federal government is set to further withdraw from health care policy. It also included the elimination of agencies such as the National Welfare Council, which provided policy-makers with critical information about the poor in Canada (Himelfarb, 2012). Under Harper's majority rule, the progressive, egalitarian state, already weakened by the 1990s, and twenty years of encroaching neo-liberalism, is more vulnerable than ever.

Conclusion

A core argument of this chapter has been that policy is shaped by the prevailing economic ideology. The debate over taxation and the role of government in the market economy—in Canada as well as in other liberal democracies—reflects the replacement of the Keynesian policy paradigm by neo-liberalism. In other words, the current state of affairs is an inevitable consequence of two decades of neo-liberal dominance—in economics and the political culture—and two decades of creeping neo-liberalism prior to that.

Over the past two decades, anti-tax ideology has gained a stranglehold on Canadian politics, narrowing the spectrum of political debate. The debate over tax cuts in Canada, as Dobbin (1998) aptly put it, is essentially "about how much and when, not *whether* to cut taxes" (p. 248). The hegemony of neo-liberalism over Canadian politics has served to denigrate the positive role of government and separate the debate over taxes from the services they pay for.

Most Canadians appreciate the value of public spending on such things as health care, education, pensions, and an array of other services. Indeed, as Mackenzie and Shillington (2009) show, public services, paid for by taxation, are in fact remarkably *efficient*: more than two-thirds of Canadian households receive in public services more than 50% of their earned income (p. 3); in other words, the value of public services received thus greatly exceeds the levels of taxes paid. And this was long after the tax-cutting mania—and thus the depletion of our public services—had begun.

Elected officials are reluctant to openly campaign for tax increases to pay for improved public services, reluctant to challenge the all too prevalent neo-liberal view that public spending is wasteful and inefficient, and therefore they are unable to build the public services needed to meet the challenges of the future. Progressive and redistributive public policy remains out of reach. It is time for a new policy.

References

Albo, G. (2002). Neo-liberalism, the state and the left: A Canadian perspective. *Monthly Review* 54(1), 46–55.

Beltrame, J. (2011, April 14). Data suggests Flaherty wrong that cutting corporate taxes raises revenue. *Canadian Business*. Retrieved from http://www.canadianbusiness.com/article/79746--data-suggests-flaherty-wrong-that-cutting-corporate-taxes-raises revenue

Boswell, R. (2011, April 25). Size matters: History shows stronger NDP could accomplish more in a minority. *Postmedia News*. Retrieved from http://www.canada.com/news/Size+matters+History+shows+stronger+could+accomplish+more+minority/4670789/story.html

Bradford, N. (2000). The policy influence of economic ideas: Interests, institutions and economics in Canada. In M. Burke, C. Mooers, & J. Shields (Eds.), *Restructuring and resistance: Canadian public policy in an age of global capitalism* (pp. 50–79). Halifax, NS: Fernwood.

Brodie, M. J., & Jensen, J. (1988). *Crisis, challenge and change: Party and class revisited.* Ottawa, ON: Carleton University Press.

Clarkson, S. (1991). Disjunctions: Free trade and the paradox of Canadian development. In D. Drache & M. S. Gertler (Eds.), *The new era of global competition: State policy and market power*. Montreal, QC: McGill-Queen's University Press.

Clarkson, S. (2002). *Uncle Sam and us: Globalization, neoconservatism and the Canadian state.* Toronto, ON: University of Toronto Press.

Cronin, J. E. (1987). The old and new politics of taxation: Thatcher and Reagan in historical perspective. In R. Miliband, L. Panitch, & J. Saville (Eds.), *Socialist register 1987: Conservatism in Britain and America. Rhetoric and reality* (pp. 263–296). London, UK: Merlin Press.

Demont, P. (2009, June 22). Ottawa's GST cut hiked deficit by as much as $10 billion. *CBC News Online*. Retrieved from http://www.cbc.ca/news/business/story/2009/06/16/f-gst-cut-estimate-deficit.html

Dobbin, M. (1998). *The myth of the good corporate citizen: Democracy under the rule of big business.* Toronto, ON: Stoddart.

Dobbin, M. (2003). *Paul Martin: CEO for Canada?* Toronto, ON: Lorimer.

Drache, D., & Cameron, D. (1985). Introduction. In D. Drache & D. Cameron (Eds.), *The other Macdonald Report*. Toronto, ON: Lorimer.

Edsall, T. (1985). *The new politics of inequality.* New York, NY: Norton.

Evans, B., & Albo, G. (2010). Permanent austerity: The politics of the Canadian exit strategy from fiscal stimulus. *Alternate Routes: A Journal of Critical Social Research, 22,* 7–28.

Friedman, M. (2002). *Capitalism and freedom: Fortieth anniversary edition* (original work published 1962). Chicago, IL: University of Chicago Press.

Glyn, A., Hughes, A., Lipietz, A., & Singh, A. (1990). The rise and fall of the golden age. In S. A. Marglin & J. B. Schor (Eds.), *The golden age of capitalism* (pp. 39–125). Oxford, UK: Clarendon Press.

Harvey, D. (2007). *A brief history of neo-liberalism.* Oxford, UK: Oxford University Press.

Himelfarb, A. (2012, April 17). Going, going, gone: Dismantling the progressive state [Web log post]. Retrieved from http://afhimelfarb.wordpress.com/2012/04/17/going-going-gone-dismantling-the-progressive-state/

Jackson, A. (2010, January). Beware the Canadian austerity model. *Global labour column*. Retrieved from http://column.global-labour-university.org/2010/01/beware-canadian-austerity-model.html

Judt, T. (2010). *Ill fares the land.* New York, NY: Penguin.

Keynes, J. M. (2006). *The general theory of employment, interest and money* (originally published in 1936). New Delhi: Atlantic.

Krugman, P. (2009). *Conscience of a liberal.* New York, NY: Norton.

Lavelle, A. (2008). *The death of social democracy: Political consequences in the 21st century.* Aldershot, UK: Ashgate.

Laxer, J. (1981). *Canada's economic strategy.* Toronto, ON: McClelland and Stewart.

Laxer, J. (1996). *In search of a new left: Canadian politics after the neoconservative assault.* Toronto, ON: Penguin.

Laxer, J. (1998). *The undeclared war: Class conflict in the age of cyber capitalism.* Toronto, ON: Penguin.

Mackenzie, H. (2004). Taxation: The Martin record. In T. Scarth (Ed.), *Hell and high water: An assessment of Paul Martin's record and the implications for the future* (pp. 55–66). Ottawa, ON: Canadian Centre for Policy Alternatives.

Mackenzie, H., & Shillington, R. (2009). *Canada's quiet bargain: The benefits of public spending* (CCPA Growing gap project, April 15, 2009). Retrieved from http://www.policyalternatives.ca/sites/default/files/uploads/publications/National_Office_Pubs/2009/Benefits_From_Public_Spending.pdf

Maddison, A. (1995). *Monitoring the world economy*. Paris: OECD Publishing.

McQuaig, L. (1998). *The cult of impotence: Selling the myth of powerlessness in the global economy*. Toronto, ON: Penguin.

McQuaig, L., & Brooks, N. (2011). *The trouble with billionaires*. Toronto, ON: Penguin.

Miliband, D. (1995). Introduction. In D. Miliband (Ed.), *Reinventing the left*. Cambidge, UK: Polity Press.

Palley, T. I. (2004, May 5). From Keynesianism to neo-liberalism: Shifting paradigms in economics. *Foreign Policy in Focus*. Retrieved from http://www.fpif.org/articles/from_keynesianism_to_neoliberalism_shifting_paradigms_in_economics

Panitch, L. (1986). The impasse of social democratic politics. In R. Miliband, J. Saville, M. Liebman, & L. Panitch (Eds.), *Socialist register 1985/86: After social democracy* (pp. 50–97). London, UK: Merlin Press.

Panitch, L. (2004). Globalization and the state. In L. Panitch, C. Leys, A. Zuege, & M. Konings (Eds.), *The globalization decade: A critical reader* (pp. 9–43). London, UK: Merlin Press.

Philipupillai, K. (2011, February 2). Why the Tories' $100-a-month childcare plan isn't enough. *This*. Retrieved from http://this.org/magazine/2011/02/09/daycare/

Pollin, R. (1998). The natural rate of unemployment: It's all about class conflict. *Dollars and Sense*, September/October.

Pollin, R. (2012). *Back to full employment*. Cambridge, MA: MIT Press.

Pressman, S. (2007). What can post-Keynesian economics teach us about poverty? In R. Holt & S. Pressman (Eds.), *Empirical post-Keynesian economics: Looking at the real world* (pp. 21–43). Armonk, NY: M. E. Sharpe.

Ruger, W. (2011). *Milton Friedman*. New York, NY: Continuum International.

Russell, F. (2011, April 13). Harper's taxing agenda. *Winnipeg Free Press*, p. A13. Retrieved from http://www.winnipegfreepress.com/opinion/westview/harpers-taxing-agenda-119751954.html?viewAllComments=y&device=mobile

Stanford, J. (2001). Social democratic policy and economic reality: The Canadian experience. In P. Arestis & M. Sawyers (Eds.), *The economics of the third way: Experiences from around the world* (pp. 79–105). Cheltenham, UK: Edward Elgar.

White, G. (1997). *The government and politics of Ontario*. Toronto, ON: University of Toronto Press.

Chapter 7

A Brief Potted History of Ottawa's Tax Cut Mania

Eugene Lang and Philip DeMont

> More than 8 out of 10 households will see their personal income taxes reduced.
> —Michael Wilson, Minister of Finance, *The Budget Speech*, February 10, 1988

> The tax measures in this Economic Statement, combined with those in the 2000 Budget, will provide $100 billion of cumulative tax relief by 2004–5. And Canadians' average personal income tax burden will be 21% less, and even lower for families with children—27%.
> —Finance Canada, *Economic Statement and Budget Update, 2000*

> This budget proposes comprehensive tax relief for individuals, valued at almost $20 billion over the next two years—more than the last four budgets combined.
> —Finance Canada, *Budget in Brief, 2006*

> You know, there's two schools in economics on this. One is that there are some good taxes and the other is that no taxes are good taxes. I'm in the latter category. I don't believe that any taxes are good taxes.
> —Prime Minister Stephen Harper, July 10, 2009

Introduction

Canadians are to be forgiven if they think they live in a high-tax country with a bloated government. "Taxes are high and need to be cut" has been the central message delivered by Canada's political class and policy elites for many years, especially at the federal level.

The ideology of tax cuts has become so entrenched in this country you'd think we've become America, where politicians who even hint at tax increases have no electoral chance whatsoever and compete against one another to see who can tell the biggest lies to Americans about the "affordability" of tax cuts; a society about to hit the fiscal wall because over the past 30 years Americans have fallen into the grips of what can only be described as "free lunch politics."

An important reflection of this American anti-tax ethos occurred in Canada in 2009 when Prime Minister Harper remarked that, in his view, no taxes are good taxes. In other words, all taxes are bad. The Prime Minister of Canada—the person most responsible for securing the public interest, the man in charge of delivering public services to Canadians, which are only possible because of taxes—said in public that he thinks all taxes are bad. It is an astounding and unprecedented statement from a national political leader.

The most revealing part of this episode is that Canada's anti-tax culture has gotten to such a point that few people challenged Harper on this statement. No one bothered to point out to the prime minister that taxes, and what they provide, are in fact one of the ultimate expressions of a society's values.

For those who argue the prime minister is merely voicing a basic, small-*c* conservative orientation, think again. "All taxes are bad" was most certainly not the conventional wisdom during the era of Brian Mulroney's Progressive Conservatives in the 1980s and early 1990s—the neo-liberal heyday. In fact, while the Mulroney government did cut some taxes significantly and brought in a major income tax reform, it also introduced entirely new types of taxes—notably the Goods and Services Tax (GST)—and increased other taxes, such as various surtaxes on income and capital.

So is Canada's tax-averse prime minister and our increasingly anti-tax political culture a reflection of the fact that taxes are too high in this country? There are different ways to answer this question. One way is by examining our fiscal history. Did Canadians pay significantly less tax in the past, meaning we need to return to the halcyon days of lower taxes? Another way to answer the question is to see how Canada stacks up tax-wise with other similarly advanced countries.

Our focus will be on the federal government, where the tax-cutting crusade has been most pronounced, especially over the past decade. We will look at personal income taxes, business taxes, consumption taxes, and payroll taxes over time to see what the trends look like. The evidence will show that the anti-tax rhetoric Canadians have been bombarded with for a generation has also coincided with unprecedented tax-cutting by Ottawa. Today, the federal government is taxing Canadians considerably less than it was in the recent past.[1] We will also show that Canada exacts low taxes on people, consumption, and business relative to other G8 and Organisation for Economic Co-operation and Development (OECD) countries.

In short, Canada is not a high-tax jurisdiction, as a lot of the political rhetoric and policy debate would lead one to believe. We live in a country with relatively low taxes compared to many other advanced democracies. And Canadians, whether they have noticed it or not, are paying significantly less tax than they were only a generation or even a decade ago.

Progressively Cutting Taxes

Federal taxes in Canada have been progressively declining for decades, particularly over the past quarter century, and even more especially over the past dozen or so years. Table 7.1 shows combined federal–provincial marginal income tax rates for some select years from the end of the Second World War to the present, as calculated by the Canadian Tax Foundation.

The most dramatic cuts have been on high-income earners. If you earned $400,000 forty years ago—which puts you among the highest income earners in Canada both then and now—you would have been paying a top marginal tax rate of over 60%. Twenty-five years ago, a person earning that kind of money would have still been paying in excess of a 50% top marginal rate. Today, according to the Canadian Tax Foundation, if you are at the top of the income ladder, you pay a top combined federal–provincial marginal rate of about 43%. And the pattern is basically the same for other income levels. Canadians have experienced a steady and progressive decline in combined federal–provincial marginal tax rates over several decades.

If we focus on federal personal income tax rates over the past 40 years, the story is much the same. Table 7.2 shows federal income tax rates for various income levels during select years since the early 1970s. The trend is clear; a steady decline in federal rates across all income levels from $20,000 to $100,000

Table 7.1 Combined federal–provincial personal income tax marginal rates

Taxable Income	1949	1973	1987	2003	2007	2011
$10,000	35%	35.2	28.5	24.32	22.2	22.2
$40,000	59	56.12	45	33.44	32.86	32.86
$400,000	84	61.34	51.08	44.08	42.92	42.92

Source: Finances of the Nation, various years. Toronto, ON: Canadian Tax Foundation.
Note: The Canadian Tax Foundation used the federal government's notional tax rate estimate as the multiplier to derive the provincial portion of the overall national income tax rate. Thus, in 1971, Ottawa applied a rate of 28% of the federal tax payable to arrive at a combined income tax level. Similarly, the federal government used a provincial rate of 4% of the federal tax payable for 1987; 52% for 1996 and 1997, and 48% for 2007 and 2011.

Table 7.2 Personal income tax for a single taxpayer—federal rate only

Income	1971	1988	1997	2000	2007
$20K	23.85%	17.51	17.5	15.9	13.99
$50K	39.60	26.78	26.8	25.00	22.00
$75K	43.20	46.11	31.30	29.00	22.00
$100K	46.80	29.87	31.30	30.50	26.00

per year. The most dramatic cuts began in the late 1980s on people who earned around $75,000 per year (a significant income at that time, and admittedly much less significant today, due to inflation). These earners have seen their federal income tax rate cut from 46 to 22% over the past 25 years. Most significantly, however, is the fact that the highest federal marginal tax rate today is 29%, kicking in on incomes of $132,000. By contrast, a quarter century ago the highest federal marginal rate was 34%, and took hold at an income of $63,000 per year (OECD, n.d.).

Corporate Tax Cuts: Getting to the Top by Racing to the Bottom

The picture with respect to federal corporate income tax rates is even more dramatic, as Table 7.3 shows. Twenty-five years ago, the general corporate income tax rate was 36%—today it is less than half that at only 15% (small businesses have had the least significant federal business tax cut—a 4% drop over the last quarter century). The decline in the general corporate rate has been consistent over the past decade, dropping under the last three federal governments, reflecting a conventional belief held by many economists that corporate tax cuts produce significant investment, job creation, and productivity benefits, thus enhancing the competitiveness of Canadian business.

Canada's Tortured Consumption Tax Story

The federal story on consumption taxes is equally revealing. In 1988, the Progressive Conservative government of Brian Mulroney announced it was introducing a new value-added tax (VAT) called the Goods and Services Tax (GST), which would replace the Manufacturers Sales Tax (MST). The introduction of a federal VAT for Canada was designed in part to enhance the competitiveness of business, which was especially important given that the country had recently entered into a free trade agreement with the United States. In this continental "free trade" world, Canadian business, especially the manufacturing sector, would be exposed to more competition and needed to be unburdened from the inefficient MST. A VAT was the solution to this economic problem.

Table 7.3 Federal corporate income tax							
	1987	1997	2000	2002	2007	2010	2012
General	36%	28	28	25	21	18	15
Manufacturing	30	21	21	21	21	18	15
Small business	15	12	12	12/21	12	11	11
Small business threshold	$200K	$225K	$225K	$225K	$400K	$500K	$500K

Source: *Finances of the Nation* (various years) (Toronto, ON: Canadian Tax Foundation).

The GST was announced in Finance Minister Michael Wilson's 1989 budget. The minister indicated that this new tax would be introduced on January 1, 1991 at a rate of 9% (Wilson, 1989, p. 13), a level at which the tax was considered "revenue neutral"—meaning it would have no impact on the fiscal position of the government—as compared to the 13.5% MST that it would replace. The desire for revenue neutrality was non-trivial at that time because the government was running a large deficit it was trying to reduce, and could therefore not afford a big reduction in revenue from its sales tax reform. Nevertheless in the end, due to intense Parliamentary controversy over the GST, the new tax was established at a rate of 7%. The GST thus has the distinction of being the first tax in Canadian history that was cut before it was even introduced. Subsequently, the GST has been cut twice more by the Harper government, so that today it stands at 5%.

Of course in Canada there are a variety of provincial sales taxes that are added to the GST, giving us a blended tax. These provincial sales taxes range from a high of 10% in Prince Edward Island to a low of zero in Alberta and the Territories. Some provinces have harmonized their sales taxes with the GST, while others have not. The three largest provinces—Ontario, Quebec, and British Columbia—have provincial sales taxes of 8%, 9.5%, and 7%, respectively, which are added to the GST. Ontario and BC are harmonized with the GST, whereas Quebec is not.

One way to get a good sense of the sales tax trend over time, given all these differential rates across the provinces, is to look at taxes on goods and services as a percentage of GDP in Canada. In other words, how much sales tax have Canadians been paying as a fraction of all the goods and services produced in the economy? In 1965, taxes on goods and services in Canada accounted for about 10.4% of GDP. Thirty years later this number had dropped to 9%. In 2009, taxes on goods and services accounted for 7.6% of GDP (OECD, n.d.). Clearly, Canadians are paying a lot less sales tax as a fraction of the economy than they were in the past.

A Wash in Payroll Taxes

Finally, a word on payroll tax trends at the federal level. Federal payroll taxes consist of Employment Insurance (EI) and Canada Pension Plan (CPP) premiums. These premiums are intended to fund EI and CPP. Over the past two decades, Canadians have seen a steady decline in EI premiums (which prior to 1996 was known as Unemployment Insurance). Since 1990, maximum EI premiums for workers, in inflation-adjusted 2011 constant dollars, peaked in 1994 at $1,726 and declined to $740 in 2008, creeping back up to $788 in 2011 (Caledon Institute of Social Policy, 2011, p. 6).

The Canada Pension Plan (CPP) premium trend has been notably different, primarily due to a major reform undertaken by the Chrétien government in the late 1990s, which increased premiums to make the plan financially self-sustaining.

According to the Caledon Institute of Social Policy, in inflation-adjusted 2011 dollars, gross CPP contributions increased from a maximum of $869.35 in 1990, to $1,273.23 in 1997, then to $2,082.00 in 2003, and then crept up slightly each year to reach $2,217.60 in 2011. The net effect of these changes is that total federal payroll taxes have increased by about $900 in inflation-adjusted terms since 1990, but have remained relatively stable at around $2,900 per year over the past decade (Caledon Institute of Social Policy, 2011, p. 6). So Canada's recent payroll tax history is a bit of a wash.

Northern Tiger Indeed: Comparing Canada's Tax Burden Internationally

The historical evidence thus reveals a broad and general trend toward lower federal taxes for Canadians over the past quarter century, across a range of different types of taxes, with the notable exception of payroll taxes. However, some will dismiss this fiscal history as irrelevant to any tax analysis, given all the changes to Canada's economy and public services over the last generation or so.

So arguably an even more meaningful way to analyze the level of taxes in Canada is to compare them to those of other advanced countries. When we do so, we find Canada's marginal income taxes, corporate taxes, sales taxes, and overall tax bite are low by international comparative standards. In fact, Canada is a world leader in taxing relatively lightly in some areas and on certain overall measures of the tax burden.

The broadest and simplest measure of the level of tax is the total tax take expressed as a percentage of GDP. According to the OECD, total tax revenue as a percentage of GDP over the past half century peaked in Canada at 35.6% in 1995, and declined to 31% in 2010 (OECD, n.d.). Over this same time frame, all other G7 countries have seen taxes as a share of GDP either remain static or slightly increase. The only other exception to this trend is the United States, with its viscerally anti-tax political culture, which has experienced about a 3% decline over this time frame. Taxes as a percent of GDP then, have declined more significantly in Canada over the past 15 years than they have in any other G7 country. And Canada's tax take as a percentage of GDP has not only declined faster but also is now the third lowest in absolute terms in the G7, trailing only the US and Japan. Taxes in Canada as a percent of GDP are also about 3 percentage points lower than the OECD average.

Comparing Canada's personal income tax rates across the OECD is much more complex, not least because we have both national and various sub-national income tax rates and income thresholds, a relative rarity in the OECD. The highest marginal provincial rates range from a peak of 21% in Nova Scotia, to a trough of 10% in Alberta. Thus, the highest combined federal–provincial personal marginal income tax rate runs from a low of 39% in Alberta to 50% in Nova Scotia. British Columbia comes in between the two extremes at 43.7%, whereas Ontario, the largest provincial economy, has a top combined marginal personal rate of almost 43% (CRA, 2013).

When we add provincial to federal rates, Canada's personal income tax levels still compare favourably to other OECD states. Ireland, hailed for many years as one of the leading low-tax jurisdictions in the advanced democracies, has a top personal marginal income tax rate of 41%. That places Alberta's combined federal–provincial top marginal rate—at 39%—lower than that of the Celtic Tiger. Other G7 countries have higher rates than Canada as well. The UK, Germany, and Italy have top marginal rates of 50%, 45%, and 43% respectively. And Australia, a country comparable to Canada in many ways, has a top marginal rate of 45% (OECD, n.d.).

Corporate tax comparisons across the OECD paint a similar picture. The OECD average corporate tax rate in 2011 was 25.37%, while the European Union standard was approximately two and a half percentage points lower, at 22.7%. Contrary to conventional wisdom, the top US corporate tax rate is actually high by international standards at 39.5%.

In contrast, Ottawa imposes a 15% levy on corporate earnings, with a slightly lower levy for small businesses. The provinces charge varied rates on top of the federal level, ranging from a low of 10% in British Columbia to a high of 16% in Prince Edward Island and Nova Scotia. For comparative purposes, the OECD uses a "representative sub-central government rate" of 11.4% for Canada, and on that basis assesses it as having a "combined corporate income tax rate" of 26.1%. This level is slightly above the OECD average, yet lower than all G7 countries save the United Kingdom, as Table 7.4 shows. Australia also has a

Table 7.4 G7 corporate income tax rate, 2012

Country	Rate %
US	39.1
Japan	38
France	34.4
Germany	30.2
Italy	27.5
Canada	26.1
UK	24

Sources: OECD Tax Database and KPMG, Corporate Tax Rates Table.

corporate rate considerably higher than Canada at 30%, which is equal to that of Mexico, one of Canada's NAFTA partners. Ottawa's corporate tax cuts over the past 10 years have clearly been significant, and have made Canada a very competitive corporate tax jurisdiction relative to many comparable countries.

Finally, when comparing Canada's consumption taxes, the pattern is even more pronounced. Most OECD countries, and all G7 countries save the US, impose some kind of value added tax. As discussed, Canada's version is the GST/HST. Nevertheless, as of 2009, among OECD countries, only Korea, Spain, and Switzerland had lower goods and services taxes as a percent of GDP than Canada. And the OECD average VAT revenue of 10.7% of GDP is three percent higher than Canada's, which stands at 7.6%.

When we compare the provinces that have harmonized their sales tax with the GST, we find that Nova Scotia currently has Canada's highest harmonized sales tax, or HST, at 15%. And, as noted previously, the larger economies of British Columbia, Ontario, and Quebec come in with combined federal provincial sales tax rates of 12%, 13%, and 13.5% respectively. By contrast, most European countries charge a value-added tax in excess of the highest Canadian consumption tax, typically in the high teens or low twenties. The unweighted OECD average VAT rate is, in fact, 18.5%. As Table 7.5 illustrates, among G7 countries excluding the US (which, as noted, does not have a VAT), Canada has the second-lowest VAT, trailing only Japan.[2]

To sum up then, even if we take the highest combined federal–provincial sales tax in Canada of 15%, our consumption tax rates are still well below the major European economies, the OECD average, and most G7 countries. Just about any way you slice it, Canada has very low VAT compared to most other advanced economies.

Table 7.5 G7 VAT rates

Country	Rates (%)
Italy	20
UK	20
France	19.6
Germany	19
Canada	12
Japan	5
US	not applicable

Note: This is the combined federal–provincial unweighted average sales tax rate.

How Canada Became a Northern Tax Tiger

So the broad trends are pretty clear. Taxes have been on the decline in Canada relative to our recent past and compared to other relevant jurisdictions for many years now. But how did we achieve this low tax status? The answer lies in what can only be described as a bipartisan tax-cutting mania that took hold in Ottawa over the past decade or so.

The origins of this go back to Michael Wilson's watershed 1988 budget, when the Mulroney government brought in major reforms aimed primarily at reducing income taxes on individuals. A federal tax structure comprised of some ten brackets and thresholds was cut down to three, allowing the government of the day to boast,

> more than 8 out of 10 households will see their personal income taxes reduced. About 850,000 lower-income individuals will have their income tax reduced to zero. Almost 9 out of 10 Canadians aged 65 and over will have income tax reductions. The vast majority of families with children will pay noticeably less personal income tax. (Wilson, 1983, p. 3)

The general direction of tax reform had thus been set in train 25 years ago. Successive governments, while often disagreeing over details and technicalities of tax policy, all basically agreed with the notion that cutting taxes was the only direction worthy of serious pursuit. A conventional wisdom had taken hold by the late 1980s, particularly among politicians, economists, and business leaders, that taxes in Canada were far too high and were impeding the country's competitiveness and productivity. Taxes simply had to come down.

The productivity/competitiveness rationale for tax cuts has remained one of the most resilient policy orthodoxies in Ottawa for two decades, transcending the political affiliation of various governments. It has been reflected in numerous federal budgets, fiscal and economic statements, government-commissioned advisory reports, and budget submissions from various public policy think tanks and business advocacy organizations. It is a rock-solid, immovable piece of the federal policy furniture.

And this orthodoxy helped give rise to the tax-cutting orientation first reflected in Wilson's 1988 budget. The tax-cutting agenda begun then was, however, interrupted by the fiscal crisis of the early to middle 1990s, and the deep and painful recession Canada experienced at that time. Fortunately, our political leaders did not succumb to the supply-side economics snake oil that many in the US embraced at that time, which argued that certain types of tax cuts could actually produce more net revenue for the government's coffers. Consequently, through the 1990s, when Ottawa was in the teeth of a fiscal crisis not dissimilar to what some European countries face today, the federal tax-cut agenda was temporarily put on hold, although the arguments about the benefits and need for tax reductions remained quite strong.

Another dominant policy orthodoxy that prevailed in Ottawa for about a decade (from the late 1990s to the recession of 2008), which gave new life and vigour to the tax-cutting agenda, was the notion that the federal government could "afford" to cut the taxes of Canadians and therefore should do so. Large deficits in the 1970s, 1980s, and early 1990s gave way to significant surpluses by the late 1990s, following some fairly draconian fiscal reforms in the mid-1990s. Suddenly, the federal government was awash in cash, charting annual surpluses that peaked at $17 billion/year. In Ottawa's *Economic Statement and Budget Update* for 2000, annual structural surpluses of over $10 billion, or around 1% of GDP, were forecast into the future. Politicians were now getting criticized for pulling in a lot more money each year than they seemed to need to conduct the business of state.

By the early 2000s, a belief emerged that was illustrated by significant growth in federal spending: not only had the deficit era permanently ended after a quarter century of red ink, but a new epoch characterized by large surpluses might be a permanent feature of the fiscal landscape. Painful recessions and the corresponding sharp reductions in revenue that resulted were a fading memory, and maybe even a thing of the past. Some thought the business cycle was over. Francis Fukuyama might have been wrong about the End of History in the early 1990s. But a decade later, as the economy rode high on the tech and real estate booms, and amid impressive US productivity growth that powered America and dragged Canada along for the ride, a case was being made that the End of Economic History might be upon us.

Ottawa's structural surplus "problem" that coincided with this economic boom provoked provincial governments to claim that a "fiscal imbalance" existed between the feds and the provinces. This allegedly meant that Ottawa had more money than it knew what to do with relative to its constitutional responsibilities, while the provinces were broke and had all kinds of unfulfilled public service demands relative to theirs (particularly in health care and education, where costs were rising rapidly). During this period, the federal government was also exposed to the accusation that the real fiscal imbalance existed between the treasury and citizens, meaning people deserved a tax cut because Ottawa could afford it and citizens were being taxed too much relative to what Ottawa needed.

The historical confluence of these two dominant policy orthodoxies—the alleged productivity and competitive benefits of cutting taxes, and the notion that the federal government had too much money relative to program spending demands, including debt servicing—aligned with the conventional political wisdom that tax cuts confer very strong benefits on politicians. This union of intellectual and political opinion in turn produced an unprecedented era of deep federal tax cuts of various kinds—a tax-cutting mania, if you will—beginning in the year 2000 under the Chrétien Liberals, and continuing through 2006–8 under the Harper Conservatives. While the Mulroney government had set the basic trajectory with their reforms during the late Reagan/Thatcher neo-liberal era, it was in fact the Chrétien and Harper governments years later that would drive tax-cutting to new and hitherto unimagined heights.

The 2000 Chrétien/Martin Budget inaugurated this new tax-cutting mania. It introduced a number of major reforms leading to significant, if not unprecedented, tax relief for Canadians and businesses, notably full indexation to the income tax system, a reduction of the middle tax bracket from 26 to 23%, an increase in the Basic Personal Exemption (the level of income one can earn without paying income tax), and a boost in the income thresholds to which the middle and upper rates apply. The government also eliminated the deficit reduction surtax on incomes above $85,000 and began the era of corporate tax cuts, slashing them by seven points, from 28 to 21% on the highest-taxed industries. Cumulatively, the 2000 budget delivered $58 billion in tax relief over five years (Department of Finance, 2000). Less than a year later, Chrétien and Martin went one step further in tax-cutting with their "Mini-Budget," brought in literally on the eve of the 2000 federal election. The $58 billion in tax relief announced eight months prior was now increased to $100 billion. Some characterized this as the largest tax cut in Canadian history. It was achieved through the lowering of all personal income tax rates, the cutting of capital gains taxes, and an acceleration of the phase-in for corporate income cuts, among other measures (Department of Finance, 2000b, para. "Reducing Taxes for Canadians"). The central policy rationale for all these tax cuts—as distinct from the political allure of cutting taxes right before an election—was affordability, now that Ottawa had moved on from a generation of deficits to an era of structural surpluses. A secondary yet important rationale was the notion that some of these tax cuts would spur innovation, productivity, and entrepreneurship, and thereby improve business competitiveness.

The next tax-cutting budget, following the brief economic slump after 9/11, was in 2005, from the short lived minority government of Paul Martin. This was a less ambitious tax reform agenda than the one in 2000, but it certainly was not trivial. Once again, the Basic Personal Exemption was increased significantly. According to the government, this reform would remove some 860,000 low-income Canadians from the tax rolls altogether. And, once again, in the effort to drive business investment and productivity growth, corporate income tax rates were further cut from 21 to 19%. The corporate surtax, introduced during the Mulroney government to help with deficit reduction, was also eliminated (Department of Finance, 2005, p. 15).

In 2006, the Liberals were defeated in a general election, giving way to the Stephen Harper Conservatives, who made no bones about their tax-cutting enthusiasms, having run in that election on a commitment to cut the reviled GST, ironically put in place by a previous Conservative government. Harper and his Finance Minister Jim Flaherty delivered on this promise quickly. Flaherty's first budget not only cut the GST from 7 to 6% but also, like his predecessors, further increased the Basic Personal Exemption and cut the lowest personal marginal income rate. The government boasted that this budget delivered almost $20 billion in tax relief to Canadians on top of what had been provided by the Chrétien and Martin governments. A vigorous competition seemed to be underway between Liberals and Conservatives to see who would cut Canadians' taxes the deepest and the fastest.

But this wasn't enough for Canada's new government. Flaherty's next budget in 2007 also contained significant tax reductions. Even after six years of deep and quite unprecedented tax-cutting, in his second budget, Flaherty stated,

> Canadians still pay too much tax. The Government is taking important steps to reduce personal income taxes to encourage people to work, save and invest. We are helping businesses succeed through lower taxes to spur innovation and growth that will lead to more jobs and higher wages for Canadian workers. (Department of Finance, 2007, p. 19)

The primary tax relief in Budget 2007 was delivered through various tax credits to families, and was titled *Working Families Tax Plan*. Senior citizens also received significant tax relief through increasing the age tax credits some fivefold and permitting income-splitting, which effectively reduced the tax rates that seniors pay. The cumulative three-year total tax relief in Budget 2007 was estimated at just over $8 billion.

Then in January 2008, the Prime Minister made good on his commitment to cut the GST by another percentage point, driving it down to 5%. This move gave Canada the distinction of being tied with Japan for the lowest central government VAT in the OECD (remember, the US has no VAT). The GST reductions and income tax cuts over their first few years in office led the Harper government to claim in 2011 that the average Canadian family of four was saving more than $3,000 each year.

Ottawa's tax-cutting mania, which had begun in 2000 with the Liberals, was not only extended by the Conservatives but also became central to their political brand. However, not unlike the Mulroney government's tax-cutting enthusiasms in the late 1980s, Harper's and Flaherty's tax reform agenda ended rather abruptly with the advent of the global financial crisis and attendant recession of 2008–9. Suddenly, and without warning, the federal government was in a significant deficit again, for the first time in a decade. The era of structural surpluses had mysteriously and unpredictably ended, almost overnight.

Notwithstanding the natural revenue loss due to the recession, plus new spending to boost the economy, those eight years of successive and deep tax-cutting played no small part in ensuring that once the economy inevitably slowed, Ottawa would end up in deficit. There was no longer any fiscal room to manoeuvre through a recession and keep the budget balanced, given the deep tax-cutting of the previous years. This was reflected in Parliamentary Budget Officer Kevin Page's 2011 report that calculated Ottawa now had a structural deficit—the part of the deficit that won't go away once the economy is operating at full capacity—of about $10 billion per year (which is, incidentally, quite a bit lower than the value of two GST points).

Tax Cuts, Smaller Government and Rising Income Inequality: Correlation or Coincidence?

It should come as no surprise that when a broad array of taxes are reduced significantly, as we have seen over the past quarter century, some things do change quite measurably. One such change is in the size of government. Among OECD countries, total government spending as a percentage of GDP—one proxy for the size of government—is 43.6%. Canada sits below this average today at 39.9%.

It was not always thus. Twenty years ago, total government spending as a percent of GDP in Canada stood at 53%, roughly where France is today (OECD, 2010). Canada has experienced a steady decline in the size of government since that time, a trend that coincided with significant tax reductions. This downward trend in the size of government is also obviously influenced by cuts to government programs and services, particularly those made in the austerity efforts of both Ottawa and the provinces during the 1990s to rein in the large fiscal deficits of that period.

Figure 7.1 G7 government spending as a percentage of GDP	
France	52.8
Italy	48.8
UK	47.3
Germany	43.7
Canada	39.7
US	38.9
Japan	37.1

Source: 2011 Index of Economic Freedom, Heritage Foundation, and *The Wall Street Journal*.

Due largely to the tax-cutting trail blazed by Ottawa over the past dozen years, the ratio of federal to provincial revenues has also changed. In 1981–82, the combined revenue take of the provincial and territorial governments was 51.6% of total provincial–territorial–federal revenues. By contrast, in 2011–12, the provincial–territorial share of revenues stood at 56%, an 8.5% increase over 30 years. This would suggest that the size and scope of the federal government has shrunk relative to that of the provinces over this time period. As noted above, total government spending as a percent of GDP in Canada today is just under 40%, with federal program spending accounting for about 14%, meaning the provinces are spending considerably more relative to Ottawa as a share of the national economy.

But perhaps the most significant economic trend in Canada that has coincided with the era of tax cuts is rising income inequality. Over the period 1981–2009, market incomes of the bottom two quintiles of Canadians fell, while the top two quintiles saw an increase of over 43% (Sharpe, 2011, p. 101). By 2007, the after-tax income share of the top 1% of Canadian households accounted for nearly 10% of total income, an increase of 3.4% over 25 years (Sharpe, 2011, p. 102). And, according to Statistics Canada, over the 2000–5 period, earnings increased by 6.2 and 2.4% for top and middle income groups respectively, while falling 3.1% for the bottom income group.

The Conference Board recently concluded in a study of income inequality in 17 OECD countries that Canada ranked twelfth. In grading Canada on income inequality, the Conference Board stated,

> After improving to a "B" grade in the mid-1990s, Canada's grade once again dropped to a "C" in the most recent decade. Canada is the only peer country whose relative grade dropped between the mid-1990s and the mid-2000s, owing to its significant increase in income inequality (the second-largest of all the peer countries). (Conference Board of Canada, 2013)

The OECD's landmark 2011 report, *Divided We Stand: Why Inequality Keeps Rising*, documented rising income inequality across all OECD countries over the past three decades and pointed to a range of causes for this phenomenon. These included technological changes and the economic returns from higher skills, regulatory reforms and institutional changes, alterations in family structures and the rise of part-time work, and less distributive tax and benefit systems. To address income inequality, the OECD offered some policy advice to governments, including investing more in human capital, but also raising marginal tax rates on higher income earners, and "improving tax compliance, eliminating tax breaks and reassessing the role of taxes on all forms of property and wealth, including the transfer of assets" (OECD, 2011, p. 4).

While the OECD does not claim that tax cuts have a direct correlation with rising income inequality, it seems more than coincidental that in this country, significant reductions in taxes coincided almost precisely with rises in income inequality.

Conclusion: Embracing a Subversive Idea

This is not to say that the bipartisan tax-cutting mania that has gripped Ottawa, while extreme by Canadian historical or even international standards, produced universally bad policy outcomes. In fact, a strong case can be made that a lot of the tax-cutting measures pursued by the Mulroney, Chrétien, Martin, and Harper governments were appropriate and progressive, notably the cuts to marginal rates for low-income Canadians, increases to the Basic Personal Exemption, and restoration of full indexation to the income tax system. Reasonable people can disagree on the merits of many of the other tax cuts ushered in over the past quarter century, although most experts tend to think that the GST reductions were a classic example of retail politics trumping sound economic and fiscal policy.

That said, many of these same experts also believe that the corporate tax cuts pursued with extreme vigour by the Chrétien, Martin, and Harper governments were sound, indeed necessary to stimulate investment and productivity growth, thereby improving the flagging competitiveness of Canadian business. Unfortunately, evidence of increased business investment and stronger productivity growth associated with these tax cuts is hard to find. Oddly enough, Canadian labour productivity growth has in fact declined during the era of corporate tax cuts—dropping to 0.8% from about 1.8% in the previous decade of higher corporate taxes—precisely the opposite of what the theory and the experts claimed would happen (Statistics Canada, 2009, Chart 1).

It is also highly debatable economically, and fails to meet any reasonable test of fairness, that the highest federal marginal personal income tax rate should kick in at $132,000 per year—meaning someone earning half a million or a million dollars a year pays the same federal tax rate as those earning one-fifth or one-tenth that level. Perhaps, in going from ten to three rates a generation ago (then back up to four rates more recently), we have flattened our tax system too much and undermined its progressivity, contributing to rising income inequality.[3]

And we could certainly have a debate around the alleged "affordability" of all these tax cuts, as the federal government today stares down a $23 billion deficit, is cutting spending significantly to rein it in, and faces profound fiscal pressures in future years due to the aging of Canadian society. While it is true that most of the tax cuts were made when Ottawa was riding high on a decade-long period of fiscal surpluses, any prudent government with a sense of economic history should have realized that these surplus years were an anomaly, and that an economic slump was just around the corner, meaning federal coffers were likely to be constrained soon and tax-cutting had to be cautious and measured. It is worth bearing in mind that recessions—and the resulting drying up of revenue—are a very common feature of Canadian economic history, not some rare occurrence. Since the end of the Second World War, Canada has experienced some 13 recessions, meaning on average this country faces an economic slump about every five years. Unfortunately, economic history plays almost no part in federal policy-making or budget planning, and is something most politicians are completely oblivious to.

What is not up for debate, however, is the fact that at the federal level this country has gone through an unprecedented and fairly lengthy bipartisan period of tax-cutting, so much so that today Canada's taxes are considerably lower than they were in the past, and are low relative to many other advanced industrial countries. Political rhetoric and a large body of elite opinion aside, Canada is a relatively low-tax jurisdiction and has become so primarily over the last decade. Given that reality, the idea of "let's raise taxes" is not as subversive as many will claim.

Notes

1 We will not examine the litany of tax deductions and credits that litter the federal tax system, but suffice to say that all of these have been on the rise in recent years and further reduce the taxes Canadians pay. These issues are taken up later in the book by Lee and Ivanova.
2 Currently, a bill to double Japan's VAT to 10% is before the Japanese Parliament's Upper House.
3 With only four brackets federally, Canada has a flatter and arguably less progressive income tax system than many other OECD countries. Australia, for example, has five brackets, while the US and Japan have six different taxation levels.

References

Caledon Institute of Social Policy (2011, November). *Trends in Canada's payroll taxes* (Caledon Social Statistics Series). Retrieved from http://www.caledoninst.org/Publications/PDF/964ENG.pdf

Canada Revenue Agency (CRA). (2013). *FAQ: Federal and Provincial/Territorial Tax Rates for 2013* [Web page]. Retrieved from http://www.cra-arc.gc.ca/tx/ndvdls/fq/txrts-eng.html

Conference Board of Canada (2013). *Income Inequality Report Card* [Web page]. Retrieved from http://www.conferenceboard.ca/hcp/details/society/income-inequality.aspx

Department of Finance Canada. (2000a, February 28). *The Budget in Brief.* Retrieved from http://fin.gc.ca/budget00/pdf/briefe.pdf

Department of Finance Canada. (2000b, October 18). *Economic Statement and Budget Update.* Retrieved from http://www.collectionscanada.gc.ca/webarchives/20071116002448/http://www.fin.gc.ca/ec2000/pdf/overe.pdf

Department of Finance Canada. (2005). *The budget speech, February 23, 2005: Delivering on commitments.* Retrieved from http://fin.gc.ca/budget05/speech/speech-eng.asp

Department of Finance Canada. (2007, March 19). *Budget in brief, 2007: Aspire to a stronger, safer, better Canada.*

KPMG. (2013). *Corporate tax rates table.* Retrieved from http://www.kpmg.com/global/en/services/tax/tax-tools-and-resources/pages/corporate-tax-rates-table.aspx

Organisation for Economic Co-operation and Development (OECD). (2010). *OECD Economic Outlook No.88*(2). doi: 10.1787/eco_outlook-v2010-2-en

Organisation for Economic Co-operation and Development (OECD). (2011, December). *Divided We Stand: Why Inequality Keeps Rising.* Retrieved from http://www.oecd.org/social/socialpoliciesanddata/49170768.pdf

Organisation for Economic Co-operation and Development (OECD). (2013). Personal Income Tax [Database]. Retrieved from http://www.oecd.org/tax/tax-policy/oecdtaxdatabase.html.

Sharpe, A. (2011, November). Income redistribution in Canada. In *The Canada we want in 2020: Towards a strategic policy roadmap for the Federal Government* (pp. 95–101). Ottawa, ON: Canada 2020.

Statistics Canada. (2009). *Trends in real gross domestic product, labour productivity and hours at work, business sector,* Chart 1. Retrieved from http://www.statcan.gc.ca/pub/15-206-x/2009025/ct001-eng.htm

Wilson, M. (1989). Minister of Finance *Budget Speech.* Ottawa, ON: Parliament of Canada.

Chapter 8

Tax Cuts and Other Cheap Parlour Tricks

Trish Hennessy

The year I turned 40, I had more than a landmark birthday to celebrate. I had a cap and gown to put on and a graduation ceremony to attend. To my delight, I beheld a spellbinding speech by Nobel Prize–winning economist Amartya Sen, who happened to accept a honourary degree the night I received my master's (What's Happening, 2004).

Sitting among the graduates, I felt accomplishment and gratitude. I imagined my paternal grandmother immigrating to Canada from Scotland as a wee lass, setting up a rough-and-tumble life with a handsome Irish lad who worked his way up the Montreal printing press scene to keep his growing brood fed. I imagined my mother, scraping by as a girl in a dilapidated shack in the dustbowl of the Prairies during the Great Depression. She had no indoor plumbing, no electricity, none of the luxuries my generation takes for granted.

I display each of my university degrees with pride. My grandparents and parents are a reminder of my good fortune, the value of hard work, and *my great big secret*: how affordable access to a university education helped me to avoid becoming a farmer's wife. (God love the farmers, but I would have made a terrible farmer's wife).

Of course, no one succeeds in life without help. In my case, I'd like to thank the academy. Literally—the countless professors (public sector workers funded by taxpayers) who took the time to explain the form of an essay, the laws of supply and demand, the explanatory power of feminism, the works of Rousseau, Marx, and Gramsci.

Most of all, I'd like to thank the people of Canada, because I simply could not have done it without the taxes that quietly subsidized my learning obsession. Thanks to a decision made by Canadians less than 100 years ago to democratize the halls of higher learning, all I had to do was want an education, and I got one.

Yes, I paid tuition. Actually, sometimes I didn't. In the early days, there were grants and bursaries, and I was grateful for them. But even in years when I didn't rely on luck or student loans to cover my tuition, Canadians who pay taxes turned out to be my anonymous benefactors. If you're alive and have received a post-secondary education—in 2011, Canada had the highest proportion of workers with a college or university degree of any OECD nation other than Korea (OECD, 2011)—you also have taxpayers to thank. In Canada, our governments subsidize the true cost of higher learning. They can't do that without taxpayers.

Actually, scrub that word, "taxpayer." It's filth. It has been dragged through the muck of divisive, opportunistic, and simplistic election campaigns; abused beyond belief with hackneyed political slogans and the dogged repetition of mantras such as "respect for taxpayers" or "there's only one taxpayer" (Lorinc, 2011; Respecting Taxpayers, 2012; Goldsbie, 2012). Politicians who chase the elusive vote of the taxpayer harp on the "tax burden," so they present themselves as the answer to those seeking "tax relief"—and who isn't? It's often couched in language designed to soothe, to reassure an anxious electorate: "A re-elected Conservative Government will continue to keep taxes down for families so they can keep more of their hard-earned money to spend on what matters to them" (Wintery Knight, 2011).

The tax-fighting politician talks only about the dollars in your pocket. He deliberately disconnects your act of social citizenship through tax contribution from its deeper, more meaningful role. Entire election campaigns and budget cycles focus on income tax cuts, corporate tax cuts, sales tax cuts, tax-free savings accounts, income-splitting, tax credits for children's activities, public transit passes, and all manner of budget line items. We elect bean-counters these days, not visionaries.

What goes unspoken: winning election platforms have been founded on the sole promise of "low-tax plans" (Conservative Party, April 3, 2011) without any acknowledgement of the true cost. But Canadians have paid a stiff price for the tax-hater's agenda. Relentless tax cut campaigns have reduced Canada's total tax rate to a level lower than that of competing G8 nations (CCPA, 2011). Based on Organisation for Economic Co-operation and Development (OECD) data, the amount of revenue as a percentage of GDP dropped from 36% in 1995 to 33% in 2007, the equivalent of a $50 billion annual loss in tax revenues that once paid for infrastructure, income supports, public services, education, and health care. It had fallen to 31% by 2010. At least $50 billion a year lost in the ether (Mackenzie, 2009). The share of GDP Canada spends on social programs has dropped steadily (Finn, 2012), as has our commitment to being a caring, more equitable society. But countering low-tax politics with myth-busting facts and figures simply doesn't cut it. Progressives have tried this approach, valiantly. The tax-haters keep talking circles around the so-called tax and spenders.

I try, when I can, to find out what Canadians think about these issues first hand through focus groups facilitated by Environics Research. But listening to

Canadians talk about taxes in focus groups can be frustrating. I hear echoes of the many lines Canadians have been fed for more than a decade of political jostling over who is the best "manager" of your tax dollars (not the collective *ours*, but the individual *yours*). It's interesting how, in these focus groups, people cannot identify just how much money Canada's tax cut agenda has cost the public coffers. Nor can they identify how much they've personally benefited from tax cuts. Some days, I try to imagine how scurrilous it would be for a left-leaning government in Canada to embark on such a costly political agenda for, say, a 10-year period, and still find itself unable to convince Canadians that the majority have benefited from it. But this has been the infuriating reality of tax-cut politics: many Canadians are still wondering, *where's mine?*

The Canadian quagmire: we are consumed with aspiring to a comfortable, middle-class lifestyle. We'll mortgage ourselves up to the eyeballs for it. We'll work night and day for it. And yet, despite decades of pandering to the *working family*—political code in Canada for middle class—many in the middle class still feel underappreciated and politically neglected. Cognitive linguist George Lakoff has written extensively about the challenges progressives face in changing the conversation so that it reflects progressive values. Among his salient observations: Stress, worry and fear "tend to activate the norepinephrine system, the system of negative emotions. The result . . . is a reduced capacity to notice" (Lakoff, 2008, p. 41). In the political context, this helps explain why Canadians might overlook the greater costs associated with tax-fighting politics: partly because they are so worried about their own bottom line. They're encouraged to worry about it by both the politician and the pundit.

We are, as Canadians who pay taxes, a privileged bunch. We enjoy an average of $41,000 in free public services that many likely couldn't otherwise afford (Mackenzie & Shillington, 2009, p. 3), considering the average, unattached Canadian's income hovered at $32,100 in 2012 (Statistics Canada, 2012). Governments have given up billions of dollars in public revenues to tax cuts while cutting back public transit service, threatening to close libraries, failing to significantly reduce health care wait times, abandoning rural highways to potholes, and shutting down schools. Progressives ask, how can Canadians keep voting against their own best interests? By which sleight of hand are they continuously fooled?

Raymond Joseph Teller, one half of the Penn and Teller magic duo, says that among the magician's great secrets is the ability to exploit the human weakness for pattern recognition. In politics, this is accomplished through repetition of the message. *Your tax dollars at work. Tax cuts create jobs.* As every federal Conservative today well knows, don't go off script or your career will suffer. The magician also knows to keep the trickery outside the frame. He removes his coat and throws it aside—our eyes follow— while he cleverly pulls the card from his sleeve without notice. In politics, we see the politician sitting at a hockey game dressed in a CANADA sweatshirt or wearing a blue sweater vest, and we're too distracted to notice that he's performing the equivalent of sawing a tax in half before our very eyes. Can we really have decades of tax cuts and maintain the level of public health care, education, garbage collection, transit service, pothole patrol, affordable tuition, regulated child care, food safety inspection, and on and on? We cannot. But, as Penn the magician puts it, "Nothing fools you better than the lie you tell yourself" (Teller, 2009, pp. 23–24). Part of the magic of tax cuts is that we want to believe we can have them without any great sacrifice on our part. It's certainly the parlour trick Canadians have come to expect at election time.

The promise of a tax cut maintains its magical lure in Canada. It distracts us from imagining what we have in common. It reduces us to virtual ATMs, to individual citizens as consumers, vulnerable to a good sales pitch. Add the modern dimension of bitterly negative personal attack ads, and Conservative politicians in Canada have made quick work of *tax-and-spend* candidates. So much so that political strategists will say with assurance that you can't win on a platform to raise taxes. Cue the attack on the last two federal Liberal leaders: when Stéphane Dion tried as Liberal leader to introduce a carbon tax plan that many people would ordinarily consider sensible, he was reviled by Stephen Harper, the prime minister, as "insane" (PM: Dion's Carbon Tax, 2008). Conservative advertising in that election harped on "Dion's tax on everything." This was in ALL CAPS for added effect, and chased with the question, "Will *you* be fooled into paying more?" (CBC Radio, 2011). Dion's replacement, Michael Ignatieff, faced similar roughhousing when it came to taxes: "Michael Ignatieff's high-tax agenda will stall our recovery, kill jobs and set families back," was a talking point spouted by many a Conservative in the 2011 federal election (Conservative Party, April 26, 2011).

Cue the automatic *you're either with us, or you're against us* talking point. Cue the line about how corporations and wealthy individuals are the job creators in Canada upon whom we rely. The line about how corporate and individual tax cuts create jobs. If you've heard it once, you've heard it a thousand times, because that is just how diligent Canada's conservative politicians have been at marketing the low-tax agenda. Cue Jim Flaherty: "If we want more jobs, higher wages, an improved standard of living for all of us, Canada needs to be an attractive place for job-creators to do business and invest" (Whittington & Delacourt, 2011). Cue John Baird: "We are reducing taxes for businesses because it creates jobs and it creates economic growth. Our tax rates for job creators is one of the measures sustaining our fragile economic recovery" (Kennedy, 2011). Cue the rote recitation of the mantra *tax burden* (Tim Hudak MPP, 2010). As former MP Glen Pearson has written, "politics increasingly calls out to the petty in us" (2012). This political fascination with tax avoidance, it's making us think small.

Once, not so long ago, the political narrative was a little more generous. We cared a little more about who was let in and who was left out. Then, over the course of two decades, a counterinsurgency took hold in influential circles of Canada, and it fuelled a stark reversal in direction. Alberta and Ontario waged Texan-style political campaigns in the 1990s that made dartboards of the poor, eschewed government as wasteful and inefficient, revered "the market," attacked public service, and made iron-clad the political rule that the best thing government could do was to give you back "your money" in the form of tax cuts. Such was the cult-like devotion that legislators in most Canadian provinces came to enact into law the binding force of "balanced budgets"—code for constraining future governments from returning to the higher act of public service.

The hypocrisy of managerial politics is that many of its staunchest proponents deliver their low-tax promises by sacrificing the quality of public service and threatening their ability to quickly return to balanced budgets after a recession. They have been, in fact, terrible managers of our public purse. Across Canada today, governments everywhere have maintained tax cuts, prolonging the deficits stemming from the Great Recession of 2008–9 and advancing, instead, job-killing austerity plans that further diminish the quality of our public services. They are not simply rejecting the social bargain our parents and grandparents had struck in the postwar era; they are putting our very future at risk. And they are using the tools of polarizing politics to get their way. In a shrinking pool of public provisions, they pit resident against resident, worker against worker in a competitive and highly individual pursuit. Will it be iron-clad protection of our public pension system for low-income seniors? Low tuition for aspiring youth? Stronger supports for those who fall onto hard times? Or will it be another corporate tax cut? The managerial political class knows which side its bread is buttered on.

This aggressive, unrelenting, two-decade-long tax-hating narrative has cost Canada tens of billions annually in lost public revenues. Conveniently, these losses have actually become the *rationale* for cutting public programs, grist for the Conservative austerity push. It has accelerated the divide between those who have lots and those who do not. It has also reshaped Canadians' expectations of their elected leaders and diminished their hope for the future. The narrative supporting what once would have been considered a radical policy shift has made enemies of those who rely most on public service. In Alberta circa the 1990s, welfare applicants were offered bus tickets to British Columbia, such was the overt hostility toward that province's most vulnerable. The tax-hating narrative has also cast government in the most negative light possible. Government as bumbling idiot: wasting your money on inefficient red tape that hinders business development, or on public servants who cannot compete with the cutthroat rate of the private sector. Government as pig at the trough: addicted to spending. The tax fighter's loathing of taxes is rivaled by his disgust of government. The two are inextricably linked.

For progressives believing in the Canadian promise that every generation has the right to do better than the last and that government is here to serve the majority, this has been a bleak era. Everything our predecessors fought for and won in the name of social progress has been under intense and often successful political assault for almost two decades.

It has been our most resounding defeat—and I'm not simply referring to political defeat. Politics that reduces Canadians to the one-dimensional concept of individual taxpayer has a devolutionary effect: we regress into the screaming toddlers we once were, jealously protecting our toys from other sticky fingers. Every time we send an elected official into office with the mandate to cut spending and taxes, we are that toddler, crying the second the service we like gets cut, asking people in authority to take away another person's services, protecting our own promised tax cuts, and wanting the other person's tax cuts too.

Opponents of the current iteration of conservative politics unwittingly become a part of the magic act every time they counter with a personalized attack on the tax fighter. With former Ontario Premier Mike Harris and Alberta Premier Ralph Klein in the 1990s, with Prime Minister Stephen Harper today, and even with Toronto Mayor Rob Ford, opponents of their low-tax agenda failed by doing just that—by focusing on the shortcomings or dubious intentions of the individual, without providing the antidote to the financial worry conservative politics exploit. Though they rightly identify the tax fighter as a detriment to the social programs we hold dear, they reduce the ballot box question to one of personal trust. These tactics unintentionally reinforce the strategy of individualization that helps voters consider their own needs ahead of society's. They also allow tax-fighting politicians to appear as the only ones willing to work to protect your money.

Recently, progressives have shifted tactics, focusing on the idea of fairness, a deeply held Canadian value. But what do we mean when we speak of fair taxation? What is your idea of fairness? Paying less? Struggling less? When the tax-hater objects to paying for someone else's education, the objection arises out of a sense that it isn't fair to ask this of him. Mention fairness, and some will argue they've earned what they have on the steam of their own hard work and sacrifice. It is only fair, they will say, that governments return their hard-earned money. As Benjamin Hale wrote in the *New York Times*, referring to fairness in society, "it is an illusion of prosperity to believe that each of us deserves everything we get" (2012). It's a symptom of a prosperous society that has come to tolerate the spread of income inequality and the political treatment of citizens as self-serving individuals, rather than a part of a community whose well-being relies upon the goodwill of others. It is also an early warning of a society in decline, where everyone starts looking out for Number One, wary of what lies ahead. Certainly, it was that sense of a system stripped of its fairness—a notion that it isn't working for the 99%—that fuelled the Occupy movement of 2011. Tax fairness advocates often get trapped in the focus on the 1%, whereas the Occupy movement did us a favour by reframing inequality through the broader lens of the 99%, the majority.

As a group of citizens acting in the public interest, we might look at fairness in a different light. Is it fair that a growing number of Canadians are working hard, getting an education, playing by all the rules but receiving a shrinking share of the income pie while the richest 10%, 1%, 0.01% enjoy income gains that reflect the kind of extreme inequality of the 1920s? Is it fair that the wealthiest benefit most from the tax cut agenda, and yet are called upon less and less to do their part in contributing to a healthy society? Is it fair to hand elites more tax cuts as we begin to question the affordability of public health care and public pensions for retirees? The problem with fairness as a core argument is that it is not only in the eye of the beholder; it also reinforces a political trend that undermines democracy by pitting Canadians against one another. Fairness can encourage us to protect our own turf. On its own, tapping into fairness is not enough to change the conversation. The situation calls for a narrative that inspires unity and social responsibility.

We are all, first and foremost, social citizens. From the day we came screaming into this world we were social citizens, and we survived due to the goodwill of family, but also with the help of other social citizens. Contrary to popular belief, no one gets by on his or her own. As brilliant, driven, or entrepreneurial as we might be, we all have a thank-you letter to write. I fill out my income tax form every April 30, try not to grumble about it, and call it even. Historically, that's been the Canadian way. We have largely understood the benefits of broad-based taxation, and the importance of everyone carrying their share of the load. That's how we became international peacekeepers. How we fostered medicare. How, during a notable stretch of our history called the postwar era, we dreamed that we could be an economically prosperous, middle-class country, and also a kinder, more caring one. We did all that by leveraging taxes to build a better society.

When I was a young journalist, I interviewed an Irish Canadian author who had just published a book about Irish history. He said to me, "Hennessy. You're Irish."

"Yes. Well, French/Irish/Scottish," I replied.

He asked, "From where in Ireland do your people come?"

"Um, I don't really know," I stammered.

He leaned back into his chair. "If you don't know your history," he said, "you don't know yourself."

I'm not one to quibble with obvious truths. (As it turns out, it would appear that I am a long way from Tipperary.) When it comes to understanding our own country—and especially the factors such as public services that help Canada to be ranked among the best places to live—we third-generation, middle-class Canadians are a long way from our historical roots. Given that our status on the UN Human Development Index is slipping, we could use a few reminders of our past, and not just for a sense of nostalgia. All that glittered then wasn't necessarily gold. But appreciating our history tells us why it is we came to look at taxation as a public good in the first place. It allows us to understand the role taxes have played in making Canada what it is today, and to gain a clearer idea of where we want to go as a country.

1917. That's the year Canada enacted its first income tax. It was meant to pay for Canada's First World War deficit (Birth of Income Tax, 2011). It came to be understood, especially after the Second World War, as a mechanism for building grander dreams: they called it the welfare state, but with its public services and income supports, it really was the great equalizer.

1943. That year, the average taxes paid by Canada's richest 0.01% peaked, at 71%. Given the pressing nature of the Second World War, Canada's elites rose to a higher calling. The job creators didn't leave the country, jobs didn't vanish, and rich people didn't hire expensive accountants to elude their duty—all the threats we hear today when someone suggests asking those who have more to contribute more in taxes. In the mid-1940s, Canada needed help, and those with the most to contribute did so. In contrast, by 2000, the average taxes paid by the richest 0.01% dropped to 33% (CCPA, 2012).

1965. The year I was born, something significant happened: Lester Pearson was re-elected Prime Minister on the promise to create a public pension plan (CPP, QPP) and expand universal public health care. Pearson implemented the federal Medical Care Act in 1966 (Health Care, 2012), creating a public system that places the state of our health above the state of our individual bank accounts. And this happened in my lifetime. One hundred years ago, it didn't exist.

Over time, the notion of what's radical and on the fringes of public acceptability shifts. This helps explain what we've witnessed in Canada over the last 20 or so years: an extreme shift in public perception about the role of taxation as a public good, a civic duty. There was a time not very long ago in Canadian history when it was unthinkable that mayors, premiers, and prime ministers could coast to victory on the strength of a political agenda that sacrificed public service for the sake of a tax cut. That a political leader would feel good about putting a tax cut ahead of better supports for the unemployed, for children, for the vulnerable. That a government might close a library or cancel a youth program instead of raising a tax.

Once, not so long ago, we believed our governments existed to enact policy and spending decisions reflective of the needs of the majority. Canada was a land of opportunity, a place where you could realize the liberating potential of social and economic mobility by risking it all to leave "the old country." Canada did not revere the cult of rugged individualism in quite the same way as our American neighbours did. We valued equality of opportunity, but also equality of outcome. That meant you were entitled to free and/or affordable high-quality public education and good health care, the tools you need to thrive. It was our way of giving everyone a fair chance. But it also meant that we considered individual success as tied to others. It wasn't enough to do well personally; it was a measure of success that those around us were doing well, too. It's why income inequality narratives maintain their appeal where poverty narratives fall short. We get it if it's put in relative terms. The challenge for progressives is to keep us all in the narrative.

Progressives would do well to return to the politics of empathy, to an ethic of care, to the humanized aspect of sharing a country, a province, a city, a neighbourhood. We've gotten lost in analytic critiques of government cuts, trapping ourselves in defending the indefensible: public programs that should be so much better than they are, but can't be for lack of adequate funding. In our defensiveness, we find small victories in minimizing the cuts rather than conditioning the field for better public services, and more of them, like a national child care program that reflects the fact that the vast majority of child-bearing women also hold down a paying job. Opposition politics has failed to rise above the fray. Far too often, the opposition pounces on wedge issues in a desperate effort to maintain voter support rather than lead with a visionary call to public service. Even ostensibly middle-of-the-road political leaders—the ones Canadians are urged to "strategically vote" for in order to avert a hard-right government—joined in the tax-cutting game as a means of shoring up their right flank. But the right still ascended.

It's time to walk away from the current conversation about taxes. Progressives who talk about raising taxes without connecting it to the broader social benefit lose the political argument. They disengage us from that higher calling as social citizens. As progressives, we have failed to counter the dehumanizing, polarizing narrative of the tax-haters. We have been ahistorical. We have lacked the fervour of the committed tax-cutter. We have been more comfortable in the critic's chair than we are in the visionary's chair.

Where is our Pearson? Our Pierre Elliott Trudeau? Our Tommy Douglas?

Perhaps we need not wait for the perfect political saviour. Social progressives are stirring in Canada. The Occupy movement shook things up for a time. The Quebec student movement has yielded some of the largest protests in Canadian history. A group of doctors, many of whom acknowledge they are among

Canada's richest, have formed Doctors for Tax Fairness, a group that lobbies for income-tax hikes on the rich in the service of sparing cuts to equalizing programs such as public health care. Lawyers for Tax Fairness has followed suit. Canadians for Tax Fairness is leading the way nationally, examining new ways to counter the tax-hating narrative. The opportunity is there for Canadians to change the conversation, but it requires a little magic of our own. The question, when it comes to taxation, is not how much more to tax. It is not which taxes to raise. The fundamental question is: What is taxation for?

Changing the conversation requires answering this vital question, and then making the case for taxes based on that answer. At first, income taxes were a way of paying down a deficit incurred by the First World War. During the Second World War, taxes helped finance the war effort. Taxation also became a tool to build the infrastructure required to accommodate burgeoning cities. It was seen as a means of striving for equality, by asking those who have more to contribute extra for our shared well-being, but also by asking all income earners and corporations to contribute to public services that functioned as great equalizers. Once, as Canadians, we had grander dreams.

Meanwhile, there is untapped potential within the great debate for Canada's future. Sixty-four percent: that's how many Canadians are willing to pay slightly higher taxes to protect our social programs. Sixty percent: that's how many Canadians say they'd be more likely to support a political party willing to raise taxes on the rich (Hennessy, 2012). In the focus groups, we hear this too. We hear the pragmatism. Canadians know what goes down must eventually go up. They know someone, somewhere, is going to raise their taxes. Environics Research asked Canadians a revealing poll question: What do you do that makes you feel like a good citizen? Number three on the list of responses? Pay taxes (Environics, 2012, p. 8). Many Canadians see tax contribution as an act of social citizenship, a measure of the public good.

That concept of virtue has been erased from the Canadian political discourse (Hennessy 2013). Our political leaders have not yet caught up with citizens on this front. We may have to show them the way. If we hope to change what is politically acceptable in Canadian society, then it falls to us—not as self-serving taxpayers, but as social citizens concerned about our future and knowing we can make a difference. It's the same conclusion my grandparents' and parents' generation reached decades ago. The time has come to lift the veil on the illusory power of the tax-hater. There is no rabbit in that hat. It was always a cheap parlour trick. Nothing more, nothing less.

References

The Birth of Income Tax (1917). (2007, September 11). In *Duhaime.org LawMuseum: Canadian Legal History*. Retrieved from http://www.duhaime.org/LawMuseum/Canadian LegalHistory/LawArticle-168/1917-The-Birth-of-Income-Tax.aspx

Canadian Centre for Policy Alternatives (CCPA). (2011, January 10). *Why are Canadian corporate taxes so low?* (Alternative Federal Budget). Retrieved from http://www.policyalternatives.ca/newsroom/updates/why-are-canadian-corporate-taxes-so-low

Canadian Centre for Policy Alternatives (CCPA). (2012, January 25). The 99% vs. The 1% [Infographic for the Growing Gap Initiative]. Retrieved from http://www.policyalternatives.ca/publications/commentary/infographic-99-vs-1

CBC Radio. (2011). Dion's tax on everything [Conservative election campaign advertisements]. *The House* [radio show]. Retrieved from http://www.cbc.ca/thehouse/assets_c/2011/01/tax%20on%20everything-73356.html

Conservative Party of Canada (Hamilton East–Stoney Creek). (2011, April 3). Harper announces new adult fitness tax credit [Web log post]. Retrieved from http://hescconservative.ca/harper-announces-new-adult-fitness-tax-credit/

Conservative Party of Canada (Maureen Harquail for St. Paul's, Toronto). (2011, April 26). Harper's low-tax plan supports Canadian families [Web log post]. Retrieved from http://maureenharquail.org/2011/04/26/harper%E2%80%99s-low-tax-plan-supports-canadian-families/

Environics Research. (2012, February). *Canadians on citizenship* (national survey). Retrieved from http://www.environicsinstitute.org/uploads/institute-projects/citizenship2011report.pdf

Finn, E. (2012, July). Government's forgone income. *The Monitor*. Retrieved from http://www.policyalternatives.ca/publications/monitor/governments-forgone-income

Goldsbie, J. (2012, July 20). Rob Ford explains his stance on gun crime and citizenship. *The Grid*. Retrieved from http://www.thegridto.com/city/politics/rob-ford-explains-his-stance-on-gun-crime-and-citizenship/

Hale, B. (2012, August 12). Opinion pages: The veil of opulence. *New York Times*. Retrieved from http://opinionator.blogs.nytimes.com/2012/08/12/the-veil-of-opulence/?smid=tw-share

Health care in Canada. (2012, September 7). *Wikipedia*. Retrieved from http://en.wikipedia.org/wiki/Health_care_in_Canada

Hennessy, T. (2012, May 1). *Taxing times* (CCPA fact sheet). Retrieved from http://www.policyalternatives.ca/publications/commentary/taxing-times

Hennessy, T. (2013). Carrying the torch. In R. Swift & Canadians for Tax Fairness, *The great revenue robbery*. Toronto, ON: Between the Lines.

Hudak announces tax relief for families. (2010). *Tim Hudak MPP* [Website]. Retrieved from http://timhudakmpp.com/news/hudak-announces-tax-relief-for-families/

Kennedy, M. (2011, January 25). Corporate tax cuts needed for recovery, Baird says. *Windsor Star*. Retrieved from http://www2.canada.com/windsorstar/news/business/story.html?id=650673f8-ad15-435c-b862-2a36f5055008

Lakoff, G. (2008). *The political mind*. New York, NY: Penguin Group.

Lorinc, J. (2011, June 5). Ford's "respect for taxpayers" mandate is about to get real. *Globe and Mail*. Retrieved from http://www.theglobeandmail.com/news/toronto/fords-respect-for-taxpayers-mandate-is-about-to-get-real/article4261872/

Mackenzie, H. (2009, October 26). Can we have an adult conversation about taxes? *Toronto Star*. Retrieved from http://www.thestar.com/opinion/2009/10/26/can_we_have_an_adult_conversation_about_taxes.html

Mackenzie, H., & Shillington, R. (2009). *Canada's quiet bargain: The benefits of quiet spending* (CCPA Growing Gap Project, April 15, 2009). Retrieved from Canadian Centre for Policy Alternatives, http://www.policyalternatives.ca/sites/default/files/uploads/publications/National_Office_Pubs/2009/Benefits_From_Public_Spending.pdf

Organisation for Economic Co-operation and Development (OECD). (2011). *Country Note–Canada* (Education at a Glance 2011). Retrieved from http://www.oecd.org/canada/48687311.pdf

Pearson, G. (2012, August 15). Beware the Sciopods and the Blemmyaes [Web log post]. Retrieved from http://glenpearson.ca/2012/08/beware-the-sciopods-and-the-blemmyaes/

PM: Dion's carbon tax would "screw everybody." (2008, June 20). *CBC News Canada Online*. Retrieved from http://www.cbc.ca/news/canada/story/2008/06/20/harper-carbon.html

Statistics Canada. (2012). *Average income after tax by economic family types* [Summary table]. Retrieved from http://www.statcan.gc.ca/tables-tableaux/sum-som/l01/cst01/famil21a-eng.htm

Sun News Network. (2012, April 4). *Daily Brief: Respecting Taxpayers* [Video]. Available from http://www.sunnewsnetwork.ca/video/1547579242001

Teller, R. J. (2012). Sorcery. *Lapham's Quarterly*, 5(2), 23–24.

What's happening in the Department of Economics. (Fall 2004). *Tradeoffs: Department of Economics Newsletter*. Retrieved from http://homes.chass.utoronto.ca/~floyd/newsletter/newslett.f04.html

Whittington, L., & Delacourt, S. (2011, January 27). Tory tax cuts could trigger election. *Toronto Star*. Retrieved from http://www.thestar.com/news/canada/article/929037--tory-tax-cuts-could-trigger-election?bn=1

Wintery Knight. (2011, April 29). Conservative Stephen Harper will cut taxes for families [Web log post]. Retrieved from http://winteryknight.wordpress.com/2011/04/29/conservative-stephen-harper-will-cut-taxes-for-families/

Part III ▶ A Different Take on Taxes

Of course in all matters of public policy, the details matter. As University of Toronto Professor Joseph Heath points out, the countries that have the biggest social programs and the highest taxes typically take the greatest care in how they design both their services and their taxes. Most policy experts have probably forgotten that the FDR New Deal in the US was approached as an experiment; its architects understood that innovation, learning, and constant adjustment would be key to breaking out of the Great Depression. The countries of Northern Europe have demonstrated similar innovation and a commitment to learning as they have adapted policies and taxes to changing circumstances. Some have come to rely more heavily on value-added taxes, generally viewed as regressive, and have cut corporate taxes to give themselves a competitive edge. Norway, an energy-producing country like Canada, has committed to doubling its carbon taxes and squeezes far more revenue from its natural resources than we do. Many have introduced or are introducing financial transaction taxes. And all of them tax more heavily than we do, and the rich carry a larger burden there than they do here. These countries have been equally aggressive in reforming their social programs in ways that fit their unique cultures and economies and that prepare them for the future.

In this global economy, many tax reforms would be most effective if they resulted from international agreements where all or most countries introduced carbon taxes or financial transaction taxes, for example, but as some of these higher-taxing jurisdictions have shown us, much can be achieved by any country on its own where the political will exists.

In this section, Marc Lee and Iglika Ivanova of the Canadian Centre for Policy Alternatives in BC provide a comprehensive view of what a truly progressive tax system might look like, making concrete recommendations on the right mix of taxes. Their comprehensive approach tries to balance economic, social, and environmental objectives.

Stéphane Dion, former leader of the Liberal Party of Canada, former minister of the environment and current Liberal MP, makes the case for a revenue-neutral and progressive carbon tax as key to addressing climate change, and asks what it will take to make these taxes politically saleable.

Toby Sanger, senior economist with the Canadian Union of Public Employees, makes the case for financial transaction taxes, already taken up by a number of jurisdictions, not only as a source of substantial revenue but also as an important economic measure to reduce speculation and shift emphasis to the "real economy" that produces goods and services. Recognizing some of the challenges for Canada of going it alone, he also explores more modest ways to tap into the profits of our financial institutions.

And finally, Scott Clark, former deputy minister of finance, describes how a simpler, economically smarter tax system would look. He highlights the importance of closing tax loopholes and treating "tax expenditures"—the growing and costly list of credits provided to individuals and corporations through the tax system—with the same rigour with which we treat all spending. He also provides an extended discussion of the GST/HST, raising important questions about the recent and significant cuts.

What all these authors share, notwithstanding their differences, is the conviction that the current Canadian tax system is not designed for our future, tax reform is essential, and constant cutting is not the answer.

Chapter 9

Toward a Fair Canadian Tax System

Marc Lee and Iglika Ivanova

Introduction: The Case for Progressive Tax Reform

The most comprehensive tax review undertaken in the developed world in the last decade, the Mirrlees Review in the United Kingdom, concluded that a good tax system must be both progressive and neutral. This is to say, it "can raise the revenue that government needs to achieve its spending and distributional ambitions whilst minimizing economic and administrative inefficiency, keeping the system as simple and transparent as possible, and avoiding arbitrary tax differentiation across people and forms of economic activity" (Mirrlees et al., 2011, pp. 471–472).[1] These principles of a good tax system are not new or controversial; they have been articulated by other major tax reviews in the past, though there is still an active debate in the economics and law literature on how to best operationalize them through public policy.

A good tax system must be progressive for reasons of fairness and justice, but also on economic grounds (Diamond & Saez, 2011).[2] The marginal utility of money declines as income rises—that is, the perceived and actual benefit derived from an extra dollar of income is much higher for someone panhandling on the street than it is for someone driving past in a Mercedes. It follows that social welfare is higher when resources are more equally distributed—at least, up to the point where incentives to work and invest in productive activities become severely distorted. In addition, to the extent that money can buy opportunities, particularly for young children, progressive taxation serves to redistribute opportunities and improve social mobility.

Progressive taxation is particularly important in the presence of high levels of market income inequality and concentration of wealth at the very top of the income distribution, as we are increasingly seeing in Canada. Yet, as previous chapters have pointed out, Canada has moved in the opposite direction over the past two decades: changes in the tax system and overall tax reductions have tended to reinforce growing income inequalities, rather than leaning against them (see also Conference Board of Canada, 2011).

The most recent comprehensive study of tax incidence in Canada by Marc Lee (2007) finds that tax changes between 1990 and 2005 have greatly eroded the progressivity of our tax system. By 2005, the tax system was progressive only up to the middle of the income distribution, then flattened out and actually became regressive at the very top. As a result, Canada's top 1% of households faced overall tax rates slightly lower than those in the bottom 10%, with the highest tax rates found in the middle to upper-middle part of the income distribution.

In its current state, the Canadian tax system does not pass the basic test of fairness. This needs to change. A return to more progressive taxation would restore fairness, while also providing a lever to directly reduce income inequality. Given the large and growing body of research exposing the corrosive effects of high levels of inequality, reform that seeks to improve the redistributive capacity of our tax system would yield broad-based social and economic benefits.[3]

A key step toward more progressive taxes would be to ensure that wealthier individuals contribute their fair share to the public purse. The federal income tax is the most progressive of Canada's taxes, but its progressivity is undermined because many sources of income for high earners—investment returns from stock options and capital gains, for example—are given preferential treatment and taxed more lightly than income from wages and salaries. And while statutory tax rates increase with income (through tax brackets), higher-income Canadians are also able to avail themselves of generous tax deductions like RRSP contributions that greatly lower their effective tax rates. At the same time, top earners will have long maxed out total contributions to payroll taxes; that is, the total taxes they pay for their pensions and unemployment insurance stop growing even as their total incomes soar.

Low-income households, in contrast, pay little in income tax, but are also generally unable to avail themselves of many credits and deductions that, in the end, disproportionately benefit those with high incomes. The exceptions are refundable tax credits and income-tested transfers such as the Goods and Services tax credit (GST) and the Canada child tax benefit (CCTB).[4] The challenge at the bottom of the income distribution is consumption taxes like the GST that are regressive, in that everybody pays exactly the same rate. Lower-income families consume almost all of their income (and then some, with many households in debt), so they end up paying a higher share of their total income in GST than higher-income households, who can afford to save or invest a significant share of their incomes. While exempting basic necessities and providing a small income-tested transfer (the GST credit) can improve tax fairness among the families with the lowest incomes, this system could be greatly improved by increasing the GST credit and extending its reach into middle income levels.

In what follows, we outline the major elements of a progressive tax reform strategy for Canada, drawn from our review of the rich literature on tax policy design. These reforms will lay the foundation for a modern, fair tax system that is capable of raising revenues with minimal distortions to investment in productive and sustainable economic activities, and will result in a more just distribution of income and direct improvements in the life of low-income households.

An Agenda for Progressive Tax Reform

A fair Canadian tax system must be progressive across all sources of income and all types of taxes: federal, provincial/territorial, and local. That said, large-scale progressive tax reforms are best undertaken at the federal level to ensure that all Canadians, regardless of their place of residence, are taxed under the same fair system, and to avert harmful tax competition among provinces. This is why we focus on federal reforms that will make Canada's tax system more progressive, although many of the findings and recommendations we present are also relevant for provincial governments. Federal taxes (including payroll taxes like EI and CPP premiums) raise just under half of all taxes in Canada today, but the federal government has given away considerable fiscal room to the provinces and territories over the last two decades.[5] As Robin Boadway argued in an earlier chapter, this may have to be re-evaluated to ensure that the Canadian tax system is progressive in its entirety.

Our proposal for a fair tax system draws on two major tax bases: income and value-added. These bases are often pitted against each other as alternative approaches, but we believe there is a compelling case for having two broad tax bases for political economy reasons, as there are widely acknowledged practical limits to how much any given base can be taxed due to political resistance and/or disincentive effects. We stick to the broad elements of progressive tax reform, and note that there is much room for different specific formulations.

Fundamentally, all tax and transfer policies must be considered as the interconnected elements of a single, well-integrated tax *system*. Personal income tax and transfer measures are the most progressive elements of any tax system and are, as the Mirrlees review explains, widely considered to be the "right tools for achieving distributional objectives" (2011, pp. 4–12). Value-added taxes like the GST, though inherently regressive, can be an effective way of raising revenues to fund public services as long as adequate income transfers are provided to low- and modest-income households to compensate them for their loss of purchasing power, and the tax *system* remains progressive overall.

We recommend that a fair tax reform package for Canada focus on the following seven priority areas:

1. Broaden the Income Tax Base

A fair tax system should be based on a broad or comprehensive income concept that reflects the individual's actual *command over resources*. This is also known as "horizontal equity": the principle that two people with the same amount of income in a given year pay the same rate of tax regardless of the source of that income. Bay Street accountant Kenneth Carter, who headed a Royal Commission on taxation in the 1960s, captured this notion with his comment, "a buck is a buck." This principle has been eroded in Canada substantially in recent decades in the name of promoting economic efficiency and growth by lowering, and in some cases eliminating, income tax rates on capital income.

There is an active and spirited debate in the modern tax literature on the best way to tax income from capital.[6] Many economists argue that income from capital should be taxed at a lower rate than income from labour, or not at all, to encourage savings (and thus investment and economic growth). It is not clear why this need be the case—in a fiat money system, the expansion of credit money through the banking system finances new investment, so investment is not limited by the deposits saved by households. Nor is there any evidence that the Canadian economy suffers from a shortage of capital. In fact, the accumulated cash holdings of private, non-financial corporations are at record-high levels as a result of recent corporate income tax cuts, and were valued at $567 billion in the second quarter of 2012 (Statistics Canada, 2012).[7]

Arguments for preferential treatment of capital income have been predicated on theoretical micro-efficiency gains for which there is simply no compelling evidence (Diamond & Saez, 2011). Reduced rates on capital income unfairly privilege high-income households, who tend to earn a larger share of their income from capital, and thereby increase income and wealth inequality. Broadening the tax base would allow government to raise the same amount of revenue with lower tax rates, or if desired, to raise more revenue at the prevailing rates.

Currently, different forms of income face different tax treatment under the Canadian income tax system. Wages and salaries are taxed in accordance with the four federal tax brackets and rates. In contrast, only half the value of realized capital gains from financial assets and secondary real estate sales is counted as income for tax purposes. Sales of primary residences are not subject to any capital gains tax (even though considerable gains can and have been made in hot urban real estate markets). And there is a lifetime capital gains exemption of $750,000 for farmers and small businesses.

Realized capital gains represent real dollars in sellers' pockets and should be fully included in the income tax base. Forgone revenues are substantial: partial inclusion of capital gains represented an income loss of $3.6 billion, the lifetime capital gains exemption for small business costs $560 million, and the non-taxation of capital gains on principal residences $4.2 billion in 2011.[8] Differences in tax treatment due to untaxed or lightly taxed sources of income—made in the name of efficiency—in fact create incentives for tax avoidance and evasion (for example, tax-motivated conversions of high-taxed labour income into low-taxed capital gains or dividends through corporations). Moving to a comprehensive personal income tax base would ensure that all sources of income are taxed at the same rates and reduce distortions related to the increasingly lucrative business of "tax planning."

Capital income from investments in Tax-Free Savings Accounts (TFSAs) is exempt from income tax entirely. The TFSA is a relatively new program, launched in 2009, but emerging evidence shows that even with the current maximum of $5,000 per person per year since 2009, these savings vehicles will significantly reduce the income tax base in Canada over a generation and represent pure windfall gains for the wealthiest Canadians, undermining both efficiency and fairness in the tax system (and even more so if the annual deposit limits are increased, as some have proposed).[9] This program should be eliminated, or at least restricted to investments that meet a public interest test, such as investments in the green economy. Registered Education Savings Plans (RESPs), which work on the same principle of non-taxation of capital income, privilege families with large enough incomes to invest in them, and should likewise be scrapped in favour of grants aimed at facilitating greater access for students from low-income families.

Outside of capital gains on principal residences, the most significant sources of income that are currently tax-free are: gifts and bequests, inheritances, lottery winnings, and certain employer-provided benefits, such as extended health benefits and pension plan contributions.

Capital income is distributed even more unequally than employment income. Canada Revenue Agency tax statistics show that in 2010, Canadians with income over $250,000 were more than three times as likely to report income from interest and other investments than those with income under $50,000, seven times as likely to have taxable dividend income, and almost ten times as likely to have income from capital gains.

Typically, the forms of income taxed at lower (or zero) rates tend to make up a larger share of richer Canadians' income. This reinforces widening income inequalities and reduces the revenue collection capacity of the tax system.

In light of these practical and equity concerns, we recommend broadening the income tax base to ensure that income from all sources is taxed according to the same progressive rate schedule, including self-employment income, property, savings and dividend income, and capital gains. In some cases, such as lottery winnings, sales of principal residences, other long-held assets, or family farm/business bequests, provisions for income averaging over several years should be implemented to accommodate large fluctuations in annual income.

This could include a deduction for general inflation so that only gains above it are subject to full income tax, but the key principle is that capital gains be taxed in the same manner as income from wages and salaries.[10]

2. Rationalizing Tax Expenditures

Canada's income tax system contains a large number of deductions and tax credits (both refundable and non-refundable), known collectively as "tax expenditures." Rather than actual expenditures funded by taxes, these represent forgone tax revenue and lower effective tax rates. While the top marginal federal tax rate is currently 29%, the average effective income tax rate paid by the richest 1% of Canadians was only 19.7% in 2008 (Finance Canada, 2012).

Some tax expenditures seek to achieve a public policy objective, such as increased saving for retirement, investment in research and development, investment in economic activities (such as exploration and mining), and support for charitable activities. Others are in place to assist individuals who have a reduced ability to pay taxes due to personal circumstances (such as deductions for medical expenditures and tax credits for children), or because they incur costs before they can earn income (education). Other tax expenditures represent adjustments to avoid double taxation at corporate and personal levels.

In recent years, we have seen a proliferation of relatively small tax deductions and credits that cater to very narrow groups, such as the public transit tax credit and the children's fitness and arts tax credits. These credits are wasteful, make the income tax system less transparent and more complex, yet once they are put in place there is little public accountability for the amount of money spent on them, and their effectiveness is not measured. A number of recent studies have challenged the effectiveness of several tax expenditure programs to achieve their stated goals, including many of the "boutique" tax credits and RRSPs.[11]

Whether or not these measures are desirable and effective in achieving their objectives, they have distributional impacts: they directly affect the taxes paid by different income and demographic groups, and indirectly they reduce available revenues that could be used for income transfers or public services. Indeed, a large number of current deductions and credits disproportionately benefit high earners, as evident in the tax data from the Canada Revenue Agency shown in Table 9.1. The table breaks down income, key deductions, and credits by three total income groups: greater than $250,000 income, $50,000 to $250,000 income, and less than $50,000 income.[12] It shows that while tax filers with income greater than $250,000 made up only 0.8% of all tax filers in 2010, they claimed 89% of the value of the security options deduction, 66% of all exploration and development expense tax credits, 50% of all taxable capital gains, and 40% of the federal dividend tax credit. In contrast, tax filers with income under $50,000 made up 73% of all tax filers and earned 38% of the total income in Canada, but claimed less than 0.5% of the value of the security options deduction, 2% of the exploration and development expense tax credits, 10% of the taxable capital gains, and 9% of the federal dividend tax credit.

Table 9.1 Selected individual tax statistics, 2010 tax year

	Tax filers with less than $50,000 income	Tax filers with income between $50,000 and $250,000	Tax filers with income greater than $250,000
Number of tax filers	9,767,100	6,460,690	186,100
Share of all tax filers	73.1%	26.1%	0.8%
Value of income, deductions, and credits claimed by each group as a share of the total amount claimed			
Employment income	31.9%	60.4%	7.6%
Taxable amount of dividends	11.4%	50.7%	37.8%
Taxable capital gains	9.9%	40.3%	49.8%
Registered Retirement Savings Plan income	43.5%	50.1%	6.4%
Total income assessed	37.7%	52.2%	10.1%
Registered pension plan contributions	17.9%	80.3%	1.8%
Registered Retirement Savings Plan deduction	17.9%	73.2%	8.9%
Exploration and development expenses	2.1%	31.8%	66.0%
Security options deductions	0.3%	10.3%	89.4%
Taxable income assessed	37.9%	52.0%	10.1%
Children's fitness amount	30.9%	65.1%	4.0%
Allowable charitable donations and government gifts	23.5%	51.8%	24.7%
Federal dividend tax credit	9.2%	50.5%	40.3%
Total federal and provincial tax payable	17.3%	62.9%	19.8%
Average effective income tax rate			
Federal	4.7%	12.3%	19.9%
Federal and provincial	6.8%	17.9%	29.0%

Source: Our calculations from Canada Revenue Agency, 2012 T1 Preliminary Statistics 2010 tax year, Table 2: All Returns by Total Income Class.

Finance Canada provides estimates of the value of tax expenditures in the federal income tax system in their annual *Tax Expenditures and Evaluations* reports. In total, personal income tax expenditures are projected to cost the federal treasury $143.7 billion in 2011—equivalent to 72% of total federal taxation revenues and 120% of federal income tax revenues in 2011/12.[13] Corporate income tax expenditures are estimated at an additional $27.1 billion. While it would not be desirable to eliminate many of these measures due to the structural issues or public policy considerations mentioned above, the sheer magnitude of forgone tax revenues calls for a re-evaluation of tax expenditures, their effectiveness and their distributional impacts.

Of particular interest from a distributional perspective are:

RRSP and registered pension plan deductions (net tax expenditures of $9.9 billion and $15.6 billion respectively in 2011): These deductions reduce income for tax purposes in order to encourage savings for retirement, at which time withdrawals are taxed typically at a lower rate than at the time initial income is earned. The evidence shows that these deductions disproportionately benefit individuals with higher incomes (see Table 9.1). In the case of RRSPs, which are "optional," only a small handful earn enough to take full advantage of their contribution room.[14] Clearly, families who are living paycheque to paycheque are unlikely to make much use of these measures.

Broad-based non-refundable tax credits: The basic personal amount, spouse or common-law partner amount, amount for eligible dependents, and children ($29.5 billion, $1.4 billion, $0.8 billion, and $1.5 billion, respectively)—effectively exempt the first $10,527 of individual net income after deductions from taxation, serving as a de facto bottom bracket of 0% for personal income tax (the amount exempt from taxes is higher for those with a stay-at-home or low-earning spouse and children). While this reduces the tax rate of low-income households, many do not earn enough to benefit from the full amount of this non-refundable credit (18% of tax filers reported total income under $10,000 in 2010). More importantly, the credit also clearly benefits the most affluent individuals, who pay no tax on the first $10,527 of their net income. This is a very expensive way to reduce tax rates for low- and modest-income Canadians. Eliminating or substantially reducing these credits and flowing the resulting revenue back to low- and modest-income households in the form of a transfer would greatly strengthen the progressivity of the tax system (more on this below).

Employee stock option deduction ($725 million): This deduction permits recipients of stock options to pay tax at half the statutory rate of ordinary income when they are realized. The principal beneficiaries of this measure are a very small number of people concentrated at the very top of the income distribution: already highly paid CEOs and executives, who receive enormous tax savings as a result (Sandler, 2001). For example, Toby Sanger (2010) estimates that this measure saved $24 million in taxes for Robert Gratton, former CEO of Power Corp, in just one tax year. CRA data shows that only 0.2% of all tax filers claimed a security options deduction, and 89% of the value of the deduction went to individuals with an income over $250,000 (see Table 9.1 above).

Charitable donations and gifts ($2.3 billion personal, and $390 million corporate): This tax credit enables well-off individuals and families to determine privately what types of charitable activities will be pursued by society.[15] In the words of Neil Brooks, it "allows them to buy public monuments and recognition for themselves and to give legitimacy to social indifference" (2007a).[16] In fact, the Canadian government has increased its reliance on charity to address pressing social problems, such as feeding and housing the marginalized, problems that are more appropriately tackled by elected and publicly accountable policymakers. Moreover, the credit's two tiers (a 15% credit for the first $200 and 29% above that) are structured in a way that provides greater benefit to higher-income households.

3. Increase Top Income Tax Rates

In Canada, the addition of one or more high-income tax brackets would greatly improve tax fairness, while also tackling income inequality at the top end. Canada has seen significant declines in both the top marginal income tax rate and the income level it kicks in at since the early 1970s. These rate reductions at the top have made our tax system less effective in mitigating market-driven increases in inequality, and particularly the concentration of income at the top. Economists Emmanuel Saez and Michael Veall (2005) looked at the top marginal income tax rate in Canada between 1920 and 2000, using the province of Ontario as an example, and found that by the year 2000, the top rate had fallen to the lowest it had been since the Depression Era. There were no changes to the top tax rates federally or in Ontario between 2000 and 2011, leaving the top marginal income tax rate at 46.41%.

However, this trend of lower taxes at the top may be at an end, at least provincially. Ontario introduced a new tax bracket for income over $500,000 as of July 1, 2012.[17] Quebec increased the tax rate for those making more than $100,000 per year as of January 1, 2013. And British Columbia recently raised taxes on income above $150,000 (albeit temporarily, for the 2014 and 2015 tax years).

The top income tax bracket in Canada kicked in at an income of $132,406 in 2012. While less than 5% of Canadian tax filers had total income over that

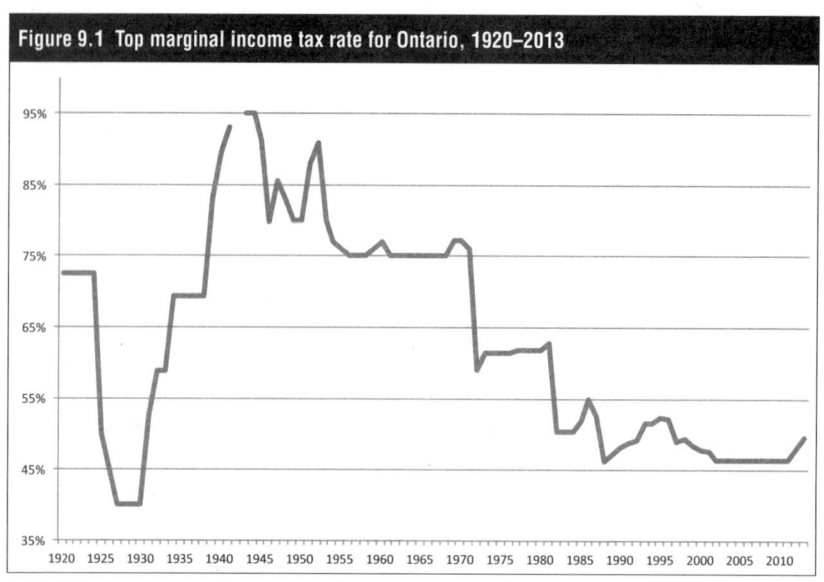

Figure 9.1 Top marginal income tax rate for Ontario, 1920–2013

Source: Data up to and including 2000 from Yalnizyan (2010). Data originally from Saez and Veall (2005). Data from 2002 to 2013 are our calculations based on Canada Revenue Agency provincial and federal tax forms for these years, and Ontario government announcements of the new tax bracket for income over $500,000, which kicked in July 2012.

threshold in 2010, the reality of increasing income concentration at the very top suggests that additional tax brackets should be set at the top 1% and 0.1% of income. Research on Canadian income distribution suggests that appropriate thresholds may be around $240,000 and $650,000.[18]

While there may be some theoretical limit to how progressive upper-bracket tax rates can be, we are not close to rates that would have adverse economic consequences. A US study by Diamond and Saez (2011) estimates the "optimal" top marginal tax rate (applying to income above the threshold for the top 1% of earners) to be 73%, taking into account real economic responses to tax changes among high-income earners, and as much as 80% if a broader income tax base is used and there are no deductions and loopholes to allow tax avoidance. These amounts are substantially higher than the prevailing US top marginal tax rate of 42.5%.

In a recent review of tax and transfer policy in Canada, Robin Boadway (2011) notes that capital income tends to be more responsive to changes in the tax rate than labour income, and he argued that this is a compelling reason for separating capital income from labour income for tax purposes. Boadway is a proponent of what is known as a "dual-income" tax system, in which labour income is taxed at steep progressive rates, while capital income is taxed according to a different rate schedule (he suggests a flat rate). This type of tax model is used by the Nordic countries, which have been successful at combining greater equality with dynamic economies (though it is not clear whether this is because of a streamlined tax system, or other factors that produce a much more equal market income distribution to begin with).

We are not persuaded that such reforms are necessary in Canada, and favour a comprehensive income tax base as the fairest way to implement a progressive tax system. That said, practical implementation issues and concerns of capital flight merit the consideration of a dual-income tax system, a second-best solution with regard to fairness. Such a shift would worsen inequality because higher-income individuals, who tend to get a higher share of their income from capital, would be paying lower effective tax rates. To compensate for this and ensure that the tax *system* overall remains progressive, dual-income taxation should be accompanied by inheritance and gift/bequest taxes and more steeply progressive personal income taxes.[19]

4. Stop the Corporate Tax "Race to the Bottom"

Corporations are legal vehicles by which individuals pool their capital in order to accumulate income. Corporation income taxes have emerged as means of ensuring that all income gets taxed, and reduce the incentive for individuals to shelter income from tax by keeping it within a corporation. At some point, however, income and capital gains must revert back to an individual (during one's lifetime or upon death), at which point they are subject to the personal income tax system.

A detailed review of corporate tax reform is beyond the scope of this chapter. However, we note that it would be possible for Canadian corporate income tax rates to rise, given that at 28.8% overall (provincial and federal combined) they are currently the lowest among G8 countries, and considerably lower than US rates (44.8%) (PricewaterhouseCooper, the World Bank, and International Finance Corp., 2012). The US taxes corporations based on their worldwide income, so Canadian corporate tax rates lower than the US rates represent a transfer of tax revenue from the Canadian to the US government (Weir, 2009, 2011).

Rhys Kesselman (2004) argues for a shift of business taxation to a "cash flow" tax base. This approach applies tax on total revenues less total expenditures, including full capital costs at the time they are incurred. This would replace arbitrary rules on depreciation and capital cost allowances that differ by sector (providing preferential treatment for natural resource sectors in Canada, for example), and that are not appropriate for capital investments with different lifecycles (mechanical boilers versus laptop computers, for example).

Such an approach would not tax funds that are transferred to individuals (these would be taxed as personal income), and would enable taxation of all currently non-taxable employer-provided non-cash benefits (including health insurance, personal use of the company car, or box seats for the Toronto Maple Leafs) under a broad-based income tax. Other formulations, such as Mirrlees, also allow for non-taxation of capital income up to a "normal" rate of return, but we see no compelling evidence why this should be a policy priority for business taxation.

A cash flow approach rightly supports the full taxation of pure economic rents, the returns from the ownership of assets. Boadway (2011, p. 25) builds on this idea as it relates to natural resource industries, which account for a significant and increasing share of Canada's economic activity. Higher tax rates on natural resources are a potential "efficient source of government revenues and a particularly important source of revenues for the federal government given its obligation to equalize provincial revenue capacities."

5. Wealth Transfer and Wealth Taxes

Inheritance taxes are based on, in the words of Sam Fleischacker (2001), "the principle that social privileges should be earned, should be a reward for contribution to society, rather than handed out by government leaders or passed down by aristocratic dynasties." Taxes on transfers of wealth (gifts and bequests) are based on the same principle, just not linked to time of death. By limiting the extent to which capital (and the opportunities it buys) is passed across generations, wealth transfer taxes equalize opportunities and increase social mobility, while reducing the concentration of income at the very top.

Taxes on transfers of wealth, whether bequests or inheritances, close the loop on comprehensive income taxation. In effect, as noted by Mirrlees et al. (2011, p. 477), "the main difference between lifetime income and lifetime expenditure is gifts and bequests. There is a good case for taxing such transfers of wealth, particularly to the next generation." Canada is one of the few developed countries that does not currently tax bequests and inheritances.

To ensure that all Canadians contribute their fair share in taxes, large inheritances and gifts should be included in the recipient's taxable income. Neil Brooks proposes a cutoff of $3 million for inclusion of inheritances and gifts in taxable income, although this threshold could arguably be lowered to $1 million. While there is room for debate on where to draw the threshold, the key point is that taxing bequests is essential for fairness and equal opportunity.

In addition to transfers of wealth, holdings of wealth should also be taxed at an annual rate. This would improve tax fairness, since wealth is even more unequally distributed than income. Provincial property taxes are, in essence, a wealth tax on real estate, which is the principal form of asset ownership for a large share of the population (BC has both a property tax and a property transfer tax). A federal tax on wealth would simply broaden the base to include financial market assets, ownership of which is highly concentrated at the top of the income distribution. Indeed, a private version of a wealth tax already exists in the form of annual fees for many whose financial wealth is held in mutual funds.

Brooks (2007a) proposes that those with wealth holdings over $3 million would pay a 1% tax on their fair market value annually. Such a tax could also have important incentive effects, by increasing the likelihood that wealthy investors will put their money to work in productive activities.

6. Use Consumption Taxes Cautiously

There are significant political economy advantages to direct consumption tax implemented as a value-added sales tax like the GST: governments tend to face less pressure to introduce loopholes, deductions, and credits to a flat VAT than to progressive income taxes. Because of the minimal tax evasion opportunities of value-added consumption taxes, they are widely recognized as large revenue generators for government and widely employed in OECD countries (with the exception of the US). In fact, the primary reason conservatives oppose VATs in the US is that they would raise too much revenue and lead to a large expansion of government.

Where consumption tax arguably fails, however, is on equity grounds. Consumption taxes are regressive because lower-income individuals end up paying a larger share of their income on tax. Even if an adequate compensation mechanism is implemented for households with low and modest incomes, consumption taxes alone cannot achieve tax fairness at the top of the distribution. The reality is that the richest spend such a small share of their income on consumption that it is practically impossible to have a progressive tax system without taxing savings as well (through a broad-based income tax).

Brooks raises another important equity concern with consumption taxes from a life cycle perspective: consumption taxes tend to be "levied on individuals at a time in their lives when they can least afford to pay, namely, when they are consuming most of their income as opposed to saving it" (2007b, p. 623), such as when they start out in the workforce, have young children, face unexpected large bills, lose their jobs, or are retired and live on their savings. It is fairer to tax individuals through income tax when they are in their peak earning years, when they can afford to save and paying taxes requires the least amount of sacrifice. In addition, consumption taxes discriminate against women, who continue to earn less than men in the twenty-first century, and therefore consume a higher share of their income than men. Women thus also end up paying a higher share of their total income in consumption tax.

Canada has moved in the direction of increasing its reliance on consumption taxes at both the provincial and federal level.[20] Theoretical rationales for shifting to consumption taxes generally do not hold up empirically, and there are important normative issues as to why, for example, not interfering with people's time preferences of consumption ought to be an aspiration of public policy. Canada remains more reliant on income tax than many OECD countries, and this should continue.

Value-added consumption taxes may be used to supplement revenues collected from a progressive, broad-based income tax, but should not form the main basis of the Canadian tax system. Conversely, carbon taxes and financial transactions taxes (discussed in other chapters) are examples of specific consumption taxes aimed at internalizing external costs, which improves the functioning of market-based economies and should be embraced.

7. Implement a Basic or Guaranteed Income

One of the ways that redistribution is achieved in the tax system is by providing direct income transfers to lower-income families (usually based on the previous year's assessed income). The five largest ones at the federal level are the Canada Child Tax Benefit (with its associated low-income National Child Benefit supplement and the Child Disability Benefit), the GST credit, the Working Income Tax Benefit, the Universal Child Care Benefit, and Old Age Security (with its Guaranteed Income Supplement).[21] Together, these programs are valued at $53.2 billion (Finance Canada, 2012).

These transfers have different income cut-offs and phase out at different rates, even though a family could qualify for more than one of these in a particular year (child benefits, WITB, and GST credit, for example). Add provincial low-income credits and transfers to the mix, and it becomes clear that Canada does not have a coherent system of supports for low-income families, but rather a patchwork of uncoordinated programs.

As a result of all benefits phasing out rapidly around incomes in the range of $25,000 to $40,000 for families with children, families in this income range face a very high marginal effective tax rate. For example, an income increase of $5,000 from $35,000 to $40,000 for a two-parent family with one child would result in a loss of CCTB and GST credits alone equivalent to a marginal tax of 17% on the extra income earned, which is on top of the federal tax rate of 15%, and the EI and CPP premium rates on that extra income.[22] That alone is a marginal tax rate of 32%. But this earnings increase, which would pull a three-person family in a large Canadian city slightly above the poverty line ($35,657 in 2011, according to LICO before tax), would likely lead to the clawing back or loss of other provincial tax credits, income-tested transfers, and subsidies the family previously qualified for. Depending on the province, the family might lose part or all of a rental assistance subsidy, child care subsidy, and assistance with the repayment of the parents' student loans. When all of these are combined, the total "tax" on the extra $5,000 earned might add up to more than 100%.[23]

The high marginal tax rates in relatively low family income ranges are a long-standing policy problem of Canada's income tax system. While much of the action happens in the provincial tax system, where tax benefits combine with stand-alone income-tested subsidy programs (for example, child care and rental assistance subsidies, which tend to phase out faster than the transfers delivered through the tax system over the same range of relatively low incomes), the federal income tax system contributes significantly to this problem.

This could be resolved by amalgamating the separate tax credits and benefits into a single income transfer (tax benefit) that would phase out gradually over a large income range similar in structure to the OAS and the CCTB. An alternative formulation is that the transfer would not be phased out, but would instead be taxable. It would be broad-based, and designed to take into account individual circumstances such as family size, the number of young children, family members with disabilities, and so on.[24]

We recommend that the benefit level be set at a significantly higher maximum level than the current GST transfer, so that this transfer would greatly increase the total income of the poorest Canadians and serve as a key pillar of a federal anti-poverty strategy. Ideally, it would be coordinated with provincial/territorial tax systems and replace the need for provincial social assistance payments and bureaucracies, making all income support federal and part of a coherent, cradle-to-grave system that all Canadians have access to, regardless of where they live. Importantly, it would not be a substitute for the provision of decent public services, but in addition to them.

The current payroll tax approach to Employment Insurance (EI) could also be rolled into this system. Employers and employees would no longer pay EI premiums, but recently unemployed workers would be eligible for a top-up on their basic income consistent with current income support levels under EI benefits. Beyond the middle of the income distribution, current EI premiums are regressive, as contributions max out at $45,900, a modest level of earnings (they are flat at incomes under this cut-off). For employers they act as a disincentive, an additional cost of hiring a new worker. Benefits have limited redistribution built into them at low-income levels, as they are based on wages earned during employment and tough eligibility requirements, which discriminate against new entrants to the labour force and workers in casual and precarious jobs that do not provide a lot of hours.

This transfer would be expensive, but could readily be funded from the additional revenues gained from broadening the base of the income tax. Such a transfer would be flexible and could easily accommodate new tax measures introduced in the future. For example, it could be merged with a new federal carbon pricing scheme (which would be regressive on its own) in a manner that offsets the regressive impact of the tax on low- to middle-income households without creating high marginal income tax rates for Canadian families with modest incomes.[25]

Conclusion

At a time of rising income inequality and unprecedented concentration of wealth in the hands of a small group of super-rich Canadians, restoring fairness should be the primary objective of the Canadian tax system. This involves broadening the income tax base to ensure that all forms of income are subject to the same progressive tax rates, raising marginal income tax rates on top incomes, eliminating tax credits and deductions that disproportionately benefit the richest Canadians, and introducing a single, streamlined income-tested transfer for low- and modest-income families.

These are, in broad strokes, the major elements for building and maintaining a fair tax system for Canada, which would be capable of raising revenues with minimal distortions to the economy, and which will result in significant reductions in income inequality and direct improvements in the life of low- and modest-income households.

The exact combination of reforms should be developed on the basis of a comprehensive review of the tax system. A Fair Tax Commission should be convened to examine how federal taxes and transfers work together as a system, and make recommendations for changes. Ideally, the commission would include an expert and well-respected team made up of both academics and practitioners, and would engage Canadians from all walks of life in a meaningful and broad-based public dialogue and deliberation process to produce a framework for tax reform.

Acknowledgements

The authors would like to thank Neil Brooks, Bruce Campbell, Trish Hennessey, Alex Himelfarb, Jordan Himelfarb, Seth Klein, David Macdonald, Hugh Mackenzie, Toby Sanger, and Armine Yalnizyan for their valuable comments and suggestions on an earlier draft of this chapter. Any errors are the responsibility of the authors.

Notes

1. This finding is consistent with other comprehensive tax reviews by Meade Report on Taxation in the UK (1978) and the Carter Royal Commission in Canada (1969).
2. This is the conclusion of the state-of-the-art economic analysis by American economists Peter Diamond and Emmanuel Saez in the *Journal of Economic Perspectives*, and a key recommendation of the Mirrlees Review in the UK, the most comprehensive tax review undertaken in the developed world in the last decade.
3. Both the International Monetary Fund (IMF) and the Organisation for Economic Co-operation and Development (OECD) have recently argued that rising income inequality is damaging for the economy; see Berg and Ostry (2011), and OECD (2011). Wilkinson and Pickett's seminal book, *The Spirit Level* (2009), provides ample empirical evidence that greater inequality leads to adverse social and health outcomes in rich countries.
4. Tax credits appear on income tax forms as reductions in tax payable. Tax benefits are paid out on an annual basis based on the previous year's income. The GST credit is thus technically a tax benefit.
5. Federal government taxes (including payroll taxes) made up 45% of all taxes collected in Canada in 2011. Data from Statistics Canada, CANSIM Table 385-0032.
6. Neil Brooks (2007b) provided a detailed summary of the arguments on both sides, which we won't reproduce here.
7. Bank of Canada Governor Mark Carney recently made national news after raising concern about corporate cash surpluses that are not being invested, which he described as "dead money" for the economy.
8. As estimated by Finance Canada (2012a). These figures are on the personal income tax side, but corporations also benefit from the partial inclusion of capital gains. The corporate income tax costs of the preferential tax treatment of capital gains were estimated at $3.9 billion in 2011.
9. See for example Milligan (2012) and Kesselman (2012).
10. A "buck is a buck," as stated by Carter during the Royal Commission on Taxation in 1969. We also reject the proposition that a deduction be granted for capital income up to a "risk-free rate of return," usually equivalent to the rate on government bonds, as there are no empirical grounds for why this should be the case.
11. These "boutique tax credits" have been shown to provide windfall gains for middle- and upper-income families rather than actual incentives that change behaviour. See Sand and Taylor (2011). The RRSP is proving inadequate as a mechanism to generate sufficient retirement savings for Canadians; see, for example, Wolfson (2011). Most current research points to the unsuitability of voluntary programs such as the RRSP to serve as a basis of a retirement income security program, due to low participation rates.
12. Some caution is required in interpretation, as tax data are based on individual filings and therefore do not adequately represent differences in household income where two or more individuals may have income.
13. Authors' calculation based on data from Finance Canada (2012a; 2012b). Note that Finance Canada figures are for 2011, while table 9.1 has data from the 2010 tax year (the latest year available for each at the time of writing). These tax expenditure totals do not take account of the interactions among the different tax expenditures, and likely understate their true cost to the federal treasury. Above and beyond these amounts are the costs of tax expenditures to provincial treasuries.
14. The RRSP deduction limit is set at 18% of earned income up to a cap of $22,450—an amount close to half of the median earnings of full-time, full-year workers in Canada, which was $46,300 in 2010.
15. A similar case can be made against tax credits for political donations, although the value of this tax expenditure is much smaller ($32 million in 2011) than charitable giving, because the tax credit is capped at $650 per year (the cap is reached with a political donation of $1,275, and no further tax credit is given for donations over that amount).
16. For a more detailed critique of the charitable tax credit, see Brooks (2001).
17. After the surtax of 13.16%, this will increase the top marginal income tax rate in Ontario to 47.97% in 2012 and 49.53% in 2013, when fully phased in.

18 Fortin, Green, Lemieux, Milligan, and Riddell (2012) estimated that the threshold for the top 1% was $230,000 in 2005, while 2010 CRA preliminary statistics show that only 0.8% of tax filers had an income over $250,000. We have used estimates for the threshold of 0.1% from Yalnizyan (2010).

19 Having a progressive income tax system with strong redistribution power is particularly important for countries with high levels of market income inequality. Countries with fewer wage disparities, like the Nordic countries, have more leeway to raise revenues in less progressive ways without exacerbating already large income inequality problems. If Canada was to consider a dual-income tax system with low capital taxation and relatively high reliance on a regressive value-added tax, it should be accompanied by labour market measures such as much higher union coverage.

20 This has been achieved by introducing the GST federally (and increasing rates of provincial sales taxes), as well as by narrowing the base of the income tax by excluding retirement savings in RRSP and RSP accounts (so that taxable income more closely resembles income consumed).

21 The UCCB is the only income transfer that is not income tested. It is provided as a taxable benefit, which means that some higher-earning families receive a lower amount net of tax (unless they are single-earner families, in which case they receive the maximum amount of the benefit regardless of the total family income).

22 Our calculations for 2012 tax year, based on Canada Revenue Agency tax forms, the CCTB online calculator for the period July 2012 to June 2013, and the GST online calculator for the period July 2012 to June 2013.

23 For a more detailed discussion of this issue, see Stapleton (2007), *Why is it so tough to get ahead?*

24 That said, we note that tax returns are filed on an individual basis, and feminist scholars have argued for transfers to individuals rather than families, as there are gender-related income distribution issues within households. For an overview of issues associated with a Guaranteed Annual Income, see Young and Mulvale (2009).

25 A study on carbon pricing in BC by Marc Lee argues for half of carbon tax revenues to be used as a new carbon transfer, and shows that it could be designed in a way that the bottom 80% of households get a positive transfer (modelled on the CCTB with a long phase-out); the bottom half of households would receive, on average, more in credits than they would pay in tax. See Lee (2011).

References

Berg, A., & Ostry, J. (2011). Equality and efficiency: Is there a trade-off between the two or do they go hand in hand? *Finance and Development, 48*(3). Retrieved from http://www.imf.org/external/pubs/ft/fandd/2011/09/berg.htm

Boadway, R. (2011). Rethinking tax-transfer policy for 21st-century Canada. In F. Gorbet & A. Sharpe (Eds.), *New directions for intelligent government in Canada: Papers in honour of Ian Stewart* (pp. 163–204). Ottawa, ON: Centre for the Study of Living Standards.

Brooks, N. (2001). The tax credit for charitable contributions: Giving credit where none is due. In J. Phillips, B. Chapman, & D. Stevens (Eds.), *Between state and market: Essays on charities law and policy in Canada* (pp. 457–481). Kingston, ON: McGill-Queen's University Press.

Brooks, N. (2007a). A democratic tax reform for Canada. *Canadian Dimension, 41*(2). Retrieved from http://canadiandimension.com/articles/1797/

Brooks, N. (2007b). An overview of the role of the VAT, fundamental tax reform, and a defense of the income tax. In R. Krever & D. White (Eds.), *GST in retrospect and prospect* (pp. 597–658). Wellington, NZ: Thomson Brookers.

Canada Revenue Agency (CRA). (n.d.). Canada Child Tax Benefit Calculator [Measurement tool]. Retrieved from http://www.cra-arc.gc.ca/bnfts/clcltr/cctb_clcltr-eng.html

Canada Revenue Agency. (n.d.). Goods and Services Tax/Harmonized Sales Tax Calculator [Measurement tool]. Retrieved from http://www.cra-arc.gc.ca/bnfts/clcltr/gstc_clcltr-eng.html

Canada Revenue Agency. (2012) Preliminary statistics for 2010 tax year, Table 2: All returns by total income class [Table]. Retrieved from http://www.cra-arc.gc.ca/gncy/stts/gb10/pst/ntrm/table2-eng.html

Diamond, P., & Saez, E. (2011). The case for a progressive tax: From basic research to policy recommendations. *Journal of Economic Perspectives*, 25(4), pp. 165–190.

Finance Canada. (2012a). *Tax Expenditures and Evaluations 2011*. Retrieved from http://www.fin.gc.ca/taxexp-depfisc/2011/taxexp11-eng.pdf

Finance Canada. (2012b). *Fiscal Reference Tables 2012*. Retrieved from http://www.fin.gc.ca/frt-trf/2012/frt-trf-12-eng.pdf.

Fleischacker, S. (2001, February 15). Why capitalists should like estate taxes. *Salon*. Retrieved from http://www.salon.com/2001/02/15/estate_tax_2/singleton/

Fortin, N., Green, D. A., Lemieux, T., Milligan, K., & Riddell, C. (2012). Canadian inequality: Recent developments and policy options. *Canadian Public Policy*, 38(2), pp. 121–145.

Gurría, A. (2011, December 5). Remarks at the press conference announcing the OECD's publication of *Divided we stand: Why inequality keeps rising*. Paris, France.

Kesselman, J. R. (2004). Tax design for a northern tiger. *IRPP Choices*, 10(1).

Kesselman, J. R. (2012). Policy forum: Expanding the tax-free savings account—Requisite companion reforms. *Canadian Tax Journal*, 60(2), pp. 375–389.

Lee, M. (2007). *Eroding tax fairness: Tax incidence in Canada, 1990 to 2005* (CCPA Growing Gap Project). Retrieved from Canadian Centre for Policy Alternatives website: http://www.policyalternatives.ca/publications/reports/eroding-tax-fairness

Lee, M. (2011). *Fair and effective carbon pricing: Lessons from BC*. Vancouver, BC: Canadian Centre for Policy Alternatives.

Milligan, K. (2012). Policy forum: The tax-free savings account—Introduction and simulations of potential revenue costs. *Canadian Tax Journal*, 60(2), pp. 355–360.

Mirrlees, J., Adam, S., Besley, T., Blundell, R., Bond, S., Chote, R., . . . Poterba, J. (2011). *The Mirrlees Review: Tax by Design*. Oxford, UK: Oxford University Press. Retrieved from http://www.ifs.org.uk/mirrleesreview/

PricewaterhouseCooper (PwC), the World Bank, & Internatonal Finance Corp. (IFC). (2012). *Paying Taxes 2012: The Global Picture*. Retrieved from www.pwc.com/payingtaxes

Saez, E., & Veall, M. (2005). The evolution of high incomes in Northern America: Lessons from Canadian evidence. *American Economic Review*, 95(3), 831–849.

Sand, B., and Taylor, P. S. (2011, March). *Harper's tax boutique: Rethinking tax expenditures in a time of deficit*. Frontier Centre for Public Policy: Backgrounder.

Sandler, D. (2001). The tax treatment of employee stock options: Generous to a fault. *Canadian Tax Journal*, 49(2), 259–319.

Sanger, T. (2010, March 3). Stock options, the buyback boondoggle and the crisis of capitalism. [Web log post]. Retrieved from http://www.progressive-economics.ca/2010/03/03/stock-options-the-buyback-boondoggle-and-the-crisis-of-capitalism/

Stapleton, J. (2007). *Why is it so tough to get ahead? How our tangled social programs pathologize the transition to self-reliance*. Toronto, ON: Metcalf Foundation.

Statistics Canada. (2012). *National balance sheet accounts* [CANSIM table 378-0121]. Retrieved from http://www5.statcan.gc.ca/cansim/a26?lang=eng&retrLang=eng&id=3780121&paSer=&pattern=&stByVal=1&p1=1&p2=-1&tabMode=dataTable&csid=

Statistics Canada. (2013). *Government finance statistics* [CANSIM table 385-0032]. Retrieved from http://www5.statcan.gc.ca/cansim/a26?lang=eng&retrLang=eng&id=3850032&paSer=&pattern=&stByVal=1&=p1=1&p2=-1&tabMode=dataTable&csid=

Weir, E. (2009, November 3). The treasury transfer effect [Web log post]. Retrieved from http://www.progressive-economics.ca/2009/11/03/treasury-transfer-effect/

Weir, E. (2011, April 20). The treasury transfer effect—You read it here first [Web log post]. Retrieved from http://www.progressive-economics.ca/2011/04/20/treasury-transfer-here-first/

Wilkinson, R., & Pickett, K. (2009). *The spirit level: Why more equal societies almost always do better.* London, UK: Allen Lane.

Wolfson, M. (2011). *Projecting the adequacy of Canadians' retirement incomes: Current prospects and possible reform options.* Montreal, QC: Institute for Research on Public Policy.

Yalnizyan, A. (2010). *The rise of Canada's richest 1%* (Growing Gap Project). Ottawa, ON: Canadian Centre for Policy Alternatives.

Young, M., & Mulvale, J. (2009). *Possibilities and prospects: The debate over a guaranteed income* (CCPA Economic Security Project). Ottawa, ON: Canadian Centre for Policy Alternatives.

Chapter 10

Carbon Taxes: Can a Good Policy Become Good Politics?

Stéphane Dion

Good policy, bad politics: this is how carbon taxes are broadly perceived, notably in Canada. It would be difficult to find a policy that generates more praise and support among policy experts and one that is more closely identified with political suicide.

After explaining why a carbon tax is good public policy, and highlighting the political obstacles to its adoption, I will consider the current propositions for making it more electorally acceptable. I will argue that these propositions would not necessarily improve the electoral attractiveness of a carbon tax, and that some of them would actually damage its effectiveness as an instrument to achieve better public outcomes. I conclude with the hope that a time will come, not too far in the future, when the merits of carbon taxes will lead to public acceptance.

The Policy Effectiveness of a Carbon Tax

A carbon tax is a tax on the full range of fossil fuels (coal, natural gas and petroleum by-products such as gasoline, diesel, propane, aviation fuel, and heating oil), with the amount determined by the amount of carbon that is emitted when the fossil fuel is burned. Putting a price on carbon would be a critical step in reducing emissions and slowing, or hopefully halting, the human-made climate change that is altering our planet. In turn, the revenue generated by a carbon tax could be used to reduce taxes on household or business income, that is, to enable governments to tax what you burn, not what you earn.

The support this policy has received and continues to receive in Canada and around the world, right across the political spectrum, is downright impressive. Environmentalists and climate scientists have endorsed it; so have many economists—Thomas Friedman, Alan Greenspan, Arthur B. Laffer, Paul Krugman, Paul Volker, Joseph E. Stiglitz, Gregory Mankiw (formerly George W. Bush's and Mitt Romney's top economic adviser) (Pigou Club Manifesto, 2006), Craig

Alexander (TD Bank Chief economist), as well as mainstream energy and fiscal policy experts, international organizations such as the OECD,[1] several corporate CEOs and business organizations like the Canadian Council of Chief Executives,[2] renowned think tanks like the US American Enterprise Institute, the Brookings Institution, the Rand Corporation, or in Canada the National Round Table on the Environment and the Economy (NRTEE),[3] the Conference Board of Canada,[4] and the Canada West Foundation.[5] Even prominent conservative politicians, such as Preston Manning in Canada[6] and George Schultz in the US (Romm, 2012), have recognized the merits of carbon taxes.

A carbon tax is categorized as a "pigouvian" tax, after British economist Arthur Pigou, who nearly one hundred years ago proposed to tax "negative externalities"—that is, the social and environmental costs of a product or activity not reflected in its market cost (Pigou, 1920). High taxes on alcohol and tobacco are typical pigouvian taxes, aiming to internalize the social costs of these products in an effort to dissuade consumers from consuming them and to encourage healthier lifestyles.

A negative externality: that is exactly what children born in 2013 will be facing when having to deal with the climate changes caused by the greenhouse gases (GHGs) emitted, at no cost, by previous generations of consumers and producers of goods, services, and commodities. As science has made clear in recent decades, the world's climate is being changed by the emission of GHGs, the most prevalent of which is carbon dioxide (CO_2). Climate change induced by human activity is one of the main threats facing humankind. By taxing this negative externality at the source of the activity, governments can force polluters to pay for the costs imposed by climate change on our children, and society as a whole; such a tax would also create an incentive for these polluters to find innovative ways to decrease their emissions in order to pay less tax.

In most of the world today, polluters can emit carbon for free. Putting a price on carbon emissions is an eminently logical way to force polluters to take the environmental cost of their operations into account, and to reduce their GHG emissions. If carbon emissions were priced in our economy, consumers and businesses would have a powerful incentive to choose goods and services with lower carbon content, and to invest in proven or innovative energy-saving and emission-reducing technologies. It would be in their own interest to curb their carbon emissions, thus reducing their tax burden.

To illustrate how this would work, imagine a corporate board meeting where senior management is asked to find ways to reduce the company's taxes. In the absence of a carbon price, a team of accountants and lawyers will be hired to find legal loopholes, or possibly ways to shift resources to lower tax jurisdictions. Such a solution might improve the company's bottom line, but it offers few benefits for the economy, or society at large. If however, there was a carbon tax in the company's jurisdiction, management would instead reduce their taxes by hiring engineers and investing in the domestic R&D needed to reduce the company's emissions. Furthermore, because governments can use part of the revenues from a carbon tax to reduce corporate income tax rates, the firm will have more capital available to make efficiency-boosting investments, thus benefiting both the firm and the broader economy.

If such decisions were taking place economy-wide, jurisdictions would benefit from a cleaner environment, increased economic activity, cleaner and more efficient processes, new export opportunities, and high-value, clean economy jobs. Thus, taxing carbon emissions would be tremendously helpful in promoting more efficient use of energy at every level, delivering innovation incentives, and making clean and renewable energy a more competitive source of power. It would also have additional environmental benefits, such as a reduction of local and transboundary air pollution and related morbidity and mortality rates.

Through carbon taxes, governments can reduce emissions more affordably and effectively than through other policy levers. While regulations and direct investment in environmental initiatives should be part of any policy mix, these would be far more effective if anchored in a clear, consistent carbon price. Without a price on carbon, conventional policy instruments, such as subsidies and command-and-control regulatory mandates, tend to pick technology winners rather than allowing private firms and individuals to choose their own made-to-measure and cost-effective ways to reduce emissions.

Relying mainly—or only—on sector-by-sector regulated performance standards, as the current federal government is doing, is not only more burdensome on the economy but also has little support from analysts as a tool to reduce emissions.[7]

A carbon tax is not the only way to levy a price on carbon. Another method is through the allocation of emission quotas, also called a carbon market or cap-and-trade system. This method imposes a cap on how many GHGs an emitter can release each year, along with the ability to purchase emitting rights beyond that cap. For example, if a coal-fired power plant wanted to exceed its allocated cap, it would need to purchase more emitting rights from one or more other emitters who have not exceeded their own caps. A widely shared view among experts and industry leaders who have analyzed both carbon pricing systems[8] is that a carbon tax is "the most efficient way to price carbon" (Oliwiler, 2012, p. 19; Hsu, 2011). Indeed, a carbon tax presents a number of policy advantages over a cap and trade system:

Greater emission coverage. A cap-and-trade system requires a large volume of data collection and monitoring of individual permit holders. Applying such a system beyond the large industrial emitters would be a complex endeavour and, in some sectors, nearly impossible. For example, addressing emission reductions in transportation with a cap-and-trade system would be a massive undertaking. In Canada, the 700 large final emitters (mostly heavy industry and power plants) produce "approximately 51% of emissions" (NRTEE, 2009, p. 44), while transportation's share is 24% (Environment Canada, 2012, p. 13). The European Union's Emission Trading Scheme (ETS) covers only 40% of European GHG emissions (Laurent & Le Cacheux, 2009, p. 24).

In contrast, a carbon tax can achieve much broader coverage since taxation can be applied to virtually all fossil fuel purchases. A carbon tax would raise revenue largely from large industrial polluters, but can also be applied to smaller emitters, including consumers. A carbon tax could reach over 75% of emissions, as is the case in British Columbia (Horne, Petropavlova, & Partington, 2012, p. 16).

Clear price for investment decisions = greater effectiveness. A key factor in successful emission reductions is providing emitters with the ability to make long-term plans for low carbon capital expenditures. Emitters need a certain, long-term price signal that they can incorporate into their projections of operating expenses that will reduce uncertainty about returns on investment decisions.

A cap-and-trade system brings price volatility that inhibits private sector investment and is vulnerable to manipulation by speculators. The price fluctuates wildly because of the unpredictable nature of supply, demand, regulatory conditions, and the volume of emission rights issued. But with a clear, meaningful, and gradually increasing carbon tax, emitters have the certainty they need to make investment decisions. A well-conceived tax starts with a low price that rises predictably over time, on a trajectory that the government makes transparent to all.

Easier implementation. Carbon cap-and-trade systems are complicated structures, difficult to administer, subject to gaming, and involve offsetting credits that may take years to negotiate and implement. Significant lead time would be necessary to negotiate the allocation of emission permits, and to develop standardized rules and baseline emission paths that define and underpin carbon as a traded commodity. This is particularly true in a decentralized federation such as Canada, given constitutional jurisdictions over natural resources and industrial activity.

In contrast, a carbon tax would be administratively simple and straightforward to implement. It could be enacted immediately by the Federal Parliament under section 91(3) of the Constitution, which enables Parliament to raise money "by any Mode or System of Taxation." It could also be introduced without hiring any new public servants, since a modern country like Canada already has an indirect tax system which also applies to fossil fuels.

Practically speaking, the only reform needed from the government would be to start taxing fossil fuels by carbon content (Mintz & Olewiler, 2008; Hohan, 2006; Yokoyama et al., 2000; Lachapelle, 2011; Laurent & Le Cacheux, 2009). For example, as it emits far more carbon when burned, coal would be taxed at a higher rate than oil, which would in turn be taxed at a higher rate than natural gas.

Use of revenues. Carbon pricing bears real costs for individuals and businesses, mostly in the form of higher energy prices. A cap-and-trade system does not generally provide any revenue with which the government may offset those costs, since emission quotas are usually allocated free of charge. While the government could sell the emitting rights by auctioning allowances for all existing emissions, this has not been done yet at a large scale.

In contrast, taxes create immediate revenue which the government could use to fund its policy priorities. It would have the resources to invest in additional emissions reduction measures, or to offset higher energy costs through broad-based, progressive tax cuts. The government could stimulate the economy and lower the cost of doing business by reducing taxes on productive activities like labour or investment. It could also target a significant share of revenues to lower-income households through refundable tax credits, to ensure that their quality of life improves rather than declines as a result of the policy. Such offsets are particularly important, given that lower-income households pay little tax and so would not benefit from reductions in tax rates alone.

In order words, a carbon tax can be the basis for comprehensive fiscal reform, combining environmental, economic, and social goals, a triple dividend the government uses to concurrently fight climate change, promote social fairness, and improve the competitiveness of the economy. Indeed, thanks to its carbon tax revenue, British Columbia lowered its corporate income tax to a rate that is among the lowest in the G8, and its personal income tax rates for those earning less than $119,000 per year are now the lowest in Canada (Bauman & Hsu, 2012).

Carbon tax revenues can be used to ensure that households are net beneficiaries. For example, in Canada a significant share of the emissions come from foreign-owned industrial sites. So while the carbon tax would be paid to a significant degree by foreign-owned companies, the resulting revenues could be recycled to disproportionately benefit Canadian households.

Carbon tax revenues may also be used to mitigate the impact of carbon pricing on those regions of the country with higher emission rates. In Canada, the two highest emitting provinces, Alberta and Saskatchewan, are benefiting from high corporate profits, which means they will disproportionately benefit from reductions in corporate tax rates that a carbon tax revenue would enable.

As I mentioned, carbon tax revenue allows for targeted tax measures to lower-income households, which is vital because in isolation, carbon pricing can be regressive. Higher carbon prices disproportionately burden low-income households, who ordinarily spend a large proportion of their income on heating and transportation (Congressional Budget Office, 2007; Sustainable Prosperity, May, July 2011). This is particularly true in a country such as Canada, with its cold climate and vast distances (Krechowicz, May 2011; NRTEE, 2009, pp. 76–77; Lee & Sanger, 2008), with already-widening inequalities (Conference Board of Canada, 2011), and where GHG emissions growth is due almost exclusively to the highest-income consumers (Osberg, 2008).

International considerations. Carbon taxes also bring advantages when we consider the international dimensions of fighting the climate change crisis. Carbon taxes are better suited to promote regional harmonization, if not an integrated world carbon price signal.

The inherent complexity of cap-and-trade systems worsens with the number of jurisdictions involved, and the rules of compliance expose them to the risk of a paralyzing domino effect: the overselling of permits by one or a few participating countries can make inaction legitimate for buyers of emission permits, as it undermines the entire pricing regime.

In contrast, a tax-based regime provides a fixed monetary incentive that is not affected by the non-compliance of one or more participants: "one country's non-compliance cannot make inaction by other countries legitimate. . . . Thus, a tax regime will always have at least some environmental effect provided that at least one country complies" (Hovi & Holtsmark, 2006, p. 138). Simply, it is harder to bypass or game a carbon tax system.

Of course, a country acting alone may be disadvantaged when facing competitors that keep their carbon emissions free. This is particularly of concern to emissions-intensive-trade-exposed industries, which have no assurance that their competitors will play by the same climate rules. If carbon pricing is to lead to carbon leakage, with economic activities moving toward jurisdictions that do not price carbon, this could result in an economic loss for the country, and without marked environmental gain for the planet as, to some extent, global emissions are not reduced, only displaced.

But here again tax regimes are better suited to address the problem than cap-and-trade systems, since the carbon tax may be linked to a corresponding reduction in other taxes— business taxes, for example—that have "approximately the same marginal deadweight loss as the carbon tax" (Nordhaus, 2001, p. 16), thereby neutralizing the economic impact of the carbon price, if not improving the economy. According to Raush and Reilly (2012) in their report for MIT, "this combination of a carbon tax with general tax cuts improves overall economic performance" (p. 17). And according to an OECD study, a carbon tax could promote employment growth when revenues are used to reduce taxation on labour (Chateau, Saint-Martin, & Manfredi, 2011).

Although the risk of carbon leakage cannot be ruled out without a universal harmonized carbon price, that risk should not be exaggerated, nor legitimize a reduction in effort (Dion & Laurent, 2012). After all, the price of carbon emissions is higher today in Europe than in America, and there is no carbon leakage between these two continents (Victor, 2011, p. 51). Many factors other than the cost of carbon, such as labour cost and quality, infrastructure, and political stability will continue to influence investment location (Andersen & Ekins, 2009).

In Canada, the current federal government decided not to adopt carbon pricing as long as the US Congress and White House do not. This marks a departure from past practice, a change from the time when Canada was willing and able to adopt different policies than its neighbour, policies that benefited Canadians, such as a more accessible and efficient health care system, more generous workers' rights, fairer and more effective anti-crime policies, tighter fiscal policy, a more reliable banking system, and lower business taxes.

In fact, trade concerns are an argument for carbon pricing, because the threat to competitiveness comes from failing to act, not from acting. Those countries—and their companies—that move toward carbon pricing will have an early adopter's advantage for trading opportunities (Sawyer & Fischer, 2010). The world will become less and less tolerant of the climate freeloaders who refuse to do their share in the fight against global warming. These environmental laggards might face new trade barriers, and their exports could be subject to boycotts in global markets. It is for this reason that the Canada West Foundation (2011, p. 25) lent its support to carbon pricing, arguing that it would reflect the seriousness with which Canada is taking its climate responsibilities, and in doing so help protect our resources from boycotts such as those organized against the oil sands in Europe and the US.

Having made the policy case for a carbon tax, I will address the issue of what its level, or "rate" should be. To be effective, a carbon tax must be high enough to create an incentive for the desired emission reductions. If the tax is too low or there are too many exemptions, business will simply "buy its way out," and fail to reduce its emissions. Multiple exemptions may reduce the tax's overall effectiveness to a negligible level (Bruvol & Larsen, 2002). The objective is to set a carbon price that raises the cost-effectiveness of research into low-carbon solutions and acts as a catalyst for the full range of actions needed to combat climate change.

Climate scientists urge decision-makers to keep global warming below the dangerous tipping point when they predict our planet will become much less hospitable for virtually all forms of life: 2° Celsius above pre-industrial levels. Ideally, the carbon price should be aligned with a required emission reduction target not to exceed this two-degree limit. The fourth report of the Intergovernmental

Panel on Climate Change (IPCC) calls for a world carbon price of between $50 and $100 per tonne of equivalent CO_2 between 2010 and 2030. According to Nordhaus (2008, p. 91), a leading climate economist, the optimal carbon tax would be $42 per tonne in 2015, rising gradually to $90 in 2050, and $202 in 2100. The International Energy Agency (IEA) sets this price at between $95 and $120 per tonne by 2030 (2011, p. 49).

In Canada, the Suzuki Foundation and the Pembina Institute recommended setting a price of $200 per tonne of CO_2, while the National Round Table on the Environment and the Economy (2009) suggested an economy-wide carbon price of $50 per tonne by 2015 that "will need to rise to $100 per tonne of CO_2 by 2020 and upward of $300 per tonne of CO_2 by 2050" (pp. 30–31, 51). The NRTEE categorizes a reduction of less than $50 dollars a tonne as low-cost, between $50 and $100 a tonne as medium-cost, and more than $100 as high-cost (NRTEE, 2009, p. 94).

As we know, the world is nowhere close to levying carbon prices at the levels described above. Or to put it another way: as leading scientists are telling us that without appropriate carbon pricing, we are risking the future of our planet, there is still little action being taken. Are carbon taxes just bad politics?

Can a Carbon Tax Ever Be Good Politics?

There is a striking and worrisome dichotomy between experts' urgent and insistent recommendation of a high carbon price and the fact that polluters worldwide (with too few exceptions) are not obliged to pay for their carbon emissions. There are only pockets of carbon pricing in a few jurisdictions. Yet where carbon taxes exist, results are encouraging.

Sweden, Finland, Norway, Denmark, and the Netherlands have been taxing carbon since the beginning of the nineties (Horne, Petropavlova, & Partington, 2012, pp. 5–6).[9] The highest rates are paid in Sweden, which currently charges a standard rate of $106 per tonne and an industry rate of $23 per tonne. Finland currently charges $78 per tonne for transportation fuels, and $39 per tonne for heating fuels. Norway's tax currently ranges from $16 to $86 per tonne, depending on the sector—they recently decided to double it for their offshore oil and gas production (Norway Ministry of Environment, 2012). In each of these economies, carbon taxes have helped to reduce greenhouse gas emissions (Sumner, Bird, & Smith, 2009), while average annual gross domestic product (GDP) growth since 1990 has outstripped that of the European Union, and matched or exceeded the average of all high-income OECD countries.

Switzerland will soon increase its rate from $39 to $65 per tonne; Ireland recently increased its rate to $26 per tonne; South Africa is planning to introduce a partial carbon tax of $15 per tonne in 2013; and Australia just decided to introduce, in July 2012, a $23 per tonne carbon tax that will increase by 2.5%

annually until 2015—at that time, the government will consider shifting to a cap-and-trade system (Horne, Petropavlova, & Partington, 2012, pp. 5–6; Jotzo, 2012).

The performance of existing cap-and-trade systems is less impressive. The largest cap-and-trade system in the world by far is the European Union's Emissions Trading Scheme, representing more than 80% of existing carbon markets. Unfortunately, its coverage is too narrow (40% of total emissions), and its price too low and too volatile to be an effective tool (around 7€ in October 2012; Clo & Vendramin, 2012). The same can be said of the Clean Development Mechanism—the UN-sponsored offset credits for international emissions markets—with a carbon price of less than $2 in October 2012. New Zealand has operated a mandatory emissions trading system since 2008, and China is launching pilot emissions trading systems with the aim of crafting a national system by 2016 (Horne, Petropavlova, & Partington, 2012, pp. 5–6).

In Canada, there has been some action at the provincial level. Nova Scotia has capped its electricity emissions, responsible for almost half of the province's emissions, with Nova Scotia Power mandated to decrease its emissions to 25% below 2007 levels by 2020. Alberta has had a cap system since 2007, whereby major emitters pay $15 per tonne emitted in excess of the government-set target of 12% emission intensity reduction. Since the cap is not very demanding and the average cost per tonne negligible, there is no meaningful incentive for companies to reduce their emissions, and Alberta is set to miss its modest target (NRTEE, 2012, p. 80).

Also in 2007, Quebec introduced a modest carbon tax called the Green Fund Duty, which raises approximately $3 dollars per tonne. The tax is levied on energy producers totalling approximately 50 companies. Quebec has committed to introducing a cap-and-trade system in 2013, in conjunction with California, with a gradually falling cap on emissions. The most ambitious initiative by far is the carbon tax established by British Columbia in 2008, which has gradually risen to its current level of $30 dollars per tonne, to be held there unless further action is taken. It is a courageous initiative, but too modest to result in appropriate emission reductions (Sustainable Prosperity, 2012). No major party has committed to pursuing this tax further than its current maximum of $30 a tonne, and it is unlikely that they will commit to do so before the next election (Richards, 2011).

At the federal level, the Harper government now rules out any form of carbon pricing as economic heresy. But in a 2007 document entitled *Turning the Corner* (Environment Canada, 2007), it proposed a cap-and-trade system which, during the 2008 federal election campaign, the Conservative Party committed to implement. In May 2008, while visiting the UK, Prime Minister Stephen Harper announced he would move immediately and launch a domestic carbon trading system, without waiting for the US: "Our plan will effectively establish a price on carbon of $65 a tonne," he bragged (Prime Minister, 2008). Unfortunately, Mr. Harper reneged on this commitment, and he now vilifies any form of carbon pricing as "job-killing taxes."

In lieu of carbon pricing, the government chose a sector-by-sector regulatory approach as the centrepiece of its climate change action plan. However, there is no overall implementation strategy to indicate how such different regulations in the sectors will enable Canada to meet the 2020 target, or how they will allow regulated companies to make appropriate investment decisions (Vaughan, 2012, pp. 38–39).

According to the Canadian Commissioner of the Environment and Sustainable Development, the Conservative government's climate change strategy appears "disjointed, confused and non-transparent" and does not even come up with the "key management tools" needed to reduce GHG emissions (Auditor General of Canada, 2011, p. 44). While Canada needs to reduce emissions by 113 million tonnes over the next eight years to meet its target of a 17% reduction below 2005 levels by 2020, "existing federal regulations are expected to reduce GHG emissions by 11 to 13 million tonnes in 2020" (Environment Canada, 2012, p. 5; Vaughan, 2012, p. 34). The proposed regulations on coal-fired plants, on their own, will only yield a further 6 million-tonne reduction (Vaughan, 2012, p. 43). The NRTEE had similar findings: "federal policies will result in 21 Mt CO_2 of incremental emission reductions by 2020" (2012, p. 71).

The Conservative government places high hopes on carbon dioxide capture and storage (CCS); but it is still unknown whether this technology is effective for coal-fired plants, and there is even less certainty about how it will work with the oil sands. According to the NRTEE, CCS likely represents 50% of the additional emission reductions required to reach the current Canadian government's 2020 target of 17% reduction below 2005 levels. However, without a price on carbon, there is little incentive for industry to invest the billions of dollars required to develop and deploy this technology. Lorraine Mitchelmore, Royal Dutch Shell Canadian President, said that CCS technology won't be widely adopted until there is a price on carbon (McCarthy, 2012; Van Loon and Mayeda, 2013). Project-specific costs range between $70 and $150 per tonne of carbon (Royal Society of Canada Expert Panel, 2010, pp. 90–91; Carter & MacGregor, 2010). With "a constant, steady carbon price of $100 to $150 per tonne of CO_2… firms would quickly move to implement CCS" (NRTEE, 2012, p. 101).

During the 2008 federal election campaign, the Liberal Party of Canada crafted an ambitious plan that made greening the Canadian economy the centrepiece of its electoral platform. Its boldest proposal to Canadian voters involved setting a price for carbon emissions with a carbon tax, and using the resulting revenue to reduce personal and business income taxes. While many economists and most environmentalists supported the fundamentals of this tax reform, the Liberals were unable to convince Canadians of the merits of the plan, nor counter the Conservative Party's misleading but effective campaign against what they portrayed as a "tax on everything." The Liberal platform was also attacked from the Left by the New Democratic Party, which argued that only big business should be subject to emission reduction targets and that taxpayers should be exempt from them—notwithstanding the fact that the NDP's proposed cap-and-trade system would have had a very real impact on Canadian individuals and families.

If the Liberals had won in 2008, 75% of Canada's GHG emissions would have been taxed, up to $10 per tonne of CO_2 in 2009, gradually rising to $40 in 2012. This green fiscal reform would have led to substantial cuts in personal and business income taxes, and to tax benefits for clean technologies, processes, practices, and activities that reduce GHG emissions. Instead, the Liberal defeat was interpreted as evidence that campaigning on a carbon tax is a sure recipe for defeat. The mere expression "carbon tax" appears to have become taboo among Canadian federal political parties, with the exception of the Green Party.

Canada is not alone in facing this reality. In fact, in no jurisdiction has a political party won an election while making a meaningful carbon tax the centrepiece of its electoral platform (Harrison, 2010 and 2012). Where carbon taxes have been implemented, it was done by already-elected governments that did not previously campaign on them. Some of those governments may have been re-elected, but they often had to concede exemptions or commit to no further tax rate increases.

Everywhere we look, the road to carbon pricing is long and bruising. In Australia, climate policy has contributed to the downfall of several prime ministers and opposition leaders since 2007. It took an unusual political constellation—a minority Labour government supported by the Green Party—to finally enact legislation that may not even survive the next election, since opposition parties averse to carbon pricing have pledged to repeal it (Jotzo, 2012).

It isn't a surprise that campaigning on a tax is tough. Some strategists advise against uttering the three-letter word at all costs, and instead call it a charge, levy, auction, or fee; but there is no proof that these semantics fool anyone. Any tax will be labelled as such, especially such a highly visible and effective tax as one on carbon.

While carbon taxes are lauded as good policy by policy experts on the Left, Right, and in between, it does not seem to be enough to convince the electorate. As Sheila Copps (2008) wrote shortly after the 2008 Liberal defeat, "whether Nobel Laureates embrace the green shift means little to voters concerned about pocketbook politics" (p. 9).

Polls regularly show that citizens may be open to the idea of a carbon tax to fight climate change (Environics, 2011). However, this support tends to vanish when questions ask more precisely about higher energy costs, particularly when referring to the retail price of gasoline or home heating fuel. For example, the National Survey on American Public Opinion on Climate Change received the lowest rate of support and the highest rate of opposition among 12 policy options with the question exploring whether "state governments should increase taxes on gasoline in order to reduce consumption" (Rabe, 2010, p. 134). In Canada, support for a carbon tax fell during the summer of 2008, just before the federal election, as the price of a barrel of oil reached its historic high of US$148. The fact that petroleum prices are likely to stay high will not make life any easier for carbon tax advocates.

Nevertheless, the future of the planet is a priority in the hearts of many citizens. The climate change crisis is a huge concern for them, and they want politicians to face this defining policy challenge of our—and our children's—lifetimes. But here again the required communications effort becomes a huge test, because although scientists can prove a high enough carbon tax has a significant impact on national GHG reductions, this remains an abstract concept for most citizens. Politicians who promote carbon taxes cannot credibly commit to deliver a substantial and rapid improvement of general climate conditions, such as fewer extreme weather events, droughts, floods, or pest infestations. Because they are spread all over the planet and over time—decades if not centuries—the positive impacts of a carbon tax on the climate are imperceptible in the course of a four-year elected mandate. Even if Canada took dramatic action and managed to cut its GHG emissions by half, such efforts would have no noticeable impact on the climate disturbances that currently threaten our country. Canada accounts for only 1.88% of global emissions, and GHGs migrate throughout the atmosphere: so 1 tonne of carbon dioxide emitted in Beijing or Paris has the same effect on Canada's climate as 1 tonne emitted in Montreal or Calgary. Therefore, acting on climate change in Canada alone cannot solve the problem—nor can acting in any single country. But acting resolutely against climate change does allow Canada to be part of the solution, and to lead in the fight against the greatest ecological challenge humankind has yet faced.

Many politicians believe that cap-and-trade systems are more politically acceptable than carbon taxes. Carbon taxes are highly visible; cap-and-trade systems are more opaque. Everybody knows what a tax does; to most people, cap-and-trade remains a mysterious concept, making it easier to bury deep inside an electoral platform. Cap-and-trade systems are so complex that nobody will even try to understand them except for a few experts, while a fiscal reform involving a carbon tax is simple enough to be attacked, even for its alleged complexity. In 2008, the Liberal tax reform plan was arguably much easier to understand than the Conservatives' and NDP's plans, based as they were on complicated cap-and-trade mechanisms. However, it was the Liberal plan that was criticized for being too complex.

In Europe, no government was elected by campaigning on the European cap-and-trade system. It is likely that few Europeans know that this system even exists, let alone understand it. The continent-wide adoption of the EU emission-trading scheme was secured through typical technocratic and opaque EU negotiations. In contrast, all attempts to establish an EU-wide carbon tax have failed, because of the political risk associated with the dreaded three-letter word.

In "tax," entrenched opponents to carbon pricing of any sort have found their preferred language of attack, denouncing cap-and-trade systems as "cap-and-tax." In Canada, the Conservative Party's attack ads have hammered the Official Opposition leaders—first, Liberal Michael Ignatieff and then, New Democrat Thomas Mulcair—as supporters of a "job-killing carbon tax" even though both leaders advocated a cap-and-trade system—the same policy the Conservatives had included in their platform in 2008.

Some suggest that the only way to make carbon taxes acceptable for voters is to make the fiscal benefit as concrete and easy to understand as possible. Carbon tax proposals can be made simple if broader policy outcomes don't matter much. For example, one can propose that the government tax carbon emissions and return the totality of the proceeds back to the public on a per capita basis—making sure to stress that every citizen will receive the same amount. A political party might then be able to campaign on the following simple commitment: "if we are elected, you will receive, every year, a 'green cheque' for X dollars." Whether or not this "tax & 100% dividend" (Hanson, 2009) would be easier to sell to voters, it is clearly not the optimal policy and could cost substantial support in many corners. The environmental community might not support a proposed carbon tax if none of its revenue is earmarked to carbon mitigation projects or green incentives. The business community might not support a carbon tax if no funding is dedicated to reducing the cost of doing business or addressing competitiveness concerns. The social activist community is likely to attack a policy that does so little to correct the inherent regressive impact of energy taxes. In short: if you care about the whole range of outcomes of the policy, you must use a more multi-dimensional approach to find policy levers.

A different approach would be, instead of earmarking the totality of revenues for corresponding tax cuts, to allocate some of them to popular government programs. Both the BC carbon tax and the 2008 Liberal plan were meant to be revenue-neutral, with legislation requiring an annual report on how all carbon tax revenue is returned to taxpayers through tax measures. Such policies are designed to make a carbon tax more politically appealing.

Those whose advise politicians to stay away from purely revenue-neutral models refer to polls showing that the public's top choices for carbon tax revenue are for programs that address environmental impact—such as public transit—and for desirable services like health care and education (Horne, Petropavlova, & Partington, 2012, pp. 21–25). However, if revenue neutrality is not guaranteed, a carbon tax risks being characterized as just another tax grab. The notion that bad things (pollution) should be taxed instead of good ones (labour, investment) is a simple and powerful one. Revenue-neutral carbon tax reforms give citizens more control over how much tax they pay in a way that benefits them and society as a whole.

Another avenue would be to build support for carbon taxes through strong intergovernmental consensus. In Canada, some are of the opinion that the federal government should levy a carbon tax and then redistribute it partly or entirely to the provincial and territorial governments, based on the contribution their taxpayers have made (Peters, Bataille, Rivers, & Jaccard, 2010; Snoddon &Wigle, 2009; Courchene & Allan, 2010; Tang, 2011). Supporters of this approach argue that it would strengthen the consensus toward a comprehensive federal climate policy, harmonize carbon pricing across Canada, and address the regional equity problems that arise in a federation where two provinces—Alberta and Saskatchewan—emit 45% of the country's GHGs, while they only represent 13% of the population.

It is difficult to see how such federal–provincial revenue-sharing would facilitate the election of a federal party running on a carbon tax, making the pitch to voters that "I will tax you and I will give the money to your provincial government with no idea how it will be spent." It seems a hard sell.

As the NRTEE (2012) points out, we should avoid designing a cross-Canada structure that creates a "joint decision trap' whereby collaboration and consensus leads to outcomes supporting the lowest common denominator" (p. 115). We should also avoid creating a disincentive for the provinces to actually reduce their emissions, which would happen if the federal government allocated carbon tax revenue to the provinces according to their volume of emissions. Then, any reduction in GHG emissions would result in reduced federal transfers. For example, it took a lot of political courage for the Ontario government to pursue its coal phase-out and pro-renewable energy policy. This would have been even more difficult if the corresponding decrease in carbon emissions from coal also cost millions of dollars from Ontario's treasury in lost federal transfers.

Conclusion: An Increasingly Pressing and Relevant Idea That Must Be Revisited

We humans are dumping far too much CO_2 and other greenhouse gases into the atmosphere, to the point where we are causing harmful and irreversible disruptions to the Earth's climate. To fight the perils of climate change, governments must set an economy-wide price on GHG emissions not as a stand-alone policy, but as a cost-effective anchor, essential to the success of a comprehensive climate plan. Carbon pricing is needed to be bold, not blind, in facing this huge challenge.

In this chapter, I have made the argument that a carbon tax is by far the most efficient and effective way to price carbon. However, above all, we need sound carbon pricing. Currently, both the federal NDP and Liberals have opted for a cap-and-trade policy. It is not the optimal solution, but it is infinitely better than the Conservative government's irresponsible vendetta against all forms of carbon pricing.

If we are to proceed with a cap-and-trade system in Canada, it should be designed in a way that emulates the most positive aspects of a carbon tax: the government should sell emission allowances through full-fledged auctions, making sure that significant revenues are returned to Canadian households and businesses; it should extend the cap beyond the large industrial emitters, broadly applying "at a point in the fuel distribution chain," to "the 36 per cent of emissions in buildings, transportation and light manufacturing" (NRTEE, 2009, p. 44). And the government should limit price volatility through cost containment measures, safety valves, and price collars (NRTEE, 2009, p. 36; Aldy & Stavins, 2011; Joshi, 2009; Fankhauser, Hepburn, & Park, 2011).

I have argued in this chapter that there is no easy path, no semantic device, no simplistic window-dressing, and no obvious way to convince voters to support a carbon tax. It may simply be that citizens need time to get familiar with the concept and its benefits. This is why its proponents should not be discouraged by a first electoral rebuff. They should forcefully highlight this policy's virtues and advocate for it on its merits, which will become all the more evident as the difficulties they address become more salient. As the planet's temperature continues to rise, and extreme weather events become more and more frequent—from heat waves and droughts, to tornadoes and flooding—there will be greater demand for governments to put a price on carbon, to ensure that polluters are no longer able to use our air as a free dumping ground.

The revenues available for recycling that a carbon tax provides will be more welcome than ever. As the world economy continues to become more competitive, there will be greater demand for lower taxes on business income and on investment in new technologies. As the sandwich generation of middle-class households faces rising living costs, as they begin looking after both their children and aging parents, there will be greater demand for lower taxes on household income. As the costs of child poverty grow, particularly with an aging workforce that will need to maximize economic opportunities for younger workers, there will be greater demand for poverty reduction strategies.

I am confident and optimistic that these simultaneous pressures will one day motivate policy-makers, whether Conservative, Liberal, or NDP, to re-evaluate carbon taxes as a policy solution. The sooner the better.

Notes

1. "Acting now to put a price on carbon..." (OECD, 2012, p. 111).
2. "Key principles include a clear, nationally consistent carbon price across the economy" (Canadian Council of Chief Executives, 2012, p. 10).
3. "An economy-wide carbon signal is the most effective way to achieve the Government of Canada's medium- and long-term emission reduction targets" (NRTEE, 2009, p. 4).
4. "Putting a price on carbon, for example, would provide broad incentives to develop and commercialize Canadian climate-friendly technologies" (Goldfarb, 2008, p. 26).
5. "This could take different forms such a carbon tax which would be the most simple to implement" (Canada West Foundation, 2011, p. 25).
6. "I've argued that for years" (Manning, 2012).
7. "It is virtually inconceivable that a standards-based approach could form the centrepiece of a meaningful climate policy" (Aldy & Stavins, 2012, p. 46). See also Simpson, Jaccard, & Rivers, 2007.
8. See the survey done by the US Congressional Budget Office (2008, February).
9. See also Sumner, Bird, & Smith (2009).

References

Aldy, J. E., & Stavins, R. N. (2012, Spring). Using the market to address climate change: Insights from theory and experience. *Daedalus, the journal of Academy of Arts & Sciences, 141*(2), pp. 45–60.

Andersen, M. S., & Ekins, P. (Eds). (2009). *Carbon energy taxation: Lessons from Europe.* New York, NY: Oxford University Press.

Auditor General of Canada. (2011, October). *Report of the Commissioner of the Environment and Sustainable Development.* Retrieved from http://www.oag-bvg.gc.ca/internet/English/parl_cesd_201110_e_35765.html

Bauman, Y., & Hsu, S-L. (2012, July 4). The most sensible tax of all. *New York Times.* Retrieved from http://www.nytimes.com/2012/07/05/opinion/a-carbon-tax-sensible-for-all.html?_r=0

Bruvoll, A., & Larsen, B. M. (2002). *Greenhouse gas emissions in Norway—Do carbon taxes work?* (Discussion paper no. 337), Statistics Norway Research Department. Oslo: Statistics Norway.

Canada West Foundation. (2011). *Changing the climate. A policy framework for Canada's new energy environment.* Retrieved from http://cwf.ca/publications-1/changing-the-climate-a-policy-framework-for-canada-s-new-energy-environment

Canadian Council of Chief Executives. (2012, July). *Framing an energy strategy for Canada–Submission to the Council of the Federation.* Ottawa, ON: Author.

Carter, J., & MacGregor, I. (2010, June 18). *Carbon capture and storage: A promising technology for the environment and the economy* (Changing the Climate series). Calgary, AB: Canada West Foundation.

Chateau, J., Saint-Martin, A., & Manfredi, T. (2011). *Employment impacts of climate change mitigation policies in OECD: A general equilibrium perspective* (OECD Environment Working Paper no. 32). Paris: OECD.

Clo, S., & Vendramin, E. (2012, May 10). *Is the ETS still the best option? Why opting for a carbon tax* (IBL Special report). Retrieved from www.brunoleonimedia.it/public/Papers/IBL-Special_Report-ETS.pdf

Conference Board of Canada. (2011). *Canadian income inequality* [Web page]. Retrieved from http://www.conferenceboard.ca/hcp/hot-topics/caninequality.aspx

Congressional Budget Office. (2007). *Trade-offs in allocating allowances for CO2 emissions.* Retrieved from http://www.cbo.gov/sites/default/files/cbofiles/ftpdocs/89xx/doc8946/04-25-cap_trade.pdf

Congressional Budget Office (2008, February). *Policy options for reducing CO_2 emissions* (No. 2930). Retrieved from http://www.cbo.gov/sites/default/files/cbofiles/ftpdocs/89xx/doc8934/02-12-carbon.pdf

Copps, S. (2008, October 20). Dion's political luck runs out. *The Hill Times*, p. 9.

Courchene, T. J., & Allan, J. R. (Eds.). (2010). *Canada: The state of federalism 2009: Carbon pricing and environmental federalism.* Kingston: McGill-Queen's University Press.

Dion, S., & Laurent, É. (2012, May 16). *From Rio to Rio: A global carbon price signal to escape the great climate inconsistency* (OFCE Working paper). Paris: French Economic Observatory.

Environics Research Group. (2011, December 1). Canadians continue to voice strong support for actions to address climate change, including an international treaty and carbon taxes. Retrieved from http://www.environics.ca/uploads/File/Environics---Climate-Change-Poll---Media-Release---Nov-30-2011(1).pdf

Environment Canada (2012, August). *Canada's emissions trends 2012.* Retrieved from http://www.ec.gc.ca/Publications/253AE6E6-5E73-4AFC-81B7-9CF440D5D2C5/793-Canada's-Emissions-Trends-2012_e_01.pdf

Fankhauser, S., Hepburn, C., & Park, J. (2011, February). *Combining multiple climate policy instruments: How not to do it* (Working paper no. 48). London, UK: Centre for Climate Change Economics and Policy.

Goldfarb, D. (2008, October). *Global climate-friendly trade: Canada's chance to clean up.* Ottawa, ON: Conference Board of Canada.

Government of Norway, Ministry of the Environment. (2012, October 8). The government is following up on the climate agreement. Retrieved from http://www.regjeringen.no/en/dep/md/press-centre/Press-releases/2012/the-government-is-following-up-on-the-cl.html?id=704137

Hanson, J. E. (2009, February 25). Carbon tax & 100% dividend vs. tax & trade. *Testimony given at Scientific Objectives for Climate Change Legislation to Committee on Ways and Means, United States House of Representatives.*

Harrison, K. (2010). The comparative politics of carbon taxation. *Annual Review of Law and Social Science*, 6, 507–529.

Harrison, K. (2012). A tale of two taxes: The fate of environmental tax reform in Canada. *Review of Policy Research*, 29(3), 383–407.

Hohan, A. (2006). The use of consumption taxes to relaunch green tax reforms. *International Review of Law and Economics*, 26, pp. 88–113.

Horne, M., Petropavlova, E., & Partington, P. J. (2012, June). *British Colombia's carbon tax. Exploring perspectives and seeking common ground.* Vancouver, BC: Pembina Institute.

Hovi, J., & Holtsmark, B. (2006). Cap-and-trade or carbon taxes? The feasibility of enforcement and the effects of non-compliance. *International Environmental Agreements: Politics, Law and Economics*, 6(2), 137–155.

Hsu, S-L. (2011). *The case for a carbon tax.* Washington, DC: Island Press.

Joshi, R. (2009). "Hybrid" carbon pricing: Issues to consider when carbon taxes and capandtrade systems interact. *Sustainable Prosperity: Issues in Carbon Pricing.* Retrieved from www.sustainableprosperity.ca

Jotzo, F. (2012, June 17). Australia's carbon pricing. *Nature Climate Change, 2,* 475–476.

International Energy Agency (IEA). (2011). *World energy outlook* [Web page]. Retrieved from www.worldenergyoutlook.org/

Krechowicz, D. (2011, May) *Effect of carbon pricing on low-income households and its potential contribution to poverty reduction* (Background paper for Sustainable Prosperity). Ottawa, ON: Sustainable Prosperity, University of Ottawa.

Lachapelle, E. (2011, February). The hidden factor in climate policy: Implicit carbon taxes (Policy Brief). *Sustainable Prosperity.* Retrieved from http://www.sustainableprosperity.ca/article900

Laurent, É, & Le Cacheux, J. (2009). *An ever-less carbonated union? Towards a better European taxation against climate change* (Studies & Research, 74, Notre Europe). Retrieved from www.notre-europe.eu

Lee, M., & Sanger, T. (2008). *Is BC's carbon tax fair? An impact analysis for different income levels* (Climate Justice Project). Vancouver, BC: Canadian Centre for Policy Alternatives.

Manning, P. (2012, June 9). Interview by E. Solomon. *The House, CBC Radio 1* [Radio show]. Retrieved from http://www.cbc.ca/thehouse/2012/06/09/house-additions-preston-manning/

McCarthy, S. (2012, September 11). President of Royal Dutch Shell Canadian division urges carbon price. *Globe and Mail.* Retrieved from http://www.theglobeandmail.com/report-on-business/industry-news/energy-and-resources/president-of-royal-dutch-shell-canadian-division-urges-carbon-price/article4534929/

Mintz, J., & Olewiler, N. (2008). *A simple approach for bettering the environment and the economy: Restructuring the federal fuel excise tax.* Ottawa, ON: Institute for the Environment.

M. K. Jaccard and Associates. (2009, October). *Exploration of two Canadian greenhouse gas emissions targets: 25% below 1990 and 20% below 2006 levels by 2020.* Toronto, ON: Suzuki Foundation and Pembina Institute.

National Round Table on the Environment and the Economy (NRTEE). (2009). *Achieving 2050: A carbon pricing policy for Canada.* Ottawa, ON: Author.

National Round Table on the Environment and the Economy (NRTEE). (2012). *The state of climate progress in Canada.* Ottawa, ON: Author.

Nordhaus, W. D. (2001, January). *After Kyoto: Alternative mechanisms to control global warming.* Paper presented at a joint session of the American Economic Association and the Association of Environmental and Resource Economists, Atlanta, Georgia.

Nordhaus, W. D. (2008). *Question of balance: Weighing the options on global warming policies.* New Haven, CT: Yale University Press.

Oliwiler, N. (2012). Smart environmental policy with full-cost pricing. *University of Calgary School of Public policy, 5*(6).

Organisation for Economic Co-operation and Development (OECD). (2012). *Environmental Outlook to 2050.*Retrieved from www.oecd.org/env/cc/49082173.pdf

Osberg, L. (2008, April). Have most North Americans already met their Kyoto obligations? Trends in the CO_2 content of consumption and the role of income inequality. *Dalhousie University* (Working Paper No. 2008-02). Retrieved from ftp://ftp.repec.org/opt/ReDIF/RePEc/.../kyoto.pdf

Peters, J., Bataille, C., Rivers, N., & Jaccard, M. (2010, November). *Taxing emissions, not income: How to moderate the regional impact of federal environmental policy* (Commentary no. 314). Toronto, ON: C. D. Howe Institute.

Pigou Club. (2006, October 20) Pigou Club Manifesto [Web log post]. Retrieved from http://gregmankiw.blogspot.ca/

Prime Minister of Canada. (2008, May 28). Prime Minister Harper addresses the Canada–UK Chamber of Commerce in London [Speech]. Retrieved from http://pm.gc.ca/eng/media.asp?id=2131

Rabe, B. G. (2010). The "impossible dream" of carbon taxes: Is the "best answer" a political non-starter? In B. G. Rabe (Ed.), *Greenhouse governance: Addressing climate change in America* (pp. 126–157). Washington, DC: Brookings Institution Press.

Raush, S., & Reilly, J. (2012, August). *Carbon tax revenue and the budget deficit: A win-win-win solution?* (Report no. 228). Cambridge, MA: MIT Joint Program on the Science and Policy of Global Change.

Richards, J. (2011). Idle speculation: Prefunding the boomers' frail elderly care and legitimizing a carbon tax. In F. Gorbet & A. Sharpe (Eds.), *New directions for intelligent government in Canada* (pp. 227–248). Ottawa, ON: Center for the Study of Living Standards.

Romm, J. (2012, July 17). Could conservatives be considering a price on carbon pollution? Retrieved from www.theenergycollective.com

Royal Society of Canada Expert Panel. (2010, December). *Environmental and health impacts of Canada's oil sands industry.* Retrieved from http://rscsrc.ca/sites/default/files/pdf/RSC_ExP_ExecutiveSummary_ENG_Dec14_10_FINAL_v5.pdf

Sawyer, D., & Fischer, C. (2010, August). *Better together? The implications of linking Canada–US greenhouse gas policies.* Toronto, ON: C. D. Howe Institute.

Simpson, J., Jaccard, M., & Rivers, N. (2007). *Hot air: Meeting Canada's climate change challenge.* Toronto, ON: McClelland and Stewart.

Snoddon, T., & Wigle, R. (2009). Clearing the air on federal and provincial climate change policy in Canada. *Choices, 15*(11). Retrieved from www.irpp.org/choices/archive/vol15no11.pdf

Sumner, J., Bird, L., & Smith, H. (2009, December). *Carbon taxes: A review of experience and policy design considerations.* Boulder, CO: National Renewable Energy Laboratory.

Sustainable Prosperity. (2011, May). *Carbon pricing, social equity and poverty reduction.* Retrieved from www.sustainableprosperity.ca/article1398

Sustainable Prosperity. (2011, July). *Carbon pricing and fairness.* Retrieved from www.sustainableprosperity.ca/article1626

Sustainable Prosperity. (2012, June 27). *British Columbia's carbon tax shift: The first four years.* Retrieved from www.sustainableprosperity.ca/article2864

Tang, M. (2011). Carbon pricing, fairness and fiscal federalism: A cost-sharing proposal for Canada. *Queen's Policy Review, 2*(2), 17–36.

Van Loon, J., & Mayeda, A. (2013, February 2). PM wrong to fight carbon tax, industry: Oil companies see advantages in greenhouse-gas levy. *Edmonton Journal.* Retrieved from http://www2.canada.com/edmontonjournal/news/business/story.html?id=08ac9937-f602-43c8-9d5a-2c0ba761e023

Vaughan, S. (2012, May 8). *Report of the Commissioner of the Environment and Sustainable Development to the House of Commons.* Retrieved from http://www.oag-bvg.gc.ca/internet/English/osh_20120508_e_36885.html

Victor, D. G. (2011). *Global warming gridlock.* New York, NY: Cambridge University Press.

Yokoyama, A., Ueta, K., Fujikawa, K., (2000). Green tax reform: Converting implicit carbon taxes to a pure carbon tax. *Environmental Economics and Policy Studies, 3*, 1–20.

Chapter 11

How Small Changes Can Make a Big Difference: The Case of Financial Transaction Taxes

Toby Sanger

The financial and economic crisis has led to a revival of interest around the world in financial transactions taxes (FTTs) and other forms of taxing finance. What started as a grassroots campaign by international development and anti-poverty activists for a small tax on currency transactions to fight global poverty has spread and become much broader in scope. Protestors from the Occupy movement to the anti-austerity demonstrations across Europe, North America, and beyond have been demanding, among other things, that governments introduce financial transactions taxes such as the "Robin Hood Tax."

The idea has now entered the mainstream, garnering the support of hundreds of thousands worldwide, including business, faith, and political leaders, Nobel-winning economists, musicians and actors, and even finance industry executives.

While the International Monetary Fund (IMF) has expressed a preference for other types of taxes, they have acknowledged that financial transactions taxes are feasible, have merit, and can be implemented without much economic disruption (IMF 2010, Chapter 7). The European Commission (EC) (2013b) has also undertaken in-depth analysis of financial transaction taxes and recommended that they be adopted in the EU—several countries have already done just that.

Despite this progress, financial transactions taxes continue to face strong opposition from the financial industry and some governments, such as the United Kingdom and Canada, intent on shielding their own financial industries from additional taxes. The international campaign for financial transactions taxes is far from over and its history has not yet been written, but the successes it has had so far against powerful opponents will no doubt provide an excellent case study to other campaigns for fair taxes.

This chapter provides a short introduction to the recent political history of financial transactions taxes, addresses economic arguments for and against them, and concludes with some comments about the campaign.

Financial Transactions Taxes, the Tobin Tax, and the Robin Hood Tax: What Are They?

Financial transactions taxes are very small taxes—a fraction of a percent—levied on transactions of stocks, bonds, foreign exchange, and other financial instruments, such as financial derivatives (options, futures contracts, swaps, etc.), while generating hundreds of billions of dollars a year in revenues. Regular bank transactions are excluded from virtually all financial transactions taxes and some also have a threshold to ensure smaller investors aren't directly affected.

Variations of financial transaction taxes include stock transaction taxes (STTs)—which are only levied on transactions of stocks—and currency transaction taxes (CTTs)—only levied on transactions of foreign exchange. CTTs have also been called the "Tobin Tax," after James Tobin, the economist who first proposed them.

The original proposal for the so-called "Robin Hood Tax" was developed by the UK international development organization *War on Want* and the *new economics foundation* in 2001, following the East Asian financial crisis of 1997–8. It was proposed as a small tax on currency transactions to help stabilize the financial system and generate billions a year in revenues that could be used to fight poverty.[1] The proposal soon attracted support from other development organizations such as Oxfam, Save the Children, and UNICEF, as well as poverty, labour, and environmental organizations eager to identify revenues that could be used to help reduce domestic and global poverty, achieve the UN's Millennium Development Goals, and fight climate change.

As the problem of financial speculation grew, culminating in the global financial crisis of 2008–9, so did the scope of the Robin Hood Tax and other proposed financial transactions taxes. The Robin Hood Tax proposal now asks for a tax of between 0.005 and 0.5% of the value of a financial product each time it is traded. Financial derivatives and foreign exchange would be taxed at a lower rate, stocks at a higher rate.

Financial transactions taxes (FTTs) are considered attractive for a number of reasons:

1. FTTs can generate *significant revenues* at national and international levels to pay for some of the costs of the financial crisis and generate funds for development. Estimates are a broad-based global FTT would raise hundreds of billions a year.
2. They can *reduce excessive financial speculation and activity*, steer more resources into productive investments, and reduce the risk of further financial crises: in short, FTTs would be good for the economy.
3. They are *very progressive,* paid for almost entirely by the finance sector and wealthy individuals, and so reduce inequality.

Because much of the trading in financial derivatives and foreign exchange is global and highly mobile, financial transactions taxes in these areas would be more effective if they were established through international agreements. However, global agreements are not necessary if domestic or regional FTTs include strong anti-avoidance measures.

Advocates for the Robin Hood Tax have proposed that at least half the funds raised be used for reducing global poverty and fighting climate change, and the other half would be kept by each country for domestic priorities. This could lead to a win-win-win outcome of reduced economic instability, stronger economic growth, and reduced inequality. If FTTs were combined with stronger regulations of tax havens, they could also reduce revenue leakage from developing countries in particular, increasing their sustainability and reducing their dependence on foreign aid.

Financial Transactions Taxes Have a Long History

Despite the wave of recent interest, financial transaction taxes aren't a new idea at all; in fact, they have a long history. One of the oldest of the existing financial transactions taxes is the United Kingdom's Stamp Duty Reserve Tax. This was first introduced more than 300 years ago in 1694. Similar stamp duty taxes had previously been collected in the Netherlands, France, Denmark, and Prussia. The UK's stamp duty tax now collects approximately £3 billion (or US$5 billion) a year for the UK Treasury from a 0.5% tax rate on stock transactions, with exemptions in certain areas.

More than 40 other countries around the world collect some form of financial transaction taxes that generate significant revenues, including countries as diverse as Switzerland, Finland, Brazil, China, India, Hong Kong, and Taiwan. China has levied a tax on trading in stocks, with the government adjusting the rate depending on how much they want to cool down or stimulate their stock market (for example, see Zhixin, 2007). Taiwan not only taxes transactions of stocks and bonds but also has a tax (at a lower rate) on transactions of financial derivatives such as options and futures. Many more countries had levied financial transactions taxes in the past, but eliminated them during the 1990s on the eve of the stock market boom that ended in the 2008 financial crisis.

The Economic Case for Financial Transaction Taxes

While governments introduced financial transactions taxes to raise revenue, there is also a strong economic argument for them. This was first articulated by John Maynard Keynes, the most renowned economist of the twentieth century. In 1936, following the Great Depression, he wrote in the path-breaking work *The General Theory* that "the introduction of a substantial government transfer tax on all transactions might prove to be the most serviceable reform available, with a view towards mitigating the predominance of speculation over enterprise in the United States" (Keynes, 1936, ch.12, s. 6, para 2).

Keynes was followed by the Nobel Prize–winning economist James Tobin, who in 1972 proposed an international tax on currency transactions (the "Tobin Tax") designed to, as he put it, "throw sand in the wheels" (1978, p. 154) of international finance, reduce speculation, and cushion exchange rate fluctuations following the breakdown of the Bretton-Woods fixed exchange rate system. More recently, other Nobel Prize–winning economists, including Joseph Stiglitz, Paul Krugman, and Amartya Sen, have joined more than 1,000 of their fellow professionals in urging governments to introduce global financial transactions taxes.

The main interest of economists in financial transactions taxes isn't for the amount of revenue they raise, or their impacts on equity and distribution, but because they believe FTTs will reduce speculation, stabilize the economy, and promote productive investments. In financial terms, they are expected to play a role similar to the way "sin taxes" on alcohol or tobacco reduce consumption, or the way environmental taxes reduce pollution or other environmentally degrading activities for social or environmental reasons.[2]

Financial Weapons of Mass Destruction

The interest in financial transactions taxes now goes beyond Keynes' and Tobin's proposals for taxing transactions of stocks and currencies, to cover a much broader range of financial instruments. Over the past two decades, trading in financial derivatives has increased exponentially worldwide, growing more than four times as fast as underlying global economic growth each year.

While financial derivatives were originally developed to *reduce* risk and are used for legitimate hedging and insurance purposes, they have also increasingly been used for speculation and consequently often have a *destabilizing* effect. Annual transactions of financial derivatives—options, futures, and swaps—now amount to more than 60 times the global GDP, and more than 10 times the value of spot transactions. The value of derivative contracts outstanding amounts to 10 times the global GDP. Clearly, much of this involves investments designed to increase profit through leverage and risky speculation, instead of hedging for insurance purposes.

Legendary investor Warren Buffett presciently warned over a decade ago that he viewed derivatives "as time bombs, both for the parties that deal in them and the economic system. . . . The range of derivatives contracts is limited only by the imagination of man (or sometimes, so it seems, madmen)" (Buffett qtd. in Berkshire Hathaway, 2002, p 13). While derivatives may reduce risks at the micro level, they allow credit risk to become dangerously concentrated in a few hands and to be highly leveraged in a way that is almost impossible to estimate: "derivatives are financial weapons of mass destruction, carrying dangers that, while now latent, are potentially lethal" (Buffet qtd. in Berkshire Hathaway, 2002, p. 15).

Financial authorities don't even have a handle on the extent of derivatives transactions, because most are traded "over the counter" (OTC) directly between institutions rather than through stock exchanges. Successive exemptions granted by regulatory agencies—moves now considered massive mistakes—meant that these growing derivatives markets were essentially deregulated under the presidencies of both Bill Clinton and George W. Bush.

As Buffett had warned, banks and financial dealers developed a bewildering array of different derivatives that allowed investors to believe they had low-risk investments in securitized mortgages, while at the same time allowing the financial industry to realize extraordinary profits. More and more money was diverted into speculative investments and away from productive investments in the real economy. Then, with credit derivatives tying it together, this financial house of cards collapsed, resulting in the financial crisis we are all still paying for.

In the wake of the crisis, financial authorities realized they should track trading in derivatives, and so now require them to be traded on exchanges or electronic trading platforms or cleared through central counterparties. But progress toward stronger regulation in most other areas has been slow, and the industry hasn't changed its practices. JP Morgan, one of the most prominent US banks fighting against stronger regulations, subsequently lost $5.8 billion on a single botched trade in derivatives.

Another growing threat is the escalation of high-frequency trading (HFT), the flipping of large amounts of shares for a fraction of a second to either capture quick profits or to move markets. These are done by computerized trading, often anonymously in the growing "dark pools" of capital away from official public exchanges. Computerized and high-frequency trading in stocks and derivatives can increase market instability; it contributed to the "flash crash" of 2010, with billions lost in the space of minutes.

High-frequency trading accounts for a growing share of trading volumes on stock markets, amounting to an estimated over 70% of all trading on exchanges in the United States, and at least 42% in Canada. Canada's main securities regulator, the Ontario Securities Commission (OSC), is increasingly concerned about the growth of high-frequency trading, as it detracts from what markets should be doing: facilitating long-term investment (Erman, 2012, p. B3).

While the negative repercussions of financial instability and a runaway financial industry may appear distant to the lives of most Canadians, they are much more real to people in other countries. In Spain and Greece, one-quarter of the workforce and over 50% of youth have become unemployed as a result of austerity measures. These were introduced ostensibly because borrowing rates and credit default swaps for these countries escalated.

Developing countries are also more exposed to the growing problem of tax havens. These have enabled corporations and wealthy individuals to stash trillions offshore in secret accounts, away from regulators and tax collectors. The problem is more acute in developing countries because of their weaker powers of law enforcement, lower levels of revenue, and more pressing development needs. Oxfam estimates that close to US$20 trillion is held in tax havens around the world just by individuals, with a loss of over US$150 billion in annual tax revenues—two times the amount needed to eliminate extreme poverty (Oxfam 2013). Estimated amounts held and revenues lost through the corporate use of global tax havens are similar in magnitude.

Progress—and Opposition—at the International Level

As proposals for financial transactions taxes have gained more widespread support, they've also faced more concerted opposition. It is especially strong in countries such as the UK, Canada, and the United States, where there's a particularly close connection between the finance industry and politicians.

The campaign for financial transaction taxes received a boost at the G20 Summit in Pittsburgh in September 2009, when leaders agreed that the "financial sector should make a fair and substantial contribution" toward paying for some of the costs of the financial crisis (G20, 2009, p. 10). In advance of the G20 Summit in Toronto, the International Monetary Fund followed up on that commitment with practical advice for different ways of taxing the financial sector. The proposals they considered included bank levies (similar to insurance premiums, with the funds to be used for bailing out banks in trouble), financial transaction taxes, and a new proposal for a financial activities tax on financial industry profits and salaries to compensate for the fact that most transactions are excluded from value-added taxes, such as Canada's GST.

These proposals were vehemently shot down by the Canadian government, with Finance Minister Jim Flaherty claiming these kinds of taxes would result in "excessive, arbitrary or punitive regulation" of the financial sector (Yew, 2010, para. 4). The Harper government dispatched various ministers on a campaign to capitals around the world to drum up opposition to these proposals just prior to the Toronto G20 Summit. Since then, Finance Minister Flaherty (2012) has also publicly criticized European countries for proceeding with FTTs.

The Canadian government's recent strident opposition to financial transactions taxes constitutes an almost complete reversal from the international leadership role it had taken on this issue a dozen years before. In March 1999, Canada's House of Commons passed a motion stating, "That, in the opinion of the House, the government should enact a tax on financial transactions in concert with the international community" (Canada, 1999, p. 13323). This motion by the Opposition New Democratic Party was supported by most of the then-governing Liberal Party, with the Conservatives in opposition.

Despite the lack of progress at the global level, European countries have moved forward with adopting FTTs. With strong support from former French President Nicolas Sarkozy and German Chancellor Angela Merkel, a proposal for a financial transactions tax was endorsed by the European Commission, which called for an FTT to be introduced across Europe by 2014. The commission estimated that a 0.1% tax on transactions of equity shares and bonds, and a 0.01% tax on financial derivatives would generate €57 billion ($US77 billion) a year in revenues (European Commission, 2013c). The majority of the 27 member nations in the European Union supported an FTT, but strong opposition by a few, such as the UK and Sweden, has prevented its adoption more broadly at the EU level.

Under its new president, François Hollande, France introduced its own FTT on August 1, 2012. Hungary also introduced an FTT that took effect in 2013. Other major member states representing 90% of the Eurozone's economic output—including France, Germany, Italy, Spain, Belgium, Austria, Greece, Portugal, Slovakia, Estonia, and Slovenia—continued to push for an enhanced cooperation agreement through the EU to introduce a common financial transactions tax. Despite opposition from the UK, this was overwhelmingly endorsed by the European Parliament in December 2012, approved by the EU's finance ministers, and then adopted by the European Commission in February 2013. The harmonized EU financial transaction tax at a rate of 0.1% on stocks and bonds, and 0.01% on financial derivatives is expected to generate a total of €30 to €35 billion per year for the countries involved (European Commission, 2013a). It is anticipated other European countries will join once it is in place.

Renewed pressure is now building on the United States to introduce an FTT. This achieved a boost when Joseph Stiglitz (2013) called for the Obama administration to introduce a tax on financial speculation as part of a more progressive tax system. In February 2013, Senator Tom Harkin and Representative Peter DeFazio introduced a bill to introduce a tax of 0.03% on transactions of stocks, bonds, and financial derivatives. It is estimated that this would raise US$350 billion over 10 years, with an average of $35 billion annually (Gongloff, 2013).

Potential Revenues from Financial Transactions Taxes

Estimates for the potential revenues generated by financial transactions taxes vary depending on the rate, instruments covered, and expected impact, but there's no question they can raise substantial sums. Existing financial transactions taxes, as limited as they are, already generate significant revenues, with the UK's Stamp Duty Reserve Tax on share transactions raising approximately US$5 billion annually. Existing FTTs in other countries generate revenues of a similar and often higher range, and have become a significant share of their country's revenues.

There's solid research building on the work by Canadian expert Rodney Schmidt that posits a tax at a rate of 0.005% just on transactions of major global currencies could generate over US$30 billion annually at a low administrative cost with little impact on markets (Leading Group on Innovative Financing, 2010). Estimates for Canada show that a transactions tax at a rate of 0.5% on equity transactions would generate over CA$4 billion annually, assuming a 50% reduction in trading volumes (Sanger, 2011, p. 25). Calculations for the United States show that a broader-based "financial speculation tax" would generate an estimated US$150 billion in revenues (Baker, Pollin, MacArthur, & Sherman, 2009, p. 2).

Arguments For and Against Financial Transaction Taxes

Beyond paying for some of the costs of the crisis, there are also a number of other compelling economic arguments for increased taxation of the financial sector.

The financial sector is too big. A number of economists now believe that the financial sector has grown "too big" for the good of the economy, as a recent IMF report (2010a, p. 20) suggested. Finance is an intermediary industry, and doesn't directly produce goods with end-use values for people, so it can divert resources from other, more productive areas. Excessive salaries and bonuses paid to engineering graduates to create new financial products and derivatives divert them away from work on more fundamental social needs (Philippon, 2008a, 2008b).

Tax changes have provided large benefits and preferences for finance. Major tax changes introduced over recent decades provided large benefits to the financial sector and to highly compensated individuals in the industry. These include preferential tax rates for capital gains and investment income, cuts to corporate taxes, and reductions in top income tax rates. Lenient regulation and prosecution also allow the banking and finance industry to avoid taxes through the extensive use of tax havens. In addition, the shift to value-added taxes (such as the GST) that exempt most financial services also benefits the industry by reducing the cost of its products compared to other goods and services.

Reducing incentives for excessive risk-taking. There is growing recognition that tax preferences, including lower rates on "investment" income and stock options, increase incentives for short-term speculation and excessive risk-taking in the financial sector, as the IMF and the European Commission have acknowledged. For centuries, bankruptcy and limited liability laws have mitigated the downside risks for corporations. Following the financial crisis, there is understandably more concern about the potential damage that can be caused to the entire economy by large financial corporations. These are considered "too big to fail," and so have an implicit public guarantee from the government that they will be rescued. This effectively allows them to engage in systemically risky activities, with often disastrous consequences and large costs for governments.

Despite these arguments in favour of financial transaction taxes, opponents have levelled a variety of criticisms against them, claiming they would

- cause significant damage to the economy
- be ultimately paid for by ordinary investors and pensioners
- unfairly tax banks and financial institutions
- be easily avoided
- need to be global to work
- reduce market liquidity and increase economic volatility
- be inferior to stronger regulation of the financial industry.

Criticism: A financial transactions tax would harm the economy, reduce economic growth, and increase unemployment

Opponents of financial transactions taxes claim they would reduce economic growth and increase unemployment. For instance, UK Prime Minister David Cameron told the annual economic forum in Davos, Switzerland that a European FTT would be economic "madness" and result in half a million job losses (World Economic Forum, 2012). Such claims fail to take into account what the revenue will be used for, how these investments might actually contribute to job creation, and—in the case of taxes such as FTTs—how such taxes might, in themselves, have a positive impact on economic behaviour.

Opponents made wide use of the European Commission's initial technical impact assessment report, which suggested a European FTT would be damaging for the economy. Since then, the EC has produced revised estimates that a European FTT would actually increase GDP by between 0.2 and 0.4% if the revenues were spent on public investment (European Commission, 2012b, p. 2). In addition, these calculations don't take into account the potential positive impacts of reduced speculation, increased productive investment, and greater stability. These criticisms of FTTs also ignore the fact that countries with some of the strongest and most dynamic financial and economic centres in the world—the UK, Switzerland, China—have had financial transaction taxes for many years. One of the major economic critiques of financial transactions taxes is that they increase the cost of raising capital by adding to the price of selling stocks and bonds. However, most financial transactions apply only to the secondary trading market for equity shares and bonds, exempting initial public offers, and so would have little impact on those who buy shares as longer-term investments. In any case, most private investment is financed from retained earnings rather than raising funds in capital markets.

Financial transactions costs have dropped significantly in recent years. However, there's little evidence that lower costs of this type have increased economic growth. In fact, some results suggest there's a negative relationship: lower transactions costs on equities are associated with lower economic growth (Baker & Jorgensen, 2012).

Financial transactions taxes would have a very small or negligible impact on smaller-scale individual investors, particularly those who hold their investments for a longer period. For smaller investors, FTT costs are likely to be far less than the trading fees charged by banks and investment dealers. They would have a much greater impact on larger-scale traders, such as high-frequency traders and day traders. The use of high-frequency trading (HFT) has grown rapidly and is now estimated to account for more than two-thirds of trading on US stock markets, and close to half on Canadian stock markets (Barker & Pomeranets, 2011). High-frequency traders have much faster access to trading platforms, and this preferential treatment allows them to exploit price differences and market timing opportunities at the expense of ordinary investors. High-frequency and other speculative traders are able to gain higher profits (and losses) when there's greater market volatility and a greater imbalance of information.

Increased volatility caused by speculators isn't just a financial market concern, but can have substantial impacts on other markets, the economy, and individuals. For example, oil speculators such as hedge funds and large investment banks that quickly flip contracts now do about 70% of the trading in oil contracts, double their share from two decades ago (Kennedy, 2012; Hall & Rankin, 2011).

Instead of having a negative impact, many now believe financial transactions taxes would have a positive impact on the economy because

1. They would reduce the role of high-frequency and speculative traders in markets, increasing market stability and thereby economic growth.
2. Lower profits and fewer resources devoted to speculation would encourage greater investment in productive activities.
3. Revenues raised from financial transactions taxes are likely to be used in areas that provide a stronger boost to the economy and job growth. For example, in virtually all areas, public investment has a stronger economic impact than corporate tax cuts. (Baker & Jorgensen, 2012)

Avinash Persaud and Stephany Griffith-Jones estimate that a 0.1% financial transaction tax on equity and bond transactions and a 0.01% tax on derivative transactions in the UK would raise approximately £9 billion (or US$14 billion) a year, increase the UK's GDP by 0.25% and increase employment with 75,000 new jobs (Griffith-Jones & Persaud, 2012, p. 16).

Criticism: FTTs reduce market liquidity and increase economic volatility

There's been considerable debate and analysis of the impact of financial transactions taxes on market liquidity and volatility. The question of whether the increased volume, speed, and variety of financial transactions have increased financial volatility and economic uncertainty is hotly debated. There's little disagreement that FTTs would reduce the volume and probably also the value of market transactions. At the micro-economic level of individual markets, an increased level in the volume of transactions often leads to less volatility and short-term variation in prices. A number of studies have also demonstrated a correlation between the introduction or increase in transactions taxes and greater short-term volatility of equity market prices. This would be expected, as changes in tax rates add to market uncertainty over the short term. But short-term market volatility isn't the same as broader, long-term financial and economic volatility.

Financial crises have become both more frequent and more painful in the last three decades.[3] Eric Lascelles, Chief Economist for RBC Global Asset Management, recently concluded our economies are likely to suffer "ever more bubbles ever more quickly" (2009) as a result of the proliferation of derivatives, increased leverage, and speculative trading strategies.

One of the main objectives of financial transactions taxes is to reduce high-frequency and speculative trading while having less impact on longer-term investments. Lower transactions volumes that provide robust liquidity are better than high speculative volumes of trading that inflate values before bursting. Financial transactions taxes are expected to limit these speculative transactions and ensure market activity is driven more by fundamental economic conditions (Stamp Out Poverty, 2012).

In fact, while it has largely been ignored in Western versions of financial transactions taxes, China, Hong Kong, and Singapore actively use changes in the rates of their "stamp duties"—taxes on transactions of stocks in China and real estate in Hong Kong and Singapore—to cool down or help stimulate these asset markets.[4] These changes are designed to reduce the booms and busts so destructive to the broader economy and responsible for the financial and economic crisis we are still suffering from. Using such taxes would certainly be more effective than warnings from the finance minister and Bank of Canada governor about taking on more debt while they keep interest rates low.

Criticism: An FTT would ultimately be paid by individuals and pensioners
Some opponents claim banks and investment dealers will ultimately just pass all the costs of financial transactions taxes onto ordinary individuals and pensioners through higher fees. The International Monetary Fund (2011) has analyzed who would ultimately end up paying the cost of FTTs and concluded they are "highly progressive," with a much higher share paid by those with higher incomes, unlike sales taxes, which are regressive (p. 23). Analysis by the European Commission shows that banks and other financial institutions, such as hedge funds, are responsible for 85% of all taxable trades (Semeta, 2012, para. 10). A large majority of these transactions are conducted for their own account, businesses, or for very wealthy individuals.

While some costs could be passed on to ordinary individuals, for the large majority it would be far less than what they pay for other types of taxes. Once the benefits of higher public spending and/or reduced taxation in other areas are accounted for, the net impact on middle- and lower-income families is likely to be positive. Competition within the industry (where it exists) could limit the degree to which businesses are able to pass the cost of the tax on to consumers.

Criticism: Banks and financial institutions are already heavily taxed and an FTT would be excessive, arbitrary, and punitive
Banks and financial firms, particularly in Canada, have been highly profitable over the last two decades. As the European Commission background paper on this issue notes, the high profitability of this sector could result from higher productivity, lack of competition, the existence of a safety net provided by governments, and banking regulation or tax exemptions (2012a).

With high profits, the financial sector has paid a higher-than-average share of domestic corporate income taxes. Despite this, there's a lot of evidence that banks and financial firms are *under-taxed* compared to other sectors of the economy:

- Comprehensive analysis of the global taxes paid by multinationals shows that the financial sector pays one of the lowest rates of tax compared to other industries (Markle & Shackleford, 2010, p. 45). This is because large banks and financial firms are able to exploit tax havens and international taxation rules more than most other industries. Calculations show that just the top five banks reduced their Canadian taxes by more than $1 billion a year through their activities in tax havens, and by $2.4 billion in 2007 alone (Lauzon & Hasbani, 2008).
- Virtually all value-added taxes, such as the GST and HST, provide exemptions for most financial services. This exemption provides major benefits for the industry as it reduces the price of its services, and increases its demand and profits. The value of this tax exemption for the Canadian financial sector amounts to approximately C$5 billion a year,

using IMF estimates. The exemption of financial services from value-added taxes is a major reason why the IMF proposed a Financial Activities Tax(Sanger, 2011, p. 25).
- Larger banks and financial firms also benefit from the "Too Big to Fail" (TBTF) guarantee that governments implicitly or explicitly provide to prevent financial crises. This guarantee allows large banks and financial firms to undertake risky and more profitable activities in the knowledge that they will always be rescued or bailed out when they experience a big loss. Calculation of the value of this subsidy guarantee varies depending on circumstances, but estimates for the 18 largest US banks put it between $6 and 34 billion for 2009 (Baker & McArthur, 2009).
- The financial sector has been one of the greatest beneficiaries of corporate tax cuts and tax preferences over the past decade in Canada. The annual value of tax savings from lower corporate tax rates since 2001 now amounts to over $6 billion a year for the finance and insurance sector, and over $3 billion a year for the banking sector alone. The cumulative tax savings for the finance and insurance sector amount to over $30 billion since 2001 (Sanger, 2011, p. 11). These tax savings do not include the value of tax preferences, such as lower tax rates on capital gains and stock options.

New taxes on finance, such as financial transaction taxes, could help compensate for some of the tax exemptions and benefits that the industry has received.

Criticism: FTTs are easily avoided and don't work

Opponents of FTTs claim they can be easily avoided and don't work, pointing to Sweden's experience with financial transaction taxes in the late 1980s (Atkinson-Small, 2011). It's true that Sweden's experiment with FTTs was a failure and simply led to trades in Swedish shares moving offshore, but that's because the tax was very poorly designed. Following the example of countries that have successful FTTs in place can minimize this type of problem. In particular, FTTs should base their tax on the residence of the financial institution or trader, not where the trade takes place, as the European Commission has proposed. They should also include the provision that the FTT must be paid in order for change of ownership to be considered legal.

Centralized clearing systems for financial transactions can make it easier and more administratively efficient to collect FTTs. As the European Commission noted,

> Taxing financial transactions is one of the least expensive ways of collecting taxes, as most transactions are carried out electronically and the tax can be collected electronically and at the source. FTT can be collected at very low cost (less than 1% of revenue raised), especially when good use can be made of existing market infrastructures, e.g., with the help of trading platforms, trade repositories or clearing houses. (2012c)

Appropriate design and enforcement can limit the benefits and risks of relocation, but they also need to be combined with stricter crackdowns on the use of tax havens to avoid taxation.

Criticism: FTTs need to be global to work
Some argue FTTs need to be global to work. While a global agreement on transactions taxes is definitely preferable, the lack of one is no barrier for countries to move forward with financial transaction taxes at the national level. The existence of financial transactions taxes in over 40 countries both small and large demonstrates that they don't need to be global to work. For more internationally mobile transactions of foreign exchange and financial derivatives, it would be especially helpful to have a global agreement, but even that is not necessary. While the majority of national FTTs just cover transactions of stocks and bonds, some also cover financial derivatives.

One example of a financial transactions tax that would be particularly well-suited to a global agreement is a currency transactions tax. The Leading Group on Innovative Financing for Development—an organization of over 70 countries, international organizations, and the Bill & Melinda Gates Foundation—recently called for an international tax on currency transactions to provide funding for international development priorities.

Criticism: FTTs are inferior to stronger regulation of the financial industry
Some argue that transactions taxes are unnecessary and would be inferior to effective regulation of the financial sector. Financial transactions taxes are certainly no substitute for effective regulation, but can actually be a good *complement* to regulation. In fact, now that financial regulators have decided they need much more information about the transactions of financial derivatives and will require them to go through centralized exchanges, demanding payment of a small tax on each transaction provides much greater enforcement powers for governments to collect and track this information.

Obstacles in Canada—and Alternatives
Despite the international campaign, there's been little progress achieved in Canada on making financial transactions taxes an issue of interest to the public, or in convincing politicians to make them a priority.

What has made Canada go from leader to laggard on financial transaction taxes and prevented FTT proponents from gaining the same level of public and political support here that they've gained in other countries? No doubt some of it is due to the fact that we haven't had the same type of banking scandals the United States and Europe have had, with direct public rescues of failed banks and more attention given to stratospheric compensation in the finance sector.

Political support and leadership has also no doubt played a role. While the federal Liberal government and the NDP both supported the motion calling for a Tobin Tax in 1999, the Harper Conservative government has aggressively opposed any proposals to increase taxation of the financial sector both domestically and internationally. And with such hostility shown by the federal government toward all taxes, and especially those on finance, opposition parties have shown less enthusiasm for the idea. At most, some federal NDP politicians have said they would support a financial transactions tax as part of a global agreement.

There are also some practical challenges related to introducing financial transactions taxes in Canada. Since the Canadian financial market operates in the same time zone as United States financial markets, and a number of larger Canadian companies are cross-listed on American exchanges, competition with those markets becomes more of an issue. While the federal government's broad powers over taxation would presumably take precedence, the regulation of securities is split between provincial and federal governments under Canada's constitution, so opponents could mount a challenge to introducing financial transactions taxes as occurred with the proposed federal Securities Act (Supreme Court of Canada, 2011).

And with the current federal government opposed, it's unlikely the provinces of Ontario or Quebec, where the securities exchanges are now located, would proceed if there is potential for alternative electronic exchanges to be established elsewhere.

While there are obstacles to having financial transactions taxes established soon in Canada without the United States also on board, there are some alternatives for taxing the financial sector that could be introduced almost immediately. One of the most attractive of these is the IMF's proposal for a Financial Activities Tax on profits and remuneration of the financial sector.

There's strong economic justification for this tax because value-added taxes, such as the GST and provincial harmonized sales taxes, largely exempt financial services, which provides a significant tax benefit for the sector. Since the value-added of a business is essentially equal to profits and remuneration, a tax on these could achieve the same thing without the complications of applying the GST to financial services.

Calculations show a Financial Activities Tax in Canada would generate approximately $5 billion a year in 2013 (Sanger, 2011, p. 25). Furthermore, this type of tax could be introduced promptly without impediment from the federal or provincial level. Quebec has had a special compensation tax for financial institutions in place for many years, which was increased in the province's Fall 2012 budget (Quebec, 2012, p. A. 115).

Something Small Can Make a Big Difference

As the preceding discussion demonstrates, financial transactions taxes and alternatives, such as Financial Activities Taxes, make a lot of sense in economic terms. But as public policy experts and economists know all too well, while good arguments should be a necessary condition for the adoption of progressive taxes, they are rarely sufficient on their own. Much more is needed to galvanize public support and achieve change in the political realm, particularly for highly progressive taxes that challenge powerful interests.

The global campaign for a financial transaction tax provides a good example. In a modern-day twist on the Robin Hood story, a small band of activists have achieved progress in getting governments to introduce new taxes on the finance industry. And, like the namesake of their tax, they've achieved success against powerful interests not simply because of the merits of their cause, but by campaigning with cunning, imagination, and humour.

Good timing has, of course, also played a major role. There has been major public antipathy against an industry that caused a crisis and then was bailed out by the public. As the resulting financial and economic crisis led to large deficits that are now being used to justify public spending cuts, the public has understandably strongly supported calls for fairer and increased taxes on the financial sector as inequality has continued to worsen. But good timing doesn't amount to anything if it isn't capitalized on.

The campaign has used a compelling storyline, and has framed the issue with the "Robin Hood" theme: a small tax on banks and the wealthiest can benefit the world's poorest. It has included continuous networking by international activists; campaigning and lobbying of governments, international agencies, leaders, and thinkers; and a letter campaign of support signed by over a thousand economists, over a thousand legislators, faith leaders, business leaders, and finance industry professionals. They've expanded support through labour, environmental, and anti-poverty organizations, gained the backing of popular musicians and actors, created humorous videos, and mobilized further public support through marches, demonstrations, media-savvy stunts, online campaigns, literature, buttons, and stickers.

Financial transactions taxes will certainly not fix all problems with finance, eliminate speculation, or generate all the revenues needed to address global poverty and environmental challenges. But they can make a significant and positive difference.

The global campaign for financial transaction taxes and fairer taxes on the financial sector continues, and at some point its story will be written. But already it has achieved remarkable successes against long odds and powerful interests. The campaign has demonstrated that a small group of committed citizens, just like a small tax, can make a big difference in the world.

Notes

1. This proposal was itself inspired by an editorial published in *Le Monde Diplomatique* during the Asian financial crisis in 1997, entitled Désarmer les marches. It called for the creation of local "Associations for the Taxation of financial Transactions and Aid to Citizens" (ATTAC) to fight for the adoption of currency transactions taxes, with funds going to reduce global poverty.
2. Economists call these "Pigovian taxes" after Arthur Pigou, who developed the economic argument for them.
3. This was noted in *The Economist* magazine in 2010 (Beyond Bretton Woods 2) and a decade ago by Stiglitz (1999).
4. See Zhixin (2007) and Wong and Tong (2013).

References

Atkinson-Small, J. (2011, October 31). Cameron must stand up against the EU tax that could destroy our finance industry. *Daily Mail Online*. Retrieved from http://www.dailymail.co.uk/debate/article-2055634/A-financial-transactions-tax-disaster-Britain.html

Baker, D. (2011). *The deficit-reducing potential of a financial speculation tax* (Centre for Economic and Policy Research [CEPR] Issue Brief). Retrieved from http://www.cepr.net/documents/publications/fst-2011-01.pdf

Baker, D., & Jorgensen, H. (2012). *The relationship between financial transactions costs and economic growth* (CEPR Report). Retrieved from http://www.cepr.net/index.php/publications/reports/the-relationship-between-financial-transactions-costs-and-economic-growth

Baker, D., & MacArthur, T. (2009, September). *The value of the "too big to fail" big bank subsidy* (CEPR Report). Retrieved from http://www.cepr.net/documents/publications/too-big-to-fail-2009-09.pdf

Baker, D., Pollin, R., MacArthur, T., & Sherman, M. (2009). *The potential revenue from financial transactions taxes* (Centre for Economic and Policy Research [CEPR] Issue Brief). Retrieved from http://www.cepr.net/documents/publications/ftt-revenue-2009-12.pdf

Barker, W., & Pomeranets, A. (2011, June). The growth of high-frequency trading: Implications for financial stability (Report). *Bank of Canada Financial System Review* (pp. 47–52). Retrieved from http://www.bankofcanada.ca/wp-content/uploads/2011/12/fsr-0611-barker.pdf

Berkshire Hathaway Inc. (2002). *2002 Annual Report*. Retrieved from http://www.berkshirehathaway.com/2002ar/2002ar.pdf

Beyond Bretton Woods 2. (2010, November 4). *The Economist*, p. 85. Retrieved from http://www.economist.com/node/17414511

Canada, House of Commons Debates (1999, March 23, 1999) 36th Parliament, 1st Session, Hansard Volume 135, No. 202A, p. 13323. Hull, QC: Government of Canada. Retrieved from http://www.parl.gc.ca/content/hoc/House/361/Debates/202/han202-e.pdf

Culp, C. L. (2010, March 16). Financial transactions taxes: Benefits and costs. *Compass Lexecon* (Research paper). Retrieved from: http://www.rmcsinc.com/articles/FTTCLC.pdf

Erman, B. (2012, August 20). OSC heads lean to the negative about high-frequency trading. *Globe and Mail*, p. B3. Retrieved from http://www.theglobeandmail.com/globe-investor/investment-ideas/streetwise/osc-head-leans-to-the-negative-about-high-frequency-trading/article4490639/

European Commission. (2012a, May). *Tax contribution of the financial sector* [Technical Fiche]. Retrieved from http://ec.europa.eu/taxation_customs/resources/documents/taxation/other_taxes/financial_sector/fact_sheet/tax-contribution-fin-sector.pdf

European Commission (2012b, May). *Taxation of the financial sector: Macroeconomic effects* [Technical Fiche]. Retrieved from http://ec.europa.eu/taxation_customs/taxation/other_taxes/financial_sector/index_en.htm

European Commission (2012c). *Tax collection* [Technical Fiche]. Retrieved from http://ec.europa.eu/taxation_customs/resources/documents/taxation/other_taxes/financial_sector/fact_sheet/tax-collection.pdf

European Commission. (2013a, February 14). Financial transaction tax under enhanced cooperation: Commission sets out the details [press release]. Retrieved from http://europa.eu/rapid/press-release_IP-13-115_en.htm

European Commission. (2013b). *Taxation of the financial sector* [website]. Retrieved from http://ec.europa.eu/taxation_customs/taxation/other_taxes/financial_sector/index_en.htm

European Commission. (2013c). *Taxation of the financial sector* [Frequently Asked Questions]. Retrieved from http://ec.europa.eu/taxation_customs/taxation/other_taxes/financial_sector/index_en.htm

Flaherty, J. (2012, May 1). The Eurozone should sort out its own mess. *The Telegraph*. Retrieved from http://www.telegraph.co.uk/finance/financialcrisis/9238854/The-eurozone-should-sort-out-its-own-mess.html

G20. (2009, September 24–25). *Leaders' Statement at the Pittsburgh Summit*. Retrieved from http://www.g20.org/documents/#p4

Gongloff, M. (2013, February 28). Senators propose transactions tax to raise cash, slow high speed trading. *Huffington Post*. Retrieved from http://www.huffingtonpost.com/2013/02/28/transaction-tax-bill-high-speed-trading_n_2783904.html

Griffith-Jones, S., & Persaud, A. (2012, February). *Financial Transaction Taxes* (Initiative for Policy Dialogue, Network Paper). Retrieved from http://policydialogue.org/publications/network_papers/financial_transaction_taxes/

Hall, K. G., & Rankin, R. A. (2011, May 13). Speculation explains more about oil prices than anything else. *McClatchy DC*. Retrieved from http://www.mcclatchydc.com/2011/05/13/114190/speculation-explains-more-about.html

International Monetary Fund (IMF). (2010, September). *Financial sector taxation: The IMF's report to the G20 and background material*. Retrieved from http://www.imf.org/external/np/seminars/eng/2010/paris/pdf/090110.pdf

International Monetary Fund. (2011). *Taxing financial transactions: Issues and evidence* (IMF Working Paper). Retrieved from http://www.imf.org/external/pubs/ft/wp/2011/wp1154.pdf

Kennedy II, J. P. (2012, April 11). The high cost of gambling on oil. *New York Times*. Retrieved from http://www.nytimes.com/2012/04/11/opinion/ban-pure-speculators-of-oil-futures.html

Keynes, J. M. (1936). *The general theory of employment, interest and money*. Retrieved from http://www.marxists.org/reference/subject/economics/keynes/general-theory/ch12.htm

Lascelles, E. (2009, November 25). Ever more bubbles, ever more quickly? *Market Musings, TD Securities* (Research note). Retrieved from https://www.tdsresearch.com/currency-rates/viewEmailFile.action?eKey=I0BOM8DKF1BK3WVFLYC3G7GHP

Lauzon, L-P., & Hasbani, M. (2008). Les banques Canadiennes et l'evasion fiscale dans les paradis fiscaux: 16 milliards de dollars d'impots eludes. Paper presented by the Chaire d'etudes socio-economiques (CESE) at the Université du Québec à Montréal (UQAM), May 2008. Retrieved from http://www.unites.uqam.ca/cese/pdf/rec_08_evasion_fiscale.pdf

Leading Group on Innovative Financing for Development, Committee of Experts. (2010). Report of the Committee of Experts to the Taskforce on International Financial Transactions for the Development of Globalizing Solidarity: *The Case for Financial Levies.* Retrieved from http://www.leadinggroup.org/IMG/pdf_Financement_innovants_web_def.pdf

Markle, K., & Shackelford, D. (2010, March). Cross-country comparisons of corporate income taxes [Table 4]. Paper presented at the New York University School of Law Colloquium on Tax Policy. Retrieved from http://www.law.nyu.edu/ecm_dlv3/groups/public/@nyu_law_website_academics_colloquia_tax_policy/documents/documents/ecm_pro_065293.pdf

Oxfam. (2013, May 22). Lost tax haven cash enough to end extreme poverty twice over (press release). Retrieved from http://www.oxfam.org.uk/blogs/2013/05/tax-haven-cash-enough-to-end-extreme-poverty

Persaud, A. (2012, March). *The economic consequences of the EU proposal for a financial transaction tax.* Report prepared by Intelligence Capital Ltd. Retrieved from http://www.stampoutpoverty.org/wf_library_post/the-economic-consequences-of-the-eu-proposal-for-a-financial-transaction-tax/

Philippon, T. (2008a). Are bankers overpaid? [Web log post]. Retrieved from http://sternfinance.blogspot.com/2008/11/are-banker-over-paid-thomas-philippon.html

Philippon, T. (2008b). *The evolution of the US financial industry from 1860 to 2007: Theory and evidence* (Working Paper, November 2008). Retrieved from http://pages.stern.nyu.edu/~tphilipp/papers/finsize.pdf

Quebec. (2012, November 20). *Budget Plan 2013–14*, Government of Quebec. Retrieved from http://www.budget.finances.gouv.qc.ca/Budget/2013-2014/en/documents/budgetplan.pdf

Sanger, T. (2011). *Fair shares: How banks, brokers and the financial industry can pay fairer taxes* (CCPA Report). Retrieved from http://www.policyalternatives.ca/publications/reports/fair-shares

Semeta, A. (2012, February 9). Rebalancing the financial transactions tax debate. *The Telegraph.* Retrieved from http://www.telegraph.co.uk/finance/newsbysector/banksandfinance/9072297/Rebalancing-the-financial-transactions-tax-debate.html

Stamp Out Poverty. (2012, April). *Financial transaction tax: Myth-busting* [Web page]. Retrieved from http://www.stampoutpoverty.org/?lid=11539

Stiglitz, J. (1999, July). Must financial crises be this frequent and this painful? *Policy Options.* Retrieved from http://www.irpp.org/po/archive/jul99/stiglitz.pdf

Stiglitz, J. (2013, January 19). Inequality is holding back the recovery. *New York Times.* Retrieved from http://opinionator.blogs.nytimes.com/2013/01/19/inequality-is-holding-back-the-recovery/

Supreme Court of Canada. (2011). *Reference re. Securities Act.* S.C.C. 66. http://scc.lexum.org/decisia-scc-csc/scc-csc/scc-csc/en/item/7984/index.do

Tobin, J. (1978). A proposal for international monetary reform. *Eastern Economic Journal,* 4(3–4), 153–159. Retrieved from http://college.holycross.edu/RePEc/eej/Archive/Volume4/V4N3_4P153_159.pdf

War on Want. (2001). *The Robin Hood Tax* [Web page]. Retrieved from http://www.waronwant.org/campaigns/financial-crisis/hide/inform/16786-the-robin-hood-tax

Wong, K., & Tong, S. (2013, February 22). HK doubles stamp duty on all properties on bubbles risk. *Bloomberg.com.* Retrieved from http://www.bloomberg.com/news/2013-02-22/hong-kong-doubles-stamp-duty-on-all-properties-on-bubble-concern.html

World Economic Forum. (2012, January 27). Davos 2012: David Cameron slams Europe's transaction tax plan. *Economic Times*. Retrieved from http://economictimes.indiatimes.com/news/international-business/world-economic-forum-davos-2012-david-cameron-slams-europes-transaction-tax-plan/articleshow/11644407.cms

Yew, M. A-T. (2010, April 21). Flaherty: No bank tax for Canada. *Toronto Star*. Retrieved from http://www.thestar.com/business/bank/article/798599--flaherty-no-bank-tax-for-canada

Zhixin, D. (2007, May 30). China triples stamp tax on stock trading. *China Daily*. Retrieved from http://www.chinadaily.com.cn/china/2007-05/30/content_883249.htm

Chapter 12

We Need to Simplify and Re-focus the Tax System

C. Scott Clark

Introduction

Between 1997 and 1998 (the first year the federal government recorded a budgetary surplus since 1969–70) and 2010–11, total federal revenues, as a share of Gross Domestic Product (GDP), declined from 18.2 to 14.6%—the lowest federal revenue share in over 45 years. All major components of federal government revenues declined as a share of GDP over this period.

The Liberal government's 2000 budget proposed the largest income tax (personal and corporate) reductions ever. Notwithstanding the decline in tax rates, the Federal Liberal government continued to record surpluses, leaving a surplus of almost $14 billion in 2006–7 for the new Conservative government. Two years later, this surplus was gone.

The Conservative government has claimed that since being elected, it has been following a "low-tax plan for jobs and growth" (Minister of Finance, 2011), and there is no doubt that taxes have been cut (Clark & Devries, 2011). Most notable was the lowering of the GST by one point in 2006 and another in 2007, against the advice of just about every economist in Canada. In keeping with the plan of the previous Liberal government to lower the corporate income tax rate (CIT) as economic and fiscal circumstances permitted, the Conservative government lowered it from 21% in 2006 to 15% in 2012.

In the case of personal income taxes (PIT), the government has reduced the lowest tax rate by 1 percentage point, increased the basic personal amount, and broadened the lowest two tax brackets. It has also chosen to provide special "tax preferences" or "tax breaks" for specific groups. These include, for example, the splitting of pension income for seniors, and special non-refundable tax credits to support participation in sports activities, arts and cultural activities, public transportation, and enhanced tax credits for groups such as volunteer firefighters.

In the 2011 election, the Conservatives campaigned on the promise to extend the special tax credit for fitness activities to adults; to allow income-splitting for families with children 18 years of age and under; and to double the tax-free savings account (TFSA) contribution from $5,000 to $10,000. These credits and cuts are to be implemented once the deficit has been eliminated.

The total loss in CIT, PIT, and GST revenues resulting from the tax cuts introduced since 2006 amounts to over $45 billion annually and growing. On this basis, the government has every right to claim that it has a "low-tax plan," but it cannot claim that it has a "low-tax plan for jobs and growth."

Whatever the size of government, and the associated level of spending and taxes, the resulting fiscal structure (tax and spending) should satisfy three conditions. First, the fiscal structure must be sustainable, as reflected in a low and possibly declining debt-to-GDP ratio. The government's current fiscal structure satisfies this first condition. Second, tax revenues should be raised in a way that best supports savings, investment, economic growth, and job creation. The current tax system does not satisfy this condition. Third, the burden of taxation must be distributed fairly, with high-income individuals paying a greater proportion of their income in tax than lower-income individuals. There is growing evidence that this condition is not being satisfied and that the tax system is becoming less progressive.

The tax system is in need of serious reform.

This chapter presents a number of recommendations on the need for tax simplification, and on the need to refocus the tax mix so that it better promotes savings, investment, economic growth, and job creation. A simplified and more growth-focused tax system can enable changes that would improve fairness and progressivity. Implementing these recommendations under ideal conditions would take years, and require a strong and sustained political commitment and broad public acceptance. These conditions are unlikely to be met by the current Conservative government, since they would require it to reverse key tax decisions implemented since 2006, which are essential to the government's economic and political strategy.

The Conservative government is committed to reducing the size and role of the federal government in the economy, by cutting spending, transferring responsibilities to the provinces, and lowering taxes. Canadians need to seriously question and debate whether this is the direction they want their federal government to take. So far, this public debate has been seriously lacking.

Nevertheless, expanding the role and size of the federal government would require raising additional revenues, as a share of the economy, to pay for the programs and services Canadians need.[1] It would require addressing the issues of how much revenues should be increased; how best to raise the additional revenues in order to best support economic growth and job creation; and how to ensure that the burden of taxation is shared fairly among Canadians.

I hope that this chapter can be part of that debate.

The Federal Income Tax System Should Be Simplified

The Income War Tax Act of 1917, which was 11 pages in length (including regulations), has grown into today's Income Tax Act (ITA), which is some 2,800 pages long, including regulations and commentary.[2] The ITA has grown not only in size but also in complexity.

> The Act today (has) special rules for all sorts of circumstances and business arrangements that were not prevalent almost one hundred years ago, and in some cases not prevalent even five years ago. The age of the global economy, the increasing complexity of transactions and the fast pace of information exchange have forced a sense of urgency, if not panic, on policy-makers to introduce ever-changing rules and regulations in an effort to respond to particular circumstances, or at least control their economic results and impact on the treasury. (Clark & Farber, 2011, p. 6)

Governments have increasingly used the tax system to carry out economic and social policies in addition to raising revenues, with the result that the ITA has become a veritable "dog's breakfast" of special "tax preferences or tax expenditures" for specific purposes, groups, industries, sectors, and regions.[3] Since 1994, over 100 personal income tax changes alone have been introduced. The Conservative government has introduced targeted tax preferences in every budget since being elected in 2006.

> Each special tax rule has its own constituency—both individuals and corporations—that has grown used to seeing the tax system as the delivery vehicle for the indirect government spending that benefits them. Removing special tax rules, especially those that have been in place for a long period of time and have a strong political constituency, is not easy to do. (Clark & Farber, 2011, p. 7)

It is not surprising, therefore, that there have been few attempts to streamline the tax system for the simple reason that it would require the government to make choices and trade-offs, resulting in winners and losers.[4] The CGA study concluded, nevertheless, that "it would be extremely valuable for the federal government to review the literally hundreds of targeted tax measures in the personal tax system to determine their relevancy and need" (Clark & Farber, 2011, p. 15). Others have also called for tax simplification, including the House of Commons Standing Committee on Finance in its 2011 pre-budget report.

In the case of CIT system, changes have been made over the past 20 years to remove impediments to investment (e.g., the elimination of capital taxes), rates have been reduced, and the system of capital cost allowances has been improved. Nevertheless, a review of the CIT system needs to be undertaken on a more selective basis. For example, there are areas (e.g., taxation and repatriation of foreign source income) which could be simplified to reduce the costs of compliance.

Examples of special PIT and CIT tax preferences include

- Registered Retirement Savings Plans (RRSPs) and pension plans, to encourage taxpayers to provide for their retirement;
- The investment tax credit, to encourage investment in particular regions and particular assets;
- The charitable donations tax credit, to encourage philanthropy;
- The registered education savings plan (RESP), to encourage saving for post-secondary education;
- The children's fitness non-refundable tax credit, to encourage sports and physical activity for children and youth;
- The scientific research and experimental development (SR&ED) tax credit to support industrial research, development, and innovation;
- The accelerated depreciation rate for manufacturing;
- Tax credits, flow-through shares, and accelerated depreciation for mining, oil, and gas companies;
- The public transit tax credit to encourage people to use public transportation; and,
- The volunteer firefighters credit to offset the cost of equipment.

The Department of Finance publishes an annual *Report of Tax Expenditures* and their estimated costs. The estimated total cost in 2011 was over $100 billion. Many of these so-called tax expenditures no doubt serve useful economic and social purposes, but the reality is that they do not receive any scrutiny from Parliament. Although the Department of Finance undertakes some reviews of tax expenditures, very few, if any, are ever eliminated.

In the 2010 and 2012 budgets, the government announced significant cuts in government spending, but there was no attempt to find any savings by eliminating ineffective and unnecessary tax expenditures. It did make some marginal changes to the scientific research and experimental development tax credit (SR&ED), but for the most part the government was doing exactly the opposite. It was proposing to extend the fitness tax credit to adults, introduce a new tax credit to support cultural activities for youth, and introduce a provision to allow families with children 18 years old or under to split income.

In responding to a public request by the Minister of Finance for pre-2012 budget submissions on how to strengthen private sector economic growth, Peter

DeVries and I recommended that the Strategic Spending Review include both the personal and corporate tax systems to identify special tax expenditures for targeted groups, sectors, and industries, and determine whether they serve any useful purpose.[5] Studies have in fact shown that many of these tax expenditures are not effective (Clark & Devries, 2011; Mintz, 2012). Not surprisingly, our recommendation was ignored, even though such a review could easily have found savings of over $5 billion annually by eliminating ineffective and unnecessary tax expenditures.

Parliamentary committees are mandated to examine program spending but not tax expenditures. Yet tax expenditures are program spending in disguise. Recent accounting changes have reclassified certain refundable tax expenditures to program spending (the scientific research and experimental tax credit and working income tax benefit, among others). It will be interesting to see if the applicable committee now reviews these. In fact, parliamentary committees should be mandated to review tax expenditures on an ongoing basis, just as they review program spending.

The Government's Tax Mix Needs to Be Re-focused

In 2010–11, personal income taxes at the federal level accounted for 47.9% of total revenues, up slightly from 47.7% in 2000–1. The share of corporate income taxes declined to 12.6% in 2010–11 from 14.6% 10 years earlier. The share of other taxes, which includes the GST, fell from 18.4 to 18.1%. The share of Employment Insurance (EI) revenues declined to 7.4 from 9.6% (Department of Finance, 2011).[6] The cuts to the CIT rate, GST rate, and EI premium rates no doubt contributed to the declines in their respective shares.

Over the coming decade, Canada's potential economic growth will decline significantly, from above 3% a decade ago to below 2% annually, mostly because of demographic factors, but also because of Canada's continuing poor productivity performance (Parliamentary Budget Office, 2010). This will slow the growth of government revenues, both federally and provincially, and put upward pressure on spending for all levels of government.

In our pre-budget 2012 submission to the Minister of Finance, Peter DeVries and I argued that the government needed to develop a medium-term growth strategy aimed at strengthening both labour force and productivity growth. As part of that strategy, the government would need to address the issue of whether the current tax mix should be refocused, so that it could better support savings, investment, and labour force participation.

Changing the Focus of Taxation

The generally accepted view among economists, at least at the theoretical level, is that shifting the focus away from income-based taxation to consumption-based taxation can have significant benefits for economic growth and job creation.

It could, for example, strengthen labour force participation, since the cost of not working would be increased through lower income taxes. The cost of consumption would increase, and this should result in increased savings, which should lead to increased investment through a lower cost of capital. Estimates of the magnitudes of these shifts remain an open question. But the implication for refocusing the tax mix is clear.

There are a number of other benefits to be gained from a greater focus on consumption-based taxation. First, a shift in focus would lead to greater revenue stability, as consumption fluctuates less than income during economic slowdowns (see Cnossen, 2012). Second, the cost of raising taxes with a consumption-based tax is cheaper than doing so through income-based taxes. Finally, a consumption-based tax is more transparent.

Shifting the focus of taxation to the GST raises three questions. First, should the current base of the GST be changed? Second, should the GST be increased, and depending on the answer to the first question, what might be an appropriate rate for the GST? And third, if the GST is increased, how should the additional revenues be used?

Should the GST Tax Base Be Broadened?

With regard to the first question, the general principle of a consumption-based tax is that the broader the range of goods and services the tax applies to, the lower the rate required to raise a desired level of revenues.

The consumption tax, or value-added tax (VAT), has been in existence for over 50 years (Charlet & Owens, 2010). In Europe, the VAT includes a standard rate and several lower rates for different commodities, so that the tax base to which the standard rate is applied is limited. Currently, EU countries cannot have a standard rate below 15% and lower rates below 5%.

Canada belongs to a group of countries that have a single standardized rate with a broader base than the EU. This group includes Australia with a standardized rate of 10%, New Zealand with a rate of 12.5%, South Africa with a rate of 14%, and Singapore with a rate of 7%. In all cases, counties have applied zero rates or exemptions for special goods or services (e.g., food). Australia, for example, has zero-rated health and medical care, educational supplies, child care, and food and beverages.

In 2011, the estimated cost of GST exemptions, rebates, and zero-ratings totalled almost $17.5 billion. The largest of these included a zero-rating for basic groceries ($3.7 billion); rebates for municipalities ($2.2 billion); rebates for educational services (tuition), and schools, colleges, and universities ($1.7 billion); exemptions for health care and hospitals ($1.2 billion); and a zero-rating for prescription drugs ($740 million).

Recently two Canadian tax experts, Michael Smart and Jack Mintz, recommended that the federal government undertake a review of the GST exemptions. They argued that these exemptions have reduced the effectiveness of the GST, and that their elimination would raise an additional $60 billion in annual revenues which could be used for other purposes (Smart, 2011; see also Beltrame, 2012).

Smart and Mintz also pointed out that the impact of some of these exemptions can be quite regressive. They argued, for example, that the exclusion of basic groceries provides a greater benefit to higher-income Canadians than it does to lower-income Canadians. Such views are not new. The extent of exemptions was hotly debated on both political and policy grounds during the development of the GST from 1988–1990, and in just about every year thereafter.[7] At no time after the introduction of the GST has any government ever indicated the slightest interest in changing the GST tax base.

The arithmetic of eliminating exemptions is easy. What is not easy is the politics. Governments know that attempting to remove special exemptions would create a political firestorm and difficult battles with a host of special interest groups and all the provinces that have a harmonized sales tax (HST).

Changing the tax base of the GST should not be a priority in tax reform.

Should the GST Be Increased?

In 1991, when the GST was introduced, the rate was set at 7%. This rate was determined after months of discussion and debate. What should be the tax base? Should the rate be set to maintain fiscal neutrality with respect to the manufacturer's sales tax (MST) that it replaced, and the planned income tax cuts? Or should the rate be set higher to gain additional revenues in order to help deal with the government's deficit and debt problems?

The original plan was to introduce the income tax changes and the GST simultaneously, and to provide revenue neutrality. The intention was to show Canadians that the income tax cuts would offset the introduction of the GST, and that low-income Canadians would be protected. Unfortunately, it didn't work out that way. The income tax cuts were introduced in 1988, and by the time the GST was introduced in January 1991, everyone had forgotten about them. It was a communications disaster, made much worse by the decision not to imbed the GST in the price of goods sold, but rather to make the GST "transparent" by adding it on at the sales register.

In my view, this decision to exclude the GST from the price has seriously undermined the use of the GST in designing appropriate tax policy. The introduction of the GST was one of the most important, and indeed politically courageous, policy actions of the postwar period. Regrettably, because of these mistakes the government made in implementation, Canadians do not see it that way. Any attempt to refocus the tax mix would probably require a decision to include the GST and HST in the price of goods and services.

The GST rate was also set so that the government could claim fiscal neutrality with respect to the income tax cuts and GST rebates for low-income families. In hindsight, it can be argued that the government should have set a higher rate and that the "surplus" revenues could have been used to deal with the growing deficit and debt problems. Also, by setting a higher rate, the government would have had a both larger and more stable source of revenue.

At the time, no one expected that the GST rate would ever be reduced. After all, it was argued, one of the benefits of a consumption-based tax is that it would allow income-based taxes to be reduced in the future.

During the 1993 election campaign, the Liberal Party ran on the promise to eliminate the GST. Fortunately, once elected, they realized that they needed it; first because of the deficit and debt crisis they inherited, and second because there was no sustainable alternative source of revenue.

With the deficit eliminated in 1997–98 and after two years of surplus, the Liberal government introduced reductions in personal income and corporate income taxes in its 2000–1 budget. By doing so, it was following a strategy to achieve a tax mix of lower income taxes and an unchanged GST. However, during its time in office, the Liberal government was never prepared to consider introducing a higher GST in order to finance an even larger reduction in income taxes.

During the 2006 election campaign, the Conservative government ran on a promise to cut the GST rate by two points. On the basis of good policy, it would have been best to do what the Liberals did in 1993, and forget that promise. But politics or ideology trumped policy, so the government cut the GST rate by one point in the 2006 budget and another point in the 2007 budget.

Should the GST be increased? The economic argument is clear. The GST should never have been reduced in the first place, and at a minimum it should be restored to 7%.

How Should the Additional GST Revenues Be Used?

Restoring the GST to 7% would generate roughly $14 billion dollars annually. In addition, simplifying the PIT and CIT income tax systems could easily raise another $5–6 billion by removing targeted tax incentives. In total, these changes would raise almost $20 billion in revenues that can be reallocated to other policy initiatives. To put this number in perspective, it is equal to 17.5% of personal income taxes collected in 2010–11; almost 60% of corporate income taxes; and more than 100% of Employment Insurance revenues.

In my view, any changes to the tax mix should be implemented on the basis of fiscal neutrality. In other words, all revenues generated through simplifying the tax system and increasing the GST should be reallocated to lowering income taxes.[8] It would allow for a reduction of three percentage points in all personal income tax rates, and a significant reduction in the high effective marginal tax rates that currently exist. Fiscal neutrality may be essential to getting broad support among Canadians for a significant refocusing of the tax mix.

Nevertheless, arguments could be made that some of the "new revenues" should be used to finance needed programs and services. Ultimately, the decision on how the revenues will be reallocated between tax cuts and spending increases will be a political one.

Improving the Fairness and Progressivity of the Tax System

The discussion so far has been in the context of "fiscal neutrality." The savings that might be found from simplifying the tax system, and the additional revenues resulting from shifting to consumption-based taxation would be offset by lower personal income taxes. These tax reform recommendations are independent of the size of government. In other words, all governments should minimize tax complexity and implement tax structures that encourage savings, investment, economic growth, and job creation. Neither of these conditions currently exist in Canada at the federal level.

Issues of tax efficiency and tax simplification get little attention in the public debate on taxes. Canadians generally believe they pay too much tax, and the debate is centred primarily on who is paying the taxes, and who should pay more so others can pay less. This lack of constructive dialogue is unfortunate, since an efficient tax system is, in my view, absolutely necessary in order to properly deal with questions of tax fairness.

Currently, with growing income inequality, there is a view that high-income earners should be paying more taxes than they are. Many believe the tax burden is inequitable and unfair. Tax fairness relates to how taxes are distributed across taxpayers with different incomes. A tax system is considered "progressive" if individuals with higher incomes pay a greater share of their incomes in taxes; the "effective tax rate" rises as income rises. This is sometimes referred to as "vertical" equity.

A major question Canadians must answer is, just how "fair" or progressive should the income tax system be? Economists cannot define fairness, and there is a concern that significantly increasing the effective tax on higher-income earners could have negative economic effects.

In an extensive review of Canada's provincial and federal tax systems between 1990 and 2005, Marc Lee (2007) concluded that "the tax rates of the richest 1% of Canadians have dropped dramatically since 1990, while poorer Canadians have seen their tax rates rise steadily," and "the overall tax system no longer meets the test of fairness across income groups" (p. 3).

A Statistics Canada study of high-income earners concluded that the share of total income for "high-income earners" increased from 21 to 25% between 1992 and 2004, while the share of income taxes they paid increased from 30 to 36%. At the same time, their effective tax rate dropped from 29 to 27% (Murphy, Roberts, & Wolfson, 2007). The study also concluded that there was considerable variation in effective tax rates, with some high-income earners facing an effective tax rate of over 45%, while others paid as little as 10%.

A policy aimed at simplifying the tax system and refocusing the tax structure provides an excellent opportunity to address the issue of tax fairness and progressivity, and the broader issue of income inequality. This is essential if the policy is to receive broad public support. The issue that must be addressed is whether the reductions in income taxes resulting from the increase in GST revenues and the revenue savings from tax simplification should be broadly based (less progressivity) for all income earners, or targeted at low- and middle-income earners (more progressivity).

There are number of areas in the ITA that could be looked at with the goal of increasing progressivity without increasing tax rates. One area, for example, would be an alternative minimum tax (AMT), which imposes constraints on the tax deductions that high-income individuals can use to ensure that they pay a "minimum" tax. These constraints could be tightened, and the tax rate increased. A second area to look at might be simplifying dividend taxation, although the system is very complex and affects many individuals who would not be considered high-income earners (e.g., seniors).

Certainly the savings found through tax simplification could be reallocated to areas such as the Canadian child tax benefit or the working income supplement. These reallocations would contribute to greater income equality.

Observations and Conclusions

In the 2012 budget, the government set out a plan to cut its direct spending by $5.2 billion annually. This followed actions in the 2010 budget to cut defence spending, cap the international assistance envelope, and freeze the operating budgets of all government departments for two years.

Why did the government feel such restraint was necessary? For years it has been telling Canadians that their nation has the best deficit and debt situation in the G7. At the federal level, there is no deficit or debt crisis as there was in

1995. The government's own fiscal forecasts published in the 2010 and 2012 budgets show that the deficit could be eliminated by 2015 or 2016, and the debt burden will continue to decline without any of the expenditure cuts.

The federal government announced in November 2011 that the growth of Canada Health Transfers (CHT) would be held to the growth of the GDP beginning in 2017; by doing this, it was able to download its structural deficit problem onto the provinces. The federal government is no longer confronted with a looming structural deficit, although the same cannot be said for a number of provincial governments.

So why did the Conservative-led government feel it necessary to introduce a major cut in spending? The reasons were ideological. The government recognized that since 2006 spending had risen dramatically, and the size of the public service had increased. During the 2008–10 recession the deficit reached an historical high, although much of that was due to the temporary stimulus spending. These developments eroded the Conservatives' claim to fiscal conservatism and smaller government, so it needed to establish a record in line with these principles. The commitment to a smaller federal government is being achieved through expenditure cuts and downloading problems to the provinces.

At present, the federal government has no fiscal anchor. With the current structure of revenues and expenses, its debt ratio could be below 25% by the end of the decade. Stabilizing the debt ratio at 25% would require lowering taxes and/or increasing spending in order to run ever-increasing deficits.

The government has been following not only a policy of low taxation but also one that provides insufficient support to economic growth and job creation. In this chapter, I have suggested a number of changes that, if implemented, would refocus the tax system and raise additional revenues that could be redirected toward providing broader and more progressive tax relief for all Canadians. These proposals include a major exercise aimed at simplifying the tax system, and a change in the tax mix with a greater emphasis on consumption-based taxation (i.e., the GST).

Any of these proposed changes would take years to implement, a strong and sustained political commitment, and probably the most extensive program of public consultation and communication undertaken since NAFTA. Most political observers say that such a thing is never going to happen with this government, and I agree.

Nevertheless, I hope that the role and size of the federal government will be increasingly discussed and debated in the coming months and years. Issues of taxation cannot be ignored in this debate. This means addressing openly and honestly the questions of what level of revenue is needed to fund the government programs and services Canadians want, how best to raise the required revenues, and how to share the burden of raising additional revenues.

It is important in this political debate to have a "policy context" against which these revenue decisions can be judged. It is better to simplify the tax system, not complicate it; it is better to depend less on income-based taxation and more on consumption-based taxation; it is better to have a tax system that supports economic growth and job creation; and finally, it is better to have a tax system that is fair and progressive.

Acknowledgements

I'd like to thank Peter Devries and Len Farber for their comments on this paper. I would also like to thank an anonymous reviewer for helpful comments. The views expressed in this paper are those of the author alone.

Notes

Much of the material in this article has been drawn from a series of articles co-authored with my colleague Peter Devries, which can be found on our blog, www.3dpolicy.ca.

1. There may still be room for some cuts to program spending, which could be reallocated to new programs. However, the amounts would be limited. Financing new programs by taxing future generations with increased debt would be unacceptable.
2. This section draws on a paper released by the Certified General Accountants Association (CGA) in August 2011 that I co-authored with Len Farber: The need for tax simplification—a challenge and an opportunity.
3. A tax preference reduces the taxes owed by an individual. A tax expenditure is a form of spending delivered through the tax system. The tax system is simply being used to determine the eligibility of the individual for the expenditure. The Department of Finance uses the term tax expenditure to refer to both; this chapter employs the same terminology.
4. There have been two reforms of the personal income tax system. The first was in 1971 following the report of the Carter Commission. The second was in 1988, which was associated with the introduction of the GST in 1990.
5. In 2011, the House of Commons Standing Committee on Finance recommended a comprehensive review of the tax system by a blue-ribbon panel.
6. The share of non-resident taxes increased from 1.2 to 2.4%, and the share of "other" revenues increased from 8.2 to 11.9%.
7. I was assistant deputy minister of fiscal policy during this time and was involved in the discussions involving the GST base and rate. Subsequently, I served as associate deputy minister (1993–1996) and deputy minister of finance (1997–2000).
8. GST low-income tax rebates would have to be increased.

References

Beltrame, J. (2012, February 24). Economists want Ottawa to tax food, prescriptions, tuition. *Canadian Press*.

Charlet, A., & Owens, J. (2010). An international perspective on the VAT. *Tax Notes International, 50*(12).

Clark, C. S., & Devries, P. (2011). A low tax plan but definitely not good tax policy [Web log post]. Retrieved from www.3dpolicy.ca

Clark, C. S., & Devries, P. Open letter to the Minister of Finance: Pre-2012 budget submission, "New strategy to strengthen economic growth and job creation" [Web log post]. Retrieved from www.3dpolicy.ca

Clark, C. S., & Farber, L. (2011, August). *The need for tax simplification—a challenge and an opportunity* (Issue in Focus Report for Certified General Accountants).

Cnossen, S. (2012). Taxing consumption or income: Du pareil au même? *University of Calgary School of Public Policy Research Papers, 5*(13).

Department of Finance Canada. (2011, October). *Fiscal Reference Tables.*

Lee, M. (2007, November). *Eroding tax fairness: Tax incidence in Canada, 1990 to 2005* (Analysis for the Growing Gap Project). Toronto, ON: Canadian Centre for Policy Alternatives.

Minister of Finance. (2011, August 19). Canada well positioned to face global economic challenges, Flaherty tells finance committee (News Release). *Department of Finance Canada: News* [Website]. Retrieved from http://www.fin.gc.ca/n11/11-069-eng.asp

Mintz, J. (2012, March 15). The chopping block 2012: Axe the tax pigs. *Financial Post.*

Murphy, B., Roberts, P., & Wolfson, M. (2007). *A profile of high-income earners* (Income Research Papers). Ottawa, ON: Statistics Canada.

Parliamentary Budget Office. (2010, January). *Estimating potential GDP and the government's structural budget balance* (Technical note). Retrieved from http://www.pbo-dpb.gc.ca/files/files/Publications/Potential_CABB_EN.pdf

Smart, M. (2011). Departures from neutrality in Canada's goods and service tax.

Part IV ▶ How to Get There

We started this project with an understanding that a real discussion about taxes and tax reform is politically risky—and that any notion of introducing new taxes or raising taxes is riskier still, some might say suicidal. But we hope by now you agree at least that we need to have the conversation. How do we change the channel? How do we get past the distrust and noise, the pandering politics? What would it take to create the room for some party, some politician, to take this on?

Paul Saurette of the University of Ottawa and Shane Gunster of Simon Fraser have been studying (not without some admiration) how conservatives in the US and Canada have managed to bring their views from the margins to the centre of political thought to the extent that they have reshaped what we consider possible in public policy. The changes in how we talk about taxes, government, public enterprise, and the private sector are no accident, and they are not simply the result of cultural drift or economic necessity. In this chapter, Saurette and Gunster examine the infrastructure conservatives built, the language they adopted, and the messages they use, and conclude that progressives have much to learn. The authors argue that we must understand just how the conservatives have succeeded, what their various narratives are, and why they work, and they offer a number of recommendations that could be just what's needed to begin to rebalance the conversation and spark a real, two-sided debate on taxes in Canada.

Chapter 13

Canada's Conservative Ideological Infrastructure: Brewing a Cup of Cappuccino Conservatism

Paul Saurette and Shane Gunster

Sometimes, they say, a cigar is just a cigar. The debate about taxes, however, is never just a debate about taxes. For as Freud and countless other political and social analysts know, the meaning and import of words, actions, and objects often go far beyond themselves because they are always embedded in a broader background that influences their reception. Policy debates take place within larger discursive and ideological contexts—contexts where philosophical principles, ideological norms, and dominant narratives invariably shape how we hear these debates, privileging certain policy positions and hampering others. Like other political issues, then, talking about taxes necessarily means engaging with values and narratives beyond those explicitly linked to taxes. This is especially true of the debate over taxes in North America.

The challenge for anyone in North America who wants to make the argument that we should raise taxes is that ours is not a hospitable ideological climate. Any third-grader can tell you that tax is not actually a four-letter word. The problem is that it sounds that way to many adults since we now hear it only after it has been refracted through the echo chamber of contemporary conservative political discourse. For over the last 40 years, the conservative movement in North America has invested heavily not only in issue-specific campaigns against taxes, endlessly repeating anti-tax concepts like "tax burden" and "tax relief" (concepts which have become embedded in our common sense and have subtly but profoundly shifted the way we imagine democratic citizenship and its associated rights and obligations); they have also sought to build and popularize a much broader philosophical world view that nurtures a generalized disdain for collective political action—of which taxes is simply one particularly concrete example.

In this environment, progressives must reignite an explicit debate over the role and importance of taxes, develop strong policy proposals for a fair tax system, marshal good, concrete arguments on behalf of it (like linking taxes and services), and powerfully communicate the ways that each of us benefit more from this system than we do from others. But this alone will not be enough. We must also work to reconstitute the broader philosophical context in a way that helps us make, and allows others to hear, the case for taxes at deeper levels.

There are no easy answers here. But if we are to make some progress on this, we need to understand the nuances of the opposing view and how we got here before proposing ways to break out. That is the goal of this chapter. We therefore begin by offering an overview of the growth of the ideological apparatus of the conservative movement in Canada over the last 15 years—showing that it has not only grown in size but also that it has become increasingly innovative in its methods, and has focused in particular on cultivating and popularizing a conservative philosophical vision. Second, we will argue that there is a powerful strain of contemporary conservatism in Canada that is distinct from the often crude and extreme anti-government discourse associated with what Thomas Frank has called "backlash populism" (e.g., the Tea Party in the US, or versions of Canadian conservatism such as the Harris Common Sense Revolution). We argue that while Canadian conservative discourse continues to employ the tropes of backlash populism in certain circumstances, they have also developed a frothier and sweeter version we call "cappuccino conservatism." We outline the key elements of this version of conservatism, and show how they create a distinctive narrative around taxation. Finally, because we believe that cappuccino conservatism has the potential to attract the support of many centrist swathes of voters (since it may well appear to be much less radical/confrontational and more consumer-friendly than the backlash populism version), we think it is imperative that progressives develop and popularize a convincing counter-vision to this variant of conservatism. As such, the chapter concludes with a discussion about a few of the things progressives can do to challenge these conservative narratives to build a perspective that re-energizes Canadians' belief in collective, public solutions to policy challenges, and a taxation system that would support this vision.

1. The Ideological Rebirth of Canadian Conservatism

There are many ways that political movements embed their political views in the fabric of a society. Most obviously, winning political power allows a movement to explicitly introduce new policies and laws, and reverse others, in ways that reflect its vision. Governing also allows a movement to make many less obvious but often even more fundamental administrative changes (e.g., long-term restructuring of government architecture; reorienting funding priorities within government departments and agencies; directing how aggressively agencies should implement and monitor existing regulations, and so on) that can have a significant impact on the political sphere. But most successful long-term political movements understand that cultivating a hospitable ideological climate—that is, making their preferred values and narratives the dominant ones by embedding them deeply into the discursive fabric of society—is also a crucial task. It is one, moreover, that is almost always a prerequisite for sustainable dominance in the electoral realm. In Canada, a number of authors have examined the first two areas (see, for example, Martin, 2010). Few, if any, have recently delved into the last one, however. In this section, therefore, we concentrate on asking to what degree, and in what ways, has the Canadian conservative movement become involved in broader ideological horticulture?

1.1 Investing in Ideological Infrastructure

The considerable size and impact of the American conservative movement's investment in articulating and popularizing its ideas and philosophical vision over the last 40 years has been well documented (see, for example, Micklethwait & Wooldridge, 2004). In contrast, the conservative movement in Canada has not traditionally been known for its valorisation of philosophical ideas or its discursive innovation. Most practitioners of the Tory tradition of conservatism in Canada have emphasized the importance of cleaving to traditional institutions (both political and social), the value of incremental and evolutionary change, and the virtues of pragmatism, compromise, and balance. Even Hugh Segal, whose appreciation for principled debate is noteworthy, claimed that "ideology is for students of history, self-absorbed think tanks and the intemperate. Modern conservative politics is about practical issues that matter to people, such as tax cuts, the state of health care, lowering the debt, restraining government and enhancing equality of opportunity" (1998, p. 20). Though differing from Red Tories in many ways, the neo-liberal New Right of the 1990s also displayed a clear disdain for idealistic philosophies and academic theories. For core to Mike Harris' "Common Sense Revolution" in Ontario or Ralph Klein's "everyman" persona in Alberta was a fundamental repudiation of the importance of philosophical ideas and a valorisation of a "common sense" model of politics (where the policy answers were assumed to be obvious and the only issue to be resolved was one of political will).[1]

The supposed absence of a robust conservative philosophical underpinning and ideological infrastructure has been a sore point for a variety of Canadian conservative activists for some time now. In a book that was a *cause célèbre* in conservative circles a few years back, two young conservative pundits, Teisha Kheiriddin and Adam Daifallah argued that the failure of the right in Canada was largely due to the lack of compelling ideas and the inability of conservatives to embed such ideas in the larger Canadian culture. According to them, "Canada's federal conservative parties have failed to develop a coherent ideology, to build an infrastructure to support and market that ideology, and to provide inspiring leadership" around those ideas (Kheiriddin & Daifallah, 2005, p. xiv). In his foreword to the book, Mark Steyn seconds this idea, claiming that Reagan and Thatcher's success was enabled by the "huge intellectual gusts at their back. They led parties with ideas, and they expressed those ideas unashamedly and optimistically" and that therefore Canadian conservatives "have to build a movement, as the Americans have done—through new magazines, and think tanks, and talk radio, and internet sites, and non-party institutions" (qtd. in Kheirridin and Daifallah, 2005, p. xii).

Over the last 15 years, however, the conservative movement in Canada has begun to appreciate the power and importance of developing and popularizing its broader vision—and has increasingly invested in this area. Consider, for example, the dramatic growth of the conservative movement's ideological infrastructure outside the realm of party politics. Even if we restrict our examination to what we might call the politicized think-tank sphere (a category that excludes advocacy groups like the National Citizens Coalition, the Canadian Taxpayers Federation, and Focus on the Family Canada; more middle-of-the-road technical think tanks such as the Canadian Tax Foundation or research-for-hire organizations such as the Conference Board of Canada; and groups that provide grants like the Donner Foundation), we can see that Kheiriddin and Daifallah's concerns are somewhat inaccurate. For while the conservative ideological machinery in Canada might be smaller than they as conservative partisans embedded in the ideological sector, would like, it is also true that the conservative movement in Canada has not only had a very strong presence in this sector for decades but also it has dramatically increased its capacity over the last decade or so.

The oldest right-of-centre think tank in Canada is the C. D. Howe Institute, founded in 1958 as the Private Planning Association of Canada, and which had 2011 revenues of $3.7 million (*Annual Report*, 2011). In the 1970s, however, the right-wing think-tank landscape grew significantly. The Canada West Foundation, founded in 1970 and with 2011 revenues of $2.7 million (Financial Statement, 2011), was perhaps the first of the new wave of more politicized right-wing think tanks to emerge in Canada. Arguably, however, it was the creation in 1974 of the Fraser Institute—arguably the largest, best-funded, and most visible political think tank over the last three decades—that truly reshaped the sector. While the institute has been an important voice since its inception in the early 1970s, what is perhaps most remarkable is its phenomenal growth over the last 15 years. In 1997, for example, the Fraser Institute had an annual budget of approximately $3.4 million, and listed 38 events it helped to organize (1998, p. 25). Ten years later in 2008, the institute had quadrupled its annual budget to $13.9 million, more than tripled the number of annual events to 130, with a total attendance of 6,500, reported a circulation of almost 80,000 for its monthly magazine and 72,000 for its student magazine, recorded almost 1 million visitors to its website (with more than 6.2 million pages viewed), and identified over 7,250 citations to its work in the media (numbers compiled from Fraser Institute, 2008). The economic downturn of the last several years has had an impact on the Fraser Institute (2011), with its annual revenue falling to just under $10 million for 2011. However, its impact metrics continue to grow. The *2011 Annual Report*, for example, claims that the institute was mentioned in 16,745 news stories in that year (of which 10,784 were online), had its op-eds published (or republished) 839 times in newspapers across North America, and had 1.9 million unique visitors to its website, with more than 17.2 million page views. While these numbers may be smaller than those gathered by its American brethren, they make the Fraser Institute by far the most significant presence in the Canadian politicized think-tank sector.[2] In comparison, the largest politicized progressive think tank in Canada is the Canadian Centre for Policy Alternatives—a largely decentralized network founded in 1980, which had annual revenues of $2.9 million in 2001, and $4.6 million in 2011 (2001 and 2011).

Equally notable is the number (and reach) of new conservative think tanks that have emerged over the last decade or so. While the last decade has not been especially kind to progressive think tanks, with the closure of the Canadian Policy Research Network and the Canadian Labour and Business Centre, among others, the opposite seems to be true for conservative ones. Even if one leaves aside the new regionally focused institutes (such as the Frontier Centre, founded in 1999) and the several newly founded smaller social conservative institutes (e.g., Institute for Canadian Values; Canadian Centre for Policy Studies), many new and highly visible conservative think tanks have opened their doors for operation since 1995. The Atlantic Institute for Market Studies (AIMS) was founded in 1995 and had an annual budget of approximately $1 million in 2009, compared to $350,000 in 1996 (numbers compiled from *2009/2010 Annual Report*, 2010). The Montreal Economic Institute (MEI) began operating in 1999 with a budget of only $200,000, while its 2011 annual revenues were $1.8 million, with over 2,500 media mentions that same year and 1.4 million visits to its website in 2010 (numbers compiled from *Annual Report 2010* and *2011*). The Institute for Marriage and Family Canada was founded in 2006 by Focus on the Family Canada (revenues not public). The MacDonald Laurier Institute opened its doors in 2010, with revenues of $855,000 that year (*Annual Report*, 2010). And the largest and most influential of the new entrants, the Manning Centre for Building Democracy, was officially founded in 2005; its annual budget is not made public. However, in 2011 Nick Gafuik (a Manning Centre Senior Fellow at the time, and previously its managing director) stated that since its inception, the centre has raised or won commitments for funding of approximately $30 million (Presentation, 2011).

At the same presentation, Gafuik estimated that the size of the partisan conservative think-tank sphere was about $25 million per year—and said that their ambition was to increase it to above $40 million per year. Neither of those figures, it is important to note, include the Conference Board of Canada (founded in 1954, with 2011 revenues of $32.6 million, and direct program expenses of $24.8 million), even though many of their economic positions are in line with the more overtly political think tanks like the Fraser Institute (Conference Board of Canada, 2011). We have not been able to find a comparable estimate for the size of the left-of-centre think-tank sector. Moreover, any comparison will necessarily be imprecise, since there is much debate about exactly which organizations would count as the type of politicized think tanks we are examining here. However, comparing the budgets and reach of the largest four or five think tanks on each side yields a "directionally correct" portrait that provides a general sense of the relative situation.

If we take the budgets of the four largest conservative think tanks with public financial statements (Fraser, Canada West, C. D. Howe, and MEI), the total for 2011 would be approximately $18 million. That total would rise to somewhere in the neighbourhood of $22 million if one assumes $4 million as the 2011 annual revenues for the Manning Centre (which would be one-seventh of the $30 million that Gafuik stated had been raised by the centre over the last seven years). In contrast, there is really only one established "generalist" progressive think tank in Canada: the Canadian Centre for Policy Alternatives, with a budget of $4.6 million in 2011. If we add the 2011 budgets of the next three largest think tanks with slightly narrower mandates that could reasonably be defined as having left-leaning policy orientations—the Wellesley Institute at $2.9M (2011), the Caledon Institute for Social Policy at $0.7M (2011), and the Vanier Institute at $0.6M (2011)—we get a relative comparison of approximately $18M for the largest right-wing think tanks versus $8.8M for left-wing think tanks, leaving liberal organizations with about 48% of the funding of conservative ones. And it seems very likely that the gap would only grow substantially if we increased it to the five largest and included the budget of the Manning Centre, as adding the next largest generalist progressive think tank, the Canadian Council for Social Development at $0.6M (2011), or the Parkland Institute at approximately $0.5M,[3] would increase the progressive ledger to $9.3M—or 42% of the $22M that we estimate the top five conservative think tanks spend.

1.2 Persuaders versus Researchers

It is not merely the size of your think-tank budget that matters, however; how you use it can matter even more. In a fascinating study published in the *Stanford*

Social Innovation Review (hosted by the Stanford School of Business), Andrew Rich has shown that conservative foundations actually have a much smaller asset base than liberal ones (approximately 15% that of liberal foundations), and that conservative think tanks receive slightly less annual funding from foundations than liberal ones do (2005, pp. 23 and 25). However, Rich suggests that in the US, conservative foundations and think tanks have compensated for their smaller asset base in a number of ways that have allowed them to win the war of ideas for the last several decades.

First, they are proudly "partisan" in the sense of being conservative, not simply in the sense of supporting the Republican party, and have clear mission statements that orient their efforts in support of specific political and policy goals. In contrast, he suggests, many progressive foundations and think tanks take pains to be neutral and thus lack comparable focus and political intensity. Second, conservative foundations have focused much of their spending on funding for think tanks. In fact, Rich's comparison of 12 major conservative and 12 major progressive foundations shows that the conservative ones spent $29 million on think tanks from an asset base of $1.7 billion compared to liberal foundations spending $38 million from an asset base of $11.5 billion—which means that conservative foundations spent almost five times as much relative to their asset base as liberal foundations did (2005, pp. 21, 23). Third, much of this conservative funding is not tied to specific studies or topics, but is given to think tanks for general operating expenses—allowing the organizations significant flexibility to pursue topics they identify as most pressing given the changing political climate. In contrast, progressive foundations tend to invest much more in grassroots programs than in building infrastructure for the "war of ideas"— and even when they do, they often invest in very narrow think tanks that deal with single issues and do not influence the overall ideological climate.

Finally, Rich shows that conservative think tanks use a great deal more of their budget for communication and popularization of their findings. He quotes Herb Berkowitz, a former vice-president of communication for the Heritage Institute, who said "our belief is that when the research product has been printed, then the job is only half done. That is when we start marketing it to the media.... We have as part of our charge the selling of ideas, the selling of policy proposals. We are out there actively selling these things, day after day. It's our mission" (qtd. in 2005, p. 25). Moreover, Rich demonstrates that the conservative movement puts its money where its mouth is, literally. For example, the largest liberal think tank, the Brookings Institution, spends only 3% of its budget on communications, whereas the Heritage Foundation spends upward of 20% on communications and government affairs (Rich, 2005, p. 25).

There is no comparable study of Canadian think tanks and foundations— and there are important differences in political culture and regulation between the two countries. But there are indications that conservative think tanks in Canada may have taken a page from their American brethren. To begin with, Canadian conservative think tanks don't need to compensate for their smaller budgets since, in contrast to the situation of similar US organizations, the conservative think tanks are generally better funded, older, and more established than their progressive counterparts. So they start with an advantage. Nevertheless, they further strengthen their impact by employing a number of the other practices Rich identifies.

Most Canadians conceptualize think tanks as research organizations—universities without students, as they are sometimes called (see Abelson, 2009, p. 18). And this is true enough for many of them. But it is a poor analogy for most of the conservative think tanks that have been founded in Canada since the 1970s. For example, although many—including the Fraser Institute—are charitable organizations, precluding them from spending more than 10% of their budget on lobbying and political activity, there is no question that these conservative think tanks are highly focused on a political mission. Making the C. D. Howe Institute appear to be an objective, grandfather-like intellectual in comparison, newer and more vociferous conservative think tanks like the Fraser Institute, the MEI, AIMS, and the MacDonald Laurier Institute are unequivocally clear about what they stand for (pro-market, smaller government) and what they are focused on (persuading policy-makers and voters alike to support pro-market policies). Moreover, despite the tax rules limiting their lobbying activities, conservative think tanks are remarkably well networked with conservative politicians and staffers. The fact that Stephen Harper wrote a congratulatory note introducing the Fraser Institute's 35th anniversary publication (*35 Big Ideas*, 2009) and Jim Flaherty—the sitting finance minister at the time—was the keynote speaker at the institute's *Canada Strong and Free* fundraising gala in November 2008 (with another 30 MPs in attendance)[4] are only particularly obvious examples of the linkages between conservative think tanks and the political realm that Donald Gutstein has outlined in detail in his book, *Not a Conspiracy Theory* (2009).[5]

Furthermore, while conservative think tanks continue to focus on influencing the "treetops"—the policy-makers and opinion leaders who are uniquely placed to directly influence government policy—they have also increasingly focused on selling their ideas to all levels of society. Seeking to influence Canadian society from tip to trunk—or from the treetops to the grassroots—conservative think tanks have been intensifying their focus on marketing. The Fraser Institute, for example, describes itself not merely as a research institute, but rather as an "independent, non-profit research and education organization" (*About us: Who we are*, n.d.). This highlights the fact that the Fraser Institute is deeply involved not only in producing research that offers a free-market perspective on public policy but also in training a wide variety of non-institute actors to further popularize this perspective. For example, the Fraser Institute offers a variety of training sessions and awards for teachers and university students. The purpose of these is to help teachers and students not only understand but also defend and spread the free-market philosophy to their own networks. According to the institute, in 2011 alone "11,520 high school students [were] influenced by their teachers' participation in Fraser Institute Teacher Workshops" (*FI in numbers*, n.d.). The strategy is clear: whether training teachers to influence the next generation of secondary students; training university students to become future conservative leaders and pundits; or offering journalists training in free market ideology, the institute is engaged in a serious, aggressive, and proactive attempt to popularize conservative ideas throughout Canadian society—especially among those who are most easily influenced (students) and those who are most influential (the media and policy-makers).

The Manning Centre has taken this approach to a new level. Describing itself as a "do-tank," the centre does not seek to generate new research nor ideas. Rather, it focuses almost exclusively on strengthening the human capital of the conservative movement (training staff, creating networking opportunities for conservatives, brokering unified positions on contentious issues, developing communication strategies, etc.) in order to solidify conservatism in Canada. Since it is not a charitable foundation, it is not bound by Canada Revenue Agency's 10% limit on political activities. Thus the organization can directly and openly lobby, train, and support conservative political parties. These types of activities—from organizing the largest annual conservative networking gathering, to connecting media and politicians to sympathetic academics willing to provide policy advice and supportive quotes, to offering training session to conservative staffers—are in fact the core of the Manning Centre's vision. As an early and particularly clear articulation of the centre's mission stated, its main goal is to help build "the democratic infrastructure, below the party level that will generate the forward looking policies and ideas that will allow the government to govern in accordance with those conservative principles" (Manning Centre, n.d.).

1.3 Envisioning the Big Picture

If the growth, diversification, and strategic intensification of conservative Canadian think tanks highlight the increased capacity of the conservative movement to develop and popularize specific policy preferences, it also seems to be the case that the movement is increasingly committed to cultivating a broader conservative philosophical vision and public discourse. Consider Hugh Segal, a central figure in conservative politics for over four decades. Segal remains, as we saw earlier, a critic of those who blindly follow narrow-minded and rigid political theories and ideologies.[6] However, in one of his recent books, he forcefully argues for the value and importance of recognizing and communicating conservative principles. According to Segal, what marks both Conservatives and NDP supporters is their commitment to principle. "While Conservatives and New Democrats may disagree intensely on how best to buttress individual freedom, collective responsibility, and equality of opportunity within society, they both stay firmly rooted in their ideologies. These two parties have had rank-and-file and elite members who have been more loyal to ideas and principles than to their fellow party members or leaders" (Segal, 2006, p. 27; compare p. 30). This, Segal believes, is a characteristic that ought to be strengthened. For in his view, election campaigns that focus the ballot question on conservative values, ideas, and principles will not only be winning electoral strategy (2006, p. 223) but could create a moderate conservative consensus that will "fuel a future Conservative era of values, freedom, progress and stability" (2006, p. 239).

It is not just ex-Red Tories who support this vision, moreover. In fact, Tom Flanagan, a key architect of the demise of Red Toryism, shares it as well. As a central and early intellectual supporter, organizer, and policy director of the Reform Party, as well as a core senior advisor to Stephen Harper and the Conservative Party of Canada (and now the Wildrose Party), Flanagan has been the dean of the conservative intellectual movement in Canada for the last two decades. Interestingly, despite his background as a professor of political theory, it would be easy to view Flanagan as someone who dismisses the importance of philosophical principles and vision when it comes to concrete politics. In his book *Harper's Team*, he is unequivocal that compromises on the level of principles were required to ensure the eventual unification into the CPC and its later electoral victory.[7] Moreover, one of his key "10 Commandments" for future conservatives is that they avoid the Reform mistake of "deducing policies from general principles, as if political reasoning were syllogistic." In Flanagan's view, since "politics is less about logic than it is about getting support. . . . [C]onservative statecraft has to be more than the logical deduction of policies from philosophical premises if it is going to succeed" (Flanagan, 2007, p. 283).

However, a closer reading suggests that Flanagan actually believes deeply in developing and popularizing a conservative political philosophy. In the conclusion to *Harper's Team*, for example, he surprisingly begins by reflecting (for the first time in the book), on the role and importance of "public philosophy." Despite his other comments, he states that he "wholeheartedly" supports those who "have argued recently that Canadian conservatives have to build for the long term, trying to affect public opinion so that conservatism becomes an entrenched public philosophy" (Flanagan, 2007, p. 274). These efforts are essential, he says, because in his view, "Canada is not yet a conservative or Conservative country; neither the philosophy of conservatism nor the party brand comes close to commanding majority support" (Flanagan, 2007, p. 274).

What is perhaps most telling, however, is the link that Flanagan sees between this concern and his practical political engagement. Why does he continue to work in the partisan arena? Flanagan chooses to discuss only one reason explicitly: he participates in the electoral realm because

> winning elections and controlling the government as often as possible is the most effective way of shifting the public philosophy. Who would deny that Canada's present climate of opinion has been fostered by the Liberal Party's long-term dominance of federal institutions? If you control the government, you choose judges, appoint the senior civil service, fund or de-fund advocacy groups, and do many other things that gradually influence the climate of opinion. (2007, p. 274)

This is a remarkable statement. Flanagan's justification of the importance of engaging in party politics and winning elections does not rest any specific concrete political issue, policy, or grievance. Rather, he inverts the traditional relationship that many politicians see between philosophy and political power so that political power is valued primarily as a means of shifting a broad public philosophy rather than philosophical principles being viewed as a means of attracting electoral success. In this sense, Flanagan's partisan work actually signals a much deeper and more profound respect for the importance of philosophical principles and discourse than a first reading of his book would suggest. The reason to win elections, in this view, is to change how people think.

Perhaps the most significant sign that the conservative movement takes its philosophical and values cultivation seriously is that even the think tanks are buying into this. The value of principled debate—and the importance of strengthening the conservative movement's ability to engage in this sort of debate—has been central to the Manning Centre's view from its inception. As an early version of the centre's vision stated, "the primary purpose of the Manning Centre for Building Democracy is to prepare Canadians for principled participation in democratic politics" as a way of "achieving a democratic society guided by conservative principles" (2007). Even more telling, however, is the role that principles and principled discourse plays in the policy prescriptions and publications of many of Canada's conservative think tanks. For they not only highlight the value the conservative movement is placing on making Canada a "conservative country," philosophically speaking. They also reveal the content of that philosophical vision. It is to this that we now turn.

2. Steaming Mad? Or Just a Warm Cup of Cappuccino Conservatism?

Most mainstream political movements, ideologies, and philosophies are amalgams and coalitions of a number of different variations and strains, and contemporary conservatism in North America is no different. In Canada alone, the conservative movement includes vocal proponents of Red Toryism, libertarianism, social conservatism, fiscal conservatism, prairie populism, corporatism, and other sub-types. These variants are not, of course, mutually exclusive and they often have enough shared values to allow them to coalesce behind common parties and positions. In theoretical terms, we might call contemporary conservatism in North America the "Rhizomatic Right," since a rhizome (for example, grass) is a networked organic assemblage that shares a common root system but has no main, unifying trunk.[8]

This rhizomatic diversity can lead to some challenges for political movements since tensions and internal friction can easily arise, diverting attention and focus away from the larger political goals. However, it can also be an advantage. For while this assembled diversity can sometimes allow a movement to put forth a single dominant narrative on a given issue or policy preference, at other times it allows a movement to have multiple narratives—each capable of resonating in different ways with different target audiences.

Political observers and actors often miss this multiplicity. They do so at their own peril, however. For tracing the ways in which, and for whom, these multiple narratives resonate is a crucial step for understanding and shaping the larger political and philosophical context where specific political debates play out.

Over the last decade, it has been increasingly accepted by many political observers that American and Canadian conservatism is now defined by what Thomas Frank has called "backlash populism." On Frank's telling, backlash populism is a conservative co-optation and inversion of the historical populism of the late nineteenth and early twentieth century, emerging in the late 1960s in response to the counter-cultural transformations of that era. Like historical "progressive" populism, conservative backlash populism rhetorically attacks a malevolent scheming elite who are allegedly poisoning the well of American democracy and eroding the foundation of society. However, in this new conservative version, it is not economic and political privilege and power that defines the "elite" class. Rather, class is a question of values and taste. In this new world of backlash populism, class is supposedly "not really about money, or birth, or even occupation. It is primarily a matter of *authenticity*, that most valuable cultural commodity. Class is about what one drives and where one shops and how one prays, and only secondarily about the work one does or the income one makes" (Frank, 2004, p. 113).

The "problem" that conservative backlash populism targets is therefore not the abuse of economic and political power—it is the snobbery, arrogance, and disdain for traditional American tastes of latte-sipping liberals. In the backlash imaginary, it [is] now a conflict in which the patriotic blue-collar "silent majority" (along with their employers) face off against a new elite, the "liberal establishment" and its spoiled, flag-burning children. This new ruling class—a motley assembly of liberal journalists, liberal academics, liberal foundation employees, liberal politicians, and the shadowy powers of Hollywood—earned the people's wrath not by exploiting workers or ripping off family farmers, but by showing contemptuous disregard for the wisdom and the values of average Americans. (Frank, 2000, p. 26)

In this view, America is defined by an increasingly polarized clash between the profoundly different values and tastes of Democratic blue-staters (latte-sipping, elitist individualists, primarily concentrated on the coasts) and Republican red-staters (the common people of America's heartland who like their coffee plain).

According to Frank, the backlash inversion of populism—and its ability to reduce class to taste, and elide issues of economic and political inequality by focusing on different preferences about social values—is at the core of the recent success of the Right in the US today. For the genius of backlash populism is that it allows its adherents, many of whom are working class, to express the anger and frustration they feel about their situation (much of which is a direct result of the insecurity and radical inequality created by structural changes to the economy over the last 30 years), but does so in a way that deflects this anger from the economic policies themselves—projecting it instead toward social issues like abortion, same-sex marriage, immigration, a supposed clash of civilizations, terrorism, and national security. In the process, conservatives constantly brand themselves as outsiders bent on shaking up a corrupt system in the interests of the people. The result is a movement that is fundamentally paradoxical, but nonetheless very helpful to the economic elite of America:

> Here, after all, is a rebellion against "the establishment" that has wound up cutting the tax on inherited estates. Here is a movement whose response to the power structure is to make the rich even richer; whose answer to the inexorable degradation of working-class life is to lash out angrily at labour unions and liberal workplace-safety programs; whose solution to the rise of ignorance in America is to pull the rug out from under public education. (Frank, 2004, p. 7)

Accustomed as we are to sleeping fitfully next to the elephant to the south, many Canadian progressives assume that the new conservative movement in Canada is simply the Tea Party North. And it is true that variations on a theme of backlash populism have been—and continue to be—an important strain of the Canadian conservative narrative. Angry about supposed government waste, angry about the laziness government hand-outs supposedly engender, angry about the control that "special interests" supposedly exercise, angry about political correctness and political dithering. This tone certainly characterized Mike Harris' Common Sense Revolution,[9] and the fact that it featured heavily in the 2010 Toronto mayoral campaign of Rob Ford and the discourse of Tim Hudak's Progressive Conservative party in Ontario illustrates that this approach continues to find prominent and influential standard-bearers in Canada's most populous province. A variety of senior federal conservative politicians continue to employ this discourse from time to time as well.[10] And it is also often present in the punditry.[11]

This portrait of backlash populism, however, does not tell the full story about the strategies the contemporary conservative movement is using to persuade Canadians of their vision. First, some aspects of the American version just don't work in Canada. Even the most virulent backlash populists in Canada rarely delve into the anti-immigrant angle so prevalent in the US. In fact, courting the new Canadian vote is central to the federal Conservatives' electoral strategy—as Jason Kenney's efforts over the last three years have ably demonstrated. Moreover, while many Canadian conservatives may oppose same-sex marriage, the movement is not using that issue, or abortion, as wedges to unify and mobilize conservatives here.

Second, and more importantly, the backlash populism portrait only captures one strain of contemporary conservative discourse in Canada. Every broad political movement is, inevitably, a coalition of movements. For this and other reasons, most political movements have multiple philosophical narratives and rhetorical strategies that they can draw on. We believe that this is the case with contemporary Canadian conservatism. In particular, we believe that in addition to the backlash populist narrative, the Canadian conservative ideological infrastructure has been developing and is increasingly employing a discourse that is quite distinct both from old Red Toryism and backlash populism (and, incidentally, the narrow libertarianism) that we see in the US. We believe, moreover, that this discursive strain offers a significantly different argument against taxes than does the backlash populist narrative—and thus that progressives need a counter-narrative that effectively challenges both.

We like to call this Canadian version "cappuccino conservatism," not merely because it highlights the irony that the coffee served at Canada's largest gathering of conservative activists several years ago (the annual Manning Centre Networking Conference) was proudly identified as Starbucks, with Tim Hortons nowhere to be seen. Nor simply because it underlines the fact that the economic policies privileged by this ideology favour the cappuccino-quaffing corporate types on Bay Street. And not even because we hope that the tongue-in-cheek nature of this term calls attention to the absurdity of talking about politics as if supposed differences in our coffee preferences are more relevant than our stances on issues of economic inequality, universal access to high-quality health care, environmental degradation, and ensuring fair prosperity and dignity for all sectors of the population. We are calling it cappuccino conservatism because, contrary to the deep social conservative strain that characterizes American backlash populism, the core political philosophy of cappuccino conservatism is the profound valorisation of *choice* that the latte liberal is supposedly so fond of. In fact, we suspect that the explicit valorisation and extension of choice (and other rhetorical innovations) by cappuccino conservatism seeks to "conservatize" Canada's political philosophy not by *replacing* progressive political values (individual choice, tolerance, pluralism, equality, etc.) that deeply resonate in Canada, but rather by *redefining* them in such a way that favours more "conservative" policies.

So what are the key characteristics of cappuccino conservatism? What is the philosophical vision of cappuccino conservatism, and what key principles and discursive strategies does it employ to construct its vision? Finally, what are the implications for reframing the debate over taxes? In the remainder of this chapter, we seek to answer these questions by analyzing the series of fascinating texts titled *Canada Strong and Free* that were published between 2005 and 2007.

We believe these to be exemplary texts that are generally representative of some of the most influential strains of conservatism in Canada's think-tank sphere for several reasons. First, they were officially authored by two of the most influential elder statesmen of the contemporary conservative movement in Canada: Preston Manning (founder and leader of the Reform Party 1987–2000; MP 1993–2002; Leader of the Official Opposition 1997–2000) and Mike Harris (former Progressive Conservative premier of Ontario 1995–2002). Second, it is a flagship series for the Fraser Institute, the most important conservative think tank in Canada. Third, not only has the Fraser Institute invested significant resources in this project over an extended period of time, but it has also been a wide and highly collaborative project with input from many sectors of the conservative movement.[12] Fourth, as we shall see below, the series explicitly seeks to reflect on both principles and policy, and thus it offers an ideal example of the interplay between the two. Fifth, comprising 11 publications (in French and English) and culminating in a final, 378-page book that summarizes the findings of the entire series (but does not include all of the prior material), the series offers an exceptionally large, diverse, and rich sample of conservative philosophy and policy thought on a wide set of issues. Finally, it is also a report that seems to have resonated in the conservative movement—as evidenced by the amount of collaborative consultation and resources put into it, the popularity of the annual "dinners" that have been organized to celebrate the launch of each new instalment, the media coverage they have received, and the fact that the institute reported it being the subject of a "vigorous exchange in the House of Commons involving then-Prime Minister Paul Martin" (Fraser Institute, 2006, p. 14.).

Given these factors, we will analyze the main tenets of cappuccino conservatism using the Manning and Harris texts as a representative example. However, since we have consistently encountered the same tendencies in many other spheres of the conservative movement, we will also briefly gesture toward the ways in which this strain has also emerged in the more formal political realm over the last few years.

2.1 Happy Shiny Canadian Conservatism

As Thomas Frank and many others have pointed out, an angry, "common-sense," and anti-intellectual tone is the defining mode of American conservative backlash populism. In contrast, what is notable about cappuccino conservatism is that it is much frothier and sweeter than its dark, acidic, and over-roasted American cousin. There are still, of course, moments and voices that recall the angry, resentful anti-political notes of backlash populism. But on the whole, cappuccino conservatism has a much greater tonal breadth—and is more willing to employ an affirmative and positive register. Here, *Canada Strong and Free* is illustrative.

First, coming as it does from a highly quantitative think tank, the *Canada Strong and Free* series is notable for the degree to which it is defined by its identification and defence of the importance of principles. The foreword of the final book version begins, for example, by highlighting the centrality of principles as framing and orienting the entire work: "'*Whereas Canada is founded upon principles*'.... With these words our *Charter of Rights and Freedoms* begins. Principles are essential to realizing our vision of a Canada as truly strong and free as our national anthem boasts. We have therefore based our public policy recommendations on the following principles" (Harris & Manning, 2005a, p. ix).

Second, it is much more forward-looking than American conservatism. Manning and Harris do not primarily harken back to some nostalgic past where everything was settled and good. Rather, the series self-consciously embraces novelty and policy innovation, and frequently celebrates itself for providing Canada with a "fresh vision with better public policies for the future" (Harris & Manning, 2005a, p. ix).

Third, *Canada Strong and Free* explicitly combines philosophical vision with practical, actionable public policies that address a wide variety of public policy "problems." The series insists that both principled vision and concrete policy suggestions are necessary to help ensure that Canada realizes its potential. What is interesting about this is that the document clearly takes the need for public policy very seriously. There is little of the dismissive tone or anti-expert sentiment that characterized Harris' vision in the 1990s.

Finally, and perhaps most importantly, for the most part the series embodies a strongly positive and affirmative tone (on one level at least—more on this below). The *Canada Strong and Free* series begins with a veneration of Canada: "We believe Canada has not yet reached its zenith—that the best is yet to come. And we believe that this will always be true. Canada is such a land of opportunity that the future can always be bigger, brighter, and better than the past, no matter how great our achievements have been" (Harris & Manning, 2005a, p. ix). They begin their first chapter (titled "Why Canada needs a fresh vision") with a proud description of the founding principles and historical successes of Canada—arguing that "without a doubt, we have accomplished great things together in the past"—and then they use this foundation to argue that to continue on this positive trajectory, a "strong clear vision for the future" is necessary to further "unite and guide Canada for the twenty-first century" (Harris & Manning, 2005a, p. 3). Given that Canadian political discourse tends not to have a strongly patriotic and self-laudatory tone, the brash confidence of their approach is notable.

Nowhere is the optimistic and engaged nature of their rhetorical strategy more evident than in the way they end their introductory chapter. For Manning and Harris neither berate us with our failures nor demand that we accept their view to avoid the certain catastrophe that awaits us if we do nothing. Rather, they *invite* us to join them in their vision. In their words, they offer us "An Invitation to Climb: Just as Canada's first residents—the aboriginal peoples—would visit high and sacred places of their territories to dream dreams and see visions of the future, you are invited to climb in your mind's eye to the high and inspirational places of our country and to look out on the horizon of what the future could hold for Canada and for all of us" (Harris & Manning, 2005a, p. 8).

The intricacies and ironies of this invitation—and its co-optation of first nations' traditions—are numerous. In the context of this chapter, however, what is most important is the stunning and self-conscious idealism and utopianism of the invitation. Where Harper's infamous speech to the US-based Council for National Policy in 1997 drips with embarrassment, anger, and contempt as he excoriates the Canada he sees,[13] and Harris' 1994 manifesto seethes with anger and resentment against politics, special interests, and the status quo (see note 9), *Canada Strong and Free* brims with optimism and positivity, focusing first of all on the successes and future potential rather than past and present failures.[14] The authors do not primarily evoke our rage, nor do they offer to execute our righteous anger. Rather, they seek to capture our idealism through a discourse of affirmation, by offering to help us to a "high and sacred place" so that we might dream inspirational visions of the future.[15]

While close observers of the Conservative Party of Canada understandably focus on the many cynical and highly polemical rhetorical tactics of the last several years, a less acknowledged fact is that the federal Conservatives have also sought to imbue their discourse with a much more upbeat and idealistic tone as well. One of the most concrete instantiations of this tone in the realm of federal politics has been the Conservative Party's not-so-subtle attempts to redefine and intensify the symbolism of Canadian patriotism. Conservative activists have long resented the fact that many Canadians ground their pride and identity in progressive accomplishments and the values they embody—for example, universal access to health care, a relatively tolerant and welcoming orientation toward new Canadians and diversity more generally, a (previously strong) international reputation for peacekeeping and judicious mediation, and so on. Rather than pout or rage against this reality (as backlash populism does) however, cappuccino conservatism seeks to reprogram the symbols of patriotism and the values that are commonly associated with the Canadian identity.

Interestingly, and again in contrast with backlash populism, although this renewed conservative patriotism is not especially nostalgic in tone, it does seek to place more emphasis on the past and the more traditional mores and norms those moments embody. And it is clearly employing a selective historical account to cultivate certain types of values and identities. One of the most notable elements of the new conservative patriotism is its drive to (re)masculinize the Canadian identity. Hence the move from peacekeeping and mediation to the more burly peace-making stance in Afghanistan and Libya; the concerted efforts to raise the profile of the War of 1812 (and define it as a Canadian, rather than a British war); and the central framing of the "North" as a question of military preparedness and sovereignty. Hence also the highly moralized legitimization of international exploits. The justification for military intervention in Afghanistan (or in the case of Iran, of suspending diplomatic relations) is about protecting women or spreading democracy, and in some ways this mimics progressive human rights tropes. But what the Conservative use of this rhetoric does is entrench a very different idea: it portrays Canada as a manly nation saving meek and helpless women abroad. In doing so, it subtly reorients the Canadian self-image toward traditional gender roles and assumptions, but in a way that seems forward-looking and positive, not resentful or behind the times.

Notably, cappuccino conservatism also seeks to embed a profound faith in the market deep into Canadian patriotism. Here the most obvious example is the degree to which the conservative movement has sought to cultivate a pride in market-driven natural resource extraction as part of our core notion of what Canada means. Whether seeking to portray Canada as an "energy superpower," or proudly identifying the oil sands as the economic engine of Canada, this posture dovetails nicely with the more masculinist and muscular foreign affairs posture—both re-idealize Canada as a rugged, upstanding, get-your-hands-covered-in-oil, salt-of-the-earth type of man.

As we will see below, cappuccino conservatism does mobilize different and much more negative tones at various moments and in different media. However, even if this more positive and inspirational tone is simply the conservative movement adding another tonal arrow to their quiver of discursive strategies, it is an important development. For altering the tone of a discourse (such as making it more positive and optimistic, and especially linking it to patriotic themes) can dramatically change its affectivity, the meaning it is given by its audience, the constituencies it can speak to, and the degree to which it can, or can't, resonate with very different audiences. In this sense, the fact that the conservative movement is developing an inspirational rhetorical approach that seeks to motivate Canadians to affirm and hold sacred conservative principles and ideals is an important innovation, even if this tone does not characterize the entirety of Canadian conservative discourse.

2.2 The Freedom to Choose ... the Market

So what are these conservatives dreaming of? What sacred and high principles underpin the cappuccino conservative vision of a Canada striving to reach its true potential? At the core of this affirmative conservative vision lies a defence and employment of the principle or moral value of "choice." We can see this clearly if we return to Harris and Manning's report, which emphasizes one principle above all others: "a dramatic expansion of *freedom of choice* in every dimension of Canadian life—economic, scientific, social, cultural, religious, political—and in the world at large" (2005a, p. 12). For Manning and Harris, this is a far-reaching principle that is violated in situations as varied as when "monopolistic practices in either the public or private sector limit our choice of goods and services"; when "freedom is limited by poverty, discrimination, and segregation (as in the case of many of our aboriginal peoples) which deny people the opportunity or the means to exercise freedoms"; when "the state commands too large a proportion of the nation's wealth and confiscates too large a proportion of the incomes of individuals and businesses"; when "governments or private monopolies restrict scientific inquiry, lifestyle choices, freedom of expression, or the ability of people to act on their most deeply held beliefs"; or when "political freedom is limited [by a context where] one party, ideology or viewpoint dominates the political landscape and voters are denied the opportunity to make choices among real public-policy options" (2005a, p. 14).

It is noteworthy that only a few of these would traditionally be found on a typical outrage list of backlash populism—and some, such as poverty and discrimination, would rarely be given even a token nod of the head, never mind listed as the third most important type of freedom limitation, even among libertarians. Moreover, the degree to which this perspective—by highlighting the importance of avoiding government, private, or community restrictions on scientific inquiry, lifestyle choices, and freedom of expression—distances itself from social conservatism is remarkable.

The importance of this broad embrace of choice is that it allows cappuccino conservatism to avoid both the cold technical arguments (often used by neoliberal perspectives) and the angry "slash and burn" anti-government/radical-privatization rhetoric (often employed by backlash populism). Instead, cappuccino conservatism talks in much friendlier and more "Canadian"-sounding ways about wanting "to implement policies that rebalance the roles of the public and private sectors in the financing and delivery of social services" and name their approach "market based approaches to public policy" (Harris & Manning, 2005a, p. 19, xi). This may not seem like a significant departure, but the use of the language of "balance" is much more nuanced and less extremist than discursive strategies used by other variants of conservatism—and it is important to note their use of a much more affirmative register, since these rhetorical alterations can have an important impact on with whom, and why, their arguments resonate.

While Harris and Manning sometimes justify their market-oriented preference with the usual claims that such solutions are more effective and efficient (2005a, p. x, 26), they primarily defend it by referring to the importance of choice as a moral and philosophical good. First, they affirm the foundational value and almost a priori status of the principles of choice and responsibility, claiming that "these principles are valuable in their own right. Individuals have the intrinsic right to determine their future course, make choices as they see fit for themselves" (Harris & Manning, 2005a, p. 13). Then they interweave these principles with assertions about the "superior outcomes" that will follow from a proper respect for the moral principle of choice to create a deeply moralized and practical argument in favour of market-oriented public policy solutions. In this view, it is axiomatic that the pre-eminent mechanism for maximizing free choice is the market. The state, in contrast, is an institution whose very nature compels it to adopt "coercive measures to ensure that individuals make the choices the state considers are appropriate," which leads to a significant erosion of liberty (Harris & Manning, 2005a, p. 13). As we outline below in the case of child care policy, this theme has been key in conservative electoral communications as well.

This rhetorical strategy is obviously not a profoundly new innovation. It has precursors—in many ways it resuscitates the utopian notes of Hayek and Friedman that were popularized by Reagan. However, what is notable is that it is quite different than the angry backlash populism so dominant in the US, and this tone of market moralism has never before been so prominent in mainstream conservative discourse in Canada. In this sense, while the philosophical themes may not be original, their intensity is distinctive in the Canadian setting.

2.3 Disciplining Responsible Choice

Up to this point, we have been focusing on the affirmative and individual choice-oriented characteristics of cappuccino conservatism. However, no discussion of cappuccino conservatism would be complete without an investigation of the fascinating ways in which this apparently affirmative and individualist foundation also requires and enables a profoundly disciplinary dimension. Perhaps the best way to unpack this element of cappuccino conservatism is to examine the role played by another of Harris and Manning's foundational principles. If their first principle is individual choice, the second is "a greater acceptance by Canadians, and better enforcement, of the *responsibilities and obligations* that attend any expansion or exercise of freedom" (Harris & Manning, 2005a, p. 12). So core is this principle that Manning and Harris assert "freedom [of choice] cannot exist without personal responsibility" (2005a, p. 13).

Why is the acceptance of responsibility and obligations a crucial rejoinder to the principle of freedom of choice? Many social (or even traditional organic) conservatives could easily answer this question with a response that highlighted the intrinsic value of community, tradition, or duty. However, what is fascinating about Manning and Harris' logic is that they do not rely on any such argument. Rather, their argument rests primarily, and only slightly paradoxically, on the first principle of choice.

Harris and Manning begin by admitting that allowing and expanding freedom of choice is risky and can have some unpleasant consequences. Individuals can abuse this freedom—transgress other people's freedom, disrespect others' rights, or ignore their responsibility to respect and protect the social and political context that allows the exercise of rights. This, in turn, causes citizens to seek protection against these types of abuse. On their reading of history, if people don't exercise responsibility themselves, the community will ask the state to step in: "traditionally in Canada, fears about the real or potential abuse of freedoms by individuals or corporations have led to demands for heavy-handed interventions by governments and an expansion of the role of the state in society" (Harris & Manning, 2005, p. 15).

This dynamic has several disastrous consequences, according to Manning and Harris. First of all, it limits freedom of choice: "as the state assumes more and more responsibility, our freedom and personal choices are eroded. When the state assumes responsibility for individual choices, it limits freedom" (Harris & Manning, 2005a, p. 13). Even worse, however, are the long-term effects of the vicious circle that state intervention initiates. For on Harris and Manning's telling, the more the state accepts responsibility for people's choices, the less responsible people will become, and thus the more interventionist the state will become. "If individuals do not bear the consequences of bad choices, more people will make them and the rest of us will be forced to bear the burden. That, in turn, forces the state to adopt coercive measures to ensure that individuals make the choices the state considers appropriate, and liberty is even further eroded" (Harris & Manning, 2005a, p. 13). Irresponsible exercise of choice therefore facilitates the growth of an interventionist state that will increasingly control all citizens' choices—even those who have the capacity for responsible self-governance. This is a truly impressive philosophical tour de force. For by its end, it appears that a larger, more interventionist state cannot be blamed on conservatives seeking moral universalism, special interests in Ottawa, big business, or institutionalized unions looking for breaks. Rather, it is the fault of individuals who have not had to accept the consequences of their bad choices. Moreover, it is the rest of us who have had to bear the consequences in the form not only of higher taxes but also of an expanding neo-totalitarian nanny state ready to coerce us into giving up our children to a Kafkaesque daycare experience.

Their use of the principle of responsibility is thus fascinating for several reasons. First, along with the principle of freedom of choice, it reinforces a market-oriented approach. For if irresponsible choice leads to state intervention, which in turn limits freedom of choice and encourages a culture that disavows freedom, it makes sense to privilege market-friendly policies that "expand private property rights and the rule of law in such a way as to give a far greater number of individual citizens, organizations, and communities the tools to protect their own rights and freedoms when those are infringed upon by others, including the state" (Harris & Manning, 2005a, p. 15).

Second, and no less important (if paradoxical), this principled invocation of responsibility allows cappuccino conservatives to simultaneously (a) champion the market for its ability to discipline (or in more affirmative tones, its ability to incentivize) individuals to cultivate certain habits, beliefs, values, and behaviours necessary for the smooth functioning of their ideal society, while also (b) denying that the market can ever be a coercive institution. From their point of view, if government intervention is a social technology that encourages dependence, laziness, and irresponsibility, the market is a social technology that trains independence, productivity, and responsibility. The market, in other words, is not merely a technically efficient mechanism for distributing goods. For cappuccino conservatism, it's a morality machine that produces virtuous citizens—or more precisely, virtuous marketizens.

And this is the real distinction between progressives and cappuccino conservatives. For once we recognize the profound role that market moralism plays in their mindset, we can see the conservative claim that the Left favours social engineering (through the state), whereas the Right favours individual freedom and choice (by expanding the reach of markets) is deeply misleading. Since both approaches use various techniques of cultivation to train our moral, political, and social subjectivities, the difference is not whether one camp or the other uses social technologies. No one—and certainly not cappuccino conservatism—is advocating radical individual freedom from social discipline. Rather, the difference lies in *which* social technologies are employed and what consequences they lead to. Progressives tend to believe that collective political measures (legislation, judicial rulings, and governmental incentive programs such as tax credits and social security) can be crucial tools of cultivation in certain cases, whereas cappuccino conservatives prefer the market to have rein to discipline social behaviour. One might say, then, that the end goal of cappuccino conservatism is to champion a very particular definition of "choice" precisely to discipline citizens not to choose to support collective action and programs organized by the state financed through universal taxation. And this is where the positive vision starts to cede to a harder-edged version. Let's see how this plays out in a concrete policy area or two.

2.4 Lazy Children-Citizens and the Indulgent Nanny State: Choice over Care

Almost all Manning and Harris' specific policy recommendations are grounded in an assertion about the philosophical value of the principles of expanded choice and individual responsibility—often unsupported by data. Take Harris and Manning's second, more policy-centric volume, titled *Caring for Canadians in a Canada Strong and Free*, which is exemplary. In this volume, they once again re-articulate the centrality of the principle of choice to creating "best in class" policies in health care, education, welfare, and child care (Harris & Manning, 2005b, p. 1). They assert, for example, that the strength of Canada's education system is due to the fact that this is the sector in which there has been the most robust freedom of choice and the least monopolistic meddling of the federal government. They thus make much of the fact that Alberta "which has gone the furthest to encourage choice and responsibility, is a world leader" in educational results (Harris & Manning, 2005b, p. 5).

Interestingly, however, they do not examine whether this correlation is a reliable indicator of causality. For example, though they offer anecdotal links between Alberta's performance and their system of choice/responsibility, they neither show that these links are generalizable, nor prove that they are the cause of increased performance. Similarly, for a report that explicitly benchmarks Canadian provinces against "best in world" performance and draws conclusions from the high performers in Canada, they do not explore the key characteristics and "best practices" of those systems that perform as well as or even better than Alberta—such as Finland, Japan, Korea, Hong Kong, and the Netherlands. Nor do they comment on the fact that despite having adopted a variety of pro-choice education policies, the US consistently scores low on the various cited benchmarking studies. Rather, in each case our faith in the principle of freedom of choice and its intrinsic link to high levels of prosperity, health, and all the rest is apparently sufficient.

The principle of choice plays a similar role in their discussion of child care policy. According to Harris and Manning, Canada needs to "put children first," which means we should create "a Canada where every parent has the freedom to bring up their children as they consider best—as well as child care choices that suit their unique needs" (2005b, p. 59). Their preferred policy solution? A market-based one that offers some government assistance to individual families, while leaving the development and delivery of child care services entirely to the private sector. And once again, an appeal to the value of choice is the bedrock of their case against publicly provided daycare. They do not, for example, provide evidence to prove that child care in the home is uniformly better for the development of the child.[16] Instead, they use the bulk of the child care section (80%) to argue against publicly funded and regulated daycare by claiming that parents deserve choice on principle, and prefer choice in reality. In their view, the most crucial issue is that a federal program would unnecessarily limit choice, since if the government set up a daycare system with public funds, it would "increasingly coerce parental choice, subsidizing some child care options and not others," and thus ensure that "thousands of Canadian children are being funnelled into formalized daycare, though this is far from their preferred options" (Harris & Manning, 2005b, p. 59). Moreover, despite the explicit policy orientation of the discussion, when evaluating which policy would be best, they choose only to report on what citizens would "prefer" in an *ideal* situation (and unsurprisingly find that most people would like to care for their children themselves or with a relative). They never explore the question of whether this is a *realistic* option for most Canadians, or what citizens would prefer given the trade-offs implied by the actual social and political context in Canada. This is not to say that there isn't merit in some of the concerns they raise, or that there aren't good reasons to consider a more decentralized approach to child care. Rather, it is to highlight the degree to which a faith in freedom of choice supports and defines their position—even to the point where it erases and trumps the discussion of other, very real, considerations.

Their discussion of child care policy highlights the ways in which cappuccino conservatism is also able to draw on harder-edged populist rhetoric. Discussing Liberal child care policies, they argue that "our government continues to divert resources to some of Canada's most prosperous families—those with two wage earners—away from single-earner families that often struggle financially to raise their children. This is particularly unfair to poorer Canadians, without the means to make other choices" (Harris & Manning, 2005, p. 59). "Most prosperous families"; "two-wage earners"; "unfair to poorer Canadians"—these terms call to mind images of wealthy city-dwelling yuppies as the primary recipients of government largesse and encourage the audience of Harris and Manning's discourse to react angrily to the unfair, self-interested, and biased nature of government policies.

They further evoke a little of the backlash populist anti-elitism by subtly creating a vision in which civil servants are explicitly counter-posed against normal people and "families." "Most importantly, our vision for child care is centred on the family. *Families*, not state bureaucrats or politicians, should make the choices that best suit their needs. This key principle has two sides: families should have the freedom, means, and responsibility for raising children—and government should not interfere in these choices, except in truly exceptional circumstances" (Harris & Manning, 2005b, p. 71). This portrait—with knowledgeable, well-meaning families on one hand and distant, interfering bureaucrats on the other—is deliberate and telling. Using italics to establish an unbridgeable gap between *families* and the state, and using the word "bureaucrat" (with all its negative connotations of uncaring, uninterested, and obstinate) rather than the term civil servant (which implies service, civility, a certain nobility, and a care for the community) are subtle but important ways in which Manning and Harris' discourse serves to evoke and cultivate suspicion and resentment toward government initiatives.

These themes have been employed at key moments in recent conservative electoral campaigns as well. During the 2006 election, for example, we had a chance to watch exactly how this affirmation of responsible choice and anger over the paternalism of the state can move from think-tank rhetoric to vote-influencing actuality. At that time, Scott Reid, the Liberal Prime Minister's director of communication, conducted an interview in which he attacked the conservative child care policy (which promised to give an annual tax refund of $1,200 for each child). In that interview, he stated that the Liberal proposal was best since it would provide the universal "care that is regulated, safe, and secure" whereas the Conservative tax refund proposal would essentially give parents "$25 a day to blow on beer and popcorn" (CBC News, 2005). Calling this comment a turning point in the election would be too strong, but it certainly had an impact. The reaction was immediate and forceful. Many voters were outraged, flooding call-in shows and writing letters strongly attacking the elitist attitudes of the Liberals. Moreover, the Conservative party immediately pursued this strategy and attacked the Liberals not merely as corrupt, but also as arrogant, out of touch, and elitist.

Why might this have resonated with some voters so strongly—even in a country where programs like medicare (despite its challenges) remain widely shared symbols of the value of collective public policy? Because it is a deeply affective and emotional vision that authorizes its audience to publicly express generalized anger (which, as Frank aptly notes, is a bumper crop in these days of economic insecurity), to identify an agent to be blamed for that anger (bureaucrats, elites, the unproductive free-riders of society who have made bad choices and now want the state to bail them out), and finally to celebrate their own moral superiority (at having made good choices), all without seeming too extreme or ungenerous, since it all starts from the idealistic valorisation of choice.

In this sense, the power of cappuccino conservatism is not only that it provides a principled and affirmative foundation for conservatism. Its force also derives from the fact that it starts from an argument about allowing more choice for all, which allows its advocates to simultaneously feel good about the privilege they have (since they earned it); angry that the government wants to take "more than its fair share" away from those who succeed (since they deserve it); annoyed at people at the bottom of society (since their very existence is provoking the emergence of a nanny state); justified about not providing more support for them (since they are the ones who chose irresponsibly and they need to learn their lessons the hard way); and comfortable with asking the state to increase punitive measures against those who transgress the law (since you need to kick the "bad apples" out of the game lest the entire game devolve into anarchy).

2.5 Taxes and the State: Drowning Government in a Bathtub? No, Just a Little Healthy Waterboarding

It is perhaps not surprising that in the US—a country whose founding myths (and contemporary conservative movement) identify a revolt against tea taxes in Boston as one of the pivotal moments in its march to revolution and independence—the size of government and the level of taxation is a topic of perpetual political contestation. Or that one of its most powerful conservative political operatives is Grover Norquist, the primary mover behind Americans for Tax Reform and the Taxpayer Protection Pledge, who is perhaps best known for saying that he wanted to shrink the US government down to the size of something he could drown in a bathtub.

But it is important to remember that the supposedly unbroken lineage of America as an anti-tax haven is not entirely historically accurate. For as recently as the 1960s and 1970s, many agreed with Lionel Trilling's suggestion that "liberalism is not only the dominant but even the sole intellectual tradition" in the United States (Mickelwait & Wooldridge, 2004, p. 43). We must remember that even in the US, the current dominance of anti-tax and anti-state conservative ideologies is not an unbroken inevitability, but rather the product of a concerted, 40-year effort by the ideological infrastructure of the conservative movement to alter the values and beliefs of the voting public.

In the US, the narrative of backlash populism has become central to this effort. Even Thomas Frank (whose primary thesis is that social issues have driven backlash populism) clearly demonstrates that a deep and virulent anti-state/anti-tax stance is intrinsic to the contemporary US conservative movement and its backlash populist narrative.[17] What is perhaps most telling about Frank's portrait is that it reveals backlash populism as a reactionary revolution that would be comic if it weren't tragic. He paints a picture of

> the angry workers, mighty in their numbers ... marching irresistibly against the arrogant. They are shaking their fists at the sons of privilege. They are laughing at the dainty affectations of the Leawood toffs. They are massing at the gates of Mission Hills, hoisting the black flag, and while the millionaires tremble in their mansions, they are bellowing out their terrifying demands. "We are here," they scream, "to cut your taxes." (Frank, 2004, p. 109)

This image is interesting for two reasons: First, that working- and middle-class populists in the US are not simply hoodwinked by social conservative issues, but instead ignore or even deny the benefits the state provides for many of them and therefore support the tax-cutting policies of upward redistribution that disproportionately benefit the very wealthy.[18] And second, that the anger of the working and middle class has been redirected away from economic elites toward other targets.

In Canada, we have certainly seen important strains of a similar narrative around the size of the state and levels of taxation. One of the most evident backlash tropes employed in Canada harkens back to the nineteenth-century US populist "producerist" critique. Originally used to criticize the "non-productive" robber barons and bankers who were viewed as living parasitically off the concrete work of farmers and workers, now it is the government that is the parasite—leeching the hard-earned money of hard-working families and even harder-working capitalists. And to add insult to injury, the government then wastes its ill-gotten revenues by giving it to lazy government workers and even lazier welfare recipients. The politics of resentment are thus key to the backlash populist narrative. And its brilliance is the understanding that in tough times, people are only too willing to project their anger and resentment onto whatever character can be portrayed as being to blame for their circumstances. Mike Harris' Common Sense Revolution thus vilified government waste, teachers and their two-month summer holidays, and welfare queens—and used this narrative to achieve almost a decade of electoral victories, cutbacks to services, and tax cuts. More recently, Tim Hudak and Rob Ford have used repeated discursive attacks on the "gravy train" of public spending, fat-cat union bosses, and coddled public service workers with gold-plated pensions.

The backlash populist narrative is not always effective, however. As Machiavelli well knew, there is no universally effective political or rhetorical strategy. Different conditions and different audiences require different approaches. And we may be seeing the limits of backlash populism these days. Yes, Rob Ford was elected on a wave of discontent. But only two years later, these same rhetorical moves seem to resonate much less intensely with the electorate. Moreover, Hudak—even though he was not weighed down by the same type of gaffes as Ford is prone to—lost the 2011 election despite having a double-digit lead at certain points before the election. And while the Harper government uses backlash populist tropes at times, this has not been the primary tone of its narrative around its cost-cutting agenda.

In this context, it is important for progressives to understand, and develop counter-narratives to, the more nuanced discourse that cappuccino conservatism employs regarding taxation and the size of government in general. Especially because the logic of cappuccino conservatism is one that can be (and has been) used by a variety of political parties to justify cuts (e.g., Paul Martin as the Minister of Finance of the federal Liberals in the mid-1990s; the last days of the McGuinty Liberals in 2012). In broad strokes, the overall orientation of cappuccino conservatism toward the state and taxation is neither surprising nor novel. The state needs to be smaller. Regulation should be lightened. Markets should be unleashed. Taxation should be lower—and under no circumstances should avenues for increasing government revenues be considered. But what is very different is the way this vision is communicated. And this is something that can make all the difference in the world in electoral politics. So, what are the key characteristics of its position on taxation and the state?

First, the cappuccino conservative perspective on taxes eschews the angry, hostile, attack-dog positioning of backlash populism. It actively embodies an affirmative and positive tone. Rather than railing against special interests and a corrupted state, Harris and Manning's *A Vision for Canada Strong and Free* explicitly affirms that "most Canadians correctly view government as a positive force in the economy" (2007, p. 115). They don't want to "slash" spending, they just want a "more modest state," "right-sized" for Canada—one where apparently, "less is more" (Harris & Manning, 2007, ch. 6 & 7). Even the pivot to critique is measured and reasonable-sounding. Suggesting that government intervention is like fertilizer (a certain amount helps growth, but too much poisons the ground and kills the crop), Manning and Harris suggest that their interest is simply in getting that balance right. In fact, one might even say that the report is rather utopian. For while even the data the report is based on clearly shows that Canada is already in the top 10 countries for a number of key metrics (including the smallness of our government and the lightness of our regulatory requirements) and fifth overall in their summary index of economic freedom (ahead of both the UK and the US), they insist this is insufficient. On these issues, "'good' is a long way from 'best'"—the authors want us to strive for true excellence (Harris & Manning, 2007, p. 107). The point, of course, is not that this is actual compassionate conservatism in action, or that they are just innocently striving for excellence as defined by the data, since they certainly do not encourage us to strive to be the most equitable society. Rather, the way they communicate and justify their tax-cutting and government-shrinking policy is very different than backlash populism—and their approach is potentially much more appealing to voters outside the conservative base.

Second, it is notable that this version of conservatism is not necessarily allergic to data. As we have argued elsewhere, one of the key elements of backlash populism is its aversion to statistical data, its preference for judging the validity of knowledge and policy based on anecdotal examples and gut feelings (what we call epistemological populism), and its use of a variety of tactics to avoid debate based on empirical evidence (see Saurette & Gunster, 2011; Saurette, 2010). Given the cuts to Statistics Canada and the ending of the long-form consensus (despite the objections of a huge coalition of groups, from civil society to the business sector), cuts to the GST (despite the objections of almost every tax expert and economist), and the passing of major crime bills (despite clear evidence that parts will be extremely costly, ineffective, and possibly unconstitutional), it seems clear that the current federal conservative government does not place a premium on policy that flows from objectively collected and publicly available data. In contrast, cappuccino conservatism only gives the appearance of being comfortable with empirical evidence. *Vision for a Canada Strong and Free* is filled with data when it comes to the discussion of the preferred size of government and taxation levels and mix. This data is rather selectively presented, and the interpretations and recommendations do not always match the data provided. But the important element is that data is used as a rhetorical mode of persuasion in this form of conservatism. It may be that there is no tension between backlash epistemological populism and cappuccino conservatism in practice; however, having access to both in different contexts is no doubt an advantage. The less objective the data the government gathers, the more it can justify its policies with reference to other rhetorical strategies, and the more it must rely on outside data when it does refer to it to justify its choices. The more it must rely on outside data, the more impact the pre-selected and interpreted data offered by the growing conservative ideological infrastructure can have. In the context of the debate about the size of government and level and mix of taxation, this selective flexibility is a notable advantage.

Third, it is important to note that cappuccino conservatism does not forward a narrowly or purely technical argument about taxation. Rather, what is crucial is that it grounds the conclusions of its data-heavy presentation by reference to principles. Often we hear people speak about their faith in the free market. And often, it seems that this is literally the case. For it frequently appears that zealous promoters of free market solutions to almost every policy challenge hold it as a religious doctrine that the free market is better in all cases. Sometimes this faith is buttressed simply by the volume and frequency of the repeated statements of belief in the market (as in the backlash populist narrative). Cappuccino conservatism, however, addresses this explicitly by reference to its core principles. In the case of Manning and Harris, they derive the principle of "economic freedom" from the already established more general principle of freedom of choice. "Economic freedom means liberating citizens to make more of their own economic decisions. The idea necessarily implies a limited government: over-sized governments, those that over-tax or substitute their decision-making for individual initiative and choice, are a major constraint on economic freedom" (Harris & Manning, 2007, p. 108).

Framing the entire discussion with the lens of choice and economic freedom turns out to be a crucial strategy, for presenting this faith as a principle protects this position against critique. "Faith" can be accused of being irrational and ungrounded. In contrast, a "principle" or "value" is given much higher standing in our public discourse. Standing on principle is, in fact, often interpreted as noble and honourable whereas making decisions purely on faith is viewed skeptically. Perhaps the most important advantage of framing the discussion first around principles of choice and then economic freedom is that it rules out many other ways of examining the question of taxation. Once choice and economic freedom are established as the only relevant principles and values, it seems utterly rational to present only that data which is related to economic freedom, evaluate it simply from that point of view, and thus offer recommendations in line with these principles. As they say, the idea of economic freedom "necessarily implies limited government." When it comes to tax policy, it also allows them to forward a set of quite radical recommendations (recommendation 7.1: accelerate the complete elimination of all corporate capital tax; 7.2: reduce corporate income tax federally from 21 to 12%, and provincially to 8%; 7.5: Move toward a single-rate income tax; 7.7: Eliminate the capital gains tax) that seem grounded in empirically based analysis about the most efficient forms and levels of taxation. But what gets lost is that the criteria they use—for example, what they call "welfare gains" or "marginal efficiency costs"—are far from the only relevant criteria. Most importantly, it ensures that there is no discussion about who gets these "welfare gains" and who pays the "marginal efficiency costs." It also pre-emptively disallows asking the question of whether these costs and benefits might be outweighed by other costs, benefits, principles, and values. All this contestability remains invisible due to the initial principled framing—and thus to the average educated audience member, these propositions have the appearance of being reasonable, measured, and empirically grounded.

3. Choosing Fair Taxation

So where do all of these findings leave progressives who want to ensure that a significant majority of Canadian voters share a vision of this country that includes a robust role for government and a system of fair taxation that sustains this capacity? We believe there are a number of implications:

1. Progressives in Canada need to invest in building a robust progressive ideological infrastructure.
   - There is simply no other option. Vocal, assertive, and profoundly political conservative think tanks have already formed a very powerful network of influence. Moreover, their relative volume is amplified by the fact that the wider traditional mediascape is dominated by outlets whose editorial positions are more sympathetic to the market utopian views of conservative think tanks than to progressive perspectives. This is a situation that is only going to intensify—especially as traditional media organizations continue to cut internal capacity and become more and more dependent on carrying content developed elsewhere (such as in think tanks).
   - This in turn requires aggressive investment in strengthening the capacity of the progressive think-tank network. We believe that many Canadians would eventually be willing to support such an effort, especially in a context where they are simultaneously politically aware but increasingly cynical about political parties. However, this effort would clearly require a kick-start of some kind. It would be nice if a dozen wealthy progressives decided to take a page out of the Koch brothers' playbook and get the ball rolling. Or if progressive political parties were willing to share their membership lists to drive a significant fundraising effort. A more probable route is to have the union movement fund the effort at the beginning. To do so, it must look beyond single-issue campaigns and understand that funding the effort to cultivate a broad progressive vision in Canada is as much in their interest as short-term, issue-specific lobbying. After all, cappuccino conservatism attacks the very idea of collective action—the core principle of the union movement. The more successful cappuccino conservatism is at dominating the public sphere, the less broad support there will be for unions, the more supportive Canadians will be of political interference in collective negotiations, and the more difficult it will be for unions to make progress for their members (which will only create a vicious circle further eroding their strength).
   - It will be important as well to fund think tanks that are not charitable organizations so that they are able to engage in a much

broader set of persuasion activities. This may make fundraising harder, but it is essential, especially since it appears that the possibility of new regulations and closer CRA examination of charities' advocacy roles will further restrict the activities of existing think tanks.

2. Progressive foundations and think tanks in Canada need to be more strategic and creative about how they allocate their resources.
   - Research is an important task of progressive think tanks. This will continue to be the case, perhaps more so than ever, given the current governments' deep cuts to data collection and analysis. However, progressive think tanks often seem to believe that the only way to get attention is to do a new study. Instead, they need to spend far more resources on getting the message out, and repeating it again and again and again and again. Repetition is crucial to persuasion.
   - They need to get better at amplifying existing progressive voices and cultivating new ones. They need to fund the best speakers to do what they do best: speak to the media as much as they can. They need to leverage their skills and work hard to get them into strategic places where their voices can influence policy-makers. They need to create effective training and mentoring opportunities for young activists who show promise and interest in becoming spokespeople for a broad progressive cause.
   - They need a think tank whose sole mission is to make the case, day in and day out, in connection with whatever debate is taking place, that Taxes are Good.

3. Any new approach must recognize that the conservative discourse around taxes is diverse, multi-layered, and constantly evolving.
   - In reality, we should probably stop talking about conservative "discourse" and start talking about conservative "discourses" on taxes.
   - It will be important to map out these discourses and identify which ones resonate with what audiences and why, and then to respond with counter-discourses capable of overturning—or at least disrupting—the "commonsensical" nature of conservative tax discourses.
   - At the very least, this means developing counter-narratives that challenge the narratives of both backlash populism and cappuccino conservatism.

4. Progressives must engage in the debate over values and principles.
   - In the Canadian context, most political principles and values are what are called essentially contested concepts—that is, concepts that are widely valued but whose definition can differ greatly, so they are thus the subject of intense ideological contestation between groups who want to define them differently (Connolly, 1993). It matters a great deal, for example, whether equality is defined as equality of opportunity or equality of condition.

- In this context, the progressive movement must challenge the conservative reduction of choice to individual market choice. It might, for example, popularize a concept of "real choice"—one that highlights the structural conditions that enable and limit the reality of who has what type of choice. It might also link choice explicitly to other progressive values, such as equality. It seems quite possible that the idea that real choice requires real equality might resonate deeply with many Canadian voters—especially given how strongly many Canadians have reacted against the growing levels of inequality (Broadbent Institute, n.d.). Given how closely taxes (as well as other things like union membership) are linked to reductions of inequality, this framing would be highly beneficial for the progressive view.
- Key will be to reinvigorate a progressive conception of responsibility. The conservative movement has been quite successful at reducing the idea of responsibility to individual responsibility for one's choices—they have used this to buttress their "tough on crime" approach, and their broader attack on the idea that collective action and the state should play a central role in society. But progressives believe deeply in responsibility as well—only they highlight the social nature of responsibility. In a sense, then, progressives entirely agree with Manning and Harris that we can't have freedom without responsibility. They just believe we have a responsibility to one another. The concrete upside of this is that it gives progressives a noble, principled, and uplifting frame for taxes.
- Yes, people should be reminded that taxes are in their self-interest since they are linked to services. But the narrative shouldn't limit it to this. Rather, why not re-energize a language of progressive citizenship? Why not speak about taxes as an obligation we have toward one another? Toward Canada? What is needed is to contest the conservative movement's reduction of Canadians to consumers of services (whether of government or the market) and reframe our identity as citizens who have bonds and obligations to one another in addition to our own self-interest.
5. Also needed is a reinvigorated progressive patriotism.
    - Many progressives seem to reject the idea of patriotism for a variety of reasons. And it is certainly true that patriotism can be deeply problematic in many ways. However, we believe that it is too important and too resonant a rhetorical appeal today to simply allow it to be owned and redefined by the conservative movement. The progressive movement made a similar mistake decades ago when we allowed the trope of the "family" to be taken over by the conservative movement—and we have been paying the price ever since.[19]
    - We are not suggesting that Canadian progressives should simply retreat into a bland protectionism/nationalism. Rather, we believe

that they should try to define a vision of patriotism that celebrates the broad set of progressive values that we as a society should strive to embody (even if we necessarily do so incompletely).
- Moreover, a progressive patriotism could play a key role in reframing taxes in a positive, noble light. Why not a progressive patriotism that reminds us how fortunate we are to be Canadian, and links that to our responsibility to do more for those who aren't as fortunate (both within and outside Canada)? Why not a progressive patriotism that trumpets our commitment to equality, to social justice, to sharing risk? Why not a patriotism that shouts: "Proud to be Canadian. Proud to pay my fair share"?
- This would not only stop the conservative movement from owning the affective pull of patriotic appeals. It would also dramatically highlight the difference between the two visions for Canada.

6. Progressives need to get angry.
    - As Machiavelli well understood, both positive emotions (love, hope) and negative ones (anger, fear) are powerful motivators. A political movement that restricts itself to either one or the other will likely be less effective and less sustainable.
    - Progressives need to get angrier, and cultivate this more widely. They need to take back populist narratives from the conservative movement. In particular, they need to develop and popularize the angry side of a progressive populism. They need to redefine the conservative casting of the villains, victims, and heroes in ways that give voice to the progressive story.
    - This is especially true in the context of taxation. Progressives need to outline a vision of what fair taxation is and convince more Canadians to feel outraged about those organizations and sectors who aren't paying their fair share. Once again, over the last 30 years, it has been the conservatives who have owned the discourse about fairness in tax—arguing angrily that it isn't fair to pay so much in tax and that our hard-earned tax dollars shouldn't be unfairly given away to people who don't work as hard. They need to redefine this and show how the radical reduction of corporate taxes and the flattening of our tax scales is unfair and has only taken place because of the concerted lobbying efforts of business interests.[20] And this should be repeated again and again, ad nauseam, both because so many Canadians don't know the facts, and because repetition is a key rhetorical strategy against the inevitable tendency to forget the past and normalize present conditions as the only world possible.

7. Finally, progressives need to become more creatively and effectively networked.
    - They need the usual suspects to participate in this effort. But they need more than just the usual suspects. As they say, no one pays attention to the old "dog bites man" story. But everyone pays attention to the "man bites dog" story. When it comes to taxes,

nothing breaks through the media saturation and expectations like having unexpected groups or individuals—whose positions are above reproach from the other side, and whose direct self-interest and high-status identity would seem to make them likely to support a tax-cutting agenda. In this sense, high profile, very successful, and wealthy individuals and groups will have to step up and become spokespeople for the Let's Raise Taxes/Let's Tax More Fairly movement. This means supporting groups like Physicians for Fair Taxation and Lawyers for Fair Taxation, and helping people create Economists for Fair Taxation, Accountants for Fair Taxation, Bay Streeters for Fair Taxation; Oil Workers for Fair Taxation; Engineers for Fair Taxation; One Percenters for Fair Taxation; Reformed Conservatives for Fair Taxation; Soldiers for Fair Taxation. You get the idea.

- And they need to be really creative in the types of priming strategies and processes they embed at various levels to start to change our perceptions of taxes. Manning and Harris want Parliament to establish a committee whose sole function is to review and strike existing laws and regulations—and they want all new regulations to come with a five-year sunset clause to force every new Parliament to re-pass them. Progressives might demand the same thing. Every tax cut and spending reduction should have a sunset clause. A new standing committee could be given responsibility is to see if there aren't ways to optimize the tax code to make it more equal and fair. The CRA could be required to send a brochure in all tax returns that outlines what services your taxes provided. Why not launch an online social media campaign titled "What your taxes allowed you to do today" with information, contests, and other methods of engagement? Let's think big and small at the same time.

These are only a few simple ideas that the progressive movement might take from an examination of the conservative movement's investment in ideological infrastructure. And some of them are not particularly new, having characterized previous eras of progressive politics. It will also be important to rethink taxes for the new and emerging challenges we face, as the contributors in other chapters have done. Our goal here has simply been to restart the conversation about how to get that wheel rolling. We hope we have contributed to this, at least in a small way.

Notes

1   This is an over-generalization and over-simplification, of course. There was much ideological, philosophical, and policy innovation in the Reform Party, for example. See Laycock's excellent book, *The new right and democracy in Canada* (2002). However, even while Reform's discourse and policy sought to profoundly redefine a variety of core philosophical and political values in Canada, this attempt was often framed as if it was nothing more than a return to straightforward and common sense practices. In this sense, while the Reform party offered new policies,

ideas, and language, they were valued not because of their novelty and innovative nature, but rather because, like cough syrup, they were necessary to counter the corrosive effects of the highfalutin' theories of the liberal political establishment and other interests.

2   We have not included the Conference Board of Canada in the politicized think-tank sector; although it is arguably part of the pro-market, pro-business ideological apparatus, it is less partisan and more technical—and thus more akin to the middle-of-the-road think tanks like the Institute for Research on Public Policy or the Public Policy Forum than the highly political think tanks discussed in this chapter.

3   This amount is estimated based on the actual 2008 budget ($0.4M plus growth of $50,000/year, as this was indicated to be the average growth rate), see Parkland Institute (2008).

4   I (Saurette) attended the Fraser Institute *Canada Strong and Free* Gala Dinner in Ottawa on November 24, 2008. The Fraser institute's overview of the event can be found in the *Fraser Forum* (December 2008), p. 3.

5   See Gutstein's 2009 book for a much more detailed overview of the history and impact of the Fraser Institute.

6   As he states, "the broader public good requires setting aside the indulgence of ideological and regional nativism." Segal, 2006, p. 6; see also p. 223.

7   See, for example, his discussion on the various negotiations around unification and the new policy adoption process (Flanagan, 2007, ch. 7).

8   The concept of the rhizome and "rhizomatic" was most famously applied to social theory by Deleuze and Guattari in *A Thousand Plateaus* (2004).

9   As the handbook for the Common Sense Revolution put it,

   The people of Ontario have a message for their politicians—government isn't working anymore. The system is broken. You sent that message when you handed the provincial government its dramatic defeat in 1990. You sent it in the referendum campaign in 1992. You sent it in the federal election. And yet, no one seems to be listening.... I have heard your message. You are looking for a Common Sense Revolution in the way our province is run.... I'm not talking about tinkering, about incremental changes, or about short-term solutions. After all, the changes we have all experienced in our personal lives have been much more fundamental than that.... It will not be easy, but it CAN be done, and it WILL be worth it.... Tinkering with the system will not be enough. It is time for fundamental change, and change is never easy. The political system itself stands in the way of making many of the changes we need right now. Our political system has become a captive to big special interests. It is full of people who are afraid to face the difficult issues, or even talk about them. It is full of people doing all too well as a result of the status quo.

   We need a revolution in this province ... a Common Sense Revolution. (Progressive Conservative Party of Ontario,1994, p. 1)

10 Vic Toews' (now infamous) "you're with us or the you're with the pedophiles" line of defence (February 2012) and Stephen Harper's speech at the June 1997 Montreal meeting of the Council for National Policy, a right-wing US think tank (see Harper, 2005), are just two of the most egregious examples. John Baird is also known to dip into this rhetorical dress-up trunk from time to time.

11 Daifallah and Kheirridan's book *Rescuing Canada's Right* is perhaps one of the most recent restatements of this perspective. We have also traced this variant in Canadian conservative talk radio; see Saurette and Gunster (2011).

12 Work on the series began in 2003 with a number of roundtable discussions on the "goals, principles and policies conducive to shaping and implementing a fresh Canadian vision for the future" (Harris & Manning, 2005a, p. ix) with various conservative stakeholders, including other think tanks such as the Montreal Economic Institute (which also helped sponsor the series). Over the last five years, Manning and Harris, with the support of many members of the Fraser Institute, have synthesized, revised, and honed the proposals.

13 For the full text of Harper's speech, see Harper 2005.

14 To be fair, *Canada Strong and Free* certainly highlights many areas where they think Canada can do things much better than they currently are. And the series does not shy away from highlighting areas where they think the country lags far behind "best in class" practices. Moreover,

there is definitely a harder edge to their prescriptions and visions, as we will discuss below. But the point is that their dominant tone and the primary strategy of affective resonance are largely positive and inspirational. For example, the fact that the series starts, above all else, in an optimistic positive tone is a huge difference since it has a significant impact framing the report and thus influences how the critical moments are taken by its readers. Even the critical moments of the report are very "solution-oriented"—the problems as they are identified do not offer a totalizing indictment of the state of the union or Canadian identity. Moreover, this report rarely identifies easy and general "scapegoats" as a way of focusing blame and inspiring an outraged and angry response.

15   Manning and Harris, of course, still identify a number of problems and challenges in their new reports. Without a problem, there would be no need for a "fresh vision," as they call it. Thus, we are not at all arguing that Canadian conservatism is abandoning its willingness to focus on the negative failures of government and even, perhaps, evoke some pseudo-populist outrage. However, two points are worth noting here. First, the tone they use to approach these issues is not one of raging against the machine or holier-than-thou outrage and populism. Rather, it is very much a "problem-solving" tone that identifies the challenges and proposes solutions. It is backed up by comparative statistics, and ends not with the demand that we dismantle and grind down government, but a positive vision of a better society. Even taking into account the fact that it is a think-tank report rather than a politician's speech, this is a very marked shift for two politicians who gained prominence and success using populist outrage in the 1990s. Second, our argument is not that we are seeing a whole-scale replacement of an undifferentiated "outraged anti-state populism" with an equally monolithic "affirmative choice-based vision." Rather, our argument is that this more affirmative orientation is an emerging framing which is supplementing—and in some cases replacing—the earlier, more negative, articulation. Or at least, that it is a new element that is being emphasized more than in the past—and that understanding this has important consequences.

16   Rather, in only one page of discussion, they simply argue that it is not clear that either home care or public care is necessarily better, based on the studies available.

17   For a critical commentary on the limits of Frank's thesis in light of voter's economic preferences, see Bartels, 2005.

18   Again, a point that Bartels' (2005) critique captures well.

19   Julie Mason pointed this out to one of us years ago, and we couldn't agree more.

20   This, of course, is not a new insight. The work of Linda McQuaig has documented precisely these elements. See for example, *Behind Closed Doors: How the rich won control of Canada's tax system ... And ended up richer* (1987); *The quick and the dead: Brian Mulroney, big business and the seduction of Canada* (1991); and *Shooting the hippo: Death by deficit and other Canadian myths* (1995).

References

Abelson, D. (2009). *Do think tanks matter?* Montreal, QC: McGill-Queen's University Press.

Atlantic Institute for Market Studies (AIMS). (2010). *2009/2010 Annual Report*. Retrieved from http://www.aims.ca/en/home/aboutus/annualreport.aspx

Bartels, L. (2005, September). *What's the matter with what's the matter with Kansas*. Paper presented at the annual conference of the American Political Science Association, Washington, DC. Retrieved from http://www.princeton.edu/%7ebartels/kansas.pdf

Broadbent Institute. (n.d.) *Equality Project*. Retrieved from http://www.broadbentinstitute.ca/en/project/equality-project

Caledon Institute for Social Policy. (2011) Canada Revenue Agency T3010 return for 2011 [Tax form]. Retrieved from http://www.cra-arc.gc.ca/ebci/haip/srch/t3010form22QuickView-eng.action?b=133564096RR0001&e=2011-11-30&n=THE+CALEDON+INSTITUTE+OF+SOCIAL+POLICY&r=http%3A%2F%2Fwww.cra-arc.gc.ca%3A80%2Feb ci%2Fhaip%2Fsrch%2Fbasicsearchresult-eng.action%3Fk=caledon%26s=regis

Canadian Council for Social Development. (2011). *2011 Audited financial statements*. Retrieved from http://www.ccsd.ca/index.php?option=com_content&view=article&id=227&Itemid=223&lang=en.

Canada West Foundation. (2011). *Financial statement 2011*. Retrieved from http://cwf.ca/about-us/annual-report

Canadian Centre for Policy Alternatives. (2011). Canada Revenue Agency T3010 return for 2001 and 2011 [Tax form]. Retrieved from http://www.cra-arc.gc.ca/ebci/haip/srch/t3010form22QuickView-eng.action?b=124146473RR0001&e=2011-12-31&n=CANADIAN+CENTRE+FOR+POLICY+ALTERNATIVES+%2F+CENTRE+CANADIEN+DERECHERCHE+EN+POLITIQUES+DE+RECHANGE&r=http%3A%2F%2Fwww.cra-arc.gc.ca%3A80%2Febci%2Fhaip%

Canadian Centre for Policy Alternatives. (2001). Canada Revenue Agency T3010 return for 2001 and 2011 [Tax form]. Retrieved from http://www.craarc.gc.ca/ebci/haip/srch/t3010form17eng.action?b=124146473RR0001&e=2001-1231&n=CANADIAN+CENTRE+FOR+POLICY+ALTERNATIVES+%2F+CENTRE+CANADIEN+DERECHERCHE+EN+POLITIQUES+DE+RECHANGE&r=http%3A%2F%2Fwww.cra-arc.gc.ca%3A80%2Febci%2Fhaip%2Fsrch%2Fadvancedsearchresult-eng.action%3Fn%3DCanadian%2BCentre%2BPolicy%2BAlternative%26amp%3Bb%3D%26amp%3Bq%3D%26amp%3Bs%3Dregistered%26amp%3Bd%3D%26amp%3Be%3D%2B%26amp%3Bc%3D%26amp%3Bv%3D%2B%26amp%3Bo%3D%26amp%3Bz%3D%26amp%3Bg%3D%2B%26amp%3Bt%3D%2B%26amp%3By%3D%2B%26amp%3Bp%3D1

CBC News Online. (2005, December 11). Liberal apologizes for saying Harper daycare bucks may buy beer, popcorn. Retrieved from http://www.cbc.ca/news/story/2005/12/11/daycare051211.html

C. D. Howe Institute. (2011). *Annual Report*. Retrieved from http://www.cdhowe.org/annual-reports

Conference Board of Canada. (2011). *2011 Annual Report*. Retrieved from http://www.conferenceboard.ca/about-cboc/annual-report.aspx

Connolly, W. (1993). *The terms of political discourse*. Princeton, NJ: Princeton University Press.

Deleuze, G., & Guattari, F. (2004). *A thousand plateaus* (Brian Massumi, Trans.). New York, NY: Continuum.

Flanagan, T. (2007). *Harper's team*. Montreal, QC: McGill-Queen's University Press 2007.

Frank, T. (2000). *One market under God*. New York, NY: Doubleday.

Frank, T. (2004). *What's the matter with Kansas*. New York, NY: Metropolitan Books.

Fraser Institute. (1998). *1998 Annual Report*. Retrieved from http://www.fraserinstitute.org/files/PDFs/annual_reports/1998_Annual_Report.pdf

Fraser Institute. (2006). *2006 Annual Report*. Retrieved from http://www.fraserinstitute.org/uploadedFiles/fraser-ca/Content/About_Us/Who_We_Are/2006-annual-report.pdf

Fraser Institute. (2008). *2008 Annual Report*. Retrieved from http://www.fraserinstitute.org/about-us/who-we-are/annual-reports.aspx

Fraser Institute. (2009). *35 Big ideas*. Retrieved from http://www.fraserinstitute.org/about-us/who-we-are/history.aspx.

Fraser Institute. (2011). *2011 Annual Report*. Retrieved from http://www.fraserinstitute.org/about-us/who-we-are/annual-reports.aspx

Fraser Institute. (n.d.). *About us: Who we are* [Web page]. Retrieved from http://www.fraserinstitute.org/about-us/who-we-are/overview.aspx

Fraser Institute. (n.d.). *The FI in numbers* [Web page]. Retrieved from http://www.fraser institute.org/about-us/who-we-are/fraser-institute-in-numbers.aspx

Gafuik, N. (2011, June 10). Presentation given at the Manning Centre Networking Conference 2011, Ottawa, Ontario.

Gutstein, D. (2009). *Not a conspiracy theory: How business propaganda hijacks democracy.* Toronto, ON: Key Porter Books.

Harper, S. (2005, December 14). Speech given at the Montreal meeting of the Council for National Policy, June 1997, Montreal, Quebec. *Globe and Mail.* Retrieved from http://www.theglobeandmail.com/news/national/text-of-harpers-speech/article 1131985/?page=all

Harris, M., & Manning, P. (2005a). *A Canada strong and free.* Part I of the *Vision statement for a new Canada* series. Toronto, ON: Fraser Institute.

Harris, M., & Manning, P. (2005b). *Caring for Canadians in a Canada strong and free.* Part II of the *Vision statement for a new Canada* series. Toronto, ON: Fraser Institute.

Harris, M., & Manning, P. (2007). *Vision for a Canada strong and free.* Part VI of the *Vision statement for a new Canada* series. Toronto, ON: Fraser Institute.

Kheirridin, T., & Daifallah, A. (2005). *Rescuing Canada's right.* Toronto, ON: Wiley.

Laycock, D. (2002). *The new right and democracy in Canada: Understanding Reform and the Canadian Alliance.* Toronto, ON: Oxford University Press.

Martin, L. (2010). *Harperland.* Toronto, ON: Viking Canada.

MacDonald Laurier Institute. (2010). *2010 Annual Report.* Retrieved from http://www.macdonald laurier.ca/about/annual-report/

Manning Centre. (2007). *Our vision* [Mission statement]. Retrieved from http://www.manning centre.ca/docs//MCBDBrochure_Apr_2007.pdf

Manning Centre. (n.d.). *What we do* [Web page]. Retrieved from http://www.manningcentre .ca/whatwedo/challenge

McQuaig, L. (1987). *Behind closed doors: How the rich won control of Canada's tax system ... And ended up richer.* Toronto, ON: Penguin.

McQuaig, L. (1991). *The quick and the dead: Brian Mulroney, big business and the seduction of Canada.* Toronto, ON: Penguin.

McQuaig, L. (1995). *Shooting the hippo: Death by deficit and other Canadian myths.* Toronto, ON: Penguin.

Micklethwait, J., & Wooldridge, A. (2004). *The right nation: Conservative power in America.* New York, NY: Penguin.

Montreal Economic Institute (MEI). (2010). *Annual Report 2010.* Retrieved from http://www .iedm.org/files/rapport2010_en.pdf

Montreal Economic Institute (MEI). (2011). *Annual Report 2011.* Retrieved from http://www .iedm.org/files/rapport2011-haute-reso_en.pdf

Parkland Institute. (2008). *Self-study report 2008.* Retrieved from http://parklandinstitute.ca/ about/index/

Progressive Conservative Party of Ontario. (1994, May). *The Common Sense Revolution* [Election campaign handbook]. Retrieved May 17, 2007 from http://www.ontariopc.com/ feature/csr/csr_text.htm

Rich, A. (2005). War of ideas: Why mainstream and liberal foundations and the think tanks they support are losing in the war of ideas in American politics. *Stanford Social Innovation Review,* Spring, 18–25.

Saurette, P. (2010, July 23). When smart parties make stupid decisions. *The Mark*. Retrieved from http://www.themarknews.com/articles/1907-when-smart-parties-make-stupid-decisions/#.UWNvOlf_Hk0

Saurette, P., & Gunster, S. (2011). Ears wide shut: Epistemological populism, argutainment and Canadian conservative talk radio. *Canadian Journal of Political Science*, 44(1), 195–218.

Segal, H. (1998, April 4). Canadian voters frown on parties seized by ideology. Modern conservatism about practical issues. *Financial Post*, p. 20.

Segal, H. (2006). *The long road back*. Toronto, ON: HarperCollins.

Vanier Institute. (2011). *2011 Annual report*. Retrieved from http://www.vanierinstitute.ca/annual_report-.UFNDWhg5t4s

Wellesley Institute. (2011). Canada Revenue Agency T3010 return for 2011. Retrieved from http://www.cra-arc.gc.ca/ebci/haip/srch/t3010form22QuickView-eng.action?b=108103862RR0001&e=2011-03-31&n=WELLESLEY+INSTITUTE&r=http%3A%2F%2Fwww.cra-arc.gc.ca%3A80%2Febci%2Fhaip%2Fsrch%2Fbasicsearchresult-eng.action%3Fk=wellesley+institute%26s=registered%2

Conclusion

For decades, politicians and citizens have been colluding in a perverse contract. In Canada—and throughout much of the English-speaking world—we have seemingly indicated to our leaders that any positive or even exploratory mention of taxes will be punished. And our leaders, in turn, have with a few exceptions lacked the courage to explain to us what we're giving up when we don't have this conversation: a say about what's important for our country, where we're going and how we are to get there.

Any reasonable discussion of taxes must take into account the public goods and services they buy. The unnatural divorce in our public discourse of these inextricably linked concepts has produced a climate in which the first question we ask of any policy proposal is "How will we ever pay for it?" And yet we never ask of any tax cut, "What will we lose as a result?" In public policy, these questions should be two sides of the same coin. Yes, we have to be rigorous about how we'll pay for new ideas, but we shouldn't preclude them, which is what we do when we take tax off the table. And we should be equally rigorous about assessing the costs of a tax cut, because no tax cut is a free good. That one question is taboo and the other orthodoxy is a reflection of today's distorted conversation—one that severely limits the political imagination and is bound to lead us in directions we would never have chosen.

This is the logical consequence of the neo-liberal model, which emerged in the US and Britain in the late 1970s and more slowly and subtly in Canada starting at around the same time. The paradigm, which has shaped discourse and policy in much of the Anglosphere ever since, sees taxes only as a burden to be relieved, no longer the price we pay for civilization. And so civilization has inevitably suffered. Absent the possibility of a balanced discussion about taxes, we have severely limited our capacity to respond to persistent financial instability and growing inequality, and we have stunted our collective aspirations. The conversation needs to change.

Of course, changing the conversation is never easy. North Americans under forty have never really known anything other than government and politics shaped by neo-liberalism, and many will understandably see this view as an immutable reality, not a paradigm at all. And those of an older vintage are invested in the current model—many have done pretty well by it. So it's not surprising that, despite the scale of our economic challenges, we keep going down the same path. Nor should it be surprising that many doubt that it can be otherwise. Our politics hasn't offered up a grand alternative.

One simple reason for this failure of leadership is fear of the political consequences. In 2008, before he was a contributor to this volume, then-Liberal leader Stéphane Dion courageously campaigned on a carbon tax and lost. He opened a door that the leaders who followed quickly closed behind him—and what might have been a prelude to a new conversation has become a cautionary tale. While there is some evidence that public attitudes toward taxes are not as negative as our politicians—even the most progressive among them—seem to think, we won't know for sure until more of our leaders show the audacity to pursue their convictions and to persist through whatever blowback follows.

And there have been encouraging, if not wholly satisfying, signs that we're on the verge of seeing just that. Emboldened perhaps by the Occupy Movement and the widespread dissatisfaction with the economic status quo it expressed, President Obama, near the end of his second term, dipped his toe into these uncertain political waters and proposed a tax hike on the super-rich as a means of addressing income inequality and a steadfastly bleak fiscal outlook; shortly thereafter, Ontario NDP leader Andrea Horwath successfully pressured the minority Liberal government in Ontario into supporting a similar levy.

Critics have rightly pointed out that these policies are somewhat misleading—such taxes won't raise the kind of revenue that's needed, and they reinforce the impression that if taxes must be raised, others should pay the price. Not withstanding, as imperfect and tentative as they are, these gestures also hold some promise insofar as they posit tax as a tool for good—in this case, a means of addressing rampant and spreading economic unfairness.

This is the challenge for progressives. How do we re-associate the idea of taxes with what they buy and what we lose when they're cut? How do we remind citizens that when we talk about carbon tax, we're talking about the preservation or further degradation of our environment? That when we talk about financial transactions taxes, we're talking about a potentially enormous, progressive source of revenue that simultaneously constrains financial speculation? That when we talk about inheritance taxes and income tax brackets, we're talking about fairness and inequality and thus, potentially, the health of our society? That when we talk about the increasing decentralization of our tax system, we're talking about abdicating our ability to pursue national goals and to take care of our fellow nationals? And conversely, as we tackle our most pressing issues—like health care, education, and the policy implications of our changing demographic reality—that we paralyze ourselves by putting our most powerful tool off limits?

As this book demonstrates, another kind of conversation is both necessary and possible—one in which the positive connotation is restored to the word "tax." To break out of our broken discourse, we must begin, as the neo-liberals did, with a concerted effort by like-minded, outlying citizens, academics, think tanks, pundits, and politicians to say the unthinkable, again and again, until it becomes thinkable. For progressives, that means repeating far and wide, over and over again, that tax is not a four-letter word; rather, it's the price we pay for the country we want.

Contributors

Robin Boadway
Robin Boadway received his Ph.D. in economics from Queen's University and has taught there since 1973, with year-long interruptions to take up a postdoctoral fellowship at the University of Chicago (1976–77) and visiting scholar positions at the University of Oxford (1980–81) and Université Catholique de Louvain (1986–87). He was president of the Canadian Economics Association (1996–97) and served as the editor of the *Canadian Journal of Economics* (1987–93) and *Journal of Public Economics* (2003–2008). Professor Boadway was made a Fellow of the Royal Society of Canada in 1986 and an Officer of the Order of Canada in 2008, and was the Distinguished CES Fellow at the University of Munich in 2009. He is currently President of the International Institute of Public Finance.

C. Scott Clark
Scott Clark is currently President of C. S. Clark Consulting and Adjunct Research Professor in the Department of Economics, Carleton University. He served as deputy minister of finance (1997–2000) and senior adviser to the prime minister (2001). Mr. Clark was Canada's executive director to the International Monetary Fund (1989–1992), Canada's G7 deputy (1992–1994), and Canada's executive director to the European Bank for Reconstruction and Development (2001–2006). He has a Ph.D. in economics from the University of California at Berkeley. Mr. Clark is a frequent commentator on public policy issues on CBC radio and TV, CTV, and BNN. He comments regularly on public policy issues (with Peter Devries) at www.3dpolicy.ca.

Philip DeMont
Philip DeMont, an economist, veteran financial journalist, and former Ontario government adviser, is co-author (with Eugene Lang) *of Turning point: Moving beyond neoconservatism.*

Stéphane Dion

Stéphane Dion was minister of intergovernmental affairs between 1996 and 2003. In that capacity, he was instrumental in bringing countless federal–provincial negotiations to fruition. As minister of the environment from 2004 to 2005, he was successful in including significant green investments in the federal budget and successfully chaired the UN Conference on Climate Change, held in Montreal in 2005. In 2006, having been elected as leader of the Liberal Party of Canada, he proposed "the green shift," which would have included a revenue-neutral carbon tax. Following the 2008 election, he retained his seat as Member of Parliament for Saint-Laurent-Cartierville, a seat he has won seven times in a row since 1996. Before entering politics, Dr. Dion taught political science at Université de Moncton and Université de Montréal. As an academic and politician, he has authored numerous publications on a wide array of Canadian and international issues, including the complexities of climate change negotiations, global environmental policies, and universal carbon pricing. Born in Quebec City, he studied at Université Laval before obtaining a doctorate in sociology from the Institut d'études politiques in Paris, France. He was awarded an honourary doctorate by the Carlos III University of Madrid. He is a member of the Yale Climate & Energy Institute External Advisory Board.

Matt Fodor

Matt Fodor is a Ph.D. candidate in the Department of Political Science at York University. His research interests include social democracy, Canadian politics and the impact of neo-liberalism on politics, and public policy. He has published numerous articles and papers in these areas.

Frank Graves

Frank Graves, as founder of EKOS Research Associates Inc., is one of the country's leading applied social researchers, directing some of the largest and most challenging social research assignments conducted in Canada. Under his leadership EKOS has earned a reputation for creative and rigorous research in the areas of public policy, social policy, and program evaluation, and is regarded as a leader in innovative survey techniques and methodology. Mr. Graves graduated from Carleton University with an M.A. in sociology and has completed doctoral coursework in sociology.

Shane Gunster

Shane Gunster teaches in the School of Communication at Simon Fraser University. His current research interests include communication about environmental issues (especially climate change) and the politics of energy.

Trish Hennessy

Trish Hennessy is Director of the Canadian Centre for Policy Alternatives' (CCPA) Ontario office, and the Founding Director of the CCPA's Income Inequality Project. She is a former newspaper journalist and has an M.A. in sociology from OISE/University of Toronto, a B.S.W. from Carleton University, and a B.A. in sociology from Queen's University.

Alex Himelfarb

Alex Himelfarb is Director of the Glendon School of Public and International Affairs, at York University, and leads the Centre for Global Challenges. From 2002 to 2006 he served as Clerk of the Privy Council and Secretary to the Cabinet, the most senior federal public servant, when he was nominated as Ambassador of Canada to the Italian Republic with concurrent accreditation to the Republic of Albania and the Republic of San Marino, and as High Commissioner for Canada to the Republic of Malta. From 1972 to 1981 he taught Sociology at the University of New Brunswick. He also serves on a number of boards, including the Trudeau Foundation, the World Wildlife Fund, the Public Service Foundation, the Couchiching Institute, the Canadian Alliance to End Homelessness (Chair), and Canadians for Fair Taxes (National Advisory Council). He is a graduate of the University of Toronto, where he obtained a Ph.D. in Sociology.

Jordan Himelfarb

Jordan Himelfarb is an opinion editor at *The Toronto Star*. Previously he was the editor of *The Mark* and the Arts and Ideas editor of *This Magazine*. His writing has appeared in most of Canada's foremost newspapers and magazines, and he is the recipient of a 2012 certificate of merit for editorial writing from the National Newspaper Awards. He is also co-editor of the music website Said the Gramophone, one of *Time* magazine's top blogs of 2009.

Iglika Ivanova

Iglika Ivanova is an economist and public interest researcher at the BC office of the Canadian Centre for Policy Alternatives. She is a frequent media commentator and public speaker on BC public policy issues, and has authored numerous studies and articles for the CCPA. Ms. Ivanova researches and writes on issues of government finance, taxation, and privatization, and how they relate to the accessibility and quality of public services in BC. Her other research investigates issues and trends in the Canadian labour market, particularly income inequality and low-wage work. She has an M.A. in Economics from the University of British Columbia.

Eugene Lang

Eugene Lang is President, J.E. Lang Consulting Inc., co-founder of Canada 2020, and BMO Visiting Fellow, School of Public and International Affairs, Glendon College, York University. An award-winning and bestselling author, Mr. Lang has co-written two books and has published over 100 articles and essays on fiscal and economic issues and defence and foreign policy. He worked in the federal government for twelve years as Economic Policy Advisor to the Deputy Prime Minister, Senior Economist, Finance Canada, Chief of Staff to the Secretary of State (Finance), and Chief of Staff to two Ministers of National Defence. He was educated at the University of Western Ontario, Queen's University, and the London School of Economics, where he studied as a Chevening Scholar.

Marc Lee

Marc Lee is senior economist for the Canadian Centre for Policy Alternatives, where he writes on a variety of economic and social policy issues. He has published on a wide range of topics, from poverty and inequality to globalization and international trade, to public services and regulation. Marc is the co-director of the Climate Justice Project, a five-year research partnership with the University of British Columbia, examining the links between climate change policies and social justice. Despite being "classically trained" with an M.A. in economics, Marc was the past chair of the Progressive Economics Forum, a national network of heterodox economists.

Hugh Mackenzie

Hugh Mackenzie is principal in an economic consulting business, Hugh Mackenzie and Associates, based in Toronto. He has worked for over 40 years in a variety of capacities related to public policy development in the trade union movement, the private sector, and at all three levels of government. He is presently part of a team at the Canadian Centre for Policy Alternatives conducting a series of research studies on income and wealth inequality in Canada. As part of the CCPA Alternative Budget project, he produces an annual review of the Ontario budget. He is the author of a regular series of in-depth analyses of the funding of elementary and secondary education in Ontario. He holds a master's degree in economics from the University of Wisconsin (Madison).

Toby Sanger

Toby Sanger works as the Economist for the Canadian Union of Public Employees (CUPE) and previously served as the chief economist for the Yukon government, principal economic policy advisor to the Ontario Minister of Finance, economic advisor to First Nations, and as a consulting economist. Among other projects, he initiated the successful Ontario Savings Bond and the Yukon

Micro-Loan Programs. He produces CUPE's quarterly *Economy at Work* publication, and has published on a wide range of issues, including *Fair shares: How banks, brokers and the financial industry can pay fairer taxes* (Canadian Centre for Policy Alternatives, 2011).

Paul Saurette

Paul Saurette is Associate Professor, School of Political Studies, University of Ottawa. He received his Ph.D. in Political Science from Johns Hopkins University. His current research focuses on theories of ideology and the conservative movement in Canada. He is the author of *The Kantian Imperative* (2005) as well as a forthcoming book on the new rhetorical strategies of the anti-abortion movement in Canada. He is also working on a book about the communication strategies of the conservative movement more broadly. He has worked as a researcher and consultant to a variety of political, think-tank, charitable, governmental, and private-sector organizations, and is currently an online columnist for *The Toronto Star*.

Jim Stanford

Jim Stanford is one of Canada's best-known economists. He works for the Canadian Auto Workers union, and writes a regular economics column for *The Globe and Mail*. He received his Ph.D. in economics from the New School for Social Research in New York City, and is the author of *Economics for Everyone* (Canadian Centre for Policy Alternatives, 2008). He was the founding chairperson of the Progressive Economics Forum, Canada's network of progressive economists. He tweets regularly on economics via @jimstanford.

Index

Alberta: carbon emissions, 175; corporate income tax collection, 43; education levels, 249; emissions cap, 179; fiscal capacity, 46; natural resource revenues, 39; welfare system, 141
Albo, Greg, 102, 114
Alexander, Craig, 172
alternative minimum tax, 220
American Enterprise Institute, 104, 172
Americans for Tax Reform, 252
anti-tax movements, 145–46; Americans for Tax Reform, 252; in Canada, 115; ideological comparisons, 227–28; Occupy Movement, 12, 95, 97, 143, 145, 191, 268; Republican no-tax pledges, 1; Tea Party, 3–4, 87, 95, 97; view of government, 141–42
Atlantic Institute for Market Studies, 231, 234
austerity: costs of, 5–9; European rejection of, 12; and public sector, 28–29
Australia: carbon tax program, 178–79; climate policy, 181; deficit reduction, 111; value added taxes (VAT), 216
Austria, 31
automatic stabilizers, 28, 31

backlash populism, 228, 238–39, 242, 246–47, 251; as politics of resentment, 253–54
Baird, John, 140, 262n10
Bank of Canada, "zero inflation" policy, 109
Berkowitz, Herb, 233

Bill & Melinda Gates Foundation, 204
Bloc, 86
Boadway, Robin, 11, 16, 39–53, 153; dual-income tax system, 160–61, 168n19
bonds, 192
"boutique tax cuts," 113–14, 156, 167n11
Brazil, 193
Bretton-Woods exchange rate system, 194
British Columbia: carbon tax, 114, 174, 175, 179; HST referendum, 2; top income tax rate, 159
Brookings Institution, 172, 233
Brooks, Neil, 159, 162, 163
Buffett, Warren, 2, 81n1, 194–95
Bush, G. W., 1, 171, 195
business, private. *See* corporations
Business Council on National Issues (BCNI), 106–7, 107–8
Business Roundtable, 104

Caledon Institute of Social Policy, 124, 232
California: emissions cap, 179; tax referenda, 16
Cameron, D., 108, 199
Canada: alignment with US carbon pricing, 177; anti tax culture, 2, 120, 140–42, 145–46; backlash populism, 237–42; conservatism, rebirth of, 228–37; Constitution Act (1982), 39, 53n1; decline in tax revenue, 56; deficit/surplus positions, 6–7; financial transaction taxes, 196–97, 204–5; "free lunch politics," 119–20; impact of decentralization, 51–53; Income Tax

Act, 213; "just society," 88–89; long-term economic performance, 89; neoliberalism, rise of, 106–9, 111–12; the "North," 244; North American Free Trade Agreement (NAFTA), 109, 110, 122; peace-keeping, 244; spending as percent of GDP, US comparison, 65; taxes and economic performance, international comparisons, 30–35; tax policy, evolution of, 99; as tax tiger, 127–31
Canada Assistance Plan, 44, 110
Canada Child Tax Benefit, 152, 164, 165, 167n4, 168n24
Canada Health Act, 49
Canada Health and Social Transfer (CHST), 44, 110
Canada Health Transfer (CHT), 44, 46, 52–53, 221
Canada Pension Plan (CPP), 23, 29, 123–24, 144, 153, 167n5
Canada Revenue Agency (CRA), 43, 235
Canada Social Transfer (CST), 44, 46, 52–53
Canada Strong and Free (Manning, Harris), 241–45, 254–56, 262n12, 262–63n14
Canada West Foundation, 172, 177, 230
Canadian Alliance, 113
Canadian Centre for Policy Alternatives, 4, 231, 232; Canadian economy, developments in, 62–64; GST, alternate uses for, 114; public services, distribution of value, 72–75
Canadian Council for Social Development, 232
Canadian Council of Chief Executives, 172
Canadian Labour and Business Centre, 231
Canadian Policy Research Network, 231
Canadian Tax Foundation, 121, 230
Canadian Taxpayers Federation, 230
cap-and-trade system, 185; vs. carbon taxes, 173–77; complexity of, 182–83; emission allowance auctions, 185; performance of, 179; *Turning the Corner*, 179

capital: international mobility of, 36; outward flight of, 25–26; taxation on, 22, 23, 36n5
capital gains, 22, 36n5; deemed realization of, 44; federal revenue losses, 154–55, 167n8; income averaging, 155–56, 167n10; reduction in, 111
capital income, treatment of in tax base, 154–56
capital investment, 26, 37n13
Capitalism and Freedom (Friedman), 101
capitalist economies: and corporate investment, 20–21; impact of taxes on profitability, 26, 37n13; and postwar economic expansion, 25, 103–4
capital spending, 31
cappuccino conservatism, 228; and backlash populism, 238–39; and "choice," 245–49; distinction between progressives, 248–49; implications of for progressives, 257–61; key characteristics, 241, 242–45, 262n12; vs. latte liberalism, 241; market moralism, and marketizens, 248; taxes and the state, 254–56
carbon dioxide capture and storage, 180
carbon leakage, 176, 177
carbon market, 173
carbon tax, 11, 268; British Columbia, 114, 174, 175, 179; climate change action plan (Harper), 179–80; economic impact of, 176–77; emission coverage, 173–74; implementation of, 52, 174–75; as innovation incentive, 172–73, 174, 176; international programs, 178–79; optimal level of, 177–78; personal attack ads, 140; as pigouvian tax, 172; policy advantages of, 173–77; as policy solution, 184–86; political acceptability of, 181–84; as political suicide, 171; in progressive tax reform, 166, 168n25; as revenue neutral tax, 183, 184, 185; trade concerns, 177; use of revenues, 175–76, 183–84; as wealth tax, 23; worldwide support for, 171–72
Caring for Canadians in a Canada Strong and Free (Manning, Harris), 249–52

Carney, Mark, 37n14, 167n7
Carter, Kenneth, 154, 167n10
C. D. Howe Institute, 107, 109, 112, 230, 234
Centre for Policy Studies (UK), 104
Centre for the Study of Living Standards, 82n5
charitable donations and gifts, 159, 167n15, 214
children: child allowances, 27; child care, and choice, 249–52, 263n16; Child Disability Benefit, 164; child tax benefit, 61; fitness and arts tax credits, 156, 214
China: emissions trading system, 179; financial transaction taxes, 193, 201
choice: disciplinary dimension of responsible choice, 247–49; moral value of, 245–46; over care, 249–52
Chrétien, Jean: Family Allowance, ending of, 59; progressive legislation, 113; tax policy, 58
citizenship: children-citizens, 249–52; marketizens, 248; obligations and benefits, 15–16; vs. rights of taxpayers, 105–6. *See also* social citizenship
citizenship democracy vs. dollar democracy, 75–76
Clark, Joe, 107
Clark, Scott, 11
Clarkson, S., 108, 110
class, and authenticity, 238–39
Clean Development Mechanism, 179
climate change: and environmental taxes, 23; and fossil fuel emissions, 171, 184–85; green shift, and pocketbook politics, 181; as negative externality, 172; political acceptability of, 181–84; and Robin Hood Tax, 192–93; as threat to global economy, 93, 95; world carbon price, 177–78
Clinton, Bill, 195
common good: and free market ideology, 3; and social citizenship, 15–16; and social responsibility, 143–46
Common Sense Revolution, 58, 59, 80, 111–12, 229, 240, 243, 253, 262n9

Conference Board of Canada, 9, 172, 230, 232, 262n2
conservatism: anti-tax campaigns, 227–28; and backlash populism, 228, 238–39, 251; cappuccino conservatism, 228, 240–42; choice, moral value of, 245–46; choice over care, 249–52; data as rhetorical mode of persuasion, 255; disciplinary dimension of responsible choice, 247–49; market-based approaches to public policy, 245–47; marketing of, 230–32; and politics of resentment, 253–54; and populism, 57–58; public philosophy, role and importance of, 235–37; and the "Rhizomatic Right," 238, 262n8; sunset clauses, 261; taxes, and the state, 252–57; tax policy recommendations, 256–57; variants within, 238. *See also* cappuccino conservatism
Conservative Party: 2011 election promises (ON), 2; attack ads, 142–43, 181, 183; choice, moral value of, 245–46; commitment to principle, 235–36; ideological infrastructure, 229–32; patriotism, redefinition of, 244–45; preferred size of government, 86–87; Red Tories, 107, 229, 236, 238; separation of taxes from public services, 57–58, 66; tax reduction policy, 2
Constitution Act: federal role in social citizenship, 48–49; revenue raising powers of government, 39–40, 45, 46, 53n1
consumption-based taxation, 216, 221
consumption taxes, 61, 84, 122–23; international comparison of, 126, 134n3, 134n4; progressive tax reform, 163–64, 168n20; as regressive tax, 152. *See also* GST; HST; Financial Activities Tax; sales tax
Copps, Sheila, 181
corporate income tax: accelerated cuts to, 58; cash flow approach, 161–62; foreign source income, 214; international comparison of, 124–26, 161; public

opinion research, 84; reductions in, 129, 133, 211; as revenue source, 215; simplification, need for, 214–15; tax-transfer harmonization, 43–45
corporate tax policy: competitiveness, and tax cuts, 111; and economic growth, 20–21; federal corporate tax rates, 122; and federal share of resource rents, 52; HST/GST inputs, 22; industry-specific tax credits, 45; and investment incentive, 214; and tax-transfer harmonization, 43–45
corporations: capital spending, 31; "dead money," 26, 37n14, 154, 167n7; deregulation of, 105; impact of taxes on profitability, 26; investment spending, 26, 37n13; and North American Free Trade Agreement (NAFTA), 109; subsidies, as income distribution, 24
corporatism, 238
Council for National Policy, 243
Cronin, J. E., 105
Crow, John, 109, 110
culture programs, 24–25
currency transaction taxes, 192, 204
cyclical stabilization, and government spending, 27–28

Daifallah, Adam, 229–30
d'Aquino, Thomas, 107–8
debt, federal: debt-to-GDP ratio, 212; and economic growth, 6–7
decentralization: arguments against, 41–42; arguments for, 41, 53n2; and fiscal federalism, 16; and fiscal policy, 39–40, 53n2; impact on Canadian federation, 51–53; and tax-transfer harmonization, 43–45
deductions, and tax expenditure rationalization, 156–59
DeFazio, Peter, 197
deficits and deficit reduction: G7 countries, 111; preferred approach to, 85–86; as pretext for service cuts, 59; program eliminations, 79; and tax reduction policy, 2
DeMont, Philip, 3, 99, 119–35
DeMott, Benjamin, 9

Denmark: carbon tax program, 178; deficit reduction, 111; productivity growth, 31; stamp duty taxes, 193
DeVries, Peter, 215
Dexter, Darrell, 114
Diamond, P., 160
Dion, Stéphane, 11, 140, 171–89, 268
direct government production, 24, 27, 31
disability support programs, 27
discrimination, and backlash populism, 245
disposable income, in-kind benefits as percentage of, 71–72, 81n3
distortion: and cost-based accounting, 80; and measurement of income distribution, 60; in public services valuation, 79–80
dividend income, 36n5
Dobbin, M., 110, 112, 115
Doctors for Tax Fairness, 146, 261
dollar democracy vs. citizenship democracy, 75–76
Donner Foundation, 230
Drache, D., 108
Drummond, Don, 79
Drummond Report, 79–80
dual-income tax system, 160–61, 168n19
Dutch disease, 47–48

Economic Council of Canada, 107
economic cycle: automatic stabilizers, and cyclical deficits, 27–28; macroeconomic stabilization, 31; pattern of, 58
economic efficiency, and tax burdens, 31–32
economic growth: and consumption-based taxation, 216, 221; and corporate investment, 20–21; and debt reduction, 6–7; decline of, and government revenues, 215; and financial transaction taxes, 200; and low taxation, 221; public investment in, 25; public opinion research, 96–97; and tax incentives, 25–26, 36n8
economic recovery, and cyclical deficits, 28
economic stagnation, 2–4, 89, 104
Economists for Fair Taxation, 261
Edsall, Thomas, 104

education: and choice, 249–52; early learning investments, 79, 82n6; as government consumption, 24–25; in-kind benefits, and disposable income, 71–72; as priority service, 7; and social citizenship, 42; as social investment, 95, 137–38. See also post-secondary education
efficiencies, and budgetary choices, 7–9, 10–11
elder care, 71, 133
election campaigns: attack ads, 142–43, 181; choice vs. state paternalism, 251–52; importance of winning, 237; language of, 138, 140–41; politics of empathy, 145; strategic voting, 145; strategy of individualization, 142
Employment Insurance (EI), 153, 165, 167n5; decline in premiums, 123–24, 215, 222n7; as income security program, 26–27, 61; as regressive tax, 23, 29
employment stability, 17
End of History, 128
Environics Research, 138–40, 146
environmental taxes, 268; Clean Development Mechanism, 179; distributional impact of, 23; Emission Trading Scheme (ETS), 174, 179, 183; Green Fund Duty, 179; green shift, and pocketbook politics, 181; as innovation incentive, 172–73; low carbon capital expenditures, 174. See also carbon tax
epistemological populism, 255
equality of opportunity, 42
equality of outcomes, 42
equalization payments, 24; and CHT/CST system, 52–53; and the fiscal gap, 50; and horizontal imbalance, 45–48; and HST revenues, 43; and regional shocks, 42
Established Programs Financing (EPF), 110
estate tax. See inheritance tax
ethics, and accountability, 96–97
Europe: austerity measures, 6; taxation choices, impact on society, 12; tax debates, emergence of, 16

European Commission: financial transaction taxes, 191, 197, 199, 202
European Union: corporate tax rates, 125–26; Emission Trading Scheme (ETS), 174, 179, 183; financial transaction taxes, 197; value added taxes (VAT), 216
Evans, B., 114
extreme inequality, consequences of, 9–10
fairness: of Canadian tax system, 152; and income inequality, 142–43; inheritance taxes, 162; intergenerational future choices, 10–11; of progressive tax system, 151; and social responsibility, 143–46. See also tax fairness
Fair Tax Commission, 166
federal budget: bipartisan tax cutting budgets, 127–31; deficit/surplus positions, 6–7; and fiscal prudence, 7–9; vertical balance, and federal–provincial transfers, 40, 41–42, 48–51
federal government: Constitutional revenue-raising power, 39–40, 53n1; household income, and per capita value of public services, 74; preferred priorities, 85–86; program spending as share of GDP, 62–64; taxation powers, 16; Tax Collection Agreements, 40, 43. See also government revenue; government spending
federal–provincial transfers: conditional transfers, 49; and vertical balance, 40, 41–42, 48–51
Federation of Canadian Municipalities, 76–77
Finance Canada: *Tax Expenditures and Evaluations*, 158, 167n13
Financial Activities Tax, 196, 203, 205, 206
financial crises, increased frequency of, 201
financial derivatives: deregulation of, 195; destabilizing effect of, 194–95, 201; financial transaction taxes, 192, 197
financial sector: public antipathy against, 206; tax preferences and benefits, 198; "too big to fail" assurance, 198, 203
financial transaction taxes, 11, 191–210, 268; arguments for, 193–94, 198–99;

avoidance of, 203–4; in Canada, 204–5; as complement to regulation, 204; costs to individuals, 202; criticisms against, and responses to, 199–204; currency transaction taxes, 192, 204; estimated revenues, 197–98, 200–201; Financial Activities Tax, 203, 205; financial derivatives, 193, 194–96; global agreement on, 204; history of, 193; and market liquidity, 201; opposition to, 191, 196–97; as pigouvian tax, 194, 207n2; punitive nature of, 202–3; revenue generation, 192; and revenue leakage, 193; Robin Hood Tax, 192–93, 206; speculation, reduction in, 192, 194; Stamp Duty Reserve Tax, 193; stock transaction taxes, 192, 193; support for, 192–93, 196–97, 206; and tax havens, 193, 196, 198, 204; Tobin Tax, 192, 205

Finland: carbon tax program, 178; deficit reduction, 111; education levels, 249; financial transaction taxes, 193; productivity growth, 31

fiscal competition, and revenue decentralization, 43–44

fiscal federalism, and decentralization, 16

fiscal gap, and vertical balance, 48–51

fiscal imbalance, 128–29

fiscal interventions: direct government production, 27, 28; incentives, 25–26, 36n8; income distribution, 29–30; income security programs, 26–27, 37n15; investment spending, 27

fiscal issues, in public opinion research, 96–97

fiscal policy: impact on economic behaviour, 25–30; societal direction of, 17, 18–19, 22, 35–36

fiscal prudence: austerity, and neo-liberal ideology, 8–9; budgetary choices of revenue and spending, 7–9, 10–11

Flaherty, Jim, 113, 114, 130, 140, 196, 234

Flanagan, Tom, 236–37

Fleischacker, Sam, 162

Focus on the Family Canada, 230, 231

Fodor, Matt, 3, 99

Ford, Rob, 2, 4, 67, 142, 240, 253, 254

foreign aid, 24

foreign source income, 214

France: financial transaction taxes, 197; stamp duty taxes, 193

Frank, Thomas, 228, 238–39, 242, 252, 253

Fraser Institute, 107, 112, 230–31, 232, 234–35, 262n2; *Canada Strong and Free* (Manning, Harris), 241–45, 262–63n14, 262n12; Teacher Workshops, 235

free market ideology: and Canadian patriotism, 244; deadweight losses from taxes, 19; economic freedom, principle of, 256; Fraser Institute, 234–35; incentives, as fiscal intervention, 25–26, 36n8; and neo-liberalism, 2–4; rise of, 103–6; role of the state, 103; sales taxes, 22–23; social welfare, reductions in, 30; and tax revenue, 16

Friedman, Milton, 3, 101, 104–5, 246

Friedman, Thomas, 171

Frontier Centre for Public Policy, 114, 231

Fukuyama, Francis, 128

G7/G8 countries: and Canadian tax policy, 120; tax as share of GDP, 124; total tax rate, 138, value added taxes (VAT), 126

G20 Summit(s), 196

Gafuik, Nick, 231–32

game theory, trust/distrust as social trap, 4–5

GDP: and carbon tax programs, 178; direct government production as percentage of, 27; federal program spending as share of, 62–64; federal tax-to-GDP ratio, 114; financial transaction taxes, impact on, 199; government spending as percentage of, 65, 111; government spending G7 countries, 131; provincial own-source revenue as share of, 62–64; public programs as share of, 62; revenue as percentage of, 7, 138; sales tax as percentage of, 123; tax burden as share of, international comparisons, 30–35; tax revenue as percentage of, 56; total federal revenue as percentage of, 211; total tax as percentage of, 124; value added taxes (VAT) as percentage of, 126, 134n3, 134n4

General Theory of Employment, Interest and Money, The (Keynes), 101–2, 193–94
Germany: financial transaction taxes, 197; productivity growth, 31
global economy: and Income Tax Act, 213; threats to, 93
global financial crisis (2008–9), 130–31
globalization: and fiscal policy, 36; and neo-liberal market fundamentalism, 102; "Third Way," as response to, 106
Goldwater, Barry, 64
government: cost of as percentage of GDP, 20; as major employer, 28–29; public trust/distrust in, 4–5, 12, 98; role of in neo-liberal ideology, 103
government, size of, 131, 212, 222n2; in public opinion research, 86–87, 91, 92; small-government agenda, and free market ideology, 2–4
government revenue: capital gains, and revenue losses, 154–55, 167n8; corporate income tax, 22; effect of cuts on, 5, 7; effect of recession on cyclical deficits, 27–28; environmental taxes, 23; GST, 22–23, 114, 153; HST, 22–23; investment income, 23; non-tax sources, 23; payroll taxes, 23, 36n6, 153, 167n5; as percentage of GDP, 211; personal income taxes, 22; ratio of federal to provincial, change in, 132; sales taxes, 22; as share of GDP, 63; tax sources, 22–23; value added taxes (VAT), 22–23, 153; wealth taxes, 23
government spending, 3–5; carbon tax revenues, 175–76, 183–84, 185; categories of, 23–25; consumption of public services, 24–25; deficit/surplus positions, 6–7; as direct production, 24, 27, 31; economic benefits of, 35–36; economic impacts of, 30–35; fiscal interventions, 25–30; G7 countries, 131; ideological reasons for cuts, 221; infrastructure and physical capital investment, 25, 27, 31; interest payments, 24; multiplier effect of second-order expansion, 28; as percentage of GDP, 111; perception of waste, 92, 95; and productivity, 15; scrutiny of, 214–15, 222n6; and societal well-being, 29–30; and tax expenditures, 214–15; transfer payments, 24, 25, 26–27, 31; transparency in, 5
Gratton, Robert, 159
Graves, Frank, 3, 16, 83–98
Great Depression, and Keynesian economics, 102
Greece, 195–96
Green Party: climate policy, 181; size of government, 86
Greenspan, Alan, 171
Griffith-Jones, Stephany, 200–201
GST (Goods and Services Tax): cost of exemptions, 5, 11, 22, 216–17; introduction of, 109, 120, 122–23; potential benefits to local governments, 76–77, 81n4, 82n5; progressive tax reform, 163–64, 168n20; public opinion research, 84; rate increase, 217–18; reduction of, 58, 114, 130, 211; as revenue neutral tax, 123, 217–18; tax base expansion, 216–17; tax credit, 152, 164, 167n4; tax-transfer harmonization, 43; use of revenues, 218–19, 222n9. *See also* consumption taxes; HST; sales taxes
Guaranteed Income Supplement, 61, 164
Gunster, Shane, 12, 102, 227–63
Gutstein, Donald, 234

Hale, Benjamin, 142
Harkin, Tom, 197
Harper, Stephen, 236, 243; attack ads, 140, 142; back-to-work legislation, 114; climate change action plan, 179–80; and Fraser Institute, 234; GST cuts, 76–77, 81n4, 82n5; on taxes, 119, 120; tax policy, 58, 113–14
Harper's Team (Flanagan), 236
Harris, Mike, 80, 142, 262n15; *Canada Strong and Free* (Manning, Harris), 241–45, 254–56, 262n12, 262–63n14; *Caring for Canadians in a Canada Strong and Free* (Manning, Harris), 249–52; Common Sense Revolution, 58, 59, 80, 111–12, 228, 229, 240, 243,

284 | Index

253, 262n9; *Vision for a Canada Strong and Free* (Manning, Harris), 255
Harvey, D., 103
Hayek, F. A., 245–46
head taxes, 59
health care: and choice, 249–52; extension of, 50–51; funding through payroll taxes, 23; as government consumption, 24–25; in Harper government, 114; in-kind benefits, and disposable income, 71–72; Medical Care Act, 144; as priority service, 7; and progressive tax reform, 268–69; public opinion research, 96–97; and social citizenship, 42; and transfer payments, 24; user fees, 23
Heath, Joseph, viii, 149
Hennessy, Trish, 3, 99, 137–48
Heritage Foundation, 104
Heritage Institute, 233
high-income earners, 15; alternative minimum tax, 220; capital income, and wealth inequality, 22, 36n5, 154–56; charitable donations and gifts, 159, 167n15; employee stock option deduction, 158–59; and income distribution, 29–30; increased taxation of, 2, 92, 94, 146, 268; individual tax statistics, 156–59; investment income, 152; tax deductions, use of, 152; top income tax rate, 159–61
high-income tax brackets, 159–60, 167n17
Hollande, François, 197
Holmes, Oliver Wendell, 69, 70
Hong Kong: education levels, 249; financial transaction taxes, 193, 201
horizontal equity, 154
horizontal imbalance, 41; and decentralized revenue-raising, 45–48; and the fiscal gap, 52
Horvath, Andrea, 268
household income, per capita value of public services, 72–75
House of Commons Standing Committee on Finance, 213
HST (Harmonized Sales Tax): British Columbia referendum, 2; as income source, 11, 22; opposition to, 114; provincial discretion over, 39–40, 123; public opinion research, 84; tax-transfer harmonization, 43; value added taxes (VAT), comparison of, 126, 134n3, 134n4. *See also* consumption taxes; GST; sales taxes
Hudak, Tim, 240, 253, 254
Human Development Index (HDI), 34–35, 37n24
Hungary, 197

Idle No More, 12
Ignatieff, Michael, 140, 183
incentives: economic consequences of taxing and spending, 31; as fiscal intervention, 25–26, 36n8
income: tax expenditure rationalization, 156–59; tax rates compared to, 33–34
income averaging, 155–56, 167n10
income distribution: guaranteed income, implementation of, 164–66; and income inequality, 31; income tax transfer system, 50, 153; market income, 29–30; and power imbalances, 34; proportional value of taxes and public services, 75–76; and quality of life, 17, 22; stages of, 29–30; total after-tax income, 29–30; total income (before tax), 29; transfer payments, 24, 25; and the wealthy, 29–30
income elasticity of demand, 33–34
income inequality: and capital income, 154–56; consequences of, 9–10, 151–52, 167n3; distributional impact of public spending, 29–30, 37n19; equality of opportunity, 42; equality of outcome, 42; and fairness in society, 142–43; growth of in Canada, 151–52, 167n3; international comparison of, 132, 133; as justification for service cuts, 59–61; measurement of, 66; and progressive tax reform, 268–69; ratio of, 30; rise of the 1%, 92–94; shifts in public outlook, 89; and tax cuts, 1–2, 111; and tax rates, 34; vertical equity, 219
income security programs, 26–27
income tax. *See* corporate income tax; personal income taxes

India, 193
inequality. *See* income inequality
inflation, 2–4, 104–5, 106
infrastructure: costs, 15; as government investment, 25, 27; underinvestment in, 80
inheritance tax, 23, 44, 162–63, 268
Institute for Canadian Values, 231
Institute for Economic Affairs (UK), 104
Institute for Marriage and Family Canada, 231
Institute for Research on Public Policy, 262n2
International Energy Agency, 178
International Monetary Fund (IMF): Financial Activities Tax, 203, 205; financial transaction taxes, 191, 196, 199, 202; job creation, and spending cuts, 8–9
International Panel on Climate Change, 177–78
investment, economic definition of, 25
investment spending, 27
investment tax credit, 214
Ireland, 178
Ivanova, Iglika, 11, 151–66

Jackson, A., 111
Japan: education levels, 249; public services, 48; tax as share of GDP, 124; value added taxes (VAT), 126, 130
job creation: and austerity measures, 5–9; and consumption-based taxation, 216, 221; economic growth, and taxation, 12; impact of spending cuts on, 8–9; and low taxation, 221; *Red Book* platform, 110; tax cuts as economic growth stimulus, 3
job creators, privileging of, 102, 140
Joseph, Keith, 104
JP Morgan Bank, 195
Judt, Tony, 103
"junk politics," 9

Kelowna Accord, 113
Kenney, Jason, 240
Kesselman, Rhys, 161–62
Keynes, John Maynard: financial transaction taxes, 193–94; income inequality, and progressive taxation, 101–2
Keynesianism: and monetarism, 105–6; vs. neo-liberalism, 101–2, 115; and the welfare state, 102–3, 104
Kheiriddin, Teisha, 229–30
Klein, Ralph, 142, 229
Korea: education levels, 138, 249; value added taxes (VAT), 126
Krugman, Paul, 8, 171, 194

labour: backward bending supply, 26, 36n12; decommodification of, 26–27, 37n15; government as major employer, 28–29; tax burdens, and productivity growth, 31, 32, 37n23; tax rates, and economic growth, 25–26, 36n9, 36n10; wage trends, 28–29
labour unions: curtailment of power, 105, 114; public views of, 107
Laffer, Arthur B., 171
Lakoff, George, 139
Lalonde, Marc, 108
Lang, Eugene, 3, 99, 119–35
Lascelles, Eric, 201
Lawyers for Tax Fairness, 146, 261
Layton, Jack, 113
Leading Group on Innovative Financing for Development, 204
Lee, Marc, 11, 151–66, 220
Liberal Party: 2011 election promises (ON), 2; child care, 250–51; financial transaction tax, proposed, 197; green fiscal reform, 180–81; preferred size of government, 86–87; *Red Book* platform, 110
libertarianism, 238
lobby groups: Business Council on National Issues (BCNI), 106–7, 107–8; National Citizens Coalition (NCC), 107, 112. *See also* think tanks
low-income households: consequences of reduced services, 58; consumption taxes, impact on, 152; distributional impact of public spending, 29–30, 37n19; and environmental taxes, 23; guaranteed income, implementation of, 164–66; individual tax statistics,

156–59; non-refundable tax credits, 158; refundable tax credits, 175, 176; tax deductions, use of, 152

Macdonald, Donald S., 108
Macdonald Commission, 108–9
MacDonald Laurier Institute, 231, 234
MacEachen, Allan, 108
Machiavelli, 254, 260
Mackenzie, Hugh, 4, 16, 55–67, 111, 115
macroeconomic stabilization, 31
Maddison, Angus, 104
Manitoba, 112
Mankiw, Gregory, 171
Manning, Preston, 172, 262n15; *Canada Strong and Free* (Manning, Harris), 241–45, 254–56, 262n12, 262–63n14; *Caring for Canadians in a Canada Strong and Free* (Manning, Harris), 249–52; *Vision for a Canada Strong and Free* (Manning, Harris), 255
Manning Centre for Building Democracy, 231–32, 235, 237
Manning Centre Networking Conference, 240
Manufacturers Sales Tax, 122
market fundamentalism, 3; and Keynesianism, 101–2
market income, 29–30; and concentration of wealth, 151; and income distribution, 60; income inequality, and tax fairness, 66, 76, 81n4, 82n5
market moralism, social technology of, 248
Martin, Paul: as Minister of Finance, 110–11, 129; as Prime Minister, 113, 241
McGuinty, Dalton, 59, 112
McQuaig, L., 110
media: personal attack ads, 140; role of in neo-liberal strategy, 112; role of in perceptions of waste, 4–5; and think tank influence, 257
Medical Care Act, 144
Merkel, Angela, 197
Mexico: corporate tax rates, 126; government corruption, perceptions of, 87; North American Free Trade Agreement (NAFTA), 109

middle-income households: individual tax statistics, 156–59; non-refundable tax credits, 158; service targeting, impact on, 60
migration, and regional shocks, 42, 50
Mintz, Jack, 217
Mirrlees Review (UK), 151, 153, 162, 167n1
Mitchelmore, Lorraine, 180
monetarism, 105–6, 110
money, marginal utility of, 151
Montreal Economic Institute, 231, 234, 262n12
Mulcair, Thomas, 183
Mulroney, Brian: North American Free Trade Agreement (NAFTA), 109, 122; Old Age Security benefits, claw back, 59; tax policy, 120
multiplier effect of second-order expansion, 28
municipal governments: household income, and per capita value of public services, 75; property taxes, 39

National Child Benefit, 113
National Child Benefit supplement, 164
National Citizens Coalition (NCC), 107, 112, 230
national identities, Canada–US comparison, 87, 88
National Round Table on the Environment and the Economy, 172, 178, 180, 184
National Survey on American Public Opinion on Climate Change, 182
National Welfare Council, 114
natural rate of employment theory, 104–5
natural resource revenues: cash flow tax approach, 161–62; and Dutch disease, 47–48; Heritage Fund use, 47, 53; provincial imbalances in, 39, 46–48; resource rents, 47, 53n7; as source of imbalance, 52
NDP, 110; 2011 election promises (ON), 2; alignment with tax cut policies (BC), 56–57; cap-and-trade system, 181; commitment to principle, 235–36; financial transaction tax, proposed, 197; opposition to taxes, 114; size of

government, 86–87; social programs, funding, 113
negative externalities, 172
neoclassical economics: tax rates, and economic growth, 25–26, 36n8, 36n9, 36n10
neo-conservatism. *See* neo-liberalism
neo-liberalism: austerity, and fiscal prudence, 8–9; as counter-revolution, 88–89, 99; "deficit-phobia," 18; free market ideology, 2–4, 16, 36; and globalization, 102; and Keynesianism, 101–2, 115; of New Right, 229, 230; opposition to government, 20, 36n4; privatization of programs and services, 24; public services, connection to taxes, 55, 56–57, 267; rise of free-market economy, 103–6; role of the state, 103; and societal direction of fiscal policy, 17, 18–19, 22
Netherlands: carbon tax program, 178; deficit reduction, 111; education levels, 249; productivity growth, 31; stamp duty taxes, 193
new economics foundation, 192
Newfoundland and Labrador: fiscal capacity of, 46; natural resource revenues, 39
New Right, 229
New Zealand: deficit reduction, 111; emissions trading system, 179; value added taxes (VAT), 216
Nordhaus, W. D., 178
Norquist, Grover, 252
North American Free Trade Agreement (NAFTA), 109, 110, 122
Norway, 178
Not a Conspiracy Theory (Gutstein), 234
Nova Scotia: electricity emissions, 179; HST exemptions, 114

Obama, Barack, 1, 2, 5, 197, 268
Occupy Movement, 12, 95, 97, 143, 145, 191, 268
OECD countries: and Canadian tax policy, 120; and carbon taxes, 172, 176; deficit reduction, 111; *Divided We Stand*, 132, 133; economic performance, comparisons, 30–35; Human Development Index (HDI), 34–35, 37n24; income inequality, 9, 34; income security, 31–33; in-kind benefits, and disposable income, 71–72, 81n3; revenue as percentage of GDP, 138; taxation, comparison of, 124–26; tax levels, and income, 33–34; value added taxes (VAT), 126
Old Age Security benefits, 59, 114, 164, 165
Ontario: 2011 election promises, 2; Common Sense Revolution, 58, 59, 80, 111–12, 228, 229, 240, 243, 253, 262n9; fiscal capacity of, 46; full day kindergarten, 79; high-income tax brackets, 159–60, 167n17; McGuinty government, 112; pro-renewable energy policy, 184; tax policy, 58–59; transit investments, cancellation of, 80
Ontario Alternative Budget project, 81n2
Ontario Economic Council, 107
Ontario Securities Commission: high-frequency trading, and market instability, 195–96
outsourcing of programs and services, 24
Oxfam, 192

Page, Kevin, vii, 8, 131
Parkland Institute, 232
Parliamentary Budget Office, vii, 8, 131
payroll taxes, 23, 29, 61, 123–24, 153, 167n5
Pearson, Glen, 140
Pearson, Lester, 144
Pembina Institute, 178
Penn and Teller, 139–40
Persaud, Avinash, 200–201
personal income taxes: Basic Personal Exemption, increase in, 129, 130, 133; combined federal–provincial marginal rates, 121–22, 134n2; Conservative changes to, 211–12; deficit reduction surtax, 129; defined, 22; fairness, and income distribution, 52; federal rate, 121–22; flat rate, 22; full indexation of, 129; and income inequality, 133, 134n5; international comparison of, 124–25; as progressive tax, 153;

progressive tax rate, 22, 61; provincial rate structure, 40; public opinion research, 84; as revenue source, 215; simplification, need for, 213–15, 222n5; Tax Collection Agreements, 40, 43; tax-transfer harmonization, 43–45
personal tax-transfer system, and regional shocks, 42
physical capital, 25
Pickett, Jane, 9
Pigou, Arthur, 172
pigouvian taxes, 172, 207n2
politics of empathy, 145
Pollin, Robert, 104
populism, 57–58, 238. *See also* backlash populism
populist "producerist" critique, 253–54
post-secondary education, 51; out-of-province students, discrimination against, 49; and RESPs, 155, 214; as social investment, 137–38; tuition increases, justification for, 59
postwar economies, expansion of, 103–4
poverty: and backlash populism, 245; carbon tax revenues, and poverty reduction strategies, 185; federal anti-poverty strategy, 165; guaranteed income, implementation of, 164–66; and Robin Hood Tax, 191, 192–93; and welfare income, 44
prairie populism, 238
Prince Edward Island, 46
Private Planning Association of Canada, 230
privatization of programs and services, 24
productivity: decline of, and government revenues, 215; effect of tax cuts on, 15, 133; and employment stability, 17; and government investment spending, 27; labour productivity, and tax rates, 31, 32, 37n23
Progressive Conservative Party, 107, 113
progressives: counter-narrative development, 254, 257–61; creative networking, 260–61; distinction between cappuccino conservatives, 248–49; ideological comparisons on taxation, 227–28; patriotism, redefinition of, 259–60; resource allocation, 258; values and principles, debate over, 258–59
progressive taxation, 11; financial transaction taxes, 192, 202, 206; income taxes, 29, 153; and Keynesianism, 101–2; principles of, 151–52; and regressive taxes, 61
progressive tax reform, 268–69; cash flow tax approach, 161–62; charitable donations and gifts, 159, 167n15, 214; consumption taxes, 163–64, 168n20; dual-income tax system, 160–61, 168n19; employee stock option deduction, 158–59; Fair Tax Commission, 166; federal reforms, 153, 167n5; guaranteed income, implementation of, 164–66; income averaging, 155–56, 167n10; income tax base, broadening of, 153, 154–56; increase to top income tax rates, 159–61; RRSPs, 152, 156, 158, 167n11, 167n14; tax credits, 156–59, 167n11; tax expenditures, rationalizing, 156–59; wealth transfer, wealth taxes, 162–63. *See also* tax reform; tax simplification
progressivity: conditions to be satisfied, 212; erosion of in Canadian tax system, 152; and tax simplification, 219–20
property taxes: municipal government, 39; as wealth tax, 23, 162–63
provincial budgets: vertical balance, and federal–provincial transfers, 40, 41–42
provincial governments: Constitutional revenue-raising power, 39–40, 53n1; and decentralized revenue-raising, 45–48; federal transfer payments, 24; fiscal gap, and public service provision, 48–51; household income, and per capita value of public services, 74; natural resource revenues, 39; own-source revenue, as share of GDP, 62–64; potential benefits of tax cuts, 76–77; rise of neo-liberalism, 111–12; taxation powers, 16; Tax Collection Agreements, 40, 43; and tax-transfer harmonization, 43–45
provincial program spending, and social citizenship, 42

Prussia, 193
public interest test, 155
public opinion research: American dominance, future of, 90; Canada–US comparison, 87, 88; climate change, 182; contextual shifts in outlook, 89–97; debt crisis, 92, 93; deficit, preferred approach to, 85–86; differences by social location, 86–87; education, 95; future well-being of world economic zones, 91; gender differences, 95–96; global economy, 93; government priorities, 85–86; income inequality, and the 1%, 92–94; issues for discussion, 93; long-term economic performance, concerns over, 89; perceived changes in quality of life, 90; personal income taxes, 84; political values and ideology, 96–97; preferred size of government, 86–87, 91, 92; propositional form of questions, 84–86; public meanings of taxation, 83–88; public understanding of tax cuts and benefits, 138–40; shifts in public outlook, 88–89; tax increases, 146; tax rates, attitudes towards, 84; trust/distrust of government, 97–98; type of tax, 83–84; on use of carbon tax revenues, 184
public pensions, 24
public policy, alternatives, 6
Public Policy Forum, 262n2
public sector, stability of in economic cycle, 27–28
public services: and austerity measures, 5–9, 141–42; benefits of, 19–20; citizenship democracy vs. dollar democracy, 75–76; connection to taxes, 55–56; daily examples of, 69–70, 81n2; funding of, 1–2, 3–5, 17; as government consumption, 24–25; in higher-income countries, 33–34; and horizontal imbalance, 45–48; household income, and per capita value of public services, 72–75; and Human Development Index (HDI), 34–35, 37n24; implications of valuation, 79–80; in-kind benefits, and disposable income, 71–72, 81n3; invisibility of, 81; justifications for cuts, 59–61; per capita benefit of, 61; per capita value of by family type, 72–73; public preparedness to pay for, 66–67; transfer payments, and standard of living, 60–61, 67n1; undervaluing of, 56, 66; valuation of, 77–78, 115; and vertical balance, 48–51
public transit: tax credit, 156, 214; user fees, 23
public vs. private spending, 3

quality of life: perceived changes in, 90; and societal direction of fiscal policy, 17, 18–19, 22; and societal well-being, 29–30
Quebec: corporate income tax collection, 43; early learning investments, 79, 82n6; and federal–provincial transfers, 49; financial sector compensation tax, 205; fiscal capacity of, 46; Green Fund Duty, 179; personal income tax collection, 43; top income tax rate, 159

Rae, Bob, 59
Rand Corporation, 172
Raush, S., 176
Reagan, Ronald, 65, 88–89, 99, 102, 103, 105–6, 230, 246
Reaganomics, 113
redistributive equity, and revenue decentralization, 41–42, 43–45
Red Toryism, 107, 229, 236
Reform Party, 110, 113, 229, 236, 261–62n1
regional development, and resource revenues, 47–48
regional shocks, adjustment mechanisms, 42, 50
Registered Education Savings Plans (RESPs), 155, 214
regressive taxation: consumption taxes, 152; distributional impact of, 23; payroll taxes, 23, 29, 36n6; proportional taxation, 81n4; sales taxes, 29; use of for progressive purpose, 61
Reid, Scott, 251
Reilly, J., 176
Report of Tax Expenditures, 214–15

resource rents, 52
responsibility, social nature of, 259
revenue leakage, 193
"Rhizomatic Right," 238, 262n8
rich. *See* high-income earners
Rich, Andrew, 233
Robin Hood Tax, 191, 192–93, 206
Romney, Mitt, 171
Royal Dutch Shell, 180
RRSPs, 152, 156, 158, 167n11, 167n14, 214

Saez, Emmanuel, 159, 160
sales taxes, 22–23; international comparison of, 124, 126; provincial sales tax rates, 123; as regressive tax, 29; tax-transfer harmonization, 43
Sanger, Toby, 11, 159, 191–210
Sarkozy, Nicolas, 197
Saskatchewan: carbon emissions, 175; fiscal capacity of, 46; natural resource revenues, 39; NDP government tax cuts, 112
Saurette, Paul, 12, 102, 227–63
Save the Children, 192
Scandinavia: public services, 48; tax rates, and economic growth, 26
Schmidt, Rodney, 198
Schultz, George, 172
Segal, Hugh, 229, 235–36
Sen, Amartya, 137, 194
Shillington, Richard, 61, 115
Singapore: financial transaction taxes, 201; value added taxes (VAT), 216
small business, income tax rates, 125–26
small-government agenda. *See* government, size of
Smart, Michael, 217
social citizenship, 11, 259; and common good, 15–16, 138, 146; and revenue decentralization, 41–42, 44; and vertical balance, 48–49
social conservatism, 238
social housing, 71
social insurance, and decentralization, 42
social issues, in public opinion research, 96–97
social programs: funding through payroll taxes, 23; provincial vs. federal spending, 132; universality, end of, 109, 110
social responsibility, and fairness in society, 143–46
social safety net, 2–3, 80
social solidarity, and federal/provincial revenue balance, 11
social technology, and collective political measures, 248–49
social transfers, 24
social welfare: in free market ideology, 30; and resource distribution, 151
South Africa: carbon tax program, 178; value added taxes (VAT), 216
Spain: financial instability, repercussions of, 195–96; value added taxes (VAT), 126
speculative investment: and financial transaction taxes, 192, 194, 198–99, 199–201; repercussions of, 194–96
spending and taxing: fiscal policy of, 18–22; international economic impacts, 30–35
Stamp Duty Reserve Tax, 193
standard of living: Human Development Index (HDI), 34–35, 37n24, 144; perceived changes in, 90; and public service benefits, 75; and societal well-being, 29–30, 144–45; transfer payments, and public services, 60–61, 67n1
Stanford, Jim, 11, 15, 17–38
Stanford Social Innovation Review, 233
Statistics Canada: public services benefits per capita, 72
Steyn, Mark, 230
Stiglitz, Joseph, 8, 171, 194, 197
stock market: high-frequency trading, and market instability, 195–96, 200; securities regulation, 205
stock transaction taxes, 192
student protests, 12, 145
subsidies, as income distribution to business, 24
supply-side economics, 113, 127–28
surpluses, as pretext for tax cuts, 59
Suzuki Foundation, 178
Sweden: carbon tax program, 178; deficit reduction, 111; financial transaction

taxes, 203; productivity growth, 31
Switzerland: carbon tax program, 178; financial transaction taxes, 193; value added taxes (VAT), 126

Taiwan, 193
taxation: attitudinal shifts in, 1, 2–5, 64–65, 66–67; and benefit from public services, 70–77; and the common good, 15–16; contextual shifts in outlook, 89–97; international comparison of, 124–26; lower taxes, emotional appeal of, 97–98; perception of as public good, 144–45, 146; and program spending, 17; public meanings of, 83–88; shifts in public outlook, 88–89; tax rates, attitudes towards, 84
tax avoidance and evasion, incentives for, 155
tax bases, 153, 154–56
Tax Collection Agreements, 40, 43
tax conversation: ideological comparisons, 227–28; need for, 2, 267–69; in UK and Europe, 16
tax credits, 152, 156–59, 167n4, 167n11, 211, 214
tax cuts: "affordability" of, and surplus revenues, 128–29, 133–34; beneficiaries of, 58; "boutique tax cuts," 113–14, 156, 167n11; and carbon tax revenue, 175–76; as "free lunch politics," 119–20, 267; Harper government, 113–14; and income inequality, 132–33; productivity/competitiveness rationale for, 127–28; separation of consequences of, 55
tax deductions, 152
tax efficiency, and revenue decentralization, 41–42
taxes: and civilized society, 69, 81n1; conservative language of, 57; and economic performance, international comparisons, 30–35; as investment in future, 10–11; types of, 22–23
tax expenditures, scrutiny of, 214–15, 222n6
tax fairness: as condition of progressivity, 212, 260; lobbies for, 146; and market income inequity, 76, 81n4, 82n5; progressive counter-narrative development, 254, 257–61; question of, 142–43, 146; in redistribution of resources, 60–61; and tax efficiency, 219–20
tax-free income, 155
Tax-Free Savings Accounts (TFSAs), 155, 212
tax harmonization, and revenue decentralization, 41–42, 43–45
tax havens: effect on developing countries, 196; and financial transaction taxes, 193, 198, 204
taxpayer, rights of vs. rights of citizenship, 105–6
tax policy: appropriateness of tax-cutting measures, 133–34; Chrétien government, 109, 113, 124, 129; Clark government, 107; and corporate investment, 20–21; and decentralization, 39–40; Harper government, 112, 113–14, 129, 130–31, 179–80, 196–97, 205, 211–13, 213–15, 220–22, 222n2; incentives, as fiscal intervention, 25–26, 36n8; Martin government, 113, 129, 211; Mulroney government, 109, 120, 127, 129; and neo-liberalism, 2–4, 20–22; non-resident taxes, 215; and progressive tax reform, 267–69; public understanding of tax cuts and benefits, 138–40; service implications of cuts, 16; spending and taxing, 18–22; tax cuts, as free good, 2–5; transparency in, 5; Trudeau government, 106–8; *Working Families Tax Plan*, 130
tax preferences and benefits, 198, 213–14, 222n4
tax reform: business opposition to, 108; and GST tax base, 216–17; of income tax base, 154–56; Mirrlees Review (UK), 151, 153; of Mulroney government, 120, 127; tax reductions on wealthy, 109. *See also* progressive tax reform; tax simplification
tax simplification: fairness, and tax efficiency, 219–20; GST rate increase,

217–18; GST revenues, use of, 218–19, 222n9; GST tax base expansion, 216–17; need for, 213–15; recommendations for, 212; savings reallocation, 220; tax mix refocusing, 215, 216–19
tax systems, principles of, 151–52
tax-transfer harmonization, 43–45
Tea Party, 3–4, 87, 95, 97
Teller, Raymond Joseph, 139–40
Thatcher, Margaret, 36, 88–89, 99, 102, 104, 105–6, 230; on society, 3, 103
think tanks: American Enterprise Institute, 104, 172; Atlantic Institute for Market Studies, 231, 234; Brookings Institution, 172, 233; Caledon Institute of Social Policy, 232; Canada West Foundation, 172, 177, 230; Canadian Centre for Policy Alternatives, 231, 232; Canadian Council for Social Development, 232; Canadian Labour and Business Centre, 231; Canadian Policy Research Network, 231; Canadian Tax Foundation, 230; Canadian Taxpayers Federation, 230; C. D. Howe Institute, 107, 109, 112, 230, 234; Centre for Policy Studies (UK), 104; charitable status, 257–58; communication and marketing budgets, 232–33; Conference Board of Canada, 9, 172, 230, 232, 262n2; conservative ideology, marketing of, 230–32, 234–35, 237; Donner Foundation, 230; Focus on the Family Canada, 230, 231; Fraser Institute, 107, 112, 230–31, 232, 234–35, 241, 262n2; Frontier Centre for Public Policy, 114, 231; funding of, 234; Heritage Foundation, 104; Heritage Institute, 233; impact metrics, 230–32; Institute for Canadian Values, 231; Institute for Economic Affairs (UK), 104; Institute for Marriage and Family Canada, 231; Institute for Research on Public Policy, 262n2; MacDonald Laurier Institute, 231, 234; Manning Centre for Building Democracy, 231–32, 235, 237; Montreal Economic Institute, 231, 234, 262n12; National Citizens Coalition (NCC), 230; National Round Table on the Environment and the Economy, 172, 178, 180, 184; network of influence, 257; Parkland Institute, 232; political activity of, 234, 235; progressive, resource allocation, 258; public communication strategy, 102; Public Policy Forum, 262n2; Rand Corporation, 172; as research organizations, 234; Vanier Institute, 232; Wellesley Institute, 232. *See also* lobby groups
Thoreau, Henry David, 67
Tobin, James, 192, 194
Tobin Tax, 192, 194, 205
Toews, Vic, 262n10
total income (before tax), 29
transfer payments: 1995 cutback, 110; household incomes, and consumer spending, 31; as income distribution, 24, 25; provincial revenue from, 39; and standard of living, 60
transparency, of tax policy and spending, 5, 216
Trilling, Lionel, 252
Trudeau, Pierre, 106–8
trust/distrust of government, 4–5, 12, 98
Turning the Corner (Environment Canada), 179

unemployment, correlation to taxes in OECD countries, 31–33
Unemployment Insurance (UI), 23, 24, 123–24
UNICEF, 192
United Kingdom: financial transaction taxes, 196–97; Mirrlees Review, 151, 153, 162, 167n1; rise of neo-liberalism, 103, 104; Stamp Duty Reserve Tax, 193, 198; tax debates, emergence of, 16; Thatcher government, 3, 36, 88–89, 99, 102, 103, 104, 105–6
United Nations: Clean Development Mechanism, 179; Human Development Index (HDI), 34–35, 37n24; Millennium Development Goals, 192
United States: American dominance, future of, 90; backlash populism,

228, 238–39, 252–53; Bush (G. W.) administration, 1, 65, 195; carbon pricing, 177; Clinton administration, 65, 195; and conservatism, 237–42; conservative think tanks, partisanship of, 233; corporate tax rates, 125–26; debt ceiling crisis, 1; Democratic postwar governments, 64; education levels, 250; financial transaction taxes, 196–97; government spending as percent of GDP, 65; Great Society, 64, 88–89; income inequality, public opinion on, 92; National Survey on American Public Opinion on Climate Change, 182; New Deal, 64; Obama administration, 1, 2, 5, 197, 268; Occupy Movement, 12, 95, 97, 143, 145, 191, 268; positive role of government, 5; preferred size of government, 87; public view of taxes, 1, 87, 88; Reagan administration, 65, 88–89, 99, 102, 103, 105–6; recovery plan as class warfare, 2; Republican no-tax pledges, 1; separation of taxes from public services, 64–65; tax as share of GDP, 124; tax cuts as "free lunch politics," 119–20; taxes, and the state, 252–53; tax referenda, 16; Tea Party, 3–4, 87, 95, 97
Universal Child Care Benefit, 164, 168n21
user fees, 23, 77–78
US Federal Reserve: Volcker shock at, 105

value added taxes (VAT), 22–23, 122–23, 153, 163–64, 168n20; broadening of tax base, 216–17; financial services exemptions, 202–3. *See also* GST (Goods and Services Tax); HST (Harmonized Sales Tax); sales taxes
Vander Zalm, Bill, 56
Vanier Institute, 232
Veall, Michael, 159

vertical balance: and federal–provincial transfers, 40, 48–51; importance of, 41–42
vertical equity, 219
Vision for a Canada Strong and Free (Manning, Harris), 255
Volker, Paul, 171
volunteer firefighters credit, 214

wage trends, and employment practices, 28–29
War on Want organization, 192
waste: and bureaucratic control, 8; elimination of, and lower taxes, 56; perceptions of government spending, 4–5, 92, 95
wealth, and income distribution, 29–30
wealth taxes, 23, 162–63
wealthy (the): increased taxation of, 2, 92, 94, 146, 268
welfare state, and Keynesian economics, 102–3, 104
welfare system: Alberta, 141; and choice, 249–52; as income security program, 24, 26–27; re-invigoration of, 50–51; and social citizenship, 42; and tax-transfer harmonization, 44
well-being: and standard of living, 144–45; of world economic zones, 91
Wellesley Institute, 232
White, Graham, 112
Wildrose Party, 236
Wilkinson, Richard, 9
Wilson, Michael, 109, 119, 123, 127
women, impact of consumption taxes on, 163
Working Families Tax Plan (Budget 2007), 130
Working Income Tax Benefit, 164
world carbon price, 177–78

"zero inflation" policy, 109

Books in the Canadian Commentaries Series

Published by Wilfrid Laurier University Press

Uneasy Partners: Multiculturalism and Rights in Canada / Janice Gross Stein, David Roberston Cameron, John Ibbitson, Will Kymlicka, John Meisel, Haroon Siddiqui, and Michael Valpy. Introduction by the Hon. Frank Iacobucci • 2007 / xiii + 165 pp. / ISBN 978-1-55458-012-5

Rites of Way: The Politics and Poetics of Public Space / Mark Kingwell and Patrick Turmel, editors • 2009 / xviii + 192 pp. / illus. / ISBN 978-55458-153-5

Tax Is Not a Four-Letter Word: A Different Take on Taxes in Canada / Alex Himelfarb and Jordan Himelfarb, editors • 2013 / viii + 296 / illus. / ISBN 978-1-55458-832-9